AF766706

Asymmetric Power Relations and International Trade Law

The book offers an analysis of the contradictions between theory and practice in the trading system. It contextualises the colonial legal structure and its impact on the peripheral countries and their participation and gain in the multilateral trading system.

The book's core argument effectively situates Economic Partnership Agreements in the 'systemic' asymmetry, which characterises the relationship between developed and developing countries in global trade. It applies the idea of asymmetry to the relationship between the core countries—the EU/USA and the peripheral countries (ACP)—in the GATT, multilaterally and in the EU-ACP trade relationship, bilaterally. The book identifies that core provisions in the WTO regime such as the special and differential treatment as well as GATT Article XXIV have not lived up to expectations. Underscoring the asymmetrical participation and dominant role of former colonial powers, the book demonstrates how, although trade is generally considered a catalyst for economic growth, developed countries have safeguarded their domestic markets while exerting pressure on developing countries to liberalise and compete. The European Union has taken measures to address the development concerns of African, Caribbean, and Pacific countries through the Lomé Conventions and Cotonou Agreement; however, these relationships still retain and reinforce colonial paternalism, evidenced by recent trade agreements. An alternative possibility—multipolarity—holds promise for African countries, especially intra-African trade and critical engagement with China.

The book is an invaluable resource for scholars, postgraduate students, government officials, and policymakers, as it offers a comprehensive understanding of the complexities of trade negotiations and agreements.

Inebu C Agbo-Ejeh obtained her PhD in commercial law from the University of Cape Town. She holds a master of laws in international economic law from the University of Warwick (UK) and a bachelor of laws degree from the University of Jos. Dr Inebu is an advocate and solicitor of the Supreme Court of Nigeria. She has taught law at the undergraduate and postgraduate levels at Baze University, the American University of Nigeria, and the University of Seychelles. In 2019, she was awarded a UNDP-supported Centre for Trade and Regional Industrialization (CTRI) Fellowship, administered through the Centre for Comparative Law in Africa (CCLA). Her research interests primarily focus on international economic law; international trade law and investment law; and business and human rights law. She has held various administrative positions, including coordinating postgraduate and undergraduate research.

Routledge Research in International Economic Law

International Trade Regulation
Evolving Dynamics and Shifting Foundations
Zhiqiong June Wang and Jianfu Chen

India and Investor-State Dispute Settlement
Affronting Sovereignty or Indicting Capriciousness?
Prabhash Ranjan

Investor-State Dispute Settlement and International Investment Agreements
The Case of the Gulf Cooperation Council Member States
David Price and Amelia Hallam

Rules for Trade in Services 2.0
Adapting the GATS to a Changing Trade Landscape
Gabriel Gari

International Trade with the Middle East and North Africa
Legal, Commercial and Investment Perspectives
Edited by Hossein Esmaeili, Vivienne Brand and Susan Karamanian

Preferential Trade Agreements and Cultural Products
Gilbert Gagné

Foreign Investment, Human Rights and Environmental Protection
Striking a Balance for Sustainable Development
Shawkat Alam and Abdullah Al Faruque

Asymmetric Power Relations and International Trade Law
A Legal Analysis of Economic Partnership Agreements
Inebu C Agbo-Ejeh

For more information about this series, please visit www.routledge.com/Routledge-Research-in-International-Economic-Law/book-series/INTECONLAW

Asymmetric Power Relations and International Trade Law

A Legal Analysis of Economic Partnership Agreements

Inebu C Agbo-Ejeh

Routledge
Taylor & Francis Group
LONDON AND NEW YORK

First published 2025
by Routledge
4 Park Square, Milton Park, Abingdon, Oxon OX14 4RN

and by Routledge
605 Third Avenue, New York, NY 10158

Routledge is an imprint of the Taylor & Francis Group, an informa business

The research published in this book was completed at the Centre for Comparative Law in Africa, Faculty of Law, University of Cape Town, while the author was a doctoral researcher.

British Library Cataloguing-in-Publication Data
A catalogue record for this book is available from the British Library

ISBN: 978-1-032-61455-7 (hbk)
ISBN: 978-1-032-61506-6 (pbk)
ISBN: 978-1-032-61505-9 (ebk)

DOI: 10.4324/9781032615059

Typeset in Times New Roman
by Apex CoVantage, LLC

To my dear mother, Onyelu, Nathaniel, Arome-Adole, Ebokondu and Okopi.

Contents

Preface and Acknowledgement

This book provides a scholarly examination of trade within the framework of power asymmetry. The motivation behind delving into the trade dynamics between the European Union and African nations, as well as their involvement in the multilateral trading system, stems from a quest to comprehend the underlying causes that render peripheral countries at a disadvantaged position and devoid of influence during trade talks and subsequent agreements. The aim is to delve deeper and elucidate the factors contributing to this unequal partnership.

The book study employs both empirical and doctrinal methodology to suggest that the systemic asymmetry in trade relations between African, Caribbean, and Pacific (ACP) countries and their traditional trade 'partners,' the EU and USA, as well as their limited participation in the multilateral system, can be traced back to colonialism. The recent Economic Partnership Agreements between the European Union and ACP countries, with a specific focus on Ghana and Nigeria, are used as a case study to analyse the nature of power asymmetry that exists between these 'partners.'

The book explores why the rhetoric of every negotiation revolves around the development concerns of ACP countries, yet the actual content of the agreements represents the interests of the core countries. These agreements, although filled with exceptions, are inaccessible to developing countries. Furthermore, the book explores the growing relationship between Africa and China. It is argued that the relationship holds promise because China and Africa do not have a history of colonialism, and China focuses on doing business on the continent without interfering in African countries' domestic affairs. However, the book does not suggest that the relationship is a solution to Africa's challenges. Nevertheless, multipolarity offers great potential for African countries.

The book is call on peripheral countries' leaders to break away from the catastrophic incompetence that has become ingrained in their domestic, continental, and international relations and to critically evaluate every term in an agreement. Therefore, caution must be exercised to ensure that the African Continental Free Trade Area does not become overshadowed by the interests of advanced countries, but rather serves as a platform for Africa to strategically reshape its trade and economic policies. The book focuses on immediate concerns relevant to the topic, condensing its vast subject matter. Blame for the lack of capacity and corruption among African leaders was not discussed. The book does not delve into interactions between the Africa Continental Free Trade Area and other trade agreements signed by African countries and countries external to it, despite these topics being worthy of investigation. Instead, the focus is on Article XXIV of the GATT/WTO, which allows parties to deviate from multilateral obligations for bilateral arrangement—and examines the contradictions in theory and practice.

Most of the research for this book was conducted at the University of Cape Town in South Africa and at Economic Community of West Africa States (ECOWAS) in Nigeria. Information from the archives and records of the ECOWAS Commission informs the book, along with interviews conducted with various experts involved in the Economic Partnership Agreements (EPAs) negotiations in ECOWAS. Additional interviews were held with individuals from the Ministry of Trade and Investment and civil society organisations in Nigeria. Both physical visits and telephone calls were made to the Ministry of Trade and Investment in Ghana and the African Continental Free Trade Agreement (AfCFTA) Secretariat. The ECOWAS Commission provided crucial materials, and special thanks are given to Mr. Jerome Boa, the Director of External Relations, for facilitating access to these materials and connecting me with key actors during the EPAs negotiations. The officers at the Federal Ministry of Trade, Industry, and Investment in Nigeria are also acknowledged for their support. Dr Ken Ukaoha, the Director of the National Association of Nigerian Traders, deserves special recognition for his willingness to answer calls, meet in person, and provide relevant materials for the study. The Manufacturing Association of Nigeria (MAN) also engaged in an hour-long discussion, and their participation is sincerely appreciated.

Particular thanks must go to the supervisors for their guidance and expertise. Professor Ismail Faizel's insightful comments, constructive criticism, and extensive knowledge and practical experience in world trade law, regional trade, and integration greatly influenced the development of this work. Thanks are given to Professor Ada Ordor for her unwavering support, encouragement, and guidance throughout the entire process. I would like to acknowledge the valuable contributions of the external examiners, Professor Joost Pawelyn, Professor Desta Melaku, and Professor Olabisi Akinkugbe, for their insightful comments. A special mention goes to Professor Akinkugbe, who went beyond the role of an external examiner and provided constructive feedback that greatly added to this book.

I would like to express my appreciation to the professional team at Routledge, specifically Diksha Bhugra and Nicola Sharpe, for their invaluable assistance throughout this process. I am grateful to Siobhan Poole, who was my initial point of contact at Taylor and Francis and provided guidance and support until an offer was extended to publish the book. I also extend gratitude to the Government of Benue State, Nigeria, as well as Gregory Agboneni, Dr Ame Idoke, and Dr John Ochai, for their support. I would like to extend my gratitude to Mr. Bandara Ajith for his kindness and support. I appreciate the support of Chief Hilary Ibegbulem. I would like to express my thanks to Mr. Victor Iboyi for his meticulous attention to detail in ensuring the proper formatting of the document.

Family has been a pillar of strength throughout the journey. I am eternally grateful to my husband and children for their steady and resolute support, love, and patience. I am indebted to my sister, Felicia, for taking care of the children while I was away. In memory of my beloved mother, whose profound influence has greatly shaped this endeavour, I am deeply grateful for your invaluable guidance and generous support that continue to direct me. To my late dad, Christopher Agbo, thank you. Immense appreciation to Adakole Agbo for paving the way for me.

Inebu C Agbo-Ejeh

1 Asymmetry and Legal Construct

1.1 Introduction

This book adopts a multidisciplinary approach. The theoretical framework and analysis draw on insights and concepts from legal scholarship, economic theory, critical theory, and political economy to analyse the trade relations between Africa and developed countries. Blending insights from multiple perspectives on the global trade phenomenon is essential,[1] as the book explores treaties that empowered colonialists and trade before, during, and after colonialism in Africa. Petersmann notes that international economic law (IEL) has become highly complex with the steady rise in regional trade agreements (RTAs) and the increasing number of World Trade Organization (WTO) cases; thus, he recommended an integrative approach for evaluating legal analysis and contradictions between theory and practice.[2]

The current narrative is that colonialism and its influence are past events.[3] However, a number of scholars believe that the present 'economic inequality' in all its ramifications is steeped in colonial construct.[4] Nonetheless, not all agree with the aforementioned position; for instance, some argue that the multilateral system is structured for the participation and benefit of all. John Ruggie conceptualised the multilateral trading system as being an adequate balance between domestic policy and the international system, an idea he referred to as 'embedded liberalism.[5] Ruggie borrowed and brought into vogue the idea of 'embedded

1 Jeffrey L Dunoff, 'Rethinking International Trade' (1998) University of Pennsylvania Journal of International Law vol 19 (2) p 34

2 Ernst-Ulrich Petersmann, 'Narrating International Economic Law' (2014) 787. Constitutional Limit' Max Planck Institute fur Auslandisches offenthiches Recht www.zaoerv.de accessed 10 May 2018

3 Uma Kothari, 'From Colonialism to Development: Reflection of Former Colonial Officers' (2006) Commonwealth & Comparative Politics vol 44 (1) pp 118–36

4 Daron Acemoglu and James A Robinson, 'The Economic Impact of Colonialism' in Stelios Michalopoulos and Elias Papaioannou (eds), *The Long Economic and Political Shadow of History* (CEPR Press, 2017) 81–5; Olabisi O Akinkugbe and Clair Gammage, 'Doing Development Differently: Reorienting Sino-African Trade and Investment Relations After Pandemic' (2021) Asia Europe Journal www.papers.ssrn accessed 24 April 2024 p 2

5 John Gerard Ruggie, 'International Regimes, Transactions, and Change: Embedded Liberalism in the Postwar Economic Order' (1982) International Organisation vol 36 (2) pp 379–415 at 398, 388

DOI: 10.4324/9781032615059-1

liberalism.'[6] The term 'embeddedness' was first used by Karl Polanyi in his work, *The Great Transformation: The Political Origins of Our Time*.[7] Embedded liberalism as conceptualised by Ruggie offers grounds for confidence in the multilateral trading system.[8] However, a critical examination reveals that the peripheral countries are not able to afford such balancing.[9] Andrew Lang refused to share in the enthusiasm of those who promoted the ideas of embedded liberalism. According to his standpoint, Ruggie did not highlight the *peripheral* group in the multilateral trading system,[10] and who, on account of their lack of skill and poor infrastructure, have not taken advantage of the exceptions provided in the General Agreement on Tariffs and Trade/World Trade Organization (GATT/WTO) law.[11] The GATT was an international treaty with an interim application, whereas the WTO is a permanent body, whose authority is recognised by many member nations. It is a global trading rule like the GATT but more extensive in its coverage. Cox argued that the free trade compromise has instead given rise to aggressive economic imbalances between the poor and the rich countries.[12]

The principal focus of this book is to interrogate how the colonial legal construct influences Africa's poor participation and the minimal gain in the multilateral system and bilateral agreements. The colonial treaties in the past did not only promote the interest of the European powers but continue to influence Africa's relations with advanced countries to date.[13] As the colonies obtained independence, their main focus was to take charge of the economic and political affairs and influence the international regime to their benefit.[14] The independent states continue to face the challenges of the universality of norms, which is not as much about various cultural interests as a steady rise in dominating the conflicting interests, while the interests of the developed countries trump all else.[15] The inability to reconcile interests has been a problem between the European Union (EU) and African Caribbean and Pacific (ACP) countries' trade relations.

6 John Gerard Ruggie, 'International Regimes, Transactions, and Change: Embedded Liberalism in the Postwar Economic Order' (1982) International Organisation vol 36 (2) pp 379–415 at 398, 388
7 Karl Polanyi, *The Great Transformation: The Political Origin of Origin of Our Time* (Beacon Press, 1944) xxiii
8 Ruggie (n 5)
9 Yilmaz Akyus, 'Multilateral Disciplines and the Question of Policy Space' in Julio Faundez and Celine Tan (eds), *International Economic Law, Globalisation and Developing Countries* (Edward Elgar, 2012) 34–7
10 Andrew Lang, 'Reconstructing Embedded Liberalism: John Ruggie and Constructivist Approaches to the Study of the International Trade Regime' (2006) Journal of International Law vol 9 (1) p 84
11 Andrew Lang, 'Reconstructing Embedded Liberalism: John Ruggie and Constructivist Approaches to the Study of the International Trade Regime' (2006) Journal of International Law vol 9 (1) p 84
12 Robert Cox, 'Critical Theory' in Thomas G Weiss and Rorden Wilkinson (eds), *International Organisation and Global Governance* (Routledge, 2014) 164–5
13 Richard Falk, *The New States and International Legal Order vol 118 of Recueil de Cours* (A.W. Sijthoff, 1968) 186
14 Antony Anghie, *Imperialism, Sovereignty and the Making of International Law* (CUP, 2004) 198
15 Falk (n 13) at 38; R P Anand, 'Attitudes of the Asian-African States Toward Certain Problems of International Law' (1966) International and Comparative Law Quarterly vol 15 p 55 at 72

The EU-ACP's Economic Partnership Agreements are used as a case study. Although, it has been argued that the EU through Lomé Convention to Cotonou Agreements, contributed to the development of African countries.[16] However, colonial influence gave rise to 'systemic' asymmetry, which has characterised the relations, just as it had been between the developed and developing countries in global trade. The idea of asymmetry can be applied to the relationship between the core countries (the EU/USA) and the periphery countries (ACP)—in the multilateral trading system (GATT) and in the EU-ACP countries' bilateral trade relationship. Adebajo Adekeye and Kaye Whiteman argued that[17] the EU deepens asymmetry between it and the ACP countries by subverting any significance the latter have left. This was done by weakening the unanimity that existed among the group during the Economic Partnership Agreements.[18]

Woolcock argued that African countries are severely restricted by economic deficiency and have not been able to shape outcomes in the multilateral trading system and regional trade arrangement.[19] However, this does not necessarily determine that the result of the interaction between the peripheral and core will always favour the latter as demonstrated in this book.[20] The question is, would the approach of donor-client adopted by the EU to African development decline as China injected itself into the economic climate of the continent? The Chinese stratagem to African development seemed to be embraced, although with some trepidation; this deserves some investigation. For instance, Western countries continue to impose human rights, the rule of law and democracy, and other conditionalities in their partnership agreement, but China distances itself from the internal affairs of African countries. It focuses on investing in Africa for political objectives, and this alternative seems like a welcome development in Africa because it treats the African partners as equal and provides tangible infrastructure in exchange for raw materials.

To explore asymmetry in the multilateral arrangement, the book examines the EU and ACP countries' agreement in 2000 to negotiate Economic Partnership Agreements (EPAs) following Article 36 (1) of the Cotonou Agreement. The

16 I William Zartman, 'European and Africa Decolonization or Dependency' (1976) International Affairs vol 54 (2) pp 326–43; Majories Lister, 'European Development Policy: Globalisation and the Post-Lomé World' in Andrew Mold (ed), *EU Development Policy in a Changing World: Challenges for the 21st Century* (Amsterdam University Press, 2007) 69–70, 72

17 Adebajo Adekeye and White Kaye, *The EU and Africa: From Eurafrique to Afro-Europa* (Hurt & Company Ltd, 2012)

18 Adebajo Adekeye and Kaye Whiteman, *The EU and Africa: From Eurafrique to Afro-Europa* (Hurt & Company Ltd, 2012)

19 Stephen Woolcock, 'The Scope for Asymmetry in the World Trade Organisation (WTO)' in Sanoussi Bilal, Philippe De Lombaerde and Diana Tussie (eds), *Asymmetric Trade Negotiations* (Routledge, 2016) 29; Melaku Geboue Desta and Moshie Hirsch, 'African Countries in the World Trading System: International Trade, Domestic Institutions and the Role of International Law' (2005) ICLQ vol 61 pp 127–70

20 Drahos Peter, 'When the Weak Bargain With the Strong: Negotiations in the World Trade Organisation' (2003) International Negotiations 8 pp 79–109; J P Singh, 'Wiggle Room: New Issues and North-South Negotiations During Uruguay Round' Prepared for the conference on Developing Countries and the Trade Negotiation Process UNCTAD (Geneva 6–7 November 2003)

arrangement was aimed at deepening free trade and fair competition following Article XXIV of the WTO law.[21] The EU demonstrated its concerns about ACP countries through Director of Trade Peter Mandelson, who declared, 'developing countries have every right to exploit the legitimate comparative advantages that they have.'[22] He further stated that the EPAs would, inevitably, be the harbinger of the end to the colonial ideological construct of the previous trading system and usher in mutually beneficial economic development.[23] Similar to Mandelson's view, other writers have called for African countries to break the connection with the colonial past.[24] In his book *Africa Must Unite*, the foremost Ghanaian president, Kwame Nkrumah, argued, 'if the gap is ever to be narrowed, not to say closed, it can only be done by a complete break with the present "patron-client relationship." '[25] Nkrumah doubted whether there would be an economic and trade arrangement between Africa and former colonialists devoid of the colonial elements.[26]

In his contribution in a book titled *International Economic Law, Globalization and Developing Countries*, Yilmaz Akyus argued that the global economic system is defined by power asymmetries between developed and developing countries.[27] Akyus's standpoint is that the WTO rule imposed constraints on national policies, which is more problematic for developing countries.[28] The author maintained that the WTO law made provisions for equality of all members, 'yet effective constraints they impose over national policies are much tighter for developing than for industrial countries.' However, according to the famous economist and free trade advocate Jagdish Bhagwati, criticism of the multilateral trading system results from a faulty logic of how the system works.[29] Bhagwati has consistently emphasised that the onslaught of criticism of 'double standards' levelled against the WTO is nothing more than 'hypocrisy,' because industrial protection is higher in developing countries than in advanced countries.[30] To the conformist, the multilateral trading system has made adequate provision for all members to coexist.

21 Cotonou Agreement Article 37 (1)

22 Peter Mandelson, 'Open Markets, Open Trade: Europe's Global Challenge' (European Parliament, Brussels 19 September 2005) 3

23 Peter Mandelson, 'Open Markets, Open Trade: Europe's Global Challenge' (European Parliament, Brussels 19 September 2005) 3

24 Sabelo J Ndlovu-Gatsheni, 'Decoloniality as the Future of Africa' (2015) History Compass vol 13 (10) pp 485–96 at 488–9; Walter Rodney, *How Europe Underdeveloped Africa* (Bogle-L'Ouverture, 1973) 157

25 Kwame Nkrumah, *Africa Must Unite* (Praeger, 1963) 176

26 Kwame Nkrumah, *Africa Must Unite* (Praeger, 1963) 176

27 Yilmaz Akyus, 'Multilateral Disciplines and the Question of Policy Space' in Julio Faundez and Celine Tan *International Economic Law, Globalization and Developing Countries* (Edward Elgar, 2012) 34–7

28 Yilmaz Akyus, 'Multilateral Disciplines and the Question of Policy Space' in Julio Faundez and Celine Tan *International Economic Law, Globalization and Developing Countries* (Edward Elgar, 2012) 34–7

29 Jagdish Bhagwati, 'Reshaping the WTO' (2005) Far Eastern Economic Review vol 168 (2) p 24 at 2

30 Jagdish Bhagwati, *In Defense of Globalisation* (Oxford University Press, 2004) 5; Jagdish Bhagwati, *Free Trade Today* (OUP, 2002) 6, 9

Some have praised the allowances created by the trading system. The former director-general of GATT, Eric Wyndham-White, described the non-discrimination principle as the GATT's 'cornerstone.'[31] This was the post-war GATT norm. This convention of unconditional most favoured nation (MFN) is found in Article 1:1, and non-discrimination is provided in Article III of the GATT. It requires that goods, when legally imported, will be treated the same as domestic goods. Notwithstanding this essential element of the norm, several shifts from it were allowed.[32] The most significant of these exceptions are the customs union, free trade area, and 'interim' agreement to permit a transition period.[33] It was believed at the time that the exceptions would expand the trading system by complying with the requirement of 'substantially all the trade.'[34] In other words, the parties who wish to adopt this form of integration shall eliminate tariffs and other restrictions on the free flow of trade.

However, scholars have argued that from the inception of GATT, member states have found it difficult to comply with GATT Article XXIV in practice, except when compliance will favour the core countries.[35] Similarly, to Lester and Mercurio, the WTO members could not agree on the right interpretation and compliance for 'political and theoretical reasons.'[36] In the same vein, Jürgen Huber argued that from an economic perspective, advanced countries believed a fair chance should be given to developing countries. Nonetheless, politically due to tension between developing and developed countries, the latter not only tolerated but showed genuine interest in the affairs of the former. Also, core countries such as the United States and the EU needed to continue their influence in these countries; as such, many agreements did not meet the requirement of Article XXIV.[37]

Instructively, the Appellate Body has restricted flexibility in the application of GATT Article XXIV.[38] The Appellate Body held that Article XXIV:8 established a standard that must be complied with to satisfy the meaning of a customs union. Also, the Panel Report on Automotive Industry[39] indicated that GATT Article

31 Erick Wyndham-White, 'Negotiations in Prospect' in C Fred Bergsten (ed), *Toward a New World Trade Organisation Policy: The Maidenhead Paper* (Lexington Books, 1975) 321 cited in Jock A Finlayson and Mark W Zacher, 'The GATT and the Regulation of Trade Barriers: Regime Dynamics and Functions' (1981) International Organisation vol 35 (4) pp 561–602 at 566

32 Erick Wyndham-White, 'Negotiations in Prospect' in C Fred Bergsten (ed), *Toward a New World Trade Organisation Policy: The Maidenhead Paper* (Lexington Books, 1975) 321 cited in Jock A Finlayson and Mark W Zacher, 'The GATT and the Regulation of Trade Barriers: Regime Dynamics and Functions' (1981) International Organisation vol 35 (4) pp 561–602 at 566

33 General Agreement on Tariffs and Trade, October, 30, 1947 A-11, 55 U.N.T.S 194 (hereinafter, GATT) Article 7: (a)

34 GATT Article XXIV:8 (a) (i)

35 Finlayson and Zacher (n 31)

36 Simon Lester and Bryan Mercurio, *World Trade Law: Text, Materials and Commentary* (Hart, 2008) 353

37 Jürgen Huber, 'The Practice of GATT in Examining Regional Arrangements Under Article XXIV (1981) Journal of Common Market Studies vol xix (3) at 295

38 Turkey—Restrictions on Imports of Textile and Clothing Products WT/DA34/AB/R 22 October 1999 (Adopted the Dispute Settlement Body on 19 November 1999) paras 48 and 58

39 Canada—Certain Measures Affecting the Automotive Industry, WT/DS139/12WT/DS142/12/R. (4 October 2000) (Adopted 19 June 2000) 10.55-56

XXIV did not provide a reason for a breach or promote inconsistency with the MFN principle of the WTO.[40] There is no doubt that the aforementioned cases show that the adjudicating bodies will not make it easy for any country under GATT Article XXIV to undertake a measure inconsistent with the WTO. However, it would be inaccurate to state that GATT Article XXIV has not succeeded in ensuring compliance with free trade agreements (FTA); this is demonstrated in subsequent chapters. It has been argued that some core countries can ignore the requirements of Article XXIV when it is not convenient for them to comply. This is discussed later in this book.

In this book, specific terms are clarified to understand the context in which they are used. The phrases *core* and *peripheral* countries are used here to depict the unequal trade relationship between the EU and African countries. The terms 'centre' and 'peripheral' were originally coined by Raul Prebisch, the renowned Argentine economist.[41] He employed the prior terminology to elucidate the robust economic and political framework prevalent in Europe and the UK, in stark contrast to the feeble economy of Argentina. Consequently, it becomes evident that the application of a single theory of economic or political governance cannot be extended to both Argentina and Europe. Immanuel Wallerstein took the terminologies a step further[42] to develop a three-tier hierarchical structure of the world system—the *core*, *periphery*, and *semi-periphery*. *Core* countries are dominant capitalist nations, which use the labour and raw materials from the peripheral countries to good advantage. The latter classification relies extensively on the *core* countries for capital, usually categorised as underdeveloped nations. *Semi-periphery* shares the quality of the *core* and the *periphery*. For this research, the focus is on the *core-periphery*. The term *core* refers to developed countries in this research: mainly Western Europe, the United States, and other advanced countries. The term core is used interchangeably with other terms to refer to developed countries. *Peripheral* countries mean developing countries in the ACP countries. It will not include Brazil, India, China, and South Africa, as those will be referred to as advanced developing countries.

The concept of the core and periphery thus best describes the West–developing countries' relationship, although the broader relationship between the developed and developing countries has undergone some significant changes, since the first writings of Immanuel Wallerstein, with the rise of China and other emerging developing countries. As later explored in this book, the EU is advanced politically and economically, while the majority of ACP member states are categorised as least developed countries (LDC). Also, it is important to note that Eastern Europe did not colonise Africa, but for ease, the book would refer to the EU when it discusses asymmetry between the regions.

40 Canada—Certain Measures Affecting the Automotive Industry, WT/DS139/12WT/DS142/12/R. (4 October 2000) (Adopted 19 June 2000) 10.55-56

41 Edgar Dosman, *The Life and Times of Raul Prebisch 1901–1986* (McGill-Queen's University Press, 2008) 38

42 Immanuel Wallerstein, *World Systems Analysis: An Introduction* (Duke University Press, 2004) 28–31

Another term that needs clarification is 'systemic.' The word is borrowed from 'systemic racism' developed by sociologist Joe Feagin. The theory is a well-received way of explaining within the social sciences and humanities the importance of race and racism both historically and in today's world. Feagin describes the ideas and realities in his books.[43] He conceptualises 'systemic' racism as the kernel of racist realities, which permeate through the United States society—'the economy, politics, education, religion, the family, etc.—reflects the fundamental reality of systemic racism.'[44] There have been some positive reforms of the Europe–Africa relationship since the Lomé Conventions—different from the colonial period. Some positive elements in the Lomé and Cotonou Agreements are built to advance the interests of the African countries. However, in line with the aforementioned concept of systemic racism, 'systemic' power asymmetry is still embedded in the global trade and trade relationship between the EU and African countries—beginning from the colonial trade era.

This book is situated around the influence of colonial legal constructs on multilateral trading systems and bilateral agreements. It specifically links the current trading system between advanced countries and Africa to the colonial structure by using the EPAs as a case study. It does not just make a sweeping assertion about colonialism but instead explores colonial treaties and multilateral and bilateral agreements to demonstrate the similarities between the colonial and current trade asymmetries. This book expands the discussion on African countries' asymmetrical trade relations with the EU and other advanced countries. While there is a plethora of excellent current scholarship on the trade relationship between the EU and ACP countries,[45] there

43 Joe R Feagin, *Racist America: Roots, Current Realities, and Future Reparations* (Routledge New, 2001); Joe R Feagin, *Systemic Racism: A Theory of Oppression* (Routledge, 2006)

44 Joe R Feagin, *Racist America: Roots, Current Realities, and Future Reparations* (Routledge New, 2001); Joe R Feagin, *Systemic Racism: A Theory of Oppression* (Routledge, 2006) at 6

45 Christopher Stevens, Sanoussi Bilal, Francesco Rampa, et al. 'The New EPAs: Comparative Analysis of their Content and Challenges for 2008', Overseas Development Institute and the European Centre for Development Policy Management (2008) www.odi.org/sites/odi.org.uk/files/odi-assets/pu . . . xiv accessed 22 January 2021; Dan Lui & Sanoussi Bilal, 'Contentious Issues in the Interim EPAs: Potential Flexibility in the Negotiations' (2009) https://ecdpm.org/WP-content/uploads/2013/11/DP-89-contentious-issues-Interim-EPAs-Flexibility-Negotiationd-2009.pdf accessed 14 December 2020 at 3; S Bilal and V Roza, 'Addressing the Fiscal Effects of an EPA' (Study With Support of Irish Aid, Department of Foreign Affairs, 2007) www.ecdpm.org/bilal accessed 18 February 2020; Sanoussi Bilal and Christopher Stevens, 'The Interim Economic Partnership Agreements Between the EU and African States: Contents, Challenges and Prospects' (2009) www.ecdpm.or/pmr17 126 accessed 01 July 2020; Cosmas M Obote Ochieng, 'The EU—ACP Economic Partnership Agreements and "Development Questions": Constraints and Opportunities Posed by Article XXIV and Special and Differential Treatment Provisions of The WTO' (2007) JIEL vol 10 (2) pp 363–95; Cosmas Milton Obote Ochieng, 'Legal and Systemic Issues in the Interim Economic Partnership Agreements: Which Way Now?' (2009) Issue Paper No 2; Stephen Hurt, 'The EU-SADC Economic Partnership Agreement Negotiations: Locking in the Neoliberal Development Model in Southern Africa' (2012) Third World Quarterly vol 499 www.tandfonline.com/loi/ctwq20 accessed 24 May 2020; Samuel O Oloruntoba, *Regionalism and Integration in Africa: EU-ACP Economic Partnership Agreements and Euro-Nigeria Relations* (2016); Angelos Sepos, 'Imperial Power Europe? The EU'S Relations With the ACP Countries' (2010); Tony Heron, 'Asymmetric

is marginal research focusing on extensive analysis of how the negotiations and agreements were influenced by 'systemic' asymmetry with its origin in colonialism.

In 1962, Touré cautioned that trade relations between Africa and the newfound organisation, the European Economic Community (EEC), would perpetuate African countries' marginal place as 'hewers of wood and drawers of water.'[46] This unvarnished prognosis about the perpetuation of the colonial ideological construct of the trading system merits investigation of the EU and Africa EPA as a case study. Thus, the use of 'systemic' best describes the relationship between the EU and ACP countries, as demonstrated later in the chapters.

Chapter 1 of this book establishes the parameters of the subject matter, the uneven trade relations between core countries and peripheral countries. Specifically, it discusses the trade relations between the core and the ACP countries, delving into the nuances of Article XXIV of the GATT/WTO and drawing connections between the contradictions in multilateral and bilateral trade relations and the influence of colonialism.

Chapter 2 provides a theoretical framework for the analysis presented in this book. It examines Article XXIV of the GATT within the context of the EPAs between ACP countries and the EU. The discussion considers the ideological frameworks of neoliberalism and asymmetry, as well as the constructivist school of thought regarding the role of ideas. John Ruggie's analysis of the global trading system as embedded liberalism is crucial in illuminating the contradictions inherent in the trading system.

Chapter 3 traces the history of power asymmetry back to the Berlin Conference of West Africa. It explores various articles of the General Act and other treaties between European powers and indigenous peoples of Africa. While some argue against the significance of the Berlin Conference, this chapter contends that the General Act legitimised the partitioning of Africa and weakened the African trading system. Understanding the General Act and subsequent treaties between European powers and Africa is essential for comprehending trade dynamics between Africa and advanced countries.

Chapter 4 examines a series of trade agreements between Europe and ACP countries prior to and after independence. It provides an overview of trade relations between ACP countries and the EU from the late 1950s and 1960s until the present day. The analysis scrutinises trade activities between these regions and evaluates the asymmetrical power dynamics between core and peripheral countries.

Chapter 5 focuses on Ghana's negotiations and agreement on EPAs with the EU as a case study. It explores the key articles of the agreement and highlights Ghana's insufficient capacity to fulfil its obligations. While certain provisions for special and differential treatment were offered, the agreement remains asymmetrical as it primarily reflects the interests and norms of the dominant core.

Chapter 6 delves into the EPA negotiations and examines whether Nigeria effectively addressed the power imbalance that favoured the EU. The chapter specifically

Bargaining and Development Trade-offs in the CARIFORUM-European Union Economic Partnership Agreement' (2011) Review of International Political Economy vol 18 (3) pp 328–57, www.tandfonline.com/action/journalInformation?journalCode=rrip20

46 Sekou Toure, 'Africa's Future and the World' (1962) Foreign Affairs vol 41 (1) 141-151

focuses on Nigeria's interpretation of Article XXIV of the GATT. These inquiries are answered through extensive interviews conducted in Nigeria and the examination of archival documents obtained from Nigerian governmental organisations and agencies. The chapter concludes that Nigeria declined to sign the agreement due to its heavy reliance on tax-free oil exports to the EU and its plans to negotiate a new agreement with the UK after Brexit. In February 2024, the two countries signed a memorandum of understanding (MOU), which the chapter investigates while highlighting the controversies surrounding it.

Chapter 7 expands on the discourse surrounding Africa and delves deeper into the concept of multipolarity. It showcases the potential for fruitful collaboration and advantages that exist between China and Africa. Africa's leaders widely commend China's approach towards addressing the continent's developmental requirements. In contrast to Western investors, who often adopt a dominant post-colonial stance, China has adeptly comprehended and confronted the challenges confronting Africa. While Europe and the United States prioritise democracy, the rule of law, and good governance as prerequisites for offering assistance, China adheres to a policy of non-interventionism. This chapter comprehensively examines China's potential encroachment upon the sovereignty of African nations, with particular attention placed on China's interactions with Kenya. These concerns are subsequently tackled.

Chapter 8 concludes the book by emphasising the contradicting nature of the theories that underlie the trading system. It underscores the imperative for African countries to wholeheartedly embrace multipolarity in their trade relationships. The chapter accentuates the possibility of African countries establishing a patron-client style of trade relationship with China and underscores the significance of remaining watchful and discerning.

1.2 Conclusion

The book demonstrates with evidence that the current multilateral regime, of which Africa is part, according to Mandelson is based on a colonial ideological construct.[47] Thus, a genuine structure to make trade between Africa and the EU beneficial to the continent of Africa would deviate from the antiquated ideology of patron-client relations and treat African countries as equal.[48] Notwithstanding the rhetoric of the previous, the colonial relics still permeate the relations of Africa with the West, although modified and refined.

Bibliography

Adekeye A, & Kaye W, *The EU and Africa: From Eurafrique to Afro-Europa* (Hurt & Company Ltd, 2012)

Akyus Y, 'Multilateral Disciplines and the Question of Policy Space' in Julio Faundez & Celine Tan (eds), *International Economic Law, Globalisation and Developing Countries* (Edward Elgar, 2012)

47 Mandelson (n 19)
48 Mandelson (n 19)

Anand R P, 'Attitudes of the Asian-African States Toward Certain Problems of International Law' (1966) 15 International and Comparative Law Quarterly vol 55
Anghie A, *Imperialism, Sovereignty and the Making of International Law* (CUP, 2004)
Canada-Certain Measures Affecting the Automotive Industry, WT/DS139/12WT/DS142/12/R. (4 October 2000) (Adopted 19 June 2000)
Cox R, 'Critical Theory' in Thomas G Weiss & Rorden Wilkinson (eds), *International Organisation and Global Governance* (Routledge, 2014)
Drahos P, 'When the Weak Bargain With the Strong: Negotiations in the World Trade Organisation' (2003) International Negotiations vol 8 pp 79–109
Dunoff J L, 'Rethinking International Trade' (1998) University of Pennsylvania Journal of International Economic Law vol 19 (2) p 34
Ernst-Ulrich P, 'Narrating International Economic Law' (2014) Constitutional Limit' Max Planck p 787
Falk R, *The New States and International Legal Order vol 118 of Recueil de Cours* (A.W. Sijthoff, 1968)
Feagin J R, *Racist America: Roots, Current Realities, and Future Reparations* (Routledge, 2001)
Feagin J R, *Systemic Racism: A Theory of Oppression* (Routledge, 2006)
Fred Bergsten C (ed), *Toward a New World Trade Organisation Policy: The Maidenhead Paper* (Lexington Books, 1975)
General Agreement on Tariffs and Trade, Oct 30, 1947, A-11, 55 U.N.T.S 194 (hereinafter, GATT)
Institute fur Auslandisches offenthiches Recht www.zaoerv.de (accessed 10 May 2018)
Jagdish Bhagwati, *In Defense of Globalisation* (OUP, 2004) 5
Jagdish Bhagwati, 'Reshaping the WTO' (2005) Far Eastern Economic Review vol 168 (2)
Jock A Finlayson, & Mark W Zacher, 'The GATT and the Regulation of Trade Barriers: Regime Dynamics and Functions' (1981) International Organisation vol 35 (4) pp 561–602
Jurgen Huber, 'The Practice of GATT in Examining Regional Arrangements Under Article XXIV' (1981) Journal of Common Market Studies vol xix (3)
Kwame Nkrumah, *Africa Must Unite* (Praeger, 1963)
Lang A, 'Reconstructing Embedded Liberalism: John Ruggie and Constructivist Approaches to the Study of the International Trade Regime' (2006) Journal of International Law vol 9 (1) p 84
Lester S, & Mercurio B, *World Trade Law: Text, Materials, and Commentary* (Hart Publishing, 2008)
Mandelson P, *Open Markets, Open Trade: Europe's Global Challenge* (European Parliament, Brussels, 19 September 2005) 3
Ndlovu-Gatsheni S J, 'Decoloniality as the Future of Africa' (2015) History Compass vol 13 (10) pp 485–496 DOI:10.111/hic3.12264
Polanyi K, *The Great Transformation: The Political Origin of Origin of Our Time* (Beacon Press, 1944)
Ruggie J G, 'International Regimes, Transactions, and Change: Embedded Liberalism in the Postwar Economic Order' (1982) International Organisation vol 36 (2) pp 379–415
Singh J P, 'Wiggle Room: New Issues and North-South Negotiations During Uruguay Round,' Prepared for the Conference on Developing Countries and the Trade Negotiation Process UNCTAD (Geneva, 6–7 November 2003)
Turkey's Restriction on Imports of Textile and Clothing Products WT/DA34/AB/R 22 October 1999 (Adopted the Dispute Settlement Body on 19 November 1999)
Wallerstein I, *World Systems Analysis: An Introduction* (Duke University Press, 2004)

2 Theoretical Framework of the Global Trading System

2.1 Introduction

The European and African, Caribbean, and Pacific (ACP) countries agreed in 2000 to negotiate EPAs by Article 36 (1) of the Cotonou Agreement to design a trade arrangement that aligns with Article XXIV of the World Trade Organization (WTO) law by gradually removing barriers to trade between the parties and to improve cooperation in all aspect of trade. In essence, the negotiations of the EPAs heralded the end of the non-reciprocal trade preference that ACP countries benefitted from the EU. The preferences ended as the most favoured nation deviation allowed by the WTO expired at the end of 2007, in line with the provision of Article 37 (1) of the Cotonou Agreement.[1]

This chapter explores a theoretical framework from the perspectives of a free trade conformists[2] and a free trade revisionist.[3] In the typical narrative of the effects of free trade, as exemplified by the views of Ikenberry, the multilateral system harmonised liberalisation and trade growth, ensuring full employment and economic

1 William Brown, *The European Union and Africa: The Restructuring of North-South Relations* (IB Tauris, 2002) 368

2 John Gerard Ruggie, 'International Regimes, Transactions, and Change: Embedded Liberalism in the Postwar Economic Order' (1982) International Organisation vol 36 (2) pp 379–415; Jagdish Bhagwati, 'Reshaping the WTO' (2005) Far Eastern Economic Review vol 168 p 2; John G Ikenberry, 'A World Economy Restored: Experts Consensus and the Anglo-American Postwar Settlement' (Winter, 1992) International Organisation vol 46 (1) pp 289–321; Kenneth W Abbott, 'GATT as a Public Institution: The Uruguay Round and Beyond' (1992) Brooklyn Journal of International Law vol XVIII p CV1

3 Gardner Patterson, *Discrimination in International Trade: The Policy Issues 1945–1965* (Princeton University Press, 1996); Rorden Wilkinson, *What's Wrong With the WTO and How to Fix It* (Polity Press, 2014); Rorden Wilkinson eds, *Global Governance, Poverty and Inequality* (Routledge, 2010); Rorden Wilkinson, 'Language, Power and Multilateral Trade Negotiations' (2009) Review of International Political vol 16 (4), doi:10.1080/09692290802587734; Andrew Lang, 'Reconstructing Embedded Liberalism: John Ruggie and Constructivist Approaches to the Study of the International Trade Regime' (2006) Journal of International Law vol 9 (1); Robert W Cox, 'Social Forces, States, and World Orders: Beyond International Relations Theory' (1981) Millennium-Journal of International Studies vol 10 (126); Robert W Cox, *The Political Economy of a Plural World: Critical Reflections on Power, Moral, and Civilization* (Routledge, 2002)

DOI: 10.4324/9781032615059-2

stabilisation.[4] However, in its report, the International Labour Organization (ILO) states that one-third of the global workforce of three billion people is not employed.[5] Also, in advanced countries, the low employment rate ranges from 3% to 25%. The unemployment situation in peripheral countries is gloomier, where the ILO estimated that 1.3 billion people are not employed. Several of these people, according to the report, will not be employed in their lifetime.

According to Bhagwati, those who opposed the idea of free trade are the 'chaff' and should not be associated with the 'wheat' of common sense. Another primary voice of trade liberalisation is Ruggie, who constructed the idea of 'embedded liberalism.' He argues that free trade is balanced because it provides several exceptions in the GATT rules. Kenneth Abbott is known to acclaim the importance of free trade and the global order that the United States championed since 1945.[6]

In contrast to these established views, there are small but notable groups of critics: Robert Cox, Rorden Wilkinson, Mark Mazower, and Gardner Patterson. These authors argue that the multilateral trading system is asymmetrical. It is promoted by the core, led by the United States, to serve its interests. Cox elucidates that the 'dominant side are the theorists of globalisation who envisage American-style capitalism absorbing the rest of the world into a single global political economy.' Referring to the views of Bhagwati earlier, Wilkinson argues that members of the multilateral system have become so accustomed to the manner of talking deployed by supporters of free trade that this has constrained most scholars and WTO members from critically subjecting such discourse to proper examination.[7] This chapter aligns with critical international political economy scholars,[8] who deviate from the usual standard of neoliberal argument, to gain insight into the interpretation of 'embedded liberalism' as conceptualised by John Ruggie.[9]

The remaining part explores embedded liberalism, constructivist and reflectivist standpoints on the role of ideas. It further examines ideas as a weapon in the hands of the core. It then investigates systemic economic power asymmetry that exists between the core and peripheral countries and discusses the various perspectives

4 John G Ikenberry, 'A World Economy Restored: Experts Consensus and the Anglo-American Post-war Settlement' (1992) International Organisation vol 46 (1) pp 289–321 at 290

5 *ILO World Employment Report Life at Work in the Information Economy* (Geneva: International Labour Organization, 2001) 1 www.ilo.org/global/about-the-ilo/newsroom/news/WCMS_007830/lang--en/index.htm

6 Kenneth W Abbott, 'GATT as a Public Institution: The Uruguay Round and Beyond' (1992) Brooklyn Journal of International Law vol XVIII: CV1 pp 66, 85

7 Wilkinson Rorden Wilkinson, *What's Wrong With the WTO and How to Fix It* (Polity Press, 2014) 79

8 Robert Cox, 'Critical Theory' in T Weiss and R Wilkinson (eds), *International Organisation and Global Governance: What Matters & Why* (Routledge, 2014); James Scott and Rorden Wilkinson, 'Reglobalising Trade: Progressive Global Governance in an Age of Uncertainty' (2021) Globalisations vol 18 (1) pp 55–69 at 62; Jennifer Clapp and Rorden Wilkinson eds, *Global Governance, Poverty and Inequality* (Routledge, 2010); Wilkinson (n 3)

9 Hubert Buch-Hansen and Angela Wigger, *The Politics of European Competition Regulation: A Critical Political Economy Perspective* (Routledge, 2011) 7, 57–8; 72–4; Laura Horn, *Regulating Corporate Governance in the EU: Towards a Marketisation of Corporate Control* (Palgrave Macmillan, 2011) 22, 50

on trade liberalisation to understand the contradictions inherent in the multilateral trading system. In addition, it explores the various discourses employed by the dominant core to eclipse critical questioning of the proponents of the ideas of free trade.

2.2 Multilateral Trading System: Exceptions and Contradictions

The phenomenon of the GATT system up to the point of the Uruguay Round represents two echelons, in which the core (developed) countries, directed initially by the United States and later by the Organisation for Economic Co-operation and Development (OECD) countries with the United States (US) and the European Union, pre-eminently set the agenda and fashioned policy outcomes.[10] On the other hand, the developing countries were under the jurisdiction of Part IV to keep within bounds their obligations but did not influence the way the GATT rules were shaped.[11] According to Lamp, the developing countries did not ask for these exceptions but rather wanted the obligation to be shaped in a manner that favours them as well. He argues, granting '"special" treatment to developing countries was a tool for the developed countries to preserve their preferred design of the trade regime, and stick to favoured method of making trade law.'[12]

Initially, the Uruguay Round ended Part IV of the GATT, replacing it with the Single Undertaking.[13] Consequently, all WTO member states were required to be WTO rules compliant, even if peripheral (developing) countries benefitted from special and differential treatment in other forms, for example, more extended periods to enforce WTO rules and commitments to grant technical assistance from the core countries.[14] Simultaneously, Pascal Lamy perceived the steady shift in power relationships in the multilateral trading system.[15] According to the observer, neither the USA nor the EU can shape agendas and policy outcomes without the contribution

10 Saxeba Sada Shanka, 'The Uruguay Round: Expectations of Developing Countries, Intereconomics Verlag Weltarchiv, Hamburg' (1988) vol 23 (6) p 269 www.econstor.eu/bitstream/10419/140157/1/v23-i06-a04-BF02925124.PDF accessed 28 October 2021

11 Saxeba Sada Shanka, 'The Uruguay Round: Expectations of Developing Countries, Intereconomics Verlag Weltarchiv, Hamburg' (1988) vol 23 (6) p 269 www.econstor.eu/bitstream/10419/140157/1/v23-i06-a04-BF02925124.PDF accessed 28 October 2021 at 270

12 Nicolas Lamp, 'How Some Countries Become "Special": Developing Countries and the Construction of Difference in Multilateral Trade Lawmaking' (2015) JIEL vol 18 pp 743–71 at 744; Inebu Agbo-Ejeh, 'Multilateral and Bilateral Trade Agreements at the Service of "Common Interest"' in Mariela de Amstalden, Nial Moran and Henok Asmelash (eds), *International Economic Law: New Approaches and Issues* (Springer, 2023)

13 WTO, 'Part IV Negotiation', at 308–9 www.wto.org/english/res_e/booksp_e/historywto_09_e.pdf accessed 28 October 2021

14 Stephen Woolcock, 'The Scope for Asymmetry in the World Trade Organisation (WTO)' in Sanoussi Bilal, Philippe De Lombaerde and Diana Tussie (eds), *Asymmetric Trade Negotiations* (Routledge, 2016) 29

15 Pascal Lamy, 'Emerging Economies Have Shifted the Balance of Power in World Trade' (Director-General Pascal Lamy, presenting the Richard Snape Lecture in Melbourne, Australia 26 November 2012) www.wto.org/english/news_e/sppl_e/sppl258_e.htm accessed 28 October 2021

of advanced developing countries.[16] It is no more 'the world of the twentieth century dominated by the US pillar on one side and the European pillar on the other.'[17] There can be no consensus in the WTO, however, without the endorsement of the USA and the EU. Nevertheless, the rise of China and the expansion of economic ascendancy of India and countries like Brazil and South Africa have created a large heterogeneous power arrangement within the WTO system.[18] The endorsement of the Single Undertaking has raised the supposition of peripheral countries that they can have a say in trade negotiations as legitimate members of the WTO.[19]

According to Woolcock, the degree to which the precursory asymmetric power relationship between the dominant core and the peripheral countries in the multilateral trading system can be altered or remedied is contingent on the number of elements.[20] As noted, Lamy in his lecture argued that the advanced developing countries had increased their market power.[21] However, Woolcock observed that the African countries are severely restricted by economic deficiency and, as such, have not been able to shape outcomes in the multilateral trading system and regional trade arrangement with the EU.[22]

There has been a shift in the multilateral trading system from the late 1990s and early 2000s—a steady rise of the bilateral free trade agreement.[23] Viner observed that the multilateral trading system has never been devoid of bilateralism.[24] Bilateralism and regionalism in trade relations were present prior to the endorsement of GATT in 1948.[25] Even though Article I made provision for the multilateral system, the elements of the bilateral arrangement are present. For instance, tariff reductions were negotiated with principal suppliers first and subsequently multilaterised through the MFN clause.[26] The aim was to reduce the complexities of the process of negotiating tariff reduction prior to the introduction of general tariff formulae.[27] However, the consequence is that it can produce asymmetric bargaining relations between the dominant core and peripheral countries in the GATT system.[28]

As the challenges of making progress in the multilateral trading system mount, there has been a shift in focus toward bilateralism from the 2000s. It was reported on the WTO website that as of 1 January 2024, 361 RTAs were in force.[29] The EU,

16 Woolcock (n 14)
17 Lamy (n 15)
18 Lamy (n 15)
19 Woolcock (n 14)
20 Woolcock (n 14)
21 Lamy (n 15)
22 Woolcock (n 14)
23 Kenneth Heydon K and Stephen Woolcock, *The Rise of Bilateralism: Comparing American, European and Asian Approaches to Preferential Trade Agreements* (United Nations University Press, 2009) 3–4, 187–9
24 Jacob Viner, *The Customs Union Issue* edited by Paul Oslingston (OUP, 2014)
25 Jacob Viner, *The Customs Union Issue* edited by Paul Oslingston (OUP, 2014) at 4–21
26 Gardner (n 3) at 7
27 Gardner (n 3) at 7
28 Woolcock (n 14)
29 World Trade Organization, 'Regional Trade Agreements' www.wto.org accessed 15 April 2024

since the beginning of 2000, has encouraged regional integration through a bilateral trade agreement. The EU-Mercado Comun del Sur, (Southern Common Market) (MERCOSUR) negotiated and signed a full EPA plus interim EPAs with other African countries, but Nigeria has yet to sign the agreement. According to Woolcock, the proliferation of bilateralism is a 'reestablishment of the asymmetric power of the major developed countries.'[30] Whether the exceptions (embedded liberalism) provided in the EU and Africa's bilateral arrangement suffice to balance domestic policy and international establishment depends on how much the peripheral countries have taken advantage of the exceptions provided in the multilateral trading system.

In its judgment, the Appellate Body in China-Raw Material declared that the whole WTO law embodies 'balance . . . between trade and non-trade-related concerns.'[31] Besides the fundamental rules of the WTO, the law also made provisions that address incompatibility between trade liberalisation, values, and interests. The laws are termed 'exceptions,' and it permits WTO members to vary the rules in the specific circumstance in order to take into account domestic issues that are not in tandem with global trade.[32] The domestic economic concerns related to the protection of local industry from harm if there is a surge in imports, providing a safeguard for the balance of payment and regional economic integration. The deviations are found in Articles XII, XIX, and XXIV of the GATT 1994, Articles V, X, and XII of the General Agreement on Trade in Services (GATS), and provisions on safeguards.

Therefore, according to Ruggie, the regime created at Bretton Woods was premised on exigency, and leave, of state intervention into the market for the sole aim of ensuring stability at the domestic level. In the manner now indicated, the goal has become a constituent part of the trading system established after the Second World War. In this sense, the cardinal vision of the trading regime has two main prongs: the first objective was to strategise a means to safeguard domestic stability without, secondly, dismantling the international regime as happened between 1918 and 1939.[33] While the trade regime's core principle is non-discrimination, it also necessitates the obligation to preserve stability at the national level.[34] Thus, some level of protection was permissible, so long as it was proportionate to 'external disturbance.'[35] It is this balancing between a national and international

30 World Trade Organization, 'Regional Trade Agreements' www.wto.org accessed 15 April 2024 at 31

31 China-Measure Related to the Exportation of Various Raw Materials, WT/DS394/WT/DS395/WT/DS398 (2012) para 306

32 Peter Van den Bossche and Werner Zdouc, *The Law and Policy pf the World Trade Organization: Text, Cases and Materials* (4th ed, CUP, 2017) 42

33 John G Ruggie, 'International Regimes, Transactions, and Change: Embedded Liberalisation and the Post-war Economic Order', in Stephen D Krasner (ed), *International Regimes* (Cornell University Press, 1983) 202

34 John G Ruggie, 'International Regimes, Transactions, and Change: Embedded Liberalisation and the Post-war Economic Order', in Stephen D Krasner (ed), *International Regimes* (Cornell University Press, 1983) at 209

35 John G Ruggie, 'International Regimes, Transactions, and Change: Embedded Liberalisation and the Post-war Economic Order', in Stephen D Krasner (ed), *International Regimes* (Cornell University Press, 1983) at 221

regime that Ruggie termed 'embedded liberalism.' As noted in Chapter 1, the idea of embedded liberalism was first used by Karl Polanyi but was borrowed and elaborated on by John Ruggie and other modern scholars.[36] In the article, Ruggie's point centres on ideological contestations over the mainstream ideas on which the post-war international economic order was based. Ruggie observed that even though multilateralism and tariff reduction principles are part of the proviso, the multilateral trading system primarily means the 'non-discrimination' obligation on tariff reduction that was, in the beginning, malleable. More so, the text contained different forms of 'safeguards, exemptions, exceptions and restrictions'—for instance, the balance of payment, preferential trading agreements, and emergency safeguards. These frameworks are put in place to advance and protect national policies.[37]

Ruggie's idea of embedded liberalism has prompted scholars to reconsider it from various perspective, revealing new insights. Rodrik argued that the compromise of embedded liberalism had served the global economy well because there has been no 'shift' from the welfare state.[38] Nevertheless, he advocated 'creative thinking' to energise the embedded liberalism compromise to meet the economic challenge of the current time.[39] According to Nye and Donahue, the compromise reached after the Second World War harmonised well between the domestic and the global arrangement.[40] However, the authors argued, some changes like interdependence call for a re-examination of embedded liberalism. According to Hart and Prakash, the politico-economic order, which originated after World War II, was based on embedded liberalism—a connubiality of free trade with government intervention.[41] The authors maintained that the logic of embedded liberalism is to preserve the idea of free trade.[42] They interpreted government intervention as 'side-payments to domestic actors hurt by the multilateral trading regime'; embedded liberalism from their perspective is 'classical protectionism.'[43] However, Helleiner's reinterpretation of the history of the 1944 Bretton Woods Agreement

36 Mark Granovetter, 'Economic Action and Social Structure: The Problem of Embeddedness' (1985) American Journal of Sociology vol 91 pp 481–510; Peter Evans, *Embedded Autonomy: States and Industrial Transformation* (Princeton University Press, 1995) cited in Karl Polanyi, *The Great Transformation: The Political Origin of Origin of our Time* (Beacon Press, 1944) xxiv

37 Ruggie (n 35) at 212

38 Dani Rodrik, *Has Globalisation Gone Too Far* (Institute for International Economics, United States, 1997) 65–6

39 Dani Rodrik, *Has Globalisation Gone Too Far* (Institute for International Economics, United States, 1997) at 67

40 Joseph Nye and John D Donahue eds, *Governance in a Globalising World* (R R Donnelley and Sons, 2000) 17–8

41 Jeffrey A Hart and Aseem Prakash, 'The Decline of "Embedded Liberalism" and the Rearticulation of the Keynesian Welfare State' (1997) New Political Economy vol 2 (1) 65–78 at 65

42 Jeffrey A Hart and Aseem Prakash, 'The Decline of "Embedded Liberalism" and the Rearticulation of the Keynesian Welfare State' (1997) New Political Economy vol 2 (1) 65–78 at 73

43 Jeffrey A Hart and Aseem Prakash, 'The Decline of "Embedded Liberalism" and the Rearticulation of the Keynesian Welfare State' (1997) New Political Economy vol 2 (1) 65–78

offered a different observation.[44] He argued against the conventional understanding that the agreement negotiated between 1942 and 1944 by the United States and Britain focused mainly on the concerns of the core countries and sidelined the matters of interest to the poor countries.[45]

Three key figures in trade law have also made a substantial contribution to embedded liberalism. Dunoff, in his interpretation of embedded liberalism, underscores the intricacies of the multifarious aims of the post-war trade system built to protect domestic policies.[46] The multilateral system founders were committed to both 'international markets' and 'interventionist domestic policies.'[47] However, the author contended that as interdependence increases through globalisation, embedded liberalism is jeopardised, necessitating a worldwide reform economy.[48] Another trade lawyer, Robert Howse, argued that embedded liberalism had lost cohesion. According to him, the GATT embedded liberalism is no longer evident due to the system's technocratic beliefs.[49] Howse is concerned that the present form of the trading system poses a threat to domestic welfare, which at the beginning was held to form the essence of the system.[50] On his part, Steinberg discusses embedded liberalism in connection to the 'object and purpose' of the WTO agreements and refuses to entertain the argument that the trading system was purely liberal.[51] According to Pauwelyn, embedded liberalism, crafted by 'technocratic elites' of the WTO, has lost legitimacy because it ignored the call for adaptability and hence is out of touch with societal needs.[52]

44 Erick Helleiner, 'Reinterpreting Bretton Woods: International Development and the Neglected Origins of Embedded Liberalism' (2006) Development and Change vol 37 (5) 943–67; Erick Helleiner, 'The Life and Times of Embedded Liberalism: Legacies and Innovations Since Bretton Woods' (2019) Review of International Political Economy doi: 10.1080/09692290.2019.1607767

45 Erick Helleiner, 'Reinterpreting Bretton Woods: International Development and the Neglected Origins of Embedded Liberalism' (2006) Development and Change vol 37 (5) 943–4, 46

46 Jeffrey L Dunoff, 'Does Globalisation Advance Human Rights' (1999) Brooklyn Journal of International Law vol XXV (1) p 125

47 Jeffrey L Dunoff, 'Does Globalisation Advance Human Rights' (1999) Brooklyn Journal of International Law vol XXV (1) p 125 at 131

48 Jeffrey L Dunoff, 'Does Globalisation Advance Human Rights' (1999) Brooklyn Journal of International Law vol XXV (1) p 125 at 136–7; Jeffrey L Dunof, 'The Death of the Trade Regime' (1999) EJIL vol 10 (4) pp 733–62 at 738

49 Robert Howse and Kalypso Nicolaidis, 'Legitimacy Through "Higher Law"? Why Constitutionalising the WTO Is a Step Too Far', in Thomas Cottier and Petro C Mavroidis (eds), *The Role of the Judge in International Trade Regulation: Experience and Lesson for the WTO* (University of Michigan Press, 2003) 307

50 Robert Howse and Kalypso Nicolaidis, 'Legitimacy Through "Higher Law"? Why Constitutionalising the WTO Is a Step Too Far', in Thomas Cottier and Petro C Mavroidis (eds), *The Role of the Judge in International Trade Regulation: Experience and Lesson for the WTO* (University of Michigan Press, 2003) 307

51 Richard H Steinberg, 'Judicial Lawmaking at the WTO: Discursive, Constitutional, and Political Constraints' (2004) AJIL vol 247 at 262

52 Joost Pauwelyn, 'The Transformation of World Trade' (2005) Michigan Law Review vol 104 (1) pp 6 and 13

In Winikoff's perspective, the sanitary and phytosanitary (SPS) measures should be interpreted to align with the trading system's initial objective; referring to Ruggie, he argued that free trade could not be practised to the detriment of 'important social goals.'[53] The approach adopted to solve challenges in a country should be accepted in the context of embedded liberalism.[54] Diebold points out that the trading system was far from rigid.[55] The founders called for state intervention to protect against harm associated with market liberalisation.[56] In his examination of South Africa's participation in the GATT, Ismail questioned Ruggie's interpretation of embedded liberalism. According to him, it failed to resolve the contradiction in trade theory and practice.[57] Lang argued that there is a hint of mysticism around the tribute paid to the trading system by the theory of embedded liberalism.[58] In view that it constrained further interrogation of why it peripheralised the concerns of the developing countries, who struggle with the systemic economic power asymmetry between it and the dominant core.[59] According to Dillion, the narrative of embedded liberalism did not take account of the impact of colonialism and the 'exploitation' of formal colonies.[60] According to Ismail, the past eight GATT rounds had not adequately given attention to matters of interest to developing countries.[61] However, the author notes that the GATT created an exception to the general principle of MFN and national treatment by enacting special and differential treatment provisions. Nevertheless, the clause is ineffective as it is drafted in best endeavour terms.[62]

Also, quite crucial, Lang noted that the development issue did not feature in the narrative of embedded liberalism and free trade.[63] According to him, embedded liberalism

53 David Winikoff, Sheila Jasanoff, Lawrence Busch et al., 'Adjusting the GM Food Wars: Science, Risk and Democracy in World Trade Law' (2005) 30 Yale Journal of International Law vol 81 at 107

54 David Winikoff, Sheila Jasanoff, Lawrence Busch et al., 'Adjusting the GM Food Wars: Science, Risk and Democracy in World Trade Law' (2005) 30 Yale Journal of International Law vol 81 at 107, 122

55 William Diebold Jr., 'From the ITO to GATT—And Back?' in Orin Kirshner (ed), *The Bretton Woods—GATT System Retrospect and Prospect After Fifty Years* (Routledge, 1996) 152, 153, 154, 160

56 William Diebold Jr., 'From the ITO to GATT—And Back?' in Orin Kirshner (ed), *The Bretton Woods—GATT System Retrospect and Prospect After Fifty Years* (Routledge, 1996) 152, 153, 154, 160

57 Faizel Ismail, 'Empirical Analysis of Apartheid South Africa's Ideas and Practices in the GATT: 1947 TO 1994' (A Thesis Submitted to the University of Manchester for the Degree of Ph.D. Politics, 2015) 28

58 Andrew Lang, 'Reconstructing Embedded Liberalism: John Ruggie and Constructivist Approaches to the Study of the International Trade Regime' (2006) Journal of International Law vol 9 (1) p 84

59 Andrew Lang, 'Reconstructing Embedded Liberalism: John Ruggie and Constructivist Approaches to the Study of the International Trade Regime' (2006) Journal of International Law vol 9 (1) p 84.

60 Sara Dillion, 'A Farewell to "Linkage": International Trade Law and Global Sustainability Indicators' (2002) Rutgers Law Review vol 55 (1) p 87 at 152

61 Faizel Ismail, *Reforming the World Trade Organization: Developing Countries in the Doha Round* (Cuts International, 2009) 11

62 Faizel Ismail, *Reforming the World Trade Organization: Developing Countries in the Doha Round* (Cuts International, 2009) at 12; GATT Articles XXXVI, XXXVII, XXXVIII and XXXVI:8

63 Lang (n 3) at 99–100

'purchase[s] domestic stability in industrialised countries by externalising the adjustment cost to developing countries.'[64] According to Jackson, legal professionals look at the facts in the context of the real world.[65] He opined, 'globalisation is the reality of that world'; the other reality is perhaps what globalisation had brought upon peripheral countries.[66] Next, this chapter explores the extent to which ideas shape this reality.

2.3 The Role of Ideas in Using Ideas Strategically

This section draws upon the constructivist theory to gain insight into the role of ideas in promoting free trade and how ideas and interests influence the EU-ACP countries' trade relations. The mention of constructivism brings to mind a historical convention in international relations linked to the writings of John Ruggie.[67] It points to the relevant function ideas play in shaping social reality. Ruggie noted three ways by which ideas influence policy results: first is the presentation of a 'road map,' indicating how individuals determine what they prefer; the second centres on interests that '[i]deas can help individuals select one from among the set of viable outcomes.'[68] The third is 'institutionalisation'; once ideas become assigned to an institution, they would consistently set out a policy that excludes new ideas.[69] Ruggie argued that a state identity could be altered by, for instance, the formulation of a new ideology.[70] According to Shepsle, ideas are designed to catch people's attention, as 'competing elites seize on popular ideas to propagate and legitimise their interests, but ideas themselves do not play a causal role.'[71] To this rationalist view, interests come first and foremost and logically ahead of beliefs.[72]

Goldstein and Keohane categorised ideas as global views, a set of beliefs, and causal beliefs. Ideas to them can be used to influence policy 'by acting as roadmaps to assist agents in managing the absence of symmetry, as such embedded in the institution for a long time.'[73] Goldstein and Keohane state that alteration

64 Lang (n 3) at 100

65 John Jackson, 'The World Trade Organization After Ten Years: The Role of the WTO in a Globalized World' (2006) Current Legal Problems vol 59 (1) pp 427–46

66 John Jackson, 'The World Trade Organization After Ten Years: The Role of the WTO in a Globalized World' (2006) Current Legal Problems vol 59 (1) pp 427–46 at 428

67 Ruggie 1982 (n 2) at 379–415

68 Ruggie 1982 (n 2) at 379–415

69 John G Ruggie, *Constructing the World Polity: Essays on International Institutionalization* (Routledge, 1998) 17

70 John G Ruggie, *Constructing the World Polity: Essays on International Institutionalization* (Routledge, 1998) 17

71 Kenneth Shepsle ed, *Comment in Regulatory Policy and the Social Sciences* (University of California Press, 1985) 231–7; Judith Goldstein and Robert O Keohane, 'Ideas and Foreign Policy: An Analytical Framework' in Judith Goldstein and Robert O Keohane (eds), *Ideas and Foreign Policy: Beliefs, Institutions, and Political Changes* (Cornell University Press, 1993) 4

72 Judith Goldstein and Robert O Keohane, 'Ideas and Foreign Policy: An Analytical Framework' in Judith Goldstein and Robert O Keohane (eds), *Ideas and Foreign Policy: Beliefs, Institutions, and Political Changes* (Cornell University Press, 1993) 4

73 Goldstein and Keohane (n 71) at 30

of a policy arises through the power of ideas. As a new issue emerges, it calls for a fundamental reformulation of the existing ideas.[74] For instance, to move away from preferential arrangement to reciprocity, the EU commissioner crafted a narrative. Mandelson stated that the EPAs would, inevitably, herald the end of the colonial ideological construct of the previous trading system and usher in mutually beneficial economic development.[75] Also, the European Commission states that as the economic situation worsens, it must focus on trade and not rely on 'public finances.'[76] For example, Ikenberry cited the 1930s international economic breakdown, where the United States became focused on the liberalisation of the market, and the country's elite quickly embraced the idea.[77]

Ikenberry narrated that as the United States became keenly interested in economic liberalisation, the think tank acknowledged this idea and made it a reality.[78] The breakdown of the international economy led the Germans and the Japanese to form an economic alliance.[79] This triggered the United States to engage with its intellectuals and politicians to explore the viability of a regional economic bloc instead of a global economic arrangement.[80] The climactic point of the debate gave rise to the academic work of Nicholas Spykman, who expressed what is now known as 'conventional wisdom.' He highlights that the need for a westernised economic arrangement alone is inadequate to protect American interests in the world.[81] A post-war strategist was employed to consider the interests of the United States in worldwide terms.[82] The attack on Pearl Harbour further enforced the belief that the United States needed to team up with Great Britain to integrate the world.[83] Goldstein and Keohane opine[84] that ideas can have lasting influence even when their motive is questioned. Examples are found in the legal doctrine of

74 Goldstein and Keohane (n 71) at 30

75 Peter Mandelson, 'Open Markets, Open Trade: Europe's Global Challenge' (European Parliament, Brussels 19 September 2005) 3

76 EU-Commission 2013 Trade: A Key Source of Growth and Jobs for the EU-Commission Contribution to the European Council of 7–8 February' Brussels: European Commission http://eu2013.ie/media/eupresidency/content/documents/130207-Commission-Contribution-on-Trade-to-EC.pdf accessed 9 November 2021

77 John G Ikenberry, 'Creating Yesterday's New World Order: Keynesian "New Thinking" and the Anglo-American Postwar Settlement in Goldstein and Keohane' (n 76) at 63

78 John G Ikenberry, 'Creating Yesterday's New World Order: Keynesian "New Thinking" and the Anglo-American Postwar Settlement in Goldstein and Keohane' (n 76) at 63

79 John G Ikenberry, 'Creating Yesterday's New World Order: Keynesian "New Thinking" and the Anglo-American Postwar Settlement in Goldstein and Keohane' (n 76) at 63

80 John G Ikenberry, 'Creating Yesterday's New World Order: Keynesian "New Thinking" and the Anglo-American Postwar Settlement in Goldstein and Keohane' (n 76) at 63

81 Nicholas John Spykman, *American Strategy's in the World: The United States and the Balance of Power* (Harcourt, Brace, 1942) xx

82 Melvyn P Leffler, *A Preponderance of Power: National Security, The Truman Administration, and the Cold War* (Stanford University Press, 1992) 15–16, 193

83 Melvyn P Leffler, *A Preponderance of Power: National Security, The Truman Administration, and the Cold War* (Stanford University Press, 1992) 15–16, 193; Goldstein and Keohane (n 76) at 63

84 Goldstein and Keohane (n 71)

GATT. They further argued, 'administrative agencies, laws, norms, and operating procedure mediate between ideas and policy outcome.'

Mark Blyth's *Great Transformations: Economic Ideas and Institutional Change in the Twentieth Century* clearly expressed theoretical and highly developed assertion of constructivism as an alternative form of institutionalism.[85] Some scholars have noted that the work has added a reputation as 'an exponent and advocate of ideational explanation in comparative political economy.'[86] Blyth identifies five hypotheses. First is constructing a new institution;[87] second is that economic ideas bring about 'collective action.' The third is that ideas are weapons in the hands of agents whose aim is to 'delegitimate' a current institution. The fourth hypothesis argues that ideas are institutional blueprints; finally, once ideas are 'embedded' in the newly formed institution, they generate and 'coordinate expectations . . . and stability.'[88] The third hypothesis speaks to the EU green paper, which extensively delegitimises preferential trade arrangements, supporting its point with the incompatibility of the Lomé Convention with the WTO law.[89]

Drake and Nicolaidis made four claims on how ideas are created and the interests they intend to promote. First, the government consults experts to find an appropriate idea that speaks to the challenges.[90] Second, the 'epistemic community' put 'both formal and informal' direct means to reach the elites, where information can quickly be disseminated to them. Third, the 'epistemic community' can play a significant role in framing the issues and delimiting a range of defensible policy options. Fourth, the direct 'epistemic community' influence often declines once ideas and interests are clarified.[91]

After OECD[92] invented the word 'trade in service,' the Trade Policy Research Centre in London published a volume that brilliantly connected services to trade principles.[93] This discourse was endorsed very quickly in the United States for the American-based transnational corporations (TNCs). It had a special appeal, and, at the domestic level, it created a bloc for firms from different backgrounds, emphasising their common problem and justifying their demands. In foreign countries,

85 Mark Blyth, *Great Transformations: Economic Ideas and Institutional Change in the Twentieth Century* (Cambridge University Press, 2002)

86 Colin Hay, 'Reviewed Work (s): Ideas, Interests, and Institutions in the Comparative Political Economy of Great Transformations' (2004) Review of International Political Economy vol 11 (1) pp 204–26 at 207

87 Blyth (n 85) at 35

88 Blyth (n 85) at 35–42

89 Commission of the European Communities, 'Green Paper on Relations Between the European Union and the ACP Countries on the Eve of the 21 Century: Challenges and Options for a New Partnership' (Brussel, 20 November 1996, COM) (96) (570 Final) iii https://eu-lex.europa.eu/legal-content/EN/TXT/pdf/?uri=CEL . . . accessed 26 June 2020

90 William J Drake and Kalypso Nicolaidis, 'Ideas, Interests, and Institutionalization: "Trade in Service" and the Uruguay Round' (1992) International Organisation vol 46 (1) 37–100

91 William J Drake and Kalypso Nicolaidis, 'Ideas, Interests, and Institutionalization: "Trade in Service" and the Uruguay Round' (1992) International Organisation vol 46 (1) 37–100 at 41

92 OECD, *Report by the High-Level Group on Trade and Related Problems* (OECD, 1973) 63

93 Brian Griffiths, *Invisible Barriers to Invisible Trade* (Macmillan, 1975) 31

proponents armed them with a 'discursive weapon' to promote this demand coherently, giving new meaning to industry-specific policies such as 'protectionism.' The White House formed an Interagency Task Force on Services and the Multilateral Trade Negotiations. In no time, the Department of Commerce and United States Trade Representative (USTR) put in place an office of services industries to examine and investigate foreign trade barriers.

Another instance that demonstrates how the dominant core makes ideas work to protect its interests strategically is seen in the Trade-Related Aspect of Intellectual Property Rights (TRIPS). In 1984, eight associations representing more than 1,500 copyright-based companies came together under the support of a lobbying group, the International Intellectual Property Alliance (IIPA). They campaigned for more robust protection and implementation in foreign countries of US-held copyrights. The IIPA encouraged revisions to the 1974 United States Trade and Tariff Act to make intellectual property right (IPR) breaches actionable by the USTR. The US government made the connection between IPR with international trade in 1984.

In 1986 the IIPA formed a coalition with patent protection groups, mainly the Pharmaceutical Manufacturing of America (PMA), currently referred to as the Pharmaceutical Research and Manufacturers of America (PhRMA).[94] With the joint forces, they campaigned against inadequate IPR protection, which should be the reason for excluding trade preferences under an arrangement such as the Generalised System of Preferences. According to Sell, the United States has not hesitated to threaten to impose sanctions unilaterally and constrain a targeted country to ensure its IPR is effectively protected.[95] To Sell and Prakash, for an idea to become assimilated, another step taken by the agent is agenda setting—initiating issues by diffusing information and establishing a standard for its interpretation.[96]

2.4 Critical Theory: Narrative and Coercion

In critical theory analysis, Cox created a theoretical premise that every theory typically arises from circumstances or beliefs, and this 'theory is always for someone and for some purpose.'[97] In his detailed examination of the theory, he claimed that perception of the world might result from a determinable viewpoint.[98] A theory, according to Cox, must be connected to the point of view or perspective. Cox asserts that there is no such thing as a theory in itself. However, when a theory is considered separately from other things or a stance, exploring it as an ideology to unmask its perspective is preferable.[99] In this theory, Cox dichotomised critical theory and problem-solving theory.

94 PhRMA, 'Global Partnerships' April 2002b, www.world.phrma.org_2001Book-let.pdf; PhrRM, 'Health Care in the Developing World' 18 February http://world.phrma.org/exec.summary.html accessed 14 May 2021

95 Susan A Sell, *Private Power, Public Law: The Globalisation of Intellectual Property Rights* (CUP, 2003) 156

96 Sell and Prakash (n 83) at 157

97 Cox, 1981 (n 3) at 128; Cox, 2014 (n 8) at 158

98 Cox, 1981 (n 3) at 128; Cox, 2014 (n 8) at 158

99 Cox, 1981 (n 3) at 128; Cox, 2014 (n 8) at 158

Cox distinguished between problem-solving and critical theory and asserted that every theory is subjective. The positivist theory is configured for problem-solving. The formulation of the problem-solving theory is that nations do not go through fundamental changes. Instead, actions are expected to occur in a controlled and systematic way through series changes. Cox argues, 'it takes the world as it finds it,' with the established social and power relationships, the structure around which such a system is arranged, as the essential supporting structure for action.[100] The strength of the problem-solving theory that Cox identified is that it can narrow down a specific problem to a 'number of variables' to be precisely investigated.[101]

On the other hand, the critical theory further ascertained the source and how the historical experience causes a marked change. The critical theory investigates the origin of the contradiction and disagreements in the 'entities.' It assesses the possibilities for transforming the system. Dissimilar to the problem-solving theory, whose main aim is to 'smooth the functioning of the whole,'[102] critical theory is termed critical because it distances itself from the established norm of the world order and critically questions how the world originated in the first place.[103]

Critical theory subjects the current world order to thorough questioning and how such an institution came to be.[104] According to Cox, critical theory, distinct from problem-solving theory, would subject 'institutions, social and power relations to a thorough systematic examination and inquire into its historical background.' In essence, critical theory is a historical account of the past and the ongoing process, as Cox states, a 'process of historical change.'[105] This book adopts the critical theory because it allows the research to dive into the history of ACP countries' trade conventions with the EU and how colonialism shaped this relationship. The major drawback of the problem-solving approach is that it deals with specific problems without probing further into the origin of the problem. Scholars like Rittberger are critical of international organisations, realists, functionalists, and liberals, because they promote the interest of the core.[106] Anghie asserts that international organisations are evidence of intricacies and relics of colonialism bequeathed to the peripheral countries.[107]

Antonio Gramsci (1891–1937) has become highly influential as a Marxist theorist of cultural and political domination in advanced capitalism. In the *Prison Notebook*, he reflected on strings of history and theory on preconditions for passive revolution in the modern state.[108] He used Italy as a case study, where to a large

100 Cox, 1981 (n 3) at 128; Cox, 2014 (n 8) at 158
101 Cox, 1981 (n 3) at 128; Cox, 2014 (n 8) at 158
102 Cox, 1981 (n 3) at 129
103 Cox, 1981 (n 3) at 129; Cox, 2014 (n 8) at 158
104 Cox, 1981 (n 3) at 129; Cox, 2014 (n 8) at 158
105 Cox, 1981 (n 3) at 129
106 Volker Rittberger Berhard Zangl, *International Organisation: Polity, Politics and Policies* (trans) Antoinett Groom (Palgrave Macmillan, 2006) 14–22
107 Antony Anghie, 'Time Present and Time Past: Globalisation, International Financial Institutions and the Third World' (2000) NYU Int'l L & Pol vol 32 at 244–5
108 Joseph A Buttigieg ed, *Antonio Gramsci Prison Notebook* (trans) Joseph Buttigieg and Antonio Callari (vol 1, Columbia University Press, 1975) 136–7

extent consent of the masses was obtained.[109] The idea of hegemony was employed to conjure up the 'intellectual and moral approach' to leadership rooted among the rulers across society.[110] The concept has become the focal point of the notebook, which is represented as leadership and domination. The concept of hegemony as used by Gramsci is open to an array of interpretations and applications. For instance, he discussed moral and cultural hegemony in Asian countries such as China and India,[111] how every important state with political hegemony may provide a sets of idea in order to bring weak states under subordination,[112] and French hegemony in female clothes.[113]

It is one of these variations, of the blend of force and consent from the notebook, that Cox used in his work 'Gramsci, Hegemony and International Relations: An Essay in Method.'[114] The notebook illustrated how the modern hegemon assimilates threat by winning over the hostile groups. This is done by concession, the core sacrificing momentarily for the protection of its interest, to maintain support from the weak society.[115] It is in this light that Cox illustrated how the dominant core perpetuates its power in peripheral countries.[116] In his analogy, Cox elucidated how the dominant core infiltrated into the peripheral countries. He states, 'The economic life of subordinate nations is penetrated by and intertwined with the powerful nations.' The situation becomes more complex if the countries or regions are inhabited by people from different social and ethnic backgrounds and lack a uniform and coherent way of relating with 'external forces.'[117] To maintain its hold on the periphery, Cox maintains that the core, which he refers to as the hegemon, must possess three fundamental qualities: 'a social structure, an economic structure, and a political structure; and it cannot be simply one of these things but must be all three.'[118]

For the institution of the dominant core to be effective, it has to operate within international organisations' walls. It helps the dominant core function through the following articulations:

1. they are the representation of rules that promote the development of 'hegemonic world order';

109 Joseph A Buttigieg ed, *Antonio Gramsci Prison Notebook* (trans) Joseph Buttigieg and Antonio Callari (vol 1, Columbia University Press, 1975) at 228
110 Joseph A Buttigieg ed, *Antonio Gramsci Prison Notebook* (trans) Joseph Buttigieg and Antonio Callari (vol 1, Columbia University Press, 1975) at 207
111 Joseph A Buttigieg ed, *Antonio Gramsci Prison Notebook* (trans) Joseph Buttigieg and Antonio Callari (vol 1, Columbia University Press, 1975)
112 Joseph A Buttigieg ed, *Antonio Gramsci Prison Notebook* (trans) Joseph Buttigieg and Antonio Callari (vol 1, Columbia University Press, 1975) at 350
113 Joseph A Buttigieg ed, *Antonio Gramsci Prison Notebook* (trans) Joseph Buttigieg and Antonio Callari (vol 1, Columbia University Press, 1975) at 303
114 Robert W Cox, 'Gramsci, Hegemony and International Relations: An Essay in Method' (1983) Millennium-Journal of International Studies vol 12 p 163
115 Buttigieg (n 108)
116 Buttigieg (n 108) (emphasis added)
117 Buttigieg (n 108) at 169
118 Buttigieg (n 108) at 171

2. the creation of hegemonic world order;
3. they make use of ideas that legitimise the standards they set in world order;
4. they select the elites, likely to embrace their ideas and assimilate any group likely to question the hegemonic ideas.[119]

International institutions, to Cox, represent rules that promote and advance powerful economic and social forces but simultaneously allow some form of accommodation of the secondary interests (peripheral countries) at no substantial cost to the core.[120] In this instance, they allow deviation from the standard norm. Examples include GATT Articles 1 and II, exceptions the EU-ECOWAS Economic Partnership Agreement (EPA).[121] Another instance involves the Bretton Woods institutions,[122] which provided more safeguards for domestic social concerns like unemployment than did the gold standard, with the condition that the domestic policies would comply with the interests of a liberal world economy.[123]

In Cox's view, the dominant core does not leave 'elite talent' in peripheral countries behind; they are assimilated into the international institution, what Gramsci referred to as 'transformism'—a systematic approach of integration of the allied and enemy into an organisation to dominate and render weak and ineffectual.[124] Similarly, according to Cox, 'transformism' also incorporates contrary ideas that pose a threat to the ideas of the core and blend it with the 'hegemonic doctrine.'[125] This ideology permeates, as demonstrated next, the trading system at both global and regional levels.

2.4.1 Asymmetrical Order of the Trading System

The ACP countries have benefitted from a non-reciprocal preferential trade arrangement and development assistance from Europe.[126] However, according to Bilal, asymmetry is at the centre of the trade relationship between the EU and ACP countries.[127] Faundez and Tan observed that the asymmetry of economic power that grew out of the core and peripheral countries' divide, the history of slavery and colonialism, is the principal underlying cause of the continuing asymmetry

119 Buttigieg (n 108) at 172
120 Buttigieg (n 108)
121 Further discussed in subsequent chapters
122 Bretton Woods institutions are initially the World Bank and International Monetary Fund (IMF). They were established at the meeting of 43 countries in Bretton Woods, New Hampshire, USA, in July 1944. The meeting's aim and objective were to reconstruct Europe after the Second World War and encourage international economic cooperation. The GATT (now WTO) was signed in 1947. Available at: www.brettonwoodsproject.org>2019/01>art-320747 accessed 12 February 2021
123 GATT Article XIX; Cox (n 122)
124 Buttigieg (108) at 137, Cox (n 100) at 173
125 Buttigieg (108) at 137, Cox (n 100) at 173
126 Sanoussi Bilal, 'Asymmetric Trade Negotiations for Development: What Does the Experience From the ACP-EU Economic Partnership Agreement Tell Us?' in Sanoussi Bilal, Philippe De Lombaerde and Diana Tussie (eds), *Asymmetric Trade Negotiations* (Routledge, 2016) 45
127 Sanoussi Bilal, 'Asymmetric Trade Negotiations for Development: What Does the Experience From the ACP-EU Economic Partnership Agreement Tell Us?' in Sanoussi Bilal, Philippe De Lombaerde and Diana Tussie (eds), *Asymmetric Trade Negotiations* (Routledge, 2016) 45

of trade, such as the EPAs.[128] This section draws on a document obtained from the Economic Community of West Africa States (ECOWAS) Commission to examine the asymmetry between the two regions.

In their work titled *The European Union as a Global Actor*, Bretherton and Vogler expressed that the EU is an economic power and trade hub, the basis of 'its actorness.'[129] The fundamental idea that underlies this is the existence of the single market. There are 455 million consumers with a gross domestic product (GDP) of €9.6 trillion within its walls. A comparison with the United States reveals a lesser population of 291 million people, but a bigger economy with a GDP of €11 trillion.[130] This regional economic power in Europe consisted of 28 countries, but currently 27 with the United Kingdom's exit on 31 January 2021.

The European Union comprised 15 member states (Austria, Belgium, Denmark, Finland, France, Germany, Greece, Ireland, Italy, Luxemburg, Netherlands, Portugal, Spain, Sweden, and United Kingdom) when the Cotonou Agreement was signed in June 2000. However, it became 25 member states with ten (10) new members in 2004 (Cyprus, Czech Republic, Estonia, Hungary, Latvia, Lithuania, Malta, Poland, Slovakia, and Slovenia). When EPA negotiations were at an advanced stage, on 1 January 2007, Bulgaria and Romania acceded, termed the 'fifth wave' of the EU enlargement.[131] According to the human development indicator published by the United Nations Development Programme, the 25 (before the accession of Bulgaria and Romania, 2007) member countries of the European Union also have a high level of human development. The economy of the EU is, to a great extent, specialised in services which account for 70% of its GDP, although industry maintains a crucial position, representing 28% of GDP, with advanced technology being a driving force for the sector and accounting for 17% of exports of finished products. Agriculture represents only 2% of the GDP.

On the other side of the divide, West Africa's share of trade, like all African countries, slowly dropped over many years to 0.5% as of now.[132] According to the ECOWAS report, in 2005, ECOWAS + Mauritania GDP was approximated at $131 billion, representing 16% of Africa's GDP. The average growth rate, according to the report, was 4.4% in 2000–04. The region's population was 260 million inhabitants in 2004, 28.5% of the whole population in the continent, and a per capita of 502 USD.[133] Thus, the states are immersed in poverty, made worse by HIV/AIDS, malaria, and total illiteracy.[134]

128 Julio Faundez and Celine Tan, *International Economic Law, Globalisation and Developing Countries* (Edward Elgar, 2012) 15

129 Charlotte Bretherton and John Vogler, *The European Union as a Global Actor* (Routledge, 2006) 59

130 Charlotte Bretherton and John Vogler, *The European Union as a Global Actor* (Routledge, 2006) 59

131 Available at www.europa.eu accessed 12 February 2021

132 Negotiation of the Economic Partnership Agreement West Africa-European Community (Report on the Reference Framework of the Economic Partnership Agreement (EPA) Between the West Africa Region and the European Community, ECOWAS) 5 (hereinafter ECOWAS EPA Report)

133 Negotiation of the Economic Partnership Agreement West Africa-European Community (Report on the Reference Framework of the Economic Partnership Agreement (EPA) Between the West Africa Region and the European Community, ECOWAS) 5

134 Negotiation of the Economic Partnership Agreement West Africa-European Community (Report on the Reference Framework of the Economic Partnership Agreement (EPA) Between the West Africa Region and the European Community, ECOWAS) at 7

The United States, in its application for a waiver to continue the African Growth and Opportunity Act (AGOA) preference for Africa, succinctly captured the abysmal situation in Africa.[135] According to the United States, sub-Saharan African countries have occupied secondary or minor importance in the international trading system for a long time, which has in no small measure diminished the role played by the countries in the world trading system.[136] The United States application document gave a litany of challenges faced by sub-Saharan African countries. For example, the region's share in world exports was 3.1% in 1955, further declined to 1.2% in the 1990s, and continued to exist at 2.3% for the past five years.[137]

The United States acknowledged that sub-Saharan African countries are overcome by the debt burden internationally and locally and are plagued by widespread disease. The United States stated:

> Sub-Saharan Africa is home to 33 of the 39 developing countries currently classified as heavily indebted developing countries by the World Bank. About 24.7 million Africans are currently living with HIV/AIDS. Sub-Saharan Africa accounts for almost 70 percent of the global total of new HIV infections.[138]

The United States asked for an expeditious hearing and favourable consideration of the application. However, the EU remained convinced that the solution to the African problem is to subject the ECOWAS-EU partnership to the jurisdiction of GATT Article XXIV. Despite the trade preferences granted to West African countries by the EU under various Lomé Conventions, West Africa's share in EU foreign trade became stagnant.[139] These vast differences between the core and peripheral countries were strangely circumvented in Ruggie's embedded liberalism.[140] The research now examines GATT Article XXIV, free trade as promoted by the proponents, and the contradictions between idea and practice.

Britain renounced its 'deplorable agricultural protection' (the corn law) and other mercantilist protection requirements in 1846.[141] According to Chang, after abolishing the corn law,[142] it became a hegemon of the new economic order.[143] The

135 African Growth and Onortunity Act (AGOA as amended): Request for Waiver (World Trade Organization Council for Trade in Goods, G/C/W/713 (16 July 2015) accessed 6 May 2019

136 African Growth and Opportunity Act (AGOA as amended): Request for Waiver (World Trade Organization Council for Trade in Goods, G/C/W/713 (16 July 2015) at 3 accessed 6 May 2019

137 African Growth and Opportunity Act (AGOA as amended): Request for Waiver (World Trade Organization Council for Trade in Goods, G/C/W/713 (16 July 2015) at 3 accessed 6 May 2019

138 African Growth and Opportunity Act (AGOA as amended): Request for Waiver (World Trade Organization Council for Trade in Goods, G/C/W/713 (16 July 2015) accessed 6 May 2019, in fact the United States asked for an expeditious hearing and favourable consideration of the application

139 ECOWAS EPA Report (n 116) at 11; John Ravenhill, 'Asymmetrical Interdependence: Renegotiating the Lomé Convention' (1979/1980) International Law Journal vol 35 (1) pp 150–69

140 Dillion (n 60)

141 Ha-Joon Chang, 'Kicking Away the Ladder: The "Real" History of Free Trade' in Anwar Shaikh, *Globalisation and the Myths of Free trade: History, Theory, and Empirical Evidence* (Routledge, 2007)

142 Ha-Joon Chang, 'Kicking Away the Ladder: The "Real" History of Free Trade' in Anwar Shaikh, *Globalisation and the Myths of Free trade: History, Theory, and Empirical Evidence* (Routledge, 2007)

143 Ha-Joon Chang, 'Kicking Away the Ladder: The "Real" History of Free Trade' in Anwar Shaikh, *Globalisation and the Myths of Free trade: History, Theory, and Empirical Evidence* (Routledge, 2007) at 24

liberalism endorsed by Britain was based on three pillars: first was the *laissez-faire* industrial policies at home; second, to reduce barriers to allow international movement of goods, capital, and labour; and third, the principle of the gold standard and balanced budgets.[144] As a result of the turn of events caused by the First World War and the lack of stability in the world economy and politics, countries reverted to setting high barriers—occasioning the Smoot-Hawley Tariff, which Bhagwati referred to as 'the most visible and dramatic act of anti-trade folly.'[145]

The year 1932 saw the demise of free trade as promoted by Britain. High tariffs were resuscitated. The constriction and unpredictability in the world economy culminated in the Second World War.[146] The by-product of the Second World War was liberalisation through the GATT institution.[147] Chang argued that the proponents of free trade believed that if the government abstained from intervening in the operation of the market, preferring neoliberalism instead, there would be economic growth.[148] As advocates of free trade pursue unbridled market operations, others warned of the danger of exposing peripheral countries to such policy.[149] Nevertheless, Mike Moore, the former director-general of the WTO, stated, 'the surest way to do more to help the poor is to continue to open markets.'[150]

The 1987 World Development Report assessed the free market as the answer to the economic miseries that had become synonymous with advanced developing countries.[151] Reflecting on the poor economic situation in the Middle East, *New York Times* multiple award winner Thomas Friedman opined that unless these countries adjust themselves to a specific economic policy that he termed the 'Golden Straitjacket,' 'countries in the olive-tree world will not be able to join the Lexus world.'[152] For this adjustment, it is required of a country to embrace the 'golden rules.' These include privatisation of public businesses, reducing to barest minimum government bureaucracy, liberalisation of trade, and removing regulation or restrictions in the industrial sectors.[153] Chang posits that Japan would

144 Ha-Joon Chang, 'Kicking Away the Ladder: The "Real" History of Free Trade' in Anwar Shaikh, *Globalisation and the Myths of Free trade: History, Theory, and Empirical Evidence* (Routledge, 2007)

145 Jagdish Bhagwati, *Protectionism* (The MIT Press, 1985) 22

146 C Kindleberger, 'The Rise of Free Trade in Western Europe, 1820–1875' (1975) Journal of Economic History vol 35 (1)

147 Douglas A Irwin, Petros C Mavroid and Alan Sykes, *The Genesis of the GATT* (Cambridge University Press, 2008) 12, 98–100

148 Chang (n 144) at 24

149 Anwar Shaikh, 'Globalisation and the Myth of Free Trade' in Anwar Shaikh (ed), *Globalisation and the Myths of Free Trade: History, Theory, and Empirical Evidence* (Routledge, 2007)

150 M R Agosin and Tussie Diana, 'Trade and Growth: New Dilemmas in Trade Policy-An Overview' *Chapter 1 in Trade and Growth: New Dilemmas in Trade Policy* (St Martin Press, 1993) 9

151 World Development Report, *Barriers to Adjustment and Growth in the World Economy Industrialisation and Foreign Trade World Development Indicators* (Oxford University Press, 1987) 29

152 Thomas Friedman, *The Lexus and the Olive Tree* (Anchor Books, 2000) 49 cited in H-J Chang (2007) *Bad Samaritans: Rich Nations, Poor Policies and the Threat to the Developing World* (Random House Business Books, 2007) 42–44

153 Thomas Friedman, *The Lexus and the Olive Tree* (Anchor Books, 2000) 130; T F Dernburg, *Global Macroeconomics* (Harper & Row, 1989) 3

have been rated as a substandard industrial nation if the government had put on Friedman's Golden Straitjacket in his counter-argument.[154] Analysing the approach of developed countries, Chang posits that the moment the developed countries industrialised, they became unwavering in their commitments to free trade and free markets and opposed intervention from the government.[155] For example, Korea's tremendous economic achievement came about due to a real stimulus and government intervention blend.[156] The nationalists have argued that Britain only adopted free trade after utilising protectionism to grow its infant industry.[157] Germany also developed its nascent industries through protectionism.[158] It was in this light that Kofi Annan emphasised the danger of exposing developing countries to complete liberalisation.[159]

Reactions have trailed the theory of free trade, claiming that all free traders will become equally competitive, regardless of the difference in their levels of development or technology.[160] Chang's historical record gives a different account of the process of development in developed countries.[161] For instance, the United Kingdom and the United States used trade protection and subsidies in their development time.[162] In the fourteenth and fifteenth centuries, Britain and the United States championed industry protection and were involved in producing woollen goods through heavy taxation of exports of other competitors.[163] In 1699, the Wool Act banned exports of woollen goods from the colonies.[164] According to Chang, Britain and the United States, which promote free trade, were the champions of

154 Thomas Friedman, *The Lexus and the Olive Tree* (Anchor Books, 2000) 130; T F Dernburg, *Global Macroeconomics* (Harper & Row, 1989) 3; D Rodrik, 'The Global Governance of Trade: As If Trade Mattered' (Background paper to the UNDP Project on Trade and Sustainable Human Development, October New York: United Nations Development Programme (2001 UNDP) 5, 10), https://wcfia.harvard.edu/files/wcfia/files/529_rodrik5.pdf accessed 8 July 2021

155 Chang Kicking Away the Ladder . . . (n 144) at 125–29; 41–2

156 Chang Kicking Away the Ladder . . . (n 144) at 125–29; 41–2

157 Robert Gilpin, *The Political Economy of International Relations* (Princeton University Press, 1987) 184

158 Friedrich List, *The National System of Political Economy* (trans) Sampson S Lloyd (Longmans, Green, and Co, 1909)

159 Kofi Annan, The Realization of Economic, Social and Cultural Rights: Globalization and its Impact on the Full Enjoyment of Human Rights, Preliminary Report Submitted by Joseph Oloka-Onyango and Deepika Udagama in accordance with Sub-Commission Resolution [hereinafter U.N. Report] 1999/8 U.N. Commission on Human Rights, 52d Sess., Provisional Agenda Item 4, 15 U.N. D.v. E/CN.4/Sub.2/2000/13 (2000); Peter Isard, *Exchange Rate Economics* (CUP, 1995) 95

160 Peter Isard, Exchnage Rate Economics (CUP, 1995) 95; Sven W Arnt and J David Richardson eds, *Real-Financial Linkages Among Open Economies* (The MIT Press, 1987) 12

161 Ha-Joon Chang, *Kicking Away the Ladder: Development Strategy in Historical Perspective* (Anthem Press, 2002)

162 Ha-Joon Chang, *Kicking Away the Ladder: Development Strategy in Historical Perspective* (Anthem Press, 2002) at 4

163 Ha-Joon Chang, *Kicking Away the Ladder: Development Strategy in Historical Perspective* (Anthem Press, 2002) at 19–20

164 Ha-Joon Chang, *Kicking Away the Ladder: Development Strategy in Historical Perspective* (Anthem Press, 2002) at 19

protectionism.[165] Likewise, Japan and Korea used protectionism to shield their industries in the latter part of the nineteenth and twentieth centuries.[166] Britain became a promoter of free trade when it completed the strengthening of its manufacturing industries.[167] As Britain was promoting free trade, the United States was described as an ardent protectionist country globally.[168]

Some observers have noted issues besides protectionism, which prosper and advance the core and deepen economic power asymmetry between the dominant and peripheral countries. In Milanovic's account of the past, before the advent of worldwide free trade, aside from the issue of protectionism and government intervention (which advanced the economic development of developed countries), there was the situation of colonisation, use of brutal force, pillage, slavery, mass murder of indigenous people, and calculated wiping out of industries that are perceived (East India Company) as competitors.[169] Gunboat diplomacy of the West was vital in dealing with Japan, Tunisia, Egypt, Zanzibar, China, and several others. Millions went through the agony of slavery on plantations worldwide, building the core's industries.[170] According to a recent approximation, from 1865 to 1930, the 'Dutch East Indies Company . . . pillaged between 7.4% and 10.3% of Indonesia's national income per year.'[171] Mazower noted, 'the door into other people's economies was soon being forced open by British diplomats, backed by gunboats, everywhere from West Africa to Istanbul and Peking.'[172] This, according to these writers, not only caused economic power asymmetry to be instituted permanently but deteriorated industrial activity in the peripheral countries.[173] With these historical facts, the postulation of Ruggie's embedded liberalism is only structured for developed countries that meant to take advantage of it.

The GATT, which was in force beginning from January 1948, was, according to Gardner, 'a historical accident.'[174] The operation continued until the United States

165 Ha-Joon Chang, *Kicking Away the Ladder: Development Strategy in Historical Perspective* (Anthem Press, 2002) at 5
166 Ha-Joon Chang, *Kicking Away the Ladder: Development Strategy in Historical Perspective* (Anthem Press, 2002) at14, 48
167 Ha-Joon Chang, *Kicking Away the Ladder: Development Strategy in Historical Perspective* (Anthem Press, 2002) at 1
168 Ha-Joon Chang, *Kicking Away the Ladder: Development Strategy in Historical Perspective* (Anthem Press, 2002) at 61, 5
169 Branko Milanovic, 'The Two Faces of Globalisation: Against Globalisation as We Know It' (April 2002) http://papers.ssrn.com>so13>papers accessed 11 June 2021 5–6
170 Branko Milanovic, 'The Two Faces of Globalisation: Against Globalisation as We Know It' (April 2002) http://papers.ssrn.com>so13>papers accessed 11 June 2021 at 6
171 Branko Milanovic, 'The Two Faces of Globalisation: Against Globalisation as We Know It' (April 2002) http://papers.ssrn.com>so13>papers accessed 11 June 2021
172 Mark Mazower, *Governing the World: The History of an Ideas* (The Penguin Press, 2012) 97
173 Branko Milanovic, 'The Two Faces of Globalisation: Against Globalisation as We Know It' (April 2002) http://papers.ssrn.com>so13>papers accessed 11 June 2021 at 7–8; Mark Mazower, *Governing the World: The History of an Ideas* (The Penguin Press, 2012) at 511
174 Richard N Gardner, *Sterling-Dollar Diplomacy: The Origins and the Prospects of Our International Economic Order* (Oxford University Press, 1969) xxxiv

Congress had approved the International Trade Organisation (ITO).[175] However, the United States Congress opposed it, and it effectively ended in 1950[176] when President Harry Truman stated that Congressional approval would no longer be pursued concerning the ITO Charter.[177]

Before establishing the GATT/WTO, the United States was famous for protecting its market against potential competitors.[178] After the formation of GATT, according to Gardner, the world was still plagued by protectionism.[179] Wilkinson referred to it as 'covert and overt protectionism.'[180] Instructively, according to Goldstein's account, the United States enacted the escape clause as a safeguard measure before establishing GATT.[181] According to Goldstein's account, the escape clause was enacted based on the executive order of 1947 and a 1951 statute. The United States never failed to include safeguard measures in trade treaties and laws. The escape clause aims to allow an industry that has suffered an injury due to imports to be free from the obligation under the United States trade agreement to reduce its tariff.[182]

According to the author, while the United States and its allies pursued the idea of worldwide liberalisation, they made laws to protect their national industries. Goldstein argued that United States protectionism has three parts: first, the United States has a constructive view of free trade ideology but ensures a legitimate 'claim to protectionism.' Second, the United States believes that its market, after the civil war in 1934, should be inaccessible to a large extent, and yet it seeks foreign countries to open their markets. Third, United States policymakers ensure indemnification for sectors that cannot compete and assist them in adjusting due to foreign competition.[183]

175 Richard N Gardner, *Sterling-Dollar Diplomacy: The Origins and the Prospects of Our International Economic Order* (Oxford University Press, 1969) xxxiv; Melvyn P Leffler, *A Preponderance of Power: National Security, The Truman Administration, and the Cold War* (Stanford University Press, 1992) 193

176 Richard N Gardner, *Sterling-Dollar Diplomacy: The Origins and the Prospects of Our International Economic Order* (Oxford University Press, 1969) at 369–79; Rorden Wilkinson, *Multilateralism and the World Trade Organisation: The Architecture and Extension of International Trade Regulation* (Routledge, 2000) 17

177 Richard N Gardner, *Sterling-Dollar Diplomacy: The Origins and the Prospects of Our International Economic Order* (Oxford University Press, 1969) at 369–78

178 Chang 2002 (n 161) at 44; H-J Chang, *Bad Samaritans: Rich Nations, Poor Policies and the Threat to the Developing World* (Random House Business Books, 2007) 5

179 Gardner (n 174) at xviii, xxxviii

180 Wilkinson 2014 (n 3) at 24; Enzo Grill and Enrico Sassoon eds, *The New Protectionist Wave* (Macmillan Education Limited, 1990)

181 Judith Goldstein, 'Ideas, Institutions, and American Trade Policy' (1988) International Organisation vol 42 (1) pp 179–217

182 Judith Goldstein, 'Ideas, Institutions, and American Trade Policy' (1988) International Organisation vol 42 (1) pp 179–217; Ernest Preeg, *Trades and Diplomats: An Analyses of the Kennedy Round Negotiations Under the General Agreement on Tariff and Trade* (Brookings Institutions, 1973)

183 Judith Goldstein, 'Ideas, Institutions, and American Trade Policy' (1988) International Organisation vol 42 (1) at 181; GATT Article XIX 1947

United States Treasury Secretary Alexander Hamilton pioneered tariffs to protect infant industries,[184] as did founding father James Madison.[185] Abraham Lincoln formulated the policy of economic nationalism. In his biography by Phillips, Lincoln asserted in 1844: 'give us a protective tariff, and we will have the greatest nation on earth.'[186] In the same vein, William McKinley posits that America had to engage in active protectionism to be great.[187] Theodore Roosevelt extolled the virtue of tariffs because, to him, it is what makes America powerful.[188] In the 1950s, however, Dwight Eisenhower persuaded people to accept free trade to unite the West against communism to promote globalisation.[189] On his part, Ronald Reagan increased tariffs on Japanese monocycles.[190] George W Bush targeted steel imports but relented after WTO threatened to sanction the USA. According to observers, American presidents over the years have been suspicious of the multilateral trading system.[191]

Donald Trump echoed his predecessors' voice that he is not fearful of trade wars by raising tariffs in recent times. In his view, 'Trade wars are good and easy to win.'[192] The former president did not hesitate to increase tariffs on billions of dollars' worth of goods worldwide, especially in China. Trump's plan for the profit from the tariff was that $100 billion would be used to buy USA agricultural products and send to 'poor and starving countries.'[193] America was a driving force behind the formation of GATT and WTO, and it has undermined its rules extensively over the years.[194]

Prioritising the dominant core concerns, Goldstein explained that for the newfound interests in liberalism to be realised, decision-makers became enthralled about liberalism and blamed the Smoot-Hawley Tariff Act of 1929–30 for the Great Depression.[195] Goldstein argued that the Great Depression was the reason for

184 Ron Chernow, *Alexander Hamilton* (Penguin Press, 2004) 901, 703–4

185 Noah Feldman, 'James Madison Would Like a Few Words on Trade Wars' (5 March 2018) www.bloomerg.com accessed 11 June 2021

186 Donald T Phillips, *Lincoln Leadership for Today: Abraham Lincoln Approach to Twenty-First-Century Issues* (Houghton Mifflin Harcourt, 2017) 43

187 Jude Sheerin, 'What Trump Has in Common With Abe Lincoln and Ferris Bueller' BBC News, Washington, 8 March 2018 www.bbc.com (11 June 2021)

188 A Roosevelt Tariff Article (ehistory, the Ohio State University) http://ehistory.osu.edu/exhibitions/1912/tariffs/roosevel accessed 11 June 2021

189 Sheerin (n 187)

190 Sheerin (n 187)

191 Sheerin (n 187)

192 Thomas Franck, 'Trump Doubles Down: 'Trade Wars are Goods and Easy to Win'' (CNBC, 2 March 2018) www.cnbc.com>2018/03/02>trump-trade-war . . . accessed 11 June 2021

193 BBC News, 'Trade Wars, Trump Tariffs and Protectionism Explained' (10 May 2019) www.bbc.com accessed 22 April 2021

194 BBC News, 'Trade Wars, Trump Tariffs and Protectionism Explained' (10 May 2019) www.bbc.com accessed 22 April 2021; BBC News, 'US Steel and Aluminium Import Face Big Tariffs, Trump Says' (1 March 2018) www.bbc.com accessed 22 April 2021; Trump Puts 25% Tariff on Chinese Goods (15 June 2018) www.bbc.com accessed 22 April 2021; Markets Edgy on US-China Trade War Fears (23 March 2018) www.bbc.com accessed 22 April 2021

195 Goldstein (n 183)

accepting liberalism, 'but not sufficient cause, for liberalism to take on an ideological character.'[196] According to her, liberalism gathered steam because it provided for the interests of the United States.[197] This idea of liberalism, according to her, was chiefly influenced by nineteenth-century British thought and eighteenth-century American political philosophy.[198]

The escape clause was first used in a 1942 trade agreement with Mexico.[199] The idea was resurrected in the debate of the 1945 Trade Act as a trade-off by the executive after 'congressional transference of increased tariff-making authority.'[200] In return for enacting the law, Truman issued Executive Order 9381 (1/25/48), establishing that all future trade agreements must include escape clause provisions.[201] To obtain the approval of Congress, the United States policymakers agreed to include an escape clause provision, precisely as found in domestic law (GATT Article XIX). Nevertheless, President Truman deplored the inclusion of Article XIX as 'an embarrassment to be avoided in the interest of maintaining an image of American leadership and dependability in the world and foreign affairs.'[202] However, the US has invoked the provision several times, interpreting the article most flexibly.[203] With this same leniency, the GATT contracting parties had applied its rules to the European Community. According to Patterson, post-war interim arrangements were for Europe not to commit to the GATT fully until it became economically stable.[204]

Faizel Ismail examined over 800 archival documents regarding South Africa's participation in the GATT treaty of 1947.[205] He demonstrated that South Africa set a limit on its use of tariffs, and it used 'import licensing and quantitative control to develop its infant industries.' When India argued for the prohibition of trade between any country and South Africa due to its discriminatory policies towards its indigenous people, GATT 'styled itself as being politically neutral and thus indifferent to the policies of racial discrimination practised by South Africa domestically.'[206] However, this neutrality stance employed by GATT members gave way as the United States used Article XXXV, providing more clarity under

196 Goldstein (n 195) 182; Robert Pastor, *Congress and the Politics of US Foreign Economic Policy: 1929–1976* (University of California Press, 1980)
197 Goldstein (n 183) at 183
198 Goldstein (n 183) at 187
199 Gardner (n 174) at 159
200 U.S. Congress, House Committee on Ways and Means, Foreign Trade Agreements, Report to Accompany H.R. 3242, H Rept. 594 79th Cong, 1st Sess (1945) p 9 cite in Gardner (n 187) at 159
201 William Ris, 'Escape Clause Relief Under the Trade Act of 1974: New Standards, Same Results' (1977) Columbia Journal of Transnational Law vol 16 p 299
202 William Ris, 'Escape Clause Relief Under the Trade Act of 1974: New Standards, Same Results' (1977) Columbia Journal of Transnational Law vol 16 p 300
203 Goldstein (n 183) at 189
204 Goldstein (n 183) at 189
205 Faizel Ismail, 'Empirical Analysis of Apartheid South Africa's Ideas and Practices in the GATT: 1947 to 1994' (A Thesis Submitted to the University of Manchester for the Degree of Ph.D. Politics, 2015) 69
206 Patterson (n 3) at 85–6

Article XIII of the WTO to ban trade with Armenia, Moldova, Georgia, the Kyrgyz Republic, and Mongolia.[207] These differences in ideas and practice can be deciphered from the viewpoint of Cox, who states that an idea becomes common sense when the hegemonic power promotes it.[208]

Drawing on an extensive range of sources, Mutasa set out different ways the EU had engaged in actively protecting its agricultural sector.[209] Chapter 39 of the 1957 Treaty of Rome enumerated five cardinal points of the Common Agricultural Policy (CAP).[210] Some EU member states, such as Sweden and Britain, have called upon the EU to cut down on budget and subsidies for CAP.[211] However, according to Mutasa and Secchi, the European Union CAP remains strongly funded.[212] Both the peripheral and advanced developing countries are well acquainted with the EU CAP for its lack of restraint in export subsidies and its repercussions, especially in peripheral countries such as the ECOWAS region.[213] According to Mutasa, in 2008, Washington paid $20 billion to farmers; in 2019, farms received $22.6 billion subsidies from government[214] and 2023 was estimated to be $12.6 billion.[215] The direct payment to farmers in 2023 in the EU was 4.875 euros.[216] The rationale for this enormous amount was never clearly revealed.[217] Mutasa further argued that by promoting excessive production of agricultural products in the EU, the excess from the products is exported to Africa, undermining farmers and 'threatening African agriculture structure in Sub-Saharan Africa.'[218]

207 Patterson (n 3) at 86; Bernard Hoekman and Petros C Mavroidis, 'WTO Dispute Settlement, Transparency and Surveillance' (2000) The World Economy vol 23 (4) p 9
208 Cox 2002 (n 3) at 84
209 Charles Mutasa, 'A Critique of the EU's Common Agricultural Policy' in Adekeye Adebajo and Kaye White (eds), *The EU and Africa: From Eurafrique to Afro-Europa* (C Hurst & Co Publishers Ltd, 2012)
210 Charles Mutasa, 'A Critique of the EU's Common Agricultural Policy' in Adekeye Adebajo and Kaye White (eds), *The EU and Africa: From Eurafrique to Afro-Europa* (C Hurst & Co Publishers Ltd, 2012) at 239
211 Charles Mutasa, 'A Critique of the EU's Common Agricultural Policy' in Adekeye Adebajo and Kaye White (eds), *The EU and Africa: From Eurafrique to Afro-Europa* (C Hurst & Co Publishers Ltd, 2012)
212 Charles Mutasa, 'A Critique of the EU's Common Agricultural Policy' in Adekeye Adebajo and Kaye White (eds), *The EU and Africa: From Eurafrique to Afro-Europa* (C Hurst & Co Publishers Ltd, 2012); Carlo Secchi, 'Protectionism, Internal Market Completion, and Foreign Trade Policy in the European Community' in Grill and Sassoon (n 215) at 56
213 Charles Mutasa, 'A Critique of the EU's Common Agricultural Policy' in Adekeye Adebajo and Kaye White (eds), *The EU and Africa: From Eurafrique to Afro-Europa* (C Hurst & Co Publishers Ltd, 2012) 244; Carlo Secchi, 'Protectionism, Internal Market Completion, and Foreign Trade Policy in the European Community' in Grill and Sassoon (n 215) at 39–40
214 USA Facts, 'Federal Farm Subsidies: What the Data Say' www.usafacts.org accessed 15 April 2024
215 '2023 Farm Subsidies Expected to Remain at Excessively High Levels' Taxpayer for Common Sense, 31 August 2023 www.taxpayer.net
216 'The Total Amount of Direct Payments Under CAP 2023 is 4.875 Billion Euros' (La Moncloa, 31 August 2023)
217 Mutasa (n 209) at 244
218 Mutasa (n 209) at 244

According to Cox, 'Western scholarship, assuming a position of universal objectivity, has defined the characteristics of dominated civilisation and has had the power to transmit to the dominated this knowledge about themselves.'[219] To blend the uncivilised into the superior universal knowledge, he suggests, 'the elites of the dominated could thus become absorbed into alien universalism.' Using the analogy of 'orientalism,' Cox explicates that the world ruling class propounds and spreads globalisation, projected as 'American-Style capitalism,' which assimilates the rest of the world into a single global political economy.[220] Watson and Hay postulate that even though globalisation has been unmasked and revealed as a myth, 'political rhetoric' continues to have a powerful effect.[221]

This metaphor represents an extensive structure of social practices that explains how people understand themselves and their conduct.[222] Jim George considers that a discourse generates the different classes of connotations to shape reality, for a discourse makes 'real' that which is prescribed as meaningful.[223] Accordingly, examining the metaphor in the context of discourse has become a social construction centred on the link between power and knowledge. Cox's framework emphasises the point that power is applied for the effectiveness of the global market metaphor.[224] The argument is that notwithstanding whether political opponents have assimilated a specific set of ideas, it 'can prove critical to success in political contests,' while 'leaving their opponents without access to the rhetorical materials needed to craft a socially sustainable rebuttal.'[225] 'Rhetorical coercion' is present when opponents are prevailed to support a position they would ordinarily reject.[226]

Susan Strange maintained that protectionism is no threat or harm to the world's trading system.[227] She identified three widely held but false beliefs promoted by liberal economists and unmasked the ideology as a 'myth.' First, the main article of faith of liberal economics, as far as international trade is concerned, is to minimise government involvement and prevent anything that 'obstructs the flow of trade.'[228] The second myth observed by Strange is the conviction of liberal economists that

219 Cox 2014 (n 8)
220 Cox 2014 (n 8) at 165
221 Matthew Watson & Colin Hay, 'The Discourse of Globalisation and the Logic of No Alternative Rendering the Contingent Necessary in the Political Economy of New Labour' (2004) 30 (4) *Policy and Politics* 289–305 at 304
222 Jim George, *Discourses of Global Politics: A Critical (Re) Introduction to International Relations* (Lynne Rienner Publishers, 1994) 29–30
223 Jim George, *Discourses of Global Politics: A Critical (Re) Introduction to International Relations* (Lynne Rienner Publishers, 1994) 29–30
224 Cox 2002 (n 3) at 76
225 Ronald R Krebs and Patrick Thaddeus Jackson, 'Twisting Tongues and Twisting Arms: The Power of Political Rhetoric' (2007) European Journal of International Relations vol 13 (1) pp 35–66 at 36
226 Ronald R Krebs and Patrick Thaddeus Jackson, 'Twisting Tongues and Twisting Arms: The Power of Political Rhetoric' (2007) European Journal of International Relations vol 13 (1) pp 35–66 at 36
227 Susan Strange, 'Protectionism and World Politics' (Spring 1985) International Organisation vol 39 (2) pp 233–59 at 233
228 Susan Strange, 'Protectionism and World Politics' (Spring 1985) International Organisation vol 39 (2) pp 233–59 at 235

the 'individual pursuit of private gain,' tallies with society's overall well-being, as 'the hidden hand of the market ensures producers make what the consumers want at the lowest price.'[229] The third myth examined deals with the exegesis drawn by liberal economists from twentieth-century economic evolution.[230] The liberal economists attributed the Great Depression of the 1930s to the indiscriminate tariff increase that led to protectionism by countries.[231] The idea prevalent among liberal economists remains that the Great Depression of 1929 and the 1930s was not caused by trade protectionism totally but unquestionably aggravated by it as most nations promoted 'beggar-thy-neighbour policies.'[232] This is the conventional argument.

Nevertheless, Strange posits that the fall of world trade and the rise of protectionism was instead a sign of a global economic breakdown.[233] She cited several development economists such as Arthur Lewis[234] and Kindleberger[235] of the realist school of thought. Both authors posit that tariffs made a 'minimal effect on the volume of world trade or its direction.' Another widely held ideology that Strange examined and challenged was what she termed the 'bicycle theory'; namely, the ideology that if the trade liberalisation impetus were not maintained, it would be disastrous to economic growth.[236]

This manner of discourse in the world trading system has been recently criticised in detail by Wilkinson.[237] Bhagwati claims that adversaries of free trade are 'the chaff' that has to be removed from the 'wheat' of good sense. Wilkinson argued that the manner of talking and tacitly consenting to an insult without questioning resulted in 'these forms of communicating' obscure the strategic manner in which GATT/WTO has been deployed and the asymmetrical outcomes its liberalisation has produced. He explores the style in which 'the discourse' has been established to express trade negotiations differently to increase the probability of perpetuation and conclusion of such trade agreements. Like Strange's bicycle theory, Wilkinson couched the phrase 'crisis discourse' employed by those with a 'vested professional or ideological interest in it.' They maintained that if actions are not taken against protectionism immediately, the trading system would break down.[238]

229 Susan Strange, 'Protectionism and World Politics' (Spring 1985) International Organisation vol 39 (2) pp 233–59 at 238
230 Susan Strange, 'Protectionism and World Politics' (Spring 1985) International Organisation vol 39 (2) pp 233–59 at 239
231 Susan Strange, 'Protectionism and World Politics' (Spring 1985) International Organisation vol 39 (2) pp 233–59 at 239
232 Susan Strange, 'Protectionism and World Politics' (Spring 1985) International Organisation vol 39 (2) pp 233–59 at 239–41
233 Susan Strange, 'Protectionism and World Politics' (Spring 1985) International Organisation vol 39 (2) pp 233–59
234 W Arthur Lewis, *Economic Survey, 1919–1930* (1949; rpt. Allen & Unwin, 1970) cited in Susan Strange, 'Protectionism and World Politics' (Spring, 1985) International Organisation vol 39 (2) pp 233–59 at 240
235 Kindleberger (n 146) at 240–1
236 Strange (n 226) at 239–42
237 Wilkinson (n 3)
238 Rorden Wilkinson, *The WTO: Crisis and the Governance of Global Trade* (Routledge, 2006) 597

Wilkinson maintained that two things are envisaged when free trade proponents use metaphorical discourse. According to Wilkinson, the metaphorical submission is based on 'historical logic or constructed identity as fact and common sense,' synchronically pressurising first to ensure particular conduct and secondly 'safeguarding that logic' from a thorough investigation.[239]

Argentina questioned the logic of free trade. Citing the economic crisis in Argentina in the 2000s, Grugel and Riggirozzi[240] conclude that neoliberalism had comprehensively failed to deliver stable and equitable growth. Argentina introduced some significant import restrictions because it needs to export its products to achieve some level of growth as a developing country. In a speech during the MERCOSUR summit in Brasilia in December 2012, Fernandez de Kirchner refused to accept the narrative of deleterious impact of protectionism. Instead, she pointed out the imbalances in the worldwide trading system and how it tried to find workable alternative solutions.[241] Christopher Wylde[242] termed the dramatic rejection of the neoliberal ideology as 'developmentalist ideology.'[243] It is believed that the new ideology making its round in Argentina 'facilitated impressive post-crisis growth through a judicious mix of domestic policy and international circumstance.'[244] However, in 2014, the WTO panel ruling overwhelmingly supported the USA, the EU, and Japan, which had separately challenged the Argentine import restrictive measures in 2012. EU Trade Commissioner Karel De Gucht praised the panel decision, as it displayed 'an important signal that protectionism is not acceptable.'[245]

2.5 Conclusion

This chapter considers in broad brushstrokes the relationship, both economic and social, between more developed and less developed countries, typically former colonial powers and former colonies, focusing on the specific dimension of multilateral trade and placing the relationships in historical context.

The dual discourse explained earlier—the crisis discourse and the bicycle theory—is essential for this book, in the context of the EU-ECOWAS EPA. The EU

239 Rorden Wilkinson, 'Language, Power and Multilateral Trade Negotiations' (2009) Review of International Political Economy vol 16 (4) pp 597–619 at 80; Rorden Wilkinson, 'Of Butchery and Bicycles: The WTO and the "Death" of the Doha Development Agenda' (2012) The Political Quarterly vol 83 (2), at 1–7

240 Jean Grugel and Maria Pia Riggirozzi, 'The Return of the State in Argentina' (2007) International Affairs vol 83 (1) pp 87–107 at 87, 95

241 Ban Cornel and Blyth Mark, 'The BRICS and the Washington Consensus: An Introduction' (2013) Review of International Political Economy vol 20 (2) pp 241–55 at 241–2, 245

242 Christopher Wylde, 'The Developmental State Is Dead, Long Live the Developmental Regime! Interpreting Néstor Kirchner's Argentina 2003–2007' (2013) Journal of International Relations and Development pp 1–29 at 1 doi:10.1057/jird.2012.32

243 Grugel and Riggirozzi (n 239) at 92–4

244 Wylde (n 241)

245 ICTSD, 'Argentina Pledges to Appeal WTO Ruling on Import Restrictions' (10 September 2014) Bridges Weekly Trade New Digest vol 16 (30) http://ictsd.org/i/news/bridgesweekly/ accessed 30 July 2020

extensively employed the strategies wherein the ACP countries would lose favourable market access if agreements were not signed on time. Second, WTO rules had to be complied with before ACP countries could obtain viable gains from trade. The EPA is the only way to develop. To prevent scrutiny of the EU discourse, an interviewee asserts that the EU prevented ACP countries from thoroughly negotiating the text of the EPA. During the campaign for the importance of EPA, Mandelson maintained that protectionism policies are a 'dead end,' as they would stall the trade benefits of the region.[246]

The chapter explores the conformist and revisionist perspectives to analyse trade relations—to understand their structure, the behaviour of agents and actors within these contexts, and the set of outcomes over time—and which, integrated into a theoretical framework of asymmetrical economic power relations, can be used to understand the origin of asymmetry in a historical context to demonstrate that the relation between the core and peripheral is only made tolerable; in essence it remains rooted in colonialism, as the next chapter shows.

Bibliography

Abbott K W, 'GATT as a Public Institution: The Uruguay Round and Beyond Brooklyn' (1992a) Journal of International Law vol XVIII p CV1

Abbott K W, 'GATT as a Public Institution: The Uruguay Round and Beyond Brooklyn' (1992b) Journal of International Law vol XVIII p CV1 66, 85

Africa Growth and Opportunity Act (AGOA as amended): Request for Waiver (World Trade Organization Council for Trade in Goods, G/C/W/713 (16 July 2015) (accessed 6 May 2019)

Agosin M R, & Tussie D, 'Trade and Growth: New Dilemmas in Trade Policy-An Overview' in *Trade and Growth: New Dilemmas in Trade Policy* (St Martin Press, 1993)

Anghie A, 'Time Present and Time Past: Globalisation, International Financial Institutions, and the Third World' (2000) New York University Journal of International Law and Politics vol 32

Annan K, 'The Realization of Economic, Social and Cultural Rights: Globalization and Its Impact on the Full Enjoyment of Human Rights, Preliminary Report Submitted by Joseph Oloka-Onyango and Deepika Udagama in Accordance With Sub-Commission Resolution [hereinafter U.N. Report] 1999/8 U.N. Commission on Human Rights, 52d Sess., Provisional Agenda Item 4, 15 U.N. D.v. E/CN.4/Sub.2/2000/13' (2000)

Branko M, 'The Two Faces of Globalisation: Against Globalisation As We Know It' (April 2002) http://papers.ssrn.com>so13>papers (accessed 11 June 2021) 5–6

Bhagwati J, *Protectionism* (The MIT Press, 1985)

Bhagwati J, 'Reshaping the WTO' (2005) Far Eastern Economic Review vol 168 p 2

Bilal S, 'Asymmetric Trade Negotiations for Development: What Does the Experience From the ACP-EU Economic Partnership Agreement Tell Us?' in Sanoussi Bilal, Philippe De Lombaerde, & Diana Tussie (eds), *Asymmetric Trade Negotiations* (Routledge, 2016)

Blyth M, *Great Transformations: Economic Ideas and Institutional Change in the Twentieth Century* (CUP, 2002)

246 Peter Mandelson, 'Sustainable Trade Observations on Trade and Protectionism EU Trade Commissioner Speech/06/187', Brussels, 21 March 2006 at 2

Bossche P V, & Zdouc W R, *The Law and Policy of the World Trade Organisation: Text, Cases, and Materials* (4th edn, Cambridge University Press, 2017)
Bretherton C, & Vogler J, *The European Union as a Global Actor* (Routledge, 2006)
Brown W, *The European Union and Africa: The Restructuring of North-South Relations* (IB Tauris, 2002)
Chang H J, *Bad Samaritans: Rich Nations, Poor Policies and the Threat to the Developing World* (Random House Business Books, 2007)
Chang H J, *Kicking Away the Ladder: Development Strategy in Historical Perspective* (Anthem Press, 2002)
Chang H J, 'Kicking Away the Ladder: The 'Real' History of Free Trade' in Anwar Shaikh (ed), *Globalisation and the Myths of Free Trade: History, Theory, and Empirical Evidence* (Routledge, 2007)
Chernow R, *Alexander Hamilton* (Penguin Press, 2004)
Commission of the European Communities, 'Green Paper on Relations between the European Union and the ACP Countries on the Eve of the 21 Century: Challenges and Options for a New Partnership' (Brussel, 20 November 1996, COM) (96) (570 Final) iii, available at https://eu-lex.europa.eu/legal-content/EN/TXT/pdf/?uri=CEL. . . (accessed 26 June 2020)
Cornel B, & Mark B, 'The BRICS and the Washington Consensus: An Introduction' (2013) Review of International Political Economy vol 20 (2) pp 241–255
Cottier T, & Mavroidis P C (eds), *The Role of the Judge in International Trade Regulation: Experience and Lesson for the WTO* (2003) 307
Cox R W, Gramsci, 'Hegemony and International Relations: An Essay in Method' (1983) Millennium-Journal of International Studies vol 12 p 163
Cox R W, 'Social Forces, States, and World Orders: Beyond International Relations Theory' (1981) Millennium-Journal of International Studies vol 10 (126)
Cox R W, *The Political Economy of a Plural World: Critical Reflections on Power, Moral, and Civilization* (Routledge, 2002)
Dernburg T F, *Global Macroeconomics* (Harper & Row, 1989)
Diebold W J, 'From the ITO to GATT—And Back?' in Orin Kirshner (ed), *The Bretton Woods—GATT System Retrospect and Prospect After Fifty Years* (Routledge 1996) 152
Dillion S, 'A Farewell to 'Linkage': International Trade Law and Global Sustainability Indicators' (2002) Rutgers Law Review vol 55 (1) p 87
Drake W J, & Nicolaidis K, 'Ideas, Interests, and Institutionalization: "Trade in Service" and the Uruguay Round' (1992) International Organisation vol 46 (1) pp 37–100
Dunof J L, 'The Death of the Trade Regime' (1999) vol 10 (4) pp 733–762
Dunof J L, 'Does Globalisation Advance Human Rights' (1999) Brooklyn Journal of International Law vol. XXV (1) p 125
EU-Commission, *Trade: A Key Source of Growth and Jobs for the EU-Commission Contribution to the European Council of 7–8 February* (European Commission, 2013). http://eu2013.ie/media/eupresidency/content/documents/130207-Commission-Contribution-on-Trade-to-EC.pdf (accessed 9 November 2021)
European Commission, Economic Partnership Agreements (EPAs), *New ACP-EU Trade Partnerships* (July 2010). htt://eu.europa.eu/trade/wider-agenda/development/economic-partnerships (accessed 29 May 2018)
European Parliament, 'Relations With the Africa, Caribbean and Pacific Countries: From Yaoundé and Lomé to Cotonou Agreement' 'Economic Development Cooperation Started Between EU and West Africa in 1963 With Leading Successive Agreements: First Lomé Convention (1975–1980) signed between 9 EU States and 46 ACP States, following the foundation of the ACP group in Georgetown (Guyana); 1979, Second Lomé Convention (1980-1985), signed between 9 EU States and 58 ACP States; 1984, Third Lomé Convention (1985-1990) signed between 9 EU States and 58 ACP States; and 1990, Fourth Lomé Convention (1990-2000) signed between 12 EU States and 68 ACP States. The Fourth

Lomé Convention was in two stage, 1990-1994 and 1995-2000. Lomé IV bis was signed between 15 EU Members and 70 ACP States. The ACP group is presently composed of 78 states (46 African, 16 Caribbean and 14 Pacific) Article 7 of Lomé Convention which is refer to as Lomé 1; www.europarl.europ.eu/facts_2004/6-4-5-en.htm (accessed 17 June 2018)

Evans P, *Embedded Autonomy: States and Industrial Transformation* (Princeton University Press, 1995)

Faundez J, & Tan C, *International Economic Law, Globalisation and Developing Countries* (Edward Elgar, 2012)

Feldman N, *James Madison Would Like a Few Words on Trade Wars* (5 March 2018). www.bloomerg.com (accessed 11 June 2021)

Franck F, Trump Doubles Down: 'Trade Wars are Goods and Easy to Win' (CNBC, 2 March 2018). www.cnbc.com>2018/03/02>trump-trade-war. . . (accessed 11 June 2021)

Friedman T, *The Lexus and the Olive Tree* (Anchor Books, 2000) 130.

Gardner R N, *Sterling-Dollar Diplomacy: The Origins and the Prospects of Our International Economic Order* (OUP, 1969)

George J, *Discourses of Global Politics: A Critical (Re) Introduction to International Relations* (Lynne Rienner Publishers, 1994)

Gilpin R, *The Political Economy of International Relations* (Princeton University Press, 1987)

Goldstein J, 'Ideas, Institutions, and American Trade Policy' (1988) International Organisation vol 42 (1) pp 179–217

Goldstein J, & Keohane R O, 'Ideas and Foreign Policy: An Analytical Framework' in Judith Goldstein & Robert O Keohane (eds), *Ideas and Foreign Policy*: *Beliefs, Institutions, and Political Changes* (Cornell University Press, 1993)

Granovetter M, 'Economic Action and Social Structure: The Problem of Embeddedness' (1985) American Journal of Sociology vol 91 pp 481–510

Griffiths B, *Invisible Barriers to Invisible Trade* (Macmillan, 1975)

Grill E, & Sassoon E (ed), *The New Protectionist Wave* (Macmillan Education Limited, 1990)

Hart J A, & Prakash A, 'The Decline of 'Embedded Liberalism' and the Rearticulation of the Keynesian Welfare State' (1997) New Political Economy vol 2 (1) pp 65–78

Hay C, 'Reviewed Work (s): Ideas, Interests, and Institutions in the Comparative Political Economy of Great Transformations' (2004) Review of International Political Economy vol 11 (1) pp 204–226

Helleiner E, 'Reinterpreting Bretton Woods: International Development and the Neglected Origins of Embedded Liberalism' (2006) Development and Change vol 37 (5) pp 943–967

Helleiner E, 'The Life and Times of Embedded Liberalism: Legacies and Innovations Since Bretton Woods' (2019) Review of International Political Economy DOI:10.1080/09692290.2019.1607767

Heydon K, & Woolcock S, *The Rise of Bilateralism: Comparing American, European and Asian Approaches to Preferential Trade Agreements* (United Nations University Press, 2009)

Hoekman B, & Mavroidis P, 'WTO Dispute Settlement, Transparency and Surveillance' (2000) The World Economy vol 23 (4)

Horn L, *Regulating Corporate Governance in the EU: Towards a Marketisation of Corporate Control* (Palgrave Macmillan, 2011)

Howse R, & Nicolaidis K, 'Legitimacy Through 'Higher Law'? Why Constitutionalising the WTO is a Step Too Far'

Hubert B H, & Wigger A, *The Politics of European Competition Regulation: A Critical Political Economy Perspective* (Routledge, 2011)

ICTSD, 'Argentina Pledges to Appeal WTO Ruling on Import Restrictions' (10 September 2014) Bridges Weekly Trade New Digest vol 16 (30). http://ictsd.org/i/news/bridgesweekly/ (accessed 30 July 2020)

Ikenberry J G, 'Creating Yesterday's New World Order: Keynesian 'New Thinking' and the Anglo-American Postwar Settlement' in Judith Goldstein & Robert O Keohane (eds), *Ideas and Foreign Policy: Beliefs, Institutions, and Political Changes* (Cornell University Press, 1993)

Ikenberry J G, 'A World Economy Restored: Experts Consensus and the Anglo-American Postwar Settlement' (Winter 1992) International Organisation vol 46 (1) pp 289–321

ILO World Employment Report Life at Work in the Information Economy (International Labour Organization, 2001) 1. www.ilo.org/global/about-the-ilo/newsroom/news/WCMS_007830/lang--en/index.htm

Irwin D A, Mavroid P C, & Sykes A, *The Genesis of the GATT* (CUP, 2008)

Isard P, *Exchange Rate Economics* (Cambridge University Press, 1995)

Ismail F, *Reforming the World Trade Organization: Developing Countries in the Doha Round* (Cuts International, India, 2009)

Jackson J, *The World Trade Organization After Ten Years: The Role of the WTO in a Globalization* (2015)

Jean G, & Pia R, 'The Return of the State in Argentina' (2007) International Affairs vol 83 (1) pp 87–107

Kindleberger C, 'The Rise of Free Trade in Western Europe, 1820–1875' (1975) Journal of Economic History vol 35 (1)

Krebs R R, & Jackson P T, 'Twisting Tongues and Twisting Arms: The Power of Political Rhetoric' (2007) European Journal of International Relations vol 13 (1) pp 35–66

Lamy P, 'Emerging Economies Have Shifted the Balance of Power in World Trade' Director-General Pascal Lamy, presenting the Richard Snape Lecture in Melbourne, Australia, 26 November 2012. www.wto.org/english/news_e/sppl_e/sppl258_e.htm (accessed 28 October 2021)

Lang A, 'Reconstructing Embedded Liberalism: John Ruggie and Constructivist Approaches to the Study of the International Trade Regime' (2006) Journal of International Law vol 9 (1)

Leffler M P, *A Preponderance of Power: National Security, the Truman Administration, and the Cold War* (Stanford University Press, 1992)

Lewis W A, *Economic Survey, 1919–1930* (1949; rpt. London: Allen & Unwin, 1970) cited in.

List F, *The National System of Political Economy* (trans Sampson S Lloyd, 1789)

Long F, *The Political Economy of EEC Relations With African, Caribbean and Pacific States* (Pergamon Press, 1980)

Mandelson P, 'Sustainable Trade Observations on Trade and Protectionism EU Trade Commissioner Speech/06/187, Brussels, 21 March 2006'

Markets Edgy on US-China Trade War Fears (23 March 2018). www.bbc.com (accessed 22 April 2021)

Mazower M, *Governing the World: The History of an Ideas* (The Penguin Press, 2012)

Milgrom P, North D, & Weingast B, 'The Role of Institutional in the Revival of Trade: The Law Merchant, Private Judges, and the Champagne Fairs' (1990) Economics and Politics vol 2 pp 1–23

Patterson G, *Discrimination in International Trade: The Policy Issues 1945–1965* (Princeton University Press, 1996)

Ruggie J G, 'International Regimes, Transactions, and Change: Embedded Liberalisation and the Post-War Economic Order' in S D Krasner (ed), *International Regimes* (Cornell University Press, 1983)

Wilkinson R, 'Language, Power and Multilateral Trade Negotiations' (2009) Review of International Political vol 16 (4) DOI:10.1080/09692290802587734

Wilkinson R, 'Of Butchery and Bicycles: The WTO and the 'Death' of the Doha Development Agenda' (2012) The Political Quarterly vol 83 (2)

Wilkinson R (ed), *Global Governance, Poverty and Inequality* (Routledge, 2010)

William Ris W, 'Escape Clause Relief Under the Trade Act of 1974: New Standards, Same Results' (1977) Columbia Journal of Transnational Law vol 16
Winikoff D, Jasanoff S, Busch L, Grove-White R, & Wynne B, 'Adjusting the GM Food Wars: Science, Risk and Democracy in World Trade Law' (2005) Yale Journal of International Law vol 30 p 81
Woolcock S, 'The Scope for Asymmetry in the World Trade Organisation (WTO)' in Sanoussi Bilal, Philippe De Lombaerde, & Diana Tussie (eds), *Asymmetric Trade Negotiations* (Routledge, 2016)
World Development Report, *Barriers to Adjustment and Growth in the World Economy Industrialisation and Foreign Trade World Development Indicators* (OUP, 1987)
WTO, 'Part IV Negotiation', at 308–309. www.wto.org/english/res_e/booksp_e/historywto_09_e.pdf (accessed 28 October 2021)

3 The Colonial Trading System

3.1 Introduction

Trade and exchange of goods among different cultures is antediluvian.[1] Its role and importance in human development cannot be overemphasised.[2] Nonetheless, the rhetoric and mythos of African trade and civilisation were that trade was introduced mainly by European powers who infiltrated the inactive continent of Africa.[3] However, there were several trade routes in Africa, and Africans traded beyond the shore of the continent.[4] The assumption that Europeans civilised the continent of Africa underestimated the advancement made by the latter before the colonisation by the former.[5] Henry Stanley in his historical account of his voyage in search of Africa notoriously referred to it as a dark continent.[6] Nevertheless, activities on the continent before slavery and the colonial conquest demonstrated otherwise. The Greek geographer Ptolemy gave a detailed account of a settlement in Eastern Africa as a 'metropolis' around 100 AD.[7] The works of Hartwig[8] and Tosh[9] revealed that in the nineteenth century, there was trade among the people and beyond the islands of Lake Victoria.

This chapter demonstrates that globalisation, from the African standpoint, is not a new phenomenon but was modified to make exploitation tolerable to developing countries.[10] Antony Anghie, in his book, built on pioneering research carried out on

1 Philip Curtin, *Cross-Cultural Trade in World History* (CUP, 1984) 1
2 Philip Curtin, *Cross-Cultural Trade in World History* (CUP, 1984) 1
3 Philip Curtin, *Cross-Cultural Trade in World History* (CUP, 1984) at 15
4 Philip Curtin, *Cross-Cultural Trade in World History* (CUP, 1984) at 15–16
5 Peter Kowalczyk, 'Unearthing the Origins of East Africa's Lost Civilisation' (CNN, 19 October 2015) https://edition.cnn.com/2015/10/19/africa/kilwa-rhapta-felix-chami/index.html accessed 16 May 2024; Graham Connah, *Civilisations: An Archaeological Perspective* (CUP, 2006); Christopher Ehret, *The Civilisation of Africa: A History to 1800* (University of Virginia, 2002)
6 Henry M Stanley, *Through the Dark Continent* (vol 1, George Newnes Limited, 1899) pp 42 and 54
7 Kowalczyk (n 5)
8 Gerald W Hartwig, 'The Victoria Nyanza as a Trade Route in the Nineteenth Century' (1970) The Journal of African History IX vol 4 pp 535–52
9 John Tosh, 'The Northern Interlacustrine Region' in R Gray and D Birmingham (eds), *Pre-Colonial Africa Trade. Essays on Trade in Central and Eastern Africa Before 1900* (OUP, 1970)
10 Branko Milanovic, 'The Two Faces of Globalization: Against Globalization as We Know It' (2003) World Development vol 31 (4) pp 667–83 at 668

DOI: 10.4324/9781032615059-3

the after-effect of decolonisation and self-determination and called for state-directed economic growth, not a wholesale construct of globalisation, which is structured to facilitate the trade of the advanced countries.[11] The approach adopted here is to explore the lopsidedness of world trade and the distortion of African understanding of globalisation and its effect on the development of the continent,[12] which paved the way for systemic asymmetry in the current world order. The European powers were able to achieve effective occupation by either placing reliance on *terra nullius* and discovery, the absolute right to make everyone a Christian, or the freedom to unrestricted trade, and vigorous attempts were made to transmute *de facto* acts into law for the legitimisation of every action.[13]

Article VI of the Treaty of Lagos made it clear that the 'subjects of the Queen of England' were authorised to trade freely in the colony of Lagos and locals were not permitted to show favour to other countries without first extending such favours to the subjects of the Queen of England.[14] In a similar term, the colonial treaty between Britain and Asaba in Article II provides, 'the Kings, Queen, and Chiefs of Asaba agreed and promise to refrain from entering into any correspondence, Agreement, or Treaty with any foreign nation or power, except with the knowledge and sanctions of Her Britannic Majesty's Government.'[15] Other similar unequal treaties shall be explored later in this chapter.

Hugo Grotius argues vehemently in defence of Dutch monopolies against British dominance in mercantilism. He contends that the treaties entered into between the Dutch and the natives give the former the right to monopolise trade advantages.[16] Treaties were used by European powers to gain unrestricted access to the non-European market, in East and West Africa—thus power asymmetry came to be institutionalised.[17] The unequal treaties gave sweeping and blanket rights to the European powers and granted them great opportunities to exploit and dominate the economies of the conquered for several decades.[18] Kennedy in his work noted that concerning Britain's dominant power, 'with her great industrial lead, her large merchant marine, her financial expertise, [Britain] above all was uniquely suited to

11 Antony Anghie, *Imperialism, Sovereignty and the Making of International Law* (CUP, 2004)

12 Padraig Carmody, 'Between Globalisation and (Post) Apartheid: The Political Economy of Restructuring in South Africa' (2002) Journal of South of Africa Studies vol 28 (2) pp 255–75

13 Anthony Pagden, *Lords of All the World: Ideologies of Empire in Spain, Britain and France c. 1500–c. 1800* (Yale University Press, 1998) chap 1–3; Kwame Yeboa Daaku, Trade and Politics on the Gold Coast 1600–1720: A Study of the African Reaction to European Trade (Clarendon Press, 1970) 18–9

14 Treaty Between Britain and Kings and Chiefs of Lagos, signed 1 January 1852, Article VI

15 Treaty Between Britain and Kings, Queens and Chiefs of Asaba, signed at Asaba, 1884, Article II

16 Richard Tuck, *The Rights of War and Peace: Political Thought and International Order From Grotius to Kant* (OUP, 1999) 94

17 Charles H Alexandrowicz, *An Introduction to the History of the Law of Nations in the East Indies* (OUP, 1967) 5–9

18 Gerrit W Gong, *The Standard of 'Civilization' in International Society* (OUP, 1984) 5–7; Ronald Hyam, *Britain's Imperial Century 1815–1914: A Study of Empire and Expansion* (3rd ed., Palgrave Macmillan, 2002) 123–33

benefit from the greater exchange of conditions.'[19] According to Burnett, to advance their economic interests, countries external to Africa looted and pillaged it.[20] The continent was forced to contend with brutal and exploitative 'globalisers'—through the slave trade and colonialism.[21] Herbstein argued, 'the Atlantic slave trade is the bedrock upon which the mighty edifice of globalisation has been constructed.'[22] The logic of Eric William may not be accepted wholesale—that the slave trade provided funds and facilitated, generally, the British Industrial Revolution.[23]

The following parts explored the advancements made in the African trading system before the advent of the European powers. It is then argued that the *de facto* power asymmetry that existed between African and European powers attained a legal construct to maintain the status quo. Furthermore, it is argued that the negotiation and agreement reached at the Berlin Conference gave legal backing to the activities of European powers already established in Africa, hence the General Act was meant to apply retrospectively and prospectively. Drawing from the insights, the chapter then concludes that both *de facto* and *de jure* construct structured an asymmetrical power continuum between Africa and the Western world.

3.2 Precolonial Trade in Africa

The presumption that African nations were insulated from the rest of the world was a misconception.[24] According to Anthony Hopkins, West Africa was well connected to the outside world in terms of trade across deserts and oceans hundreds of years before the Industrial Revolution, which empowered the Europeans to infiltrate the continent of Africa and the rest of the world.[25] The works of Hartwig[26] and Tosh[27] and other early travellers revealed that in the nineteenth century, there was trade among the people of the islands of Lake Victoria. According to Tosh, iron and

19 Paul M Kennedy, *The Rise and Fall of British Naval Mastery* (Penguin Books Ltd, 1976) 152; John Ruggie, 'Multilateralism: The Anatomy of an Institution' (1992) International Organisation vol 46 (3) pp 561–98 at 580–82

20 Patrick Burnett and Firoze Manji, *From the Slave Trade to 'Free' Trade: How Trade Undermines Democracy and Justice in Africa* (Fahamu, 2007) 37; Anwar Shaikh, 'Globalization and the Myths of Free' in Anwar Shaikh (ed), *Globalization and the Myths of Free Trade: History, Theory, and Empirical Evidence* (Routledge, 2007) 60

21 Manu Herbstein, 'A Story of the Atlantic Slave Trade' in Patrick Burnett and Firoze Manji (eds), *From the Slave Trade to 'Free' Trade: How Trade Undermines Democracy and Justice in Africa* (Fahamu, 2007) 70

22 Manu Herbstein, 'A Story of the Atlantic Slave Trade' in Patrick Burnett and Firoze Manji (eds), *From the Slave Trade to 'Free' Trade: How Trade Undermines Democracy and Justice in Africa* (Fahamu, 2007) 70; Ibrahim Kawuley Mikail and Ainuddin Iskandar Lee Abdullah, 'The Impact of Globalization on African Culture and Politics' (2017) Journal of International Studies vol 13 (1–14) pp 2–8

23 Eric William, *Capitalism and Slavery* (University of North Carolina Press, 1944) 40–66

24 Anthony Gerald Hopkins, *An Economic History of West Africa* (2nd ed, Routledge, 2020) 125

25 Anthony Gerald Hopkins, *An Economic History of West Africa* (2nd ed, Routledge, 2020) 125

26 Gerald W Hartwig, 'The Victoria Nyanza as a Trade Route in the Nineteenth Century' (1970) The Journal of African History IX vol 4 pp 535–52

27 Tosh (n 9)

salt were scarce products in East Africa.[28] This made these commodities natural items of trade notwithstanding other local commodities.

However, the food trade is to a limited extent different, as the need and desire for it can be severe because the challenge of transporting it, under pre-colonial conditions, was higher than with portable iron and salt. Food trade thus needs sufficient transport, and if the trade destination is far, 'presumably, also a high return, one which could be attained if traded for iron, salt, or similarly valuable and portable items.'[29] The sewn canoe was a means of transport and was possessed by Kerebe, Ganda, Soga, the lacustrine Suba, and others.[30] The canoe made a large amount of trade possible, as trade was facilitated and made secure through this mode of transport. Hartwig[31] gave evidence about trade in iron, salt, and foodstuffs in the southeastern and southern lakes. Roscoe suggested that there was trade in salt from the eastern lake into Buganda; however, there was no mention of the origin of the salt.[32] Tosh pointed out the connection between trade in Ssese Island, coastal Buganda, and coastal Busoga.[33] Several scholars revealed the regionally important trade in iron in the northeast of the lake, which focused on smelting work in the Samia Hills close to the Kenya-Uganda border.[34]

Upon his visit to Cairo, Al Umar declared that Mansa Musa 'left no emir or holder of royal office without a gift or load of gold, he and his company gave out so much gold they depressed its value in Egypt and caused its price to fall.' At this point, two-thirds of the global gold supply originated in West Africa.[35] Unrestrained distribution of gold by Mansa Musa strategically placed Mali on the world map, drawn by Angelino Dulcert of Majorca in 1339 and other maps.[36] Mali, as a

28 Tosh (n 9) at 104–6

29 Michael G Kenny, 'Pre-Colonial Trade in Eastern Lake Victoria' http://dx.doi.org/10.1080/00672707909511265 accessed 10 July 2023

30 Michael G Kenny, 'Pre-Colonial Trade in Eastern Lake Victoria' http://dx.doi.org/10.1080/00672707909511265 accessed 10 July 2023

31 Gerald W Hartwig, *The Art of Survival in East Africa: The Kerebe and Long Distance Trade 1800–1895* (Lynne Rienner, 1975) 105

32 John Roscoe, *The Baganda: An Account of their Native Customs and Beliefs* (CUP, 2011, First published in 1965) 438

33 Tosh (n 9) at 109

34 David William Cohen, *The Historical Tradition of Busaga: Mukama and Kintu* (OUP, 1972) 99; Charles William Hobley, *Eastern Uganda, an Ethnological Survey 1867–1947* (Occasional Paper 1 Anthrop. Inst. of GT Britain and Ireland, 1902) 27; Joseph Thomas, *Through Masai Land: A Journey of Exploration Among the Snowclad Volcanic Mountains and Strange Tribes of Eastern Equatorial Africa* (Hansebooks, 2016) 290; Gunter Wagner, *The Bantu of Western Kenya I–II* (OUP, 1949) 9; William Robert Ochieng, *A History of the Kadimo Chiefdom of Yimbo in Western Kenya Nairobi* (East Africa Literature Bureau, 1975) 46; Jane Humphris and Louis Iles, *Pre-Colonial Iron Production in Great Lakes Africa: Recent Archaeometallurgical Research at UCL Institute of Archaeology, in the World of Iron* (Archetype, 2013) 56–5

35 Barbara Kraser, *Mansa Musa: The Most Famous African Traveler to Mecca* (Rosen Publishing, 2017) 38

36 Barbara Kraser, *Mansa Musa: The Most Famous African Traveler to Mecca* (Rosen Publishing, 2017) at 64–5

result of this popularity, became a citadel of commercial activity and learning.[37] Also, Ghana was wealthy in gold. In the eighteenth century, during the medieval time, Ghana was known as 'the land of gold.'[38] Interestingly, Ghana at this time was not involved in gold extraction but had political power in West Africa because it provided an indispensable route for trans-Saharan trade.[39]

The trans-Saharan trade course manifested that regional and international trade combined in such a way that enhanced commercial transactions.[40] The Sahel, including, the grassland belt to the south of the Sahara, produced large quantities of livestock, and leather products were exported.[41] The food basket of West Africa was the savanna to the south of Sahel—production of cereal and fish was in abundance as well, and these were traded to far distant markets, the tributaries of River Niger provided fish, and rice was locally produced.[42] The other two key products, kola nuts and gold, were traded into other distant markets, but Mali had a monopoly and political control of gold, which made it one of the richest nations in the medieval period.[43]

In the fifteenth century, Akan traded from the forest of the south to trans-Saharan areas through the direction of Dyula[44]—long-distance traders from Mali.[45] The trading system was so structured in West Africa to the extent that the Portuguese could not penetrate it.[46] It was suggested by Wilks that the Wangara had benefitted from exclusive control in the Akan gold trade, supplying gold or silver in bulk to western Sudan markets. He further noted that even though the Portuguese began to take part in the trade in the late fifteenth century, they experienced extreme difficulty to change the direction of gold supply.[47] The Portuguese and other Europeans found some West African communities who could paddle their canoes far enough into the Atlantic Ocean to became canoe men on the ships of the Europeans.[48] Most of the trade was carried out along the Keta and Nokue Lagoon before the arrival of the Europeans. The lagoon connects the Guinea coast, Ivory

37 Barbara Kraser, *Mansa Musa: The Most Famous African Traveler to Mecca* (Rosen Publishing, 2017)at 7–10; Joseph C Miller, *Way of Death: Merchant Capitalism and the Angolan Slave Trade, 1730–1830* (University of Wisconsin Press, 1988)

38 Barbara Kraser, *Mansa Musa: The Most Famous African Traveler to Mecca* (Rosen Publishing, 2017) at 5

39 Barbara Kraser, *Mansa Musa: The Most Famous African Traveler to Mecca* (Rosen Publishing, 2017) at 25

40 Roland Oliver and Anthony Atmore, *Medieval Africa 1250–1800* (CUP, 2004) 112–4

41 Emmanuel Akyeampong, Robert H Bates, Nathan Nunn, et al. (eds), *Africa's Development in Historical Perspective* (CUP, 2014) 215, 61–2

42 Hartwig (n 8) 107–8

43 Akyeampong (n 41) at 62

44 Ivor Wilks, 'Wangara, Akan and Portuguese in the Fifteenth and Sixteenth Centuries, 1 The Matt Bitu' (1982) Journal of African History vol 23 (3) pp 333–49 at 344

45 Oliver and Atmore (n 40) at 64

46 Wilks I (n 44) 472

47 Wilks I (n 44) 472

48 Akyeampong (n 41) at 245

Coast and Lagos.[49] Most textiles and clothes worn before the arrival of Europe originated in North Africa. Blue cloth and beads were exported from Benin, the present-day capital of Edo State in Nigeria to the Gold Coast before the advent of the Europeans.[50]

There was a bitter complaint among the Dutch, Portuguese, and English throughout the eighteenth century about the unsteady consumption of textiles on the Gold Coast. According to Ray Kea, this was so because the need for textile consumption was met by the production by the local manufacturers; European products were only used as a status symbol, hence demand and taste began to change.[51] On the East African coast, Kilwa was classified as one of the richest nations before the arrival of the Portuguese. Two factors accounted for its wealth;[52] first, the seasonal monsoon winds followed a predictable pattern, enabling ships to sale from Asia to Africa and back within season. Second, Kilwa was nearer to the coastal port, making it easy to transport gold from the inner part of the Zimbabwe plateau. It is important to note that Kilwa was not the only rich Swahili nation in 1500. Malindi and Mombasa were also rich and had civilisation between the period of 1300 and 1500.[53]

The increase in power of the Portuguese would ultimately lead to the ruination of Kilwa, but it was found that the wealth of the Kilwa went far into the interior.[54] Several attempts were made by the Portuguese to gain access to the inland, but they were unsuccessful for centuries.[55] The people of Zimbabwe and the state of Mwene Mutapa had well-structured and organised economies internally; the economies were arranged around agriculture and minerals.[56] The economy of Zimbabwe was strengthened and maintained by minerals such as copper and gold,

49 Robin Law, 'Between the Sea and the Lagoon: The Interaction of Maritime and Inland Navigation on the Precolonial Slave Coast' (1989) Cahiers d'etudes Africaines, 114 vol xxix-2 pp 209–37; Emmanuel Akyeampong, 'History of African Trade' (2017) African Export-Import Bank, (Afreximbank) vol 6

50 A Adu Boahen, 'Ghana Before the Coming of the Europeans' (1977) Ghana Social Science Journal vol 4 (2) pp 93–106

51 Ray A Kea, *Settlements, Trade and Politics in the Seventeenth Century Gold Coast* (John Hopkin University Press, 1982)

52 Heba Elhanafy, 'Building Africa: Kilwa Kisiwani, The Indian Occasion Trade, and Rise of Eastern Africa Cuty-State' (Charter Cities Institute, 2020) https://chartercitiesinstitute.org/blog-posts/building-africa-kilwa-kisiwani-the-indian-ocean-trade-and-the-rise-of-east-african-city-states/ accessed 16 May 2024

53 Akyeampong (n 49) 8; Derek Nurse and Thomas Spear, *The Swahili Reconstructing the History and Language of an African Society, 800–1500* (University of Pennsylvania, 1985); Randall L Pouwels, *Horn and Crescent: Cultural Change and Traditional Islam on the East African Coast, 800–1900* (CUP, 1987); John Middleton, *The World of the Swahili* (Yale University Press, 1992)

54 John E G Sutton, 'Archaeological Sites of Eastern Africa: Four Studies' (1998) The Journal of the British Institute vol xxxiii at 116

55 John E G Sutton, 'Archaeological Sites of Eastern Africa: Four Studies' (1998) The Journal of the British Institute vol xxxiii at 131

56 Ray A Kea, 'Africa in World History, 1400 to 1800' in Jerry H Bentley, Sanjay Subrahmanyam and Merry E Wiesner-Hanks (eds), *The Cambridge World History: The Construction of a Global World 1400–1800* (vol VI, CUP, 2015) 260

extensive trade around the Indian Ocean, and abundant cattle.[57] The gold was traded along with herds of cattle, and the gains from such trade were used to pay workers in the mining sector.[58] It was reported that several attempts were made to persuade the Zimbabwe people to focus on the production of ivory and gold, but these were declined.[59]

It was claimed that there was nothing much in terms of trade in South Africa prior to 1652 when the Dutch set up the East Indies Company at Table Bay at the Cape.[60] However, this is more like mythos than documentary evidence. Khoisan and Bantu were the larger group in South Africa and had trading networks. Khoisan exchanged their cattle, sheep, and hunting produce for iron from the Batswanna and in turn traded the metals to the Xhosa for dagga and tobacco. Trading intersects South Africa. The trading of cattle by pastoralist Khoi drew the attention of the European ships in the sixteenth century.[61] It was the enforced departure and appropriation of the land and cattle of the Khoisan in the Cape Province, and the subsequent wars against South-eastern Cape Province in South Africa, that laid the foundation of European superiority in South Africa for centuries.

There was also regional trade in central Africa, to some degree secluded from the outside world.[62] However, the infiltration of the Atlantic and Indian Ocean trade in the nineteenth century brought it into contact with other nations.[63] Zambia and the Democratic Republic of Congo exploited copper as early as the fourth century.[64] The Luba-Lunda kingdoms made copper goods of estimable value, and the Luba and Lunda regions traded in salt, fish, and copper.[65] Thus regional trade played an important role in cultural exchange by introducing innovative technologies and integration of nations. For instance, Mande traders and blacksmiths from medieval Mali subsumed the Akan forest into trans-Saharan trade networks and taught the advanced technology of mining.[66]

57 Ray A Kea, 'Africa in World History, 1400 to 1800' in Jerry H Bentley, Sanjay Subrahmanyam and Merry E Wiesner-Hanks (eds), *The Cambridge World History: The Construction of a Global World 1400–1800* (vol VI, CUP, 2015) 260

58 Ray A Kea, 'Africa in World History, 1400 to 1800' in Jerry H Bentley, Sanjay Subrahmanyam and Merry E Wiesner-Hanks (eds), *The Cambridge World History: The Construction of a Global World 1400–1800* (vol VI, CUP, 2015) 260 at 61

59 Michael N Pearson, *Port Cities and Intruders: The Swahili Coast, India, and Portugal in the Early Modern Era* (The John Hopkins University Press, 1998)

60 Christopher Saunders, *The Making of the South African Mind: Major Historian on Race and Class* (Barnes and Noble, 1988)

61 Akyeampong (n 49)

62 Enid Guene, 'Copper, Borders and National-Building: The Kantagese Factor in Zambian Political and Economic History' (2017) African Studies Centre Leiden vol 67 at 35–6; David Birmingham, 'Central Africa' (Britannica, 2007) www.britannica.com/place/central-Africa/Economic-organization accessed 16 May 2024

63 John D Fage and T C McCaskie, West African Britannica 2024

64 Guene (n 62) at 7–13

65 Guene (n 62) at 37, 114, 7 and 21

66 Oliver and Atmore (n 40)

The importance of trade in human history cannot be overemphasised, but it also has adverse effects if it is wrongly applied.[67] This was the situation with the export of human beings as chattel, which changed the African economies. There was some element of slavery prior to the European involvement.[68] However, according to Nunn and Inikori, the European slave trade brought about insecurity and destructive technologies; for instance, firearms, discontinuation of traditional craft, and loss of able-bodied men and women from the continent which contributed in no small measure to ultimately hampering development of the continent. Walter Rodney,[69] made this argument strongly, and in recent times the same argument has been made by other authors such as Nunn and Inikori.[70]

The impact of the Atlantic slave trade on social, economic, and political structure in Africa continues to be a subject of debate.[71] However, one thing is clear enough to Melber—the slave trade seemed to have created sempiternal impairment to the process of industrialisation on the continent.[72] Although the Atlantic trade initiated the planting of some new crops and ideologies that were beneficial to the African nations, the slave trade's negative impact permeated and persisted in the economic development of the continent to this present time.[73] Douglas Rimmer argued that the West's idea of civilising Africa failed to yield substantial benefits concerning the economic transformation of the continent.[74] Feagin believed that Africans still face 'economic exploitation,' and this to him remains the cause of underdevelopment.[75]

Notwithstanding the abolition of the slave trade, foreign powers' interests were protected to the detriment of the natives. Upon the issuance of the Royal Edict in 1792, Denmark decreed that the slave trade should be abolished beginning in 1803. Britain and the Netherlands proscribed the illegal trade in 1807 and 1814 accordingly.[76] To commence 'legitimate trade,' the Danish wasted no time in replacing the

67 Nathan Nunn, 'The Long Term Effects of Africa's Slave Trade' (2008) The Quarterly Journal of Economics vol 123 (1)

68 Frank Tannenbaum, *Slave and Citizen: The Negro in the Americas* (Alfre A Knopf, 1947); Joe R Feagin, *Systemic Racism: A Theory of Oppression* (Routledge, 2006)

69 Walter Rodney, *How Europe Underdeveloped Africa* (Bofle-L'Ouverture Publications, 1972); also, Tannebaum (n 72) at 32–3

70 Nunn (n 67); Joseph E Inikori, *The Chaining of a Continent: Export Demand for Captives and the History of Africa South of the Sahara, 1450–1870* (University of West Indies, 1992)

71 Linda M Heywood, 'Slavery and Its Transformation in the Kingdom of Kongo: 1491–1800' (2009) The Journal of African History vol 50, pp 1–22 at 1

72 Henning Melber, 'The New Scramble for Africa's Resources' in Patrick Burnett and Firoze Manji (eds), *From the Slave Trade to 'Free' Trade: How Trade Undermines Democracy and Justice in Africa* (Fahamu, 2007) 37–8; Joseph E Inikori, 'The Development of Commercial Agriculture in Pre-Colonial Africa' (African Economic History Working Paper Series, No. 9/2013) www.ecostor.eu/bitstream/10419/242638/1/aehn-wp-09.pdf accessed 1 April 2024

73 Douglas Rimmer, 'Learning About Economic Development From Africa' (2003) African Affairs vol 102 pp 469–91, at 479–79

74 Douglas Rimmer, 'Learning About Economic Development From Africa' (2003) African Affairs vol 102 pp 469–91 at 479–79

75 Joe R Feagin, *Systemic Racism: A Theory of Oppression* (Routledge, 2006) 196, 197

76 Ray A Kea, 'Plantations and Labour in the South-East Gold Coast From the Late Eighteenth to the Mid Nineteenth Century' in Robin Law (ed), *From Slave Trade to 'Legitimate' Commerce: The Commercial Transition in Nineteenth-Century West Africa* (CUP, 1995) 120

slave trade with plantations in the hinterland of West Africa. The new economic focus was on the production of tropical plants such as indigo, coffee, sugar cane, cotton, and tobacco to send to the Denmark market.[77] It was recorded that in 1850 the Danish possession was sold to the British government.[78]

The contradiction is that after Britain and other European states decided to end the slave trade, it transformed Britain into a sort of 'guardian' with an automatic license to manage the affairs of native communities. British officials and representatives of the monarch would impose treaties on African kings, queens, and chiefs to end the slave trade.[79] Christopher Brown states that the self-acclaimed champion of abolition gave Britain the upper hand to protect the 'integrity' and ownership of civilising the Africans.[80] In other words, the quest for the abolition of slavery 'displayed Britain as the purveyor of civilisation, justice, and order.' The British state was historically portrayed as being concerned with the welfare of African people to its own expense.[81] Slavery was replaced with transaction in palm oil and other cash crops.

A boom in the palm oil trade contributed to the rise of West African merchants and princes in the second half of the nineteenth century.[82] In 1840, Zanzibar was leading in the export of clove.[83] There was commercial interest rising with African boldness and self-assuredness in handling their commerce; this was one of the reasons that led to the Berlin Conference in the first quarter of the nineteenth century.[84] Another reason was the recession of 1873 to 1896, which heightened the commercial competition between African and European traders and between big and small traders. As commercial activities became unpredictable, European merchants began to advocate for the colonisation of Africa. According to John Hargreaves, the European military forces were brought to restrain and subdue socioeconomic revolt

77 Ray A Kea, 'Plantations and Labour in the South-East Gold Coast From the Late Eighteenth to the Mid Nineteenth Century' in Robin Law (ed), *From Slave Trade to 'Legitimate' Commerce: The Commercial Transition in Nineteenth-Century West Africa* (CUP, 1995) 120

78 Ray A Kea, 'Plantations and Labour in the South-East Gold Coast From the Late Eighteenth to the Mid Nineteenth Century' in Robin Law (ed), *From Slave Trade to 'Legitimate' Commerce: The Commercial Transition in Nineteenth-Century West Africa* (CUP, 1995) 120; Joseph C Miller, *The Problem of Slavery as History: A Global Approach* (Yale University Press, 2012) 142

79 Anietie A Inyang and Manasseh Edidem, 'Imperial Treaties and Origins of British Colonial Rule in Southern Nigeria, 1860–1890' (2014) Mediterranean Journal of Social Science vol 5 (20) p 1951

80 Christopher Brown, *Moral Capital: Foundations of British Abolitionism* (University of North Carolina Press, 2006)

81 Christopher Brown, *Moral Capital: Foundations of British Abolitionism* (University of North Carolina Press, 2006) at 8; see John R Seeley, *The Expansion of England* (Macmillan, 1883, John Gross, ed. 1971)

82 Emmanuel Akyeampong, 'Commerce, Credit, and Mobility in the Late-Nineteenth Century Gold Coast: Changing Dynamics in Euro-African Trade' in Emmanuel Akyeampong, Robert H Bates, Nathan Nunn and James A Robinson (eds), *Africa's Development in Historical Perspective* (CUP, 2014) 231–63

83 Emmanuel Akyeampong, 'Commerce, Credit, and Mobility in the Late-Nineteenth Century Gold Coast: Changing Dynamics in Euro-African Trade' in Emmanuel Akyeampong, Robert H Bates, Nathan Nunn and James A Robinson (eds), *Africa's Development in Historical Perspective* (CUP, 2014) 231–63 at 247

84 H P Meritt, 'Bismarck and the German Interest in East Africa 1884–1885' (1978) The Historical Journal vol 21 (1) pp 97–116

in West Africa, bringing about free trade.[85] The Berlin Conference, for some, legitimised the partition of Africa. The atmosphere was vividly captured by the Lagos newspaper editor in 1891, 'a forcible possession of our land has taken the place of a forcible possession of our person.'[86]

The economy during the colonial era was at a basic level, and infrastructure was negligible.[87] For example, in coastal colonies, the railway line led only from the port to the source of the mineral or resulted in imperial threat to the facilitation of resources.[88] The whole of Sierra Leone had 84 miles of railway.[89] There was no form of manufacturing, and it was not until the Second World War that industrialisation began slowly driven by both domestic production and imports. As discussed later in this chapter, colonies were prevented from trading with other communities except with the consent of the colonialists.[90] As the powers had the advantage of imposing bilateral relations with various colonies, diversification was not of concern to the imperial metropole, as the powers only looked for key products from all its colonies: gold and cocoa from Ghana, groundnuts from Senegal, cotton from the northern part of present-day Nigeria, palm oil and cocoa from Bonny in the south, cotton from Malawi, copper from Zambia, tea from Kenya, and so on.[91] Food security was not of concern to the metropole, as the powers preferred commodities that could earn foreign currency. Thus, the Idoma in the middle belt in colonial Nigeria had a booming domestic economy based principally on the production of yams, which were usually sold to the miners on the Jos Plateau. They were classified as economically retrograde because they declined to grow cotton for export.[92] Armed with influence and power, the next agenda of the colonialists was to constructively legitimise commerce.

3.3 Legal Construct of Colonial Trade in the Context of the Berlin Conference

On 15 November 1884, an international conference was formally opened by the chancellor of the German Empire at the official residence on Wilhelmstrasse, in

85 John D Hargreaves, 'The European Partition of West Africa' in J F A Ajayi and Michael Crowder (eds), *History of West Africa* (2nd ed., Longman, 1987) cited in Akyeampon, Bate and Nunn (n 53) at 232

86 John B Webster and Albert Adu Boahen with M Tidy, *The Revolutionary Years: West African Since 1800* (Longman, 1986) 176

87 D Acemoglu, S Johnson and J Robinson, 'Colonial Origins of Comparative Development: An Empirical Investigation' (2001) American Economic Review vol 91 pp 1369–401; Melissa Dell and Benjamin A Olken, 'The Development Effects of the Extractive Colonial Economy: The Dutch Cultivation System in Java' https://scholar.harvard.edu/files/dell/files/170414draft.pdf accessed 17 May 2024

88 Emmanuel Akeyeampong, *History of African Trade* (Africa, Export-Import Bank, 2015) 16–7

89 Emmanuel Akeyeampong, *History of African Trade* (Africa, Export-Import Bank, 2015) 16–7

90 Inyan and Edidem (n 79) at 1751; E Herslet, *The Map of Africa by Treaty: British Colonies, Protectorate and Possession in Africa* (Frank Cass & Co Ltd, 1967)

91 I Anietie A Inyang and Manasseh Edidem, 'Imperial Treaties and Origins of British Colonial Rule in Southern Nigeria, 1860–1890' (2014) Mediterranean Journal of Social Science vol 5 (20)

92 Moses Ochonu, *Colonial Meltdown: Northern Nigeria in the Great Depression* (Ohio University Press, 2009)

Berlin.[93] With the addition of the short break during Christmas and the New Year, the West Africa Conference of Berlin lasted 104 days. It ended on 26 February 1885. The conference which took place more than 138 years ago adopted the rules for the overpowering and acquisition of Africa.[94] Thus, the Berlin West African conference began the legalisation and institutionalisation of asymmetry. It was a gathering of powers from 14 countries as well as the United States of America (USA). The meeting was convoked in mid-November 1884.[95]

The agenda for the meeting was to fix the boundary of a free trade zone in the Congo basin and Niger and to proscribe import duties.[96] After a week of discussing the thorny problem of delimitation, the USA proposed that the free trade zone should be extended to the east to cover the entire part of Africa and further to the Indian Ocean.[97] At the third session of the conference, the proposal by the USA was adopted. However, the French delegate, Baron Courcel, expressed hesitancy that the 'conference Powers would be obliged to respect the existing sovereign rights of non-signatory powers on the east coast of Africa.'[98] As such, the General Act was meant to apply retrospectively as lands on the African continent had been acquired through unequal and imposed treaties by the European powers, hence the Act ratified such action and prospectively in case of native lands that may be acquired or merged an acquired native lands if it is useful to the European powers' interest.

The agenda for the conference was presented in order of priority: first were the interests of commercial and industrial nations, which a common necessity compels the finding of new outlets; second, the powers of the states over the regions of the Congo and authority which will have burdens corresponding to their rights. And last, that which some generous voices have already commended—the interests of the native populations. The question of the sovereignty of Africa and the legitimacy of occupying a foreign nation was brushed aside by Bismarck. According to Uzoigwe (1984–1985), Bismarck in his opening remarks states that the delegates were not summoned to debate about the 'sovereignty of Africa or European powers in Africa.' This made it clear as to why no African was invited to the conference. The sultan of Zanzibar attempted to persuade the organisers for an invitation to be extended to him, but he was mocked by the British. American journalist Daniel De Leon portrayed the conference as 'an event unique in the history of political

93 Global Erinnern, 'Berlin Africa Conference 1884' https://globalerinnern.org/en/event/berlin-africa-conference-1884/ accessed 25 July 2023

94 Patrick Gathara, 'Berlin 1884: Remembering the Conference that Divided Africa' (Aljazeeraa 15 November 2019) www.aljazeera.com/opinions/2019/11/15/berlin-1884-remembering-the-conference-that-divided-africa accessed 21 October 2023

95 Patrick Gathara, 'Berlin 1884: Remembering the Conference that Divided Africa' (Aljazeeraa 15 November 2019) www.aljazeera.com/opinions/2019/11/15/berlin-1884-remembering-the-conference-that-divided-africa accessed 21 October 2023

96 H P Meritt, 'Bismarck and the German Interest in East Africa, 1884–1885' (1978) Historical Journal vol 21 (1) pp 97–116 at 109

97 Sybil Eyre Crowe, *The Berlin West African Conference 1884–85* (Greenwood Press, 1970) 112–13

98 Protocol no. 3 meeting of 27 November 1884, 'Protocol and General Act of the Berlin West African Conference' F[OREIGN] o[FFICE] 84/1826, Public Record Office, London

science. . . . Diplomatic in form, it was economic in fact.' This is an apt description, although represented as a humanitarian summit to explore ways to assist the locals, the primary agenda was the economic interest of the Europeans powers.[99]

Legal scholars have tried to give a historical account of colonialism in the context of treaties.[100] As described by Anthony Nutting, the undisguised objective of the General Act's scramble for Africa was to maintain control of the process of colonisation in Africa to prevent conflict between European powers.[101] Nutting's observation was deduced from the preambular reading of the General Act, which states:

> Wishing, in the spirit of good and mutual accord, to regulate the conditions most favourable to the development of trade and civilization in certain regions of Africa, and to assure all nations of the advantages of free navigation on the two chief rivers of Africa flowing into the Atlantic.[102]

This means the objective of the General Act was to give all nations free access to waterways in Africa for the advancement of trade that would benefit the European powers and in return the continent of Africa civilised by the powers. Furthermore, the preamble reads:

> Being desirous, on the other hand, to obviate the misunderstanding and disputes which might in future arise from new acts of occupation (prises de possession) on the coast of Africa; and concerned, at the same time, as to the means of furthering the moral and material well-being of the native population.[103]

As mentioned earlier by Nutting, the second aim of the General Act was to ensure peaceful navigation and trading without conflict among the powers and to advance and inculcate in the natives a sense of morality and provide for welfare due to them.[104] In other words, the first and second paragraphs of the preamble can be

99 Daniel De Leon, 'The Conference at Berlin on the West-African Question' (1886) Political Science Quarterly vol 1 (1) pp 103–39

100 T Elias, *Africa and the Development of International Law* (Martinus Nijhoff, 1972); Charles Henry Alexandrowicz, *The European-African Confrontation: A Study in Treaty Making* (Sijthoff, 1973); Umozurike U Orji, *International Law and Colonialism in Africa* (Nwamife, 1979); Makau Wa Mutua, 'Why Redraw the Map of Africa? A Moral and Legal Inquiry' (1995) Michigan Journal of International Law vol 16 (4) p 1113; James Tuo Gathii, 'How American Support for Freedom of Commerce Legitimized King Leopold's Territorial Ambitions in the Congo' (2005) 37 Studies in Transnational Legal Policy vol 97; Anthony Anghie, *Imperialism, Sovereignty and the Making of International Law* (CUP, 2005); Martti Koskenniemi, *The Gentle Civiliser of Nations: The Rise and Fall of International Law 1870–1960* (CUP, 2002)

101 Anthony Nutting, *Scramble for Africa: The Great Trek to the Boer War* (Constable and Robinson Ltd, 1994)

102 General Act of the Berlin Conference on West Africa, 26 February 1885

103 General Act of the Berlin Conference on West Africa, 26 February 1885

104 Nutting (n 101)

summed up as economic exploitation of the continent; the General Act offers legal protection to the Europeans who were extracting mineral and raw materials in Africa and imposed on the natives docility expected of a 'Christian,' that which was adopted through superior moral values of the Europeans.[105] However, obtaining the submission of the natives did not come cheap as there were several revolts against the colonialists; for instance, tax riots in the 1920s depict the resistance faced by the British in Nigeria.[106] Nevertheless, nations, now known as Nigeria, mechanically consented to British rule but there was septic disgruntlement, which was most of the time palpable, thus the agitation of the nationalists began in earnest in the 1940s.[107]

The protection offered to the British company was substantial. For instance, in 1877 Sir George Goldie Taubman ran a successful trading company, which was at first named the United African Company and later in 1882 was renamed the National African Company. Sir Goldie was an astute imperialist, who had the ambition of building a vast British commercial empire on the continent of Africa. Beginning in the 1870s, he gained entrance into the Niger by trading in the Delta with some African traders, comprising middlemen and producers, to which the British had direct access. The French eventually had access to the interior, and fierce competition ensued among the two—British and French. Finally, in 1884, after a series of mergers and acquisitions with Britain and France trading companies, Sir Goldie and the National African Company had a trade monopoly in the Niger. The British rule in the West Africa areas was acknowledged by the powers at the Berlin Conference; in other words, the General Act had a retrospective application, and it ratified what had been done previously.[108]

The authority of Britain over Niger was recognised pursuant to Article 30 of the General Act. As Britain had taken charge of most of Niger, the Act retrospectively ratified its dominion over the area and imposed upon it the obligation to the principle of freedom of navigation as stipulated in Articles 26, 27, 28, and 29. The Article further states:

> Great Britain undertakes to protect foreign merchants and all the trading nationalities on all those portions of the Niger which are or may be under her sovereignty or protection as if they were her own subjects, provided always that such merchants conform to the rules which are or shall be made in virtue of the foregoing.[109]

105 Mieke van der Linden, *The Acquisition of Africa (1870–1914): The Nature of International Law* (Brill Nijhoff, 2016) 4

106 Obaro Ikime, 'Nigerian Reaction to the Imposition of British Colonial Rule, 1885–1918' in S I Forster, I G Wolfgang, J Mommsen, et al. (eds), *Bismarck, Europe, and Africa: The Berlin Africa Conference 1884–1885 and the Onset of Partition* (OUP, 1988) 467

107 Obaro Ikime, 'Nigerian Reaction to the Imposition of British Colonial Rule, 1885–1918' in S I Forster, I G Wolfgang, J Mommsen, et al. (eds), *Bismarck, Europe, and Africa: The Berlin Africa Conference 1884–1885 and the Onset of Partition* (OUP, 1988) 467

108 Linden (n 105) at 98

109 General Act, Article 30

Upon conclusion of the General Act, Goldie became empowered to create more colonies for the British Empire. More trading posts were established in Niger and more treaties finalised with chiefs. The treaties were altogether 37 by 1884.[110] The chiefs are claimed to have signed those treaties ceding away their whole territory to the National African Company (Limited) and heirs forever, giving the National African Company sole and exclusive rights to trade to the exclusion of all others including chiefs.[111] Similar to Britain, France pursuant to Article 31 of the General Act accepted obligations concerning 'water of the Niger, its affluent, branches and outlets, as are or may be under her sovereignty or protection.' All the signatories to the General Act committed themselves to apply the Act from a future date.

The General Act made it abundantly clear that the land, waters, and every resource in Africa were for the benefit of the powers and the natives were to obtain civilisation, which can be classed as the formalisation of economic and power asymmetry. For instance, Article 5 of the General Act states, 'Foreigners, without distinction, shall enjoy the protection of their persons and property, as well as the right of acquiring and transferring movable and immovable possessions; and national rights and treatments in the exercise of their professions.' Why did the Act not provide for the natives trading with the foreigners, or that they had the right to impose some form of tax on those who utilise their waterways or ports? Instead, Article 6 provides, 'All the powers exercising sovereign rights or influence in the aforesaid territories bind themselves to watch over the preservation of the native tribes, and to care for the improvement of the conditions of their moral and material well-being.'

The Act does not clarify what amounts to material well-being in a colonial legal construct; it cannot be anything meaningful because the natives in a series of treaties before and after the General Act would require the chiefs to sign[112] away their lands and all resources that are to lead to 'material well-being.' However, Sir Harry Johnston believed the presence of the White man was the most reasonable thing for the natives as they were being taught how to harness and control their natural resources.[113] His position was considerate when compared to the court decision in John Holt's case of 1905, the issue before the *Cour de Cassation* was whether John Holt Trading Company was vested with the proprietary right to exploit and construct a building on a piece of land in Congo occupied by the French. Another question was whether the French had obtained exclusive rights of the territory as well as property rights to the exclusion of all others. The court held that an individual cannot occupy a territory, as such proprietary rights accrue to the French; the court failed to recognise the rights of the natives before the French took the land, more so, the natives did not have the possession of the land according to the French land law.[114]

Notwithstanding that most Africans achieved independence in the 1950s and 1960s, the pernicious track laid down in the General Act for protecting the

110 Linden (n 105)

111 E Hertslet, *The Map of Africa by Treaty* (3rd ed., vol I, Frank Cass, 1967) 131–54

112 Linden (n 105) at 112–16

113 Linden (n 105) at 228

114 Linden (n 105) at 167

economic interest of the Western world continued to be trodden.[115] Former Tanzanian president, Julius Nyerere, declared, 'we have artificial "nations" carved out at the Berlin Conference in 1884, and today we are struggling to build these nations into stable units of human society . . . we are in danger of becoming the most Balkanised continent of the world.'[116] According to the authors, the European powers superimposed their domains on the African continent. By the time independence returned to Africa, the territories were bequeathed with a fractured political system that proved impossible to eradicate or render fully satisfactory.[117]

Ikime opined that both African and European powers were interested in trade, which accounted for a series of agreements.[118] At the start of 1851, the British Consul and different coastal rulers signed agreements, setting down conditions to govern trade among them. A study of these agreements shows that it was extremely imbalanced, stipulating harsh punishment that would be meted out to rulers if they breached the terms of the agreements. This was succinctly captured by Dike in the analysis of the trade treaty between Britain and Bonny in 1836. According to him, 'the treaty in 1836 signalised naval power as the new and disintegrating [also decisive] factor in Delta Society.'[119] The fact that the agreements were signed on board a British man-of-war explains why the rulers would sign such one-sided agreements: it signals the asymmetry of the military force and remains the foundation of the inability of the native rulers to protect their interests.[120]

Also, to protect the interest of the 'parties' there was established the 'Court of Equity.' It was a mix of the court of European supercargoes and main coastal traders. The purpose of the Court of Equity was to settle disputes that might arise in the course of trade transactions. However, it was noted that there was no equity in the court. For instance, in Calabar, more than half of the members of the court were Efik and the rest were the European powers. While the European members of the court had the vote, the rulers of Creek Town and Duke Town had one vote each. The president of the court, who was a European, had two votes.[121] The objective of the Court of Equity was to bring about a peaceful resolution between natives

115 A D Nzeneke, 'Free Trade and Territorial Partition in Nineteen-Century West Africa: Course and Outcome' in Forster Stig, Mommsen Wolfgang J and Robinson Ronald (eds), *Bismarck, Europe, and Africa: The Berlin Africa Conference 1884–1885 and the Onset of Partition* (OUP, 1988) 60–1

116 Jan Nijman, Peter Muller and Harm de Blij i, *Geography: Realms, Regions, and Concepts* (Wiley, 2016)

117 Jan Nijman, Peter Muller and Harm de Blij i, *Geography: Realms, Regions, and Concepts* (Wiley, 2016)

118 Obaro Ikime, 'Nigerian Reaction to the Imposition of British Colonial Rule, 1885–1918' in Forster Stig, Wolfgang J Mommsen and Robinson Ronald (eds), *Bismarck, Europe, and Africa: The Berlin Africa Conference 1884–1885 and the Onset of Partition* (OUP, 1988) 453

119 Onwuka K Dike, *Trade and Politics in the Niger Delta 1839–1885: An Introduction to the Economic and Political History of Nigeria* (Oxford, 1956) chap. 9 and 10; Ikime Obaro, Merchant Prince of the Niger Delta (Heinemann Educational, 1968)

120 Onwuka K Dike, *Trade and Politics in the Niger Delta 1839–1885: An Introduction to the Economic and Political History of Nigeria* (Oxford, 1956) chap. 9 and 10 Ikime Obaro, Merchant Prince of the Niger Delta (Heinemann Educational, 1968) 72, 186

121 Obaro Ikime, Afro-European Relations in the Western Congo Basin 1884–1885 at 458

and European powers if there was a dispute; the establishment strengthened and reinforced the position of the powers in coastal areas.[122]

Lawyers and historians perceive and understand that what brought world powers together in Berlin in 1884 was nothing exceptional.[123] But interestingly, this widely held view has not estopped a contrary opinion. International lawyers such as John Westlake[124] as well as Tony Anghie[125] have explored the relevance of the Berlin Conference and its General Act for establishing a legal and political structure to partition Africa.[126] According to Anghie, the Berlin Conference was transformationally drastic, in the sense that it created the idea that the land in Africa was legally unoccupied (*terra nullius*). According to the author, this ideology silenced the 'native resistance through the subordination of their claims to sovereignty, and providing, in the process, an effective ideology of colonial rule.'[127] He further argued that in an important respect, it was purposeful and single-minded to map out a future for Africa and this has continued to have a negative impact on every step taken by Africa in the current political dispensation.[128]

Nevertheless, some historians are unenthusiastic about the legal importance of the Berlin Conference. Sybil Crowe suggested that the relevance of the conference in international law is overestimated. The only thing that can be ascribed to it was that it was a complete failure, whatever the intention was. It established free trade 'in the basin of Congo and made provisions for free navigation of the Congo and Niger.' It was claimed the proponents of the conference intended to advance the welfare institution in Africa but the handling of that part of Africa gained notoriety for savage physical violence and carnage.[129] The Berlin Conference legalised the acquisition of territories both in the past and in the future, which is the international law that has become connected to the conference.[130] It can be argued that the General Act was also meant to put 'trespassers' on notice with respect to acquisition of any piece of territory.[131] Pakenham amplified the argument of Crowe, expressing the view that the General Act of the Berlin Conference was empty as the African continent was shared before the conference in Berlin.[132] However, a rebuttal could

122 Obaro Ikime, Afro-European Relations in the Western Congo Basin 1884–1885 at 458

123 Mathew Craven, 'Between Law and History: The Berlin Conference of 1884–1885 and the Logic of Free Trade' (2015) London Review of International Law vol 3 (1) pp 31–59 at 32

124 John Westlake, *Chapters on the Principle of International Law* (CUP, 1894) 129, 117–89

125 Anghie (n 100) at 90–97

126 China Mieville, *Between Equal Rights: A Marxist Theory of International Law (Historical Materialism)* (Haymarket Books, 2005) 253 'the conference was an important moment in the formalisation of the international legal structure of imperialism'

127 Anghie (n 100) at 91

128 Anghie (n 100) at 91

129 Crowe (n 97) 4–5; also, J D Hargreaves, *Prelude to the Partition of West Africa* (Macmillan, 1963) 337; H Wessling, 'The Berlin Conference and the Expansion of Europe: A Conclusion', in Forster, et al. (eds) (OUP, 1988) 527, 531–32; Ewans (2002) 97–8

130 Westlake (n 124)

131 Westlake (n 124), at 188–9

132 Thomas Pakenham, *The Scramble for Africa: The White Man's Conquest of the Dark Continent* (Abacus, 1991) 254

be that the General Act was enacted to apply retrospectively; in other words, it is not empty as it gave legal backing to a *de facto* act previously done before enactment.[133]

According to Crowe, the conference was all about welfare, internationalising the continent, and promotion of free trade, remaining unconvinced that it is nothing but legalising colonisation and exploitation and legitimately making the natives view themselves as peripheral to foreign powers. Thus, for Crowe, the General Act had little or no legal and political consequences.[134] However, for Anghie, the opposite was the case. Notwithstanding that the continent had been shared, the Berlin Conference legitimised and gave international recognition to the colonisation, exploitation and marginalisation of the natives.[135]

The pre-eminence of the economy was abundantly clear by debates concerning free trade and the authority to carry out the policy of colonialism in the world economic regime.[136] It was habitual for colonial powers to monopolise the trade of their colonies through the imposition of acute trade restrictions so that other nations were unable to trade or relate with these colonies, for example preventing access to raw materials and opening markets. It was well known that these restrictions increased tension at the international level.[137] The pre-occupation of the natives of the Delta in 1884 was securing for themselves the middleman position, and a treaty had to be entered into to ensure the protection of the powers. One of the numerous treaties between Britain and King and Chiefs in Africa reads:

> We, the undersigned King and Chiefs . . . with the view to the bettering of the condition of our country and people, do this day cede to the National Africa Company (Limited), their heirs and assigns, forever, the whole of our territory . . . We also give the said National African Company (Limited) full power to settle all native disputes arising from any cause whatever, and we pledge ourselves not to enter into any war with other tribes without the sanction of the said National Africa Company (Limited).
>
> We also understand that the said National African Company (limited) have full power to mine, farm, and build in any portion of our territory. We bind ourselves not to have any intercourse with any strangers or foreigners except through the said National African Company (Limited), and we give the said National African Company (Limited) full power to exclude all other strangers and foreigners from their territory at their discretion.
>
> In consideration of the foregoing, the said National African Company (Limited) bind themselves not to interfere with any of the native laws or

133 See Robert J Newton, Retroactive and Retrospective Legislation and the Rule of Law (Thesis Submitted to the School of Graduate Studies and Research, University of Ottawa, 1990)

134 Crowe (n 93); Ronald Robinson, 'The Conference in Berlin and the Future of Africa, 1884–1885' in Forset et al. (eds), (n 93) 1, 16; Carl Schmitt, *The Nomo of the Earth in the International Law of the Jus Publicum European* (trans) G L Ulmen (Telos Press Publishing, 2006) 216; J Fisch, 'Africa as terra Nullus', in Forset et al. (eds) (n 93) at 347

135 Anghie (n 100) at 91

136 Robinson (n 134) at 3; General Act, Article 7

137 Anghie (N 100) at 162

> customs of the country, consistently with the maintenance of order and good government . . . [and] agree to pay native owners of land a reasonable amount for any portion they may require. The said National African Company (Limited) binds themselves to protect the said King and Chiefs from the attacks of any neighbouring tribes.[138]

Based on the aforementioned, Wilson at Versailles strongly expressed the view that an 'open door policy' had to be stipulated and secured in the mandates.[139] The mandate's focus on economic development had a structural impact on the policies of the colonialists so that they perceived the natives from the vantage of labour and economic wealth that they could derive from them. Wolff noted that between 1870 and 1913, the manufacturing industries in Britain depended mainly on raw materials.[140] Prior to the First World War, 50% of British crude iron production utilised imported ore, and 80% and 100% of tin, copper, lead, and zinc consumed was imported.[141] However, for instance in Kenya, Britain was able to eliminate the need for substantial treasury subsidies by 1910, and to advance the development of the empire, cash crops relevant to Britain were promoted, and land and labour were made available to the British at a meagre amount.[142]

According to Broms, during the colonial period, large concessions were obtained by the powers. For instance, the Western trading and mining companies were given free hands to exploit precious mineral resources at favourable terms. Instructively, the concession was obtained by direct coercion, what the powers termed 'agreement;' while it is cloaked with law, the natives had no understanding of the terms or the implications but appeared to append their signature.[143] Interestingly, an interpreter is always at hand to interpret the terms of the agreement to the kings and chiefs but with no understanding of those clauses. For instance, one of the treaties, provides:

> I . . . native of . . . do hereby solemnly declare that I am well acquainted with the . . . language, and that on the . . . day of . . . 1885, I truly and faithfully explained the above Agreement to all the Chiefs present, and that they understood its meaning.[144]

138 Herslet (n 111) at 120

139 Woodrow Wilson, 'The Fourteen Points' (18 January 1918) 461. www.theworldwar.org/learn/peace/fourteen-points

140 Richard D Wolff, 'Economic Aspects of British Colonialism in Kenya, 1895 to 1030' (1970) The Journal of Economic History vol 30 (1) p 273

141 Richard D Wolff, 'Economic Aspects of British Colonialism in Kenya, 1895 to 1030' (1970) The Journal of Economic History vol 30 (1) p 273

142 Richard D Wolff, 'Economic Aspects of British Colonialism in Kenya, 1895 to 1030' (1970) The Journal of Economic History vol 30 (1) p 273 at 277

143 Bright Broms, 'Natural Resources, Sovereignty Over' in R Bernhardt (ed), *Encyclopedia of International Law* (vol 4, Elsevier, 1997) 111, 520–4; Anghie (n 100) at 211

144 Hertslet (n 111) at 133

The importance of the raw material for the global economy was well understood by the power. This was made clear in the Fourth Declaration of the Atlantic Charter of 1941, which emphasised: 'Will endeavour . . . to further the enjoyment by all states, great or small, victor or vanquished, of access, on equal terms to the trade and to the raw materials of the world which are needed for their economic prosperity.'[145] The raw materials under reference were mainly found in Africa and other developing nations. This prompted several developing nations, at the start of the 1950s, to make several attempts to advocate for their right and exploit their resources. These efforts were linked to other issues, such as agitation to nationalise and to take charge of their natural resources for economic advancement.[146]

3.4 Regulating Colonial Trade

The European trade and raw materials exploitation in Africa at no cost was made possible through a series of treaties. For example, Article VI of the Treaty with Asaba made it clear that the subjects of the Queen of England were allowed to trade freely in every territory of the Kings, Queen, and Chiefs of Asaba.[147] Article II stipulated, 'the Kings, Queen, and Chiefs of Asaba agree and promise to refrain from entering into any correspondence, Agreement, or Treaty with any foreign nation or power, except with the knowledge and sanction of Her Britannic Majesty's Government.'[148] Article VIII of the Treaty provides that the locals shall at all times protect and secure the property of Britain if there was a shipwreck.[149]

In the same vein, the colonial treaty with Sokoto provides,

> for the mutual advantage of ourselves and people, and those European trading under the name of the 'National African Company (Limited)' the King of the Mussulmans of the Soudan, was said to have surrendered the whole of his territory and rights to the National African Company Limited.

The latter was granted 'the sole right, among foreigners, trade in our territories, and the sole right, also among foreigners, to possess or workplaces from which are extracted articles such as lead and antimony.'[150] Article III declared, 'no communication will be held with foreigners coming from the rivers except through

145 'The Atlantic Charter' Declaration of Principles Issued by the President of the United States and the Prime Minister of the United Kingdom (14 August 1941) www.nato.int/cps/en/natohq/official_texts_16912.htm accessed 17 May 2024; Nico Schrijver, *Sovereignty Over Natural Resources: Balancing Rights and Duties* (CUP, 1997) 37

146 Nico Schrijver, *Sovereignty Over Natural Resources: Balancing Rights and Duties* (CUP, 1997) at 49

147 Treaty with Kings, Queen, and Chief of Asaba, signed at Asaba in 1884, Article VI

148 Treaty with Asaba Article II

149 Treaty with Asaba Article VIII

150 Treaty between Umoru, King of the Mussulmans of the Soudan and Sultan of Sokoto and European Trading on the Kworra and Benue, Under the name of the 'National African Company (Limited)' on the other part, 1885 Article II

the above-mentioned company.'[151] In the Treaty of Friendship and Commerce at Abeokuta in the Egba country, Article II provides for unhindered freedom to trade between the Egba country and Lagos, which was under the complete domination of the British. The Article further stated, 'in view of the injury to commerce arising from the arbitrary closing of roads'[152] the king and other authorities agreed not to close any road that may cause injury to trade between Egba and Lagos except with the approval of the Governor of Lagos shall the road be closed.

According to Burns, when the slave trade was declared unlawful by the British in the nineteenth century, merchants from Britain turned their attention to trade in palm oil, which was in large amounts and in high value. In 1806, 150 tons of palm oil were exported from the Oil River to Liverpool; in 1839 the export had risen to 13,600 tons, and in 1965 no less than 150,051 tons of palm oil, valued at £13,591,000, were exported from Nigeria, together with the large quantity consumed at the local level. There was also a large export of palm kernels, 415,506 tons valued at £26,541,000 shipped in 1965.[153] The export of palm oil and palm kernels reduced drastically upon the discovery of mineral oil.

Besides the products mentioned earlier, cocoa, groundnuts, and rubber were exported. The large number of hides and skins exported shows the quantity of livestock raised, mainly in the north; it was approximated that there were more than ten million cattle, 14 million goats, and a half million sheep in the country. The palm oil and rubber grew mainly in the southern part of Nigeria, and crude oil and timber were harvested there as well. The north had groundnuts, cotton, benniseed, shea products, and tin.[154] To facilitate trade in the aforementioned goods, the colonialists established marketing boards, the purpose of which was to ensure the organised making of crops and to stabilise prices for the producers. There was the Cocoa Marketing Board, founded in 1947, and three other boards were established in 1949—the Oil Palm Produce Marketing Board, the Cotton Marketing Board, and the Groundnut Marketing Board, which handled benniseed and soya.[155]

Article VI of the Treaty of Lagos made it clear that the 'subjects of the Queen of England' were authorised to trade freely in the colony of Lagos and locals were not permitted to show favour to other countries without first extending such favours to the subjects of the Queen of England.[156] In a similar term, the treaty between

151 Treaty between Umoru, King of the Mussulmans of the Soudan and Sultan of Sokoto and European Trading on the Kworra and Benue, Under the name of the 'National African Company (Limited)' on the other part, 1885 Article III

152 Treaty of Friendship and Commerce made at Abeokuta in the Egba Country, this 18th (eighteenth) day of January, in the year 1893 (Hereinafter Treaty with Abeokuta)

153 Palm oil is extracted from the fruit of the oil palm tree; 'hard oil' is obtained from fermented fruit and 'soft oil' without fermentation, and the latter is more valuable. The oil is obtained from the pericarp or fleshy exterior of the fruit, the nuts are then dried and cracked, the kernel is extracted, and the kernel and oil are sold, using a middleman

154 Alan Burns, *History of Nigeria* (8th edn, George Allen & Unwin, 1954) 298

155 Burns (n 154) 298

156 Treaty Between Britain and Kings and Chiefs of Lagos, signed 1 January 1852, Article VI

colonial Britain and Asaba in Article II provides, 'the Kings, Queen, and Chiefs of Asaba agree and promise to refrain from entering into any correspondence, Agreement, or Treaty with any foreign nation or power, except with the knowledge and sanctions of Her Britannic Majesty's Government.'[157]

Therefore, of greatest importance to the British and Europeans was the inclination to infiltrate the economy of Africa.[158] According to Forster, the European powers did the insincere formulation of free trade as the principle not applied in their domestic economy but applied to Africa.[159] Free trade was conceptualised to the advantage of the industrial nations.[160] The trade between Europe and Africa was an entanglement of domestic or regional monopolies, taxes, and privileges. Thus, the primary aim of the Europeans was the outlet for their products and necessarily to control domestic trade.[161] The burden of Europe was then the development of this market, good enough to accept and consume the innovatory and highly developed goods.[162]

The Europeans appointed themselves as collective 'official guardians' of the native Africans, but the primacy of interest was still given to the industrial nations. The preposterousness of the claims remains stark as their role as 'collective official guardian' gave rise to what Kipling called the 'White Man's Burden' and Lugard 'the Dual Mandate.'[163] At the time the gratis arrangements were made, Africans were not represented by any recognised leaders or spokespersons to defend their cause or interest before the Berlin Conferees. As a result of this gap, the European powers assumed the right to stipulate for Africa as a whole what it perceived as the native peoples' interest, which is to be part of industrial progress by linking them in a more structured way to the regime's global market. This the powers achieved, according to Hull, through the enforcement of unequal treaties that dismantled existing manufacturing industries and enslaved, robbed, exploited, and indiscriminately colonised Africa.[164] Once domination of Africa was completed and secured, a preferential trade was laden with conditions to assist the newly independent states, which if scrupulously applied would promote the development of the continent.[165]

3.5 Conclusion

The chapter examines the interplay between law and the structuring of asymmetrical power in Africa. Historical analysis demonstrated that international rule utilised coercion for the actualization of the interests of powerful states. Consequently,

157 Treaty Between Britain and Kings, Queens and Chiefs of Asaba, signed at Asaba, 1884, Article II
158 Stig Forster, et al. (n 129) p 266
159 Stig Forster, et al. (n 129) p 266
160 Stig Forster, et al. (n 129) p 266
161 Stigg Forster, et al. (n 129) p 266
162 Stigg Forster, et al. (n 129) at 206
163 Stigg Forster, et al. (n 129) at 273
164 Inge Van Hulle, *Britain and International Law in West Africa* (OUP, 2020) at 2
165 Angie (n 100) 67; Gong (n 18) at 210–11

the colonial legal system ensured compliance by African states through coercion. A series of treaties were signed by the Kings and Chiefs, even though the clauses of slavery and colonialism, for the African continent, was an edifice upon which power asymmetry between the West and Africa was built and has pervaded in all its relations in the world order to the detriment of its development.[166] This was done through commercial treaties wherein the rights and privileges of British merchants were negotiated and sanctioned by law.[167]

As noted previously, all the treaty articles mainly made provisions for commercial privileges and trading conditions most conducive for the British and their companies. The provision of the commercial agreement suggested that a valid agreement was seen by the writers as beneficial to the Europeans. It was also assumed that trade in slaves would be eliminated, new markets would be opened and market access given for British products, and good living conditions would be made available for the British merchants.

As expected, the treaties supported the organisation and promoted the ownership of African markets through trading privileges, which were put in place in the early decades of the nineteenth century.[168] Articles 5 and 6 provide that British subjects have the right to trade without let or hindrance with African communities in any article of their choice. The communities are to be opened to facilitate imports and exports of British goods. Article 4 provides for freedom of religion—the British are allowed to practice the Christian faith without any form of hindrance in any territory of Africa. Article 10 of the treaties gave power to the British to send agents to an African territory to monitor and ensure compliance with the agreement.[169]

Based on evidentiary support, the chapter demonstrates that globalization is far from being a new phenomenon in Africa, as the continent was trading within the interior, regionally, and with other nations long before the advent of slavery and colonialism. The Berlin Conference and the series of treaties 'between' European and natives of Africa represents, to a large extent, the legal construct that structured the establishment of power asymmetry, which has defined how the continent is treated and the level of its participation in the multilateral trading system. Despite efforts post-independence to promote interdependence between Africa and former colonial powers—often framed as a partnership of equals aimed at fostering the continent's development—this partnership remains a mere façade.

Bibliography

African Since 1800 (Longman, 1986)

Akyeampong E, Bates R H, Nunn N, & Robinson J A (eds), *Africa's Development in Historical Perspective* (CUP, 2014)

166 Angie (n 100) 67; Gong (n 18) at 274

167 Hulle (n 164) at 39–40; Treaty of Peace Between Great Britain and King of R O Woolah and Fouricaria, The Kings of Macbatee and Kambia (10 June 1861) British and Foreign State Papers, Vol II (HMO, 1820–1977) 34, Articles 7 and 5

168 Hulle (n 164) at 82

169 Hulle (n 164) at 85

Alexandrowicz C H, *An Introduction to the History of the Law of Nations in the East Indies* (OUP, 1967)
Alexandrowicz C H, *The European-African Confrontation: A Study in Treaty Making* (Sijthoff, 1973)
Anghie A, *Imperialism, Sovereignty and the Making of International Law* (CUP, 2005)
Boahen A A, 'Ghana Before the Coming of the Europeans' (1977) Ghana Social Science Journal vol 4 (2) 93–106
Broms B, 'Natural Resources, Sovereignty Over' in R Bernhardt (ed), *Encyclopedia of International Law* vol 4 (Elsevier, 1997)
Brown C, *Moral Capital: Foundations of British Abolitionism* (University of North Carolina Press, 2006)
Burnett P, & Manji F, *From the Slave Trade to 'Free' Trade How Trade Undermines Democracy and Justice in Africa* (Fahamu, 2007)
Burns A, *History of Nigeria* (8th edn, George Allen & Unwin, 1954)
Callaghy T M, Kassimir R, & Latham R (eds), *Intervention and Transnationalism in Africa* (CUP, 2001)
Cohen D W, *The Historical Tradition of Busaga: Mukama and Kintu* (OUP, 1972)
Cooper F, *Plantation Slavery on the East African Coast* (Yale University Press, 1977)
Crowe S E, *The Berlin West African Conference 1884–85* (Greenwood Press, 1970)
Curtin P D, *The Images of Africa: British Ideas and Action, 1780–1850* (Palgrave Macmillan, 1964)
Daaku K Y, *Trade and Politics on the Gold Coast 1600–1720: A Study of the African Reaction to European Trade* (Clarendon Press, 1970)
Elias T, *Africa and the Development of International Law* (Martinus Nijhoff, 1972)
Eltis D, & Jennings LC, 'Trade Between Western Africa and the Atlantic World in the Pre-Colonial Era' (1988) The American Historical Review vol 93 (4)
Feagin J R, *Systemic Racism: A Theory of Oppression* (Routledge, 2006)
Forster S I, Wolfgang I G, Mommsen J, & Robinson D (eds), *Bismarck, Europe, and Africa: The Berlin Africa Conference 1884–1885 and the Onset of Partition* (OUP, 1988)
Gathara P, 'Berlin 1884: Remembering the Conference that Divided Africa' (*Aljazeera*, 15 November 2019). www.aljazeera.com/opinions/2019/11/15/berlin-1884-remembering-the-conference-that-divided-africa
Gathii J T, 'How American Support for Freedom of Commerce Legitimized King Leopold's Territorial Ambitions in the Congo' (2005) Studies in Transnational Legal Policy vol 37 p 97
General Act Article 6 and Article VI Made Provisions for Missionaries, Scientific Explorers, 'Freedom of Conscience and Religious Toleration'
General Act of the Berlin Conference on West Africa, 26 February 1885
Gong G W, *The Standard of 'Civilization' in International Society* (OUP, 1984)
Grewe W G, *Epochs of International Law* (trans & rev, Michael Byer, Walter de Gruyter Berlin, 1984)
Hargreaves J D, 'The European Partition of West Africa' in J F A Ajayi & Michael Crowder (eds), *History of West Africa* (2nd ed, Longman, 1987)
Hargreaves J D, *Prelude to the Partition of West Africa* (Macmillan, 1963)
Hartwig G W, *The Art of Survival in East Africa: The Kerebe and Long Distance Trade 1800–1895* (Lynne Rienner, 1975)
Hartwig G W, 'The Victoria Nyanza as a Trade Route in the Nineteenth Century' (1970) The Journal of African History vol IX
Herbstein M, 'A Story of the Atlantic Slave Trade' in Patrick Burnett & Firoze Manji (eds), *From the Slave Trade to 'Free' Trade How Trade Undermines Democracy and Justice in Africa* (Fahamu, 2007)
Heywood L M, 'Slavery and Its Transformation in the Kingdom of Kongo: 191–1800' (2009) The Journal of African History vol 50

Hobley C W, *Eastern Uganda, an Ethnological Survey 1867–1947* (Occasional Paper 1 Anthrop. Inst. of GT Britain and Ireland, London 1902)
Hopkins A G, *An Economic History of West Africa* (2nd ed, Routledge, 2020) 125
Hulle I V, *Britain and International Law in West Africa* (OUP, 2020)
Humphris J, & Iles L, 'Pre-Colonial Iron Production in Great Lakes Africa: Recent Archaeo-metallurgical Research at UCL Institute of Archaeology' in *The World of Iron* (Archetype, 2013)
Hyam R, *Britain's Imperial Century 1815–1914: A Study of Empire and Expansion* (3rd edn, Palgrave Macmillan, 2002)
Ibhawoh B, 'Strong Than the Maxim Gun Law, Human Rights and British Colonial Hegemony in Nigeria' (2002) Journal of the International African Institute vol 72 (1) pp 55–83
Inikori J E, *The Chaining of a Continent: Export Demand for Captives and the History of Africa South of the Sahara, 1450–1870* (University of West Indies, 1992)
Inikori J E, 'The Development of Commercial Agriculture in Pre-Colonial Africa' African Economic History Working Paper Series, No. 9/2013. www.ecostor.eu/bitstream/10419/242638/1/aehn-wp-09.pdf (accessed 1 April 2024)
James C L R, *The Black Jacobins: Toussaint L'Ouverture and the San Domingo Revolution* (Vintage Books, 1963)
Jones G I, *The Trading States of the Oil Rivers: A Study of Political Development in Eastern Nigeria* (James Currey, 2000)
Kea R A, *Settlements, Trade and Politics in the Seventeenth Century Gold Coast* (John Hopkin University Press, 1982)
Kennedy P M, *The Rise and Fall of British Naval Mastery* (Penguin Books Ltd, 1976)
Kenneth P, *The Great Divergence: Europe, China, and the Making of the Modern World Economy* (Princeton University Press, 2000)
Kenny M G, 'Pre-Colonial Trade in Eastern Lake Victoria' http://dx.doi.org/10.1080/00672707909511265 (accessed 10 July 2023)
Kenny M G, 'Pre-Colonial Trade in Eastern Lake Victoria' http://dx.doi.org/10.1080/00672707909511265 (accessed 10 July 2023)
Koskenniemi M, *The Gentle Civiliser of Nations: The Rise and Fall of International Law 1870–1960* (CUP, 2002)
Kraser B, *Mansa Musa: The Most Famous African Traveler to Mecca* (Rosen Publishing, 2017)
Law R, 'Between the Sea and the Lagoon: The Interaction of Maritime and Inland Navigation on the Precolonial Slave Coast' (1989) Cahiers d'etudes Africaines vol 114 pp xxix-2
Law R (ed), *From Slave Trade to 'Legitimate' Commerce: The Commercial Transition in Nineteenth-Century West Africa* (CUP, 1995)
Leon D D, 'The Conference at Berlin on the West-African Question' (1886) Political Science Quarterly vol 1 (1) pp 103–139
Linden M V D, *The Acquisition of Africa (1870–1914): The Nature of International Law* (Brill Nijhoff, 2016)
List F, *The National System of Political Economy* (trans Sampson S Lloyd, Longman, Green and Co, 1885)
Martin L, *Commerce and Economic Change in West Africa: The Palm Oil Trade in the Nineteenth Century* (CUP, 1998)
Melber H, 'The New Scramble for Africa's Resources' in Patrick Burnett & Firoze Manji (eds), *From the Slave Trade to 'Free' Trade: How Trade Undermines Democracy and Justice in Africa* (Fahamu, 2007) 37–38
Meritt H P, 'Bismarck and the German Interest in East Africa, 1884–1885' (1978) Historical Journal vol 21 (1)
Middleton J, *The World of the Swahili* (Yale University Press, 1992)
Mieville C, *Between Equal Rights: A Marxist Theory of International Law (Historical Materialism)* (Haymarket Books, 2005)

Mikail I K, & Abdullah A I L, 'The Impact of Globalization on African Culture and Politics' (2017) Journal of International Studies vol 13 (1–14)
Milanovic B, 'The Two Faces of Globalization: Against Globalization as We Know It' (2003) World Development vol 31 (4) pp 667–683
Miller J C, *The Problem of Slavery as History: A Global Approach* (Yale University Press, 2012)
Miller J C, *Way of Death: Merchant Capitalism and the Angolan Slave Trade, 1730–1830* (University of Wisconsin Press, 1988)
Mutua M W, 'Why Redraw the Map of Africa?: A Moral and Legal Inquiry' (1995) Michigan Journal of International Law vol 16 (4) p 1113
Newton R J, *Retroactive and Retrospective Legislation and the Rule of Law* (Thesis Submitted to the School of Graduate Studies and Research, University of Ottawa, 1990)
Nijman J, Muller P, & Harm B, *Geography: Realms, Regions, and Concepts* (Wiley, 2016)
Nunn N, 'The Long Term Effects of Africa's Slave Trade' (2008) The Quarterly Journal of Economics vol 123 (1)
Nurse D, & Spear T, *The Swahili Reconstructing the History and Language of an African Society, 800–1500* (University of Pennsylvania, 1985)
Nutting A, *Scramble for Africa*: *The Great Trek to the Boer War* (Constable and Robinson Ltd, 1994)
Obaro Ikime, 'Nigerian Reaction to the Imposition of British Colonial Rule, 1885–1918' in Forster Stig, Wolfgang J Mommsen and Robinson Ronald (eds), *Bismarck, Europe, and Africa: The Berlin Africa Conference 1884–1885 and the Onset of Partition* (OUP, 1988)
Ochieng W R, *A History of the Kadimo Chiefdom of Yimbo in Western Kenya Nairobi* (East Africa Literature Bureau, 1975)
Ochonu M, *Colonial Meltdown: Northern Nigeria in the Great Depression* (Ohio University Press, 2009)
Oliver R, & Atmore A, *Medieval Africa 1250–1800* (CUP, 2004)
Orji U U, *International Law and Colonialism in Africa* (Nwamife, 1979)
Pagden A, *Lords of All the World: Ideologies of Empire in Spain, Britain and France c. 1500-c.1800* (Yale University Press, 1998)
Pakenham T, *The Scramble for Africa: The White Man's Conquest of the Dark Continent* (1991) 254
Palen M W, *The 'Conspiracy' of Free Trade: The Anglo-American Struggle Over Empire and Economic Globalization*, 1846–1896 (CUP, 2016)
Pearson M N, *Port Cities and Intruders: The Swahili Coast, India, and Portugal in the Early Modern Era* (The John Hopkins University Press, 1998)
Pouwels R L, *Horn and Crescent: Cultural Change and Traditional Islam on the East African Coast, 800–1900* (CUP, 1987)
Protocol No. 3 Meeting of 27 November 1884, 'Protocol and General Act of the Berlin West African Conference' F[oreign] O[ffice] 84/1826, Public Record Office, London.
Rimmer D, 'Learning About Economic Development From Africa' (2003) African Affairs vol 102 pp 469–491
Rodney W, *How Europe Underdeveloped Africa* (Bofle-L'Ouverture Publications, 1972)
Roscoe J, *The Baganda: An Account of Their Native Customs and Beliefs* (CUP, 2011 First published in1965)
Ruggie J, 'Multilateralism: The Anatomy of an Institution' (1992) International Organisation vol 46 (3) pp 561–598
Sanderson G N, 'British Informal Empire, Imperial Ambitions, Defensive Strategies and the Anglo-Portuguese Congo Treaty of February 1884'
Saunders C, *The Making of the South African Mind: Major Historian on Race and Class* (Barnes and Noble, 1988)
Schmitt C, *The Nomo of the Earth in the International Law of the Jus Publicum European* (trans G L Ulmen, Telos Press Publishing, 2006)

Schrijver N, *Sovereignty Over Natural Resources: Balancing Rights and Duties* (CUP, 1997)
Schweinfurth G, Ratzel F, Felkin R W, & Rartlaub G (eds), Emin Pasha in Central Africa: Being a Collection of His Letter/Journals (trans R W Felkin, George Philip & Sons, 1888)
Seeley J R, *The Expansion of England* (Macmillan, 1883, John Gross, ed., 1971)
Shaikh A, 'Globalization and the Myths of Free' in Anwar Shaikh (ed), *Globalization and the Myths of Free Trade: History, Theory, and Empirical Evidence* (Routledge, 2007)
Stanley H M, *Through the Dark Continent* (vol 1, George Newness Limited, 1899) pp 42 and 54
Tannenbaum F, *Slave and Citizen: The Negro in the Americas* (Alfred A Knopf, 1947)
Thomas J, *Through Masai Land: A Journey of Exploration Among the Snowclad Volcanic Mountains and Strange Tribes of Eastern Equatorial Africa* (Hansebooks, 2016)
Thornton J, *Africa and African in the Making of the Atlantic World 1400–1680* (CUP, 1992) 43–71
Tosh J, 'The Northern Interlacustrine Region' in R Gray & D Birmingham (eds), *Pre-Colonial Africa Trade: Essays on Trade in Central and Eastern Africa Before 1900* (OUP, 1970)
Treaty Between Britain and Kings and Chiefs of Lagos, signed 1 January 1852, Article VI
Treaty Between Britain and Kings, Queens and Chiefs of Asaba, signed at Asaba, 1884, Article II
Treaty Between Umoru, King of the Mussulmans of the Soudan and Sultan of Sokoto and European Trading on the Kworra and Benue, Under the name of the 'National African Company (Limited)' on the Other Part, 1885 Article II
Treaty of Friendship and Commerce Made at Abeokuta in the Egba Country, This 18th (Eighteenth) Day of January, in the year 1893 (Hereinafter Treaty with Abeokuta)
Treaty of Peace Between Great Britain and King of RO Woolah and Fouricaria, The Kings of Macbatee and Kambia (10 June 1861) British and Foreign State Papers, Vol II (HMO 1820–1977)
Treaty with Kings, Queen, and Chief of Asaba, signed at Asaba in 1884
Tuck R, *The Rights of War and Peace: Political Thought and International Order From Grotius to Kant* (OUP, 1999)
Uzoigwe G N, 'Reflection on the Berlin West Africa Conference, 1884–1885' (1984–1985) Journal of the Historical Society of Nigeria vol 12 (3/4) pp 9–22
Waddame S M, *Law Politics and the Church of England: The Career of Stephen Lushington 1782–1873* (CUP, 1992)
Wagner G, *The Bantu of Western Kenya I-II* (OUP, 1949) 9.
Webster J B, and Boahen A A with Idowu H O, *The Growth of African Civilisation, The Revolutionary Years: West African Since 1800* (Longman, 1968)
Westlake J, *Chapters on the Principle of International Law* (CUP, 1894)
Wilks I, 'Wangara, Akan and Portuguese in the Fifteenth and Sixteenth Centuries, 1 The Matt Bitu' (1982) Journal of African History vol 23 (3) pp 333–349
Wilks I, 'Wangara, Akan and Portuguese in the Fifteenth and Sixteenth Centuries, II: The Struggle for Trade' (1982) Journal of African History vol 23 (4) pp 463–472
William E, *Capitalism and Slavery* (University of North Carolina Press, 1944)
Wilson W, 'The Fourteen Points' (18 January 1918). www.theworldwar.org/learn/peace/fourteen-point
Wolff R D, 'Economic Aspects of British Colonialism in Kenya, 1895 to 1030' (1970) The Journal of Economic History vol 30 (1) p 273
Wright Q, *Mandates Under the League of Nations* (The University of Chicago Press, 1930)
Zook G F, *The Company of Royal Adventures Trading into Africa* (Negro Universities Press, 1919)

4 The European Union and ACP Countries

1957–2000s

4.1 Introduction

This chapter explores the historical account of the trade relations between the European Union (EU) and the African, Caribbean, and Pacific (ACP) countries. To gain insight into the nature of the relationship, and the extent of colonial influence on the current arrangement, the chapter draws on critical theory propounded by Cox[1] and the neocolonialism argument by Nkrumah.[2] According to Cox, questioning the state of a relationship, for instance, between the EU and ACP countries, should not be taken at face value but the past and present must be investigated.[3] Regarding the management of the absence of symmetry, insight is drawn from Goldstein and Keohane[4] and Blyth.[5] This chapter reveals the intricate economic mutation in Africa since the 'insertion' of some colonies into the Treaty of Rome, Article 182, which provides for mutual economic and social development among 'countries and territories.'[6] The question of African countries attaining development through participation in the regional and multilateral trading system has been the subject of a series of non-reciprocal arrangements.

The principal aim of this chapter is to provide context for the analysis of power asymmetry. It argued that the discourse of 'no alternative' to Economic Partnership Agreements (EPAs), employed by the EU in the EPAs, would likely deepen asymmetry between the EU and ACP countries.[7] Also, it explores the rationale for the

1 Robert Cox, 'Critical Theory' in Thomas G Weiss and Rorden Wilkinson (eds), *International Organisation and Global Governance* (Routledge, 2014)

2 Kwame Nkrumah, *Africa Must Unite* (Heinemann, 1963) 176

3 Robert W Cox, 'Social Forces, States, and World Orders: Beyond International Relations Theory' (1981) Millennium-Journal of International Studies vol 10 (126) p 128

4 Judith Goldstein and Robert O Keohane, 'Ideas and Foreign Policy: An Analytical Framework' in Judith Goldstein and Robert O Keohane (eds), *Ideas and Foreign Policy: Beliefs, Institutions, and Political Changes* (Cornell University Press, 1993) 30

5 Mark Blyth, *Great Transformations: Economic Ideas and Institutional Change in the Twentieth Century* (University of Cambridge, 2002)

6 Article 182 (ex Article 131) Part IV 'Consolidated Version of the Treaty Establishing the European Community; Official Journal of the European Communities (97/C 340/03)

7 Rorden Wilkinson, 'Of Butchery and Bicycles: The WTO and the "Death" of the Doha Development Agenda' (2012) The Political Quarterly vol 83 (2) pp 1–7; Robert O Keohane and Joseph S Nye, 'World Politics and the International Economic System' in Fred C Bergsten (ed), *The Future of the International Economic Order: An Agenda for Research* (Lexington Books, 1973) 122

DOI: 10.4324/9781032615059-4

strict application of Article XXIV to the EU-ACP EPAs because the EU defaulted on several occasions, as discussed later in this chapter, to comply with it. In discussing power asymmetry in the historical context from 1957 to the current EPA regime between EU and ACP countries, it is argued that the series of agreements did not delink their relations, as such, from the colonial past. The laws are still fraught with contradictions and imbalance; for example, while the EU insists on bringing its trade relations in line with Article XXIV, the USA still grants preference to sub-Saharan Africa under the African Growth and Opportunity Act (AGOA), which is likely to be renewed again upon its expiration in 2025.[8]

Mandelson declared during the market access symposium in Brussels that the EU-APC countries must do away with the relics of colonialism and donor beneficiaries, to adopt equality among partners, shared interests, and integration of the African countries into the world economy.[9] A week to the conference in Lisbon between the 27 countries of the EU and 53 African countries, Louis Michel stated categorically, 'the European Union's relationship with Africa has to change and why that change is so crucial to both continents.'[10] However, Nkrumah doubts the possibility of a complete break from neocolonialism.[11] Whiteman maintained that EU-Africa trade relations have not 'escaped from the burden of history.'[12] According to Raul Prebisch, free trade as promoted by the dominant core is 'post-colonial servitude.'[13] However, addressing the United Nations Conference on Trade and Development (UNCTAD) delegates in 1996, the then Director-General of the World Trade Organisation (WTO) Mr Renato Ruggiero said, 'We are writing the constitution of a single global economy' for the benefit of all.'[14] The paradox is that the fanatical zeal for trade liberalisation and the benefit of free trade has constrained peripheral countries to the bottom of the spectrum.[15]

The following provides context to the history of the EU-ACP trade relationship. It explores the launch of the reciprocal trade arrangement through the EU green paper; it looks at the legal framework of the Cotonou Agreement and examines the application of GATT Article XXIV.

8 Julian Pecquet, 'US Senate Introduces 16-Year AGOA Renewal' (12 April 2024) www.theafricareport.com/344050/us-senate-introduces-16-year-agoa-renewal/ accessed 4 May 2024

9 Peter Mandelson, 'Open Markets, Open Trade: Europe's Global Challenge' Market Access Symposium European Parliament (Brussels, 19 September 2005) 3; Louis Michel, 'Europe Africa: The Indispensable Partnership' Conference organised by the European Policy Centre Brussels November 30th 2007 (SPEECH/07/779) https://appablog.wordpress.com>2007/11/30>louis-mechel-europe-africa-the-indispensable-partnership/ accessed 20 June 2021

10 Louis Michel, 'Europe Africa: The Indispensable Partnership' Conference organised by the European Policy Centre Brussels November 30th 2007 (SPEECH/07/779) https://appablog.wo rdpress.com>2007/11/30>louis-mechel-europe-africa-the-indispensable-partnership/ accessed 20 June 2021

11 Nkrumah (n 2)

12 Adekeye Adebajo and Kaye Whiteman (eds), *The EU and Africa: From Eurafrique to Afro-Europa* (Hurt & Company, 2012) 2

13 Edgar J Dosman, *The Life and Times of Raul Prebisch 1901–1986* (Queens University School of Policy, 2008) 390–95; Mark Mazower, *Governing the World: The History of an Idea* (Penguin Press, 2011) 344

14 UNCTAD and WTO, 'A Common Goal in Global Economy' (TAD/INF/PR/9628, 8 October 1996) www.unctad.org accessed 31 August 2020; Mark Mazower, *Governing the World: The History of an Ideas* (The Penguin Press, New York, 2012) at 362

15 Rorden Wilkinson, *What's Wrong With the WTO and How to Fix* (Polity Press, 2014) 20

4.2 EC and the Associated States

The European Coal and Steel Community states met in a conference on 1–3 June 1955 in Italy, in Messina, Sicily.[16] The initiative for another meeting in Vienna for May 1956 and March 1957 was agreed upon. The 1957 conference led to the Treaty of Rome, establishing the European Economic Community (EEC).[17] At the 1956 conference in Vienna, a contentious subject was introduced during the negotiation of the Treaty of Rome.[18] The controversy was about the inclusion of some African colonies into the Treaty of Rome. Kottos reported that the history of the idea to include French and Belgian Africa in the Common Market was traceable to Pierre Moussa.[19] Moussa is a director of economic affairs at the Ministry of Overseas and an expert on the economy of the French Union.[20] Peo and Jonsson assert that Moussa asked his minister Gaston Defferre to indicate the significance of discussing the colonial matter in the scheduled negotiations.[21]

On 17 May 1956, Defferre presented a document to Guy Mollet, demanding that the French not participate in the Common Market if the colonies were not included.[22] In his note to Mollet, Defferre pointed out that the overseas territories be integrated into the Eurafrican Common Market. The Overseas Countries and Territories (OCTs) enter into this Common Market while benefitting from special clauses, which justifies their state of development.[23] Explaining the proceedings of the Venice Conference the next day, *Le Figaro* reported to its readers, 'the Eurafrica idea, long considered to be a myth, will inscribe itself on African soil.'[24] For Peo and Jonsson, the argument influenced by geopolitical factors was the usual 'Eurafrican dictum of a common colonial market that offered Europe an opportunity

16 Miriam Camps, Britain and the European Community, 1955–1963 (1964) cited in Gardner Patterson, *Discrimination in International Trade: The Policy Issues* (Princeton University Press, 1966) 139

17 Miriam Camps, Britain and the European Community, 1955–1963 (1964) cited in Gardner Patterson, *Discrimination in International Trade: The Policy Issues* (Princeton University Press, 1966) 139

18 J.J. Van Der Lee, 'Association Relations Between the European Economic Community and African States' (1967) African Affairs vol 66 (264) pp 197–212

19 Laura Kottos, 'A European Commonwealth: Britain, the European League for Economic Co-operation, and European Debates on Empire, 1947–1957' (2012) Journal of Contemporary European Studies vol 20 (4) pp 497–515

20 Laura Kottos, 'A European Commonwealth: Britain, the European League for Economic Co-operation, and European Debates on Empire, 1947–1957' (2012) Journal of Contemporary European Studies vol 20 (4) pp 497–515

21 Laura Kottos, 'A European Commonwealth: Britain, the European League for Economic Co-operation, and European Debates on Empire, 1947–1957' (2012) Journal of Contemporary European Studies vol 20 (4) pp 497–515

22 Gaston Defferred, 'Letter a Guy Mollet' 17 May 1956 cited in Hansen Peo and Stefan Jonsson (eds), *Eurafrican: The Untold History of European Integration and Colonialism* (Bloomsbury Publishing, 2014) 147–238

23 Gaston Defferred, 'Letter a Guy Mollet' 17 May 1956 cited in Hansen Peo and Stefan Jonsson (eds), *Eurafrican: The Untold History of European Integration and Colonialism* (Bloomsbury Publishing, 2014) 147–238

24 L'Europ sans L'Afrique', Le Figaro, 31 May 1956. cited in Hansen Peo and Stefan Jonsson (eds), *Eurafrican: The Untold History of European Integration and Colonialism* (Bloomsbury Publishing, 2014) 147–238

to regain its geopolitical position' against the Union of Soviet Socialist Republic (USSR) and the United States of America (USA).[25]

Throughout the negotiation, France refused to be persuaded against Eurafrica. Instead, France encouraged the other countries to view it as a 'collective' undertaking: first to protect the general interests of Europe, which hung on the 'interdependence' between the states; second, it was a great 'historical opportunity' and an 'offer' made not only to the European parties but also to Africans.[26] Following France's astute and compelling argument, the Six (the Six or the Six founders refers to the six founding member states of the European Union: Belgium, France, West Germany, Italy, Luxembourg and the Netherlands) succumbed to the proposal.[27] It unanimously agreed to associate the French and Belgian dependent territories in Africa and Madagascar, Italian Somaliland, and Netherlands' New Guinea with the Common Market.[28] After endorsement of the French proposal, terms and conditions were provided in the Treaty of Rome. Part IV of the Treaty of Rome, Article 131, provides: 'the Community had an obligation to promote the economic and social development of the associates' countries and territories and to establish close economic relations between them and the Community as a whole.'[29] Also, Article 132 (3) requires, 'members shall contribute' to the investment required for these countries' progressive development of the territories.[30]

The provision paints the picture of African interests as being of vital importance. Van der Lee, former Honorary Director-General of the Commission of the European Economic Community, maintained that the system of association as provided in the Treaty of Rome was to assist the associate countries to trade preferentially and develop social and economic infrastructure through investment aid from the Community.[31] Connecting this Community's beneficence to Cox's neo-Gramsci theory, he opined that the core countries would make specific allowance for peripheral countries in its established order, although at no substantial cost to the former.[32]

25 L'Europ sans L'Afrique', Le Figaro, 31 May 1956. cited in Hansen Peo and Stefan Jonsson (eds), *Eurafrican: The Untold History of European Integration and Colonialism* (Bloomsbury Publishing, 2014) at 156

26 L'Europ sans L'Afrique', Le Figaro, 31 May 1956. cited in Hansen Peo and Stefan Jonsson (eds), *Eurafrican: The Untold History of European Integration and Colonialism* (Bloomsbury Publishing, 2014) at 156; Theresa Hayter, French Aid (1966) 9–12, Treaty Establishing the European Economic Community (adopted 25 March 1957 Article 131–136); Conrad Rein, 'The European Union and the African Union: A strategic Partnership?' (2015) European Foreign Affairs Review vol 20 (4) at 553; Martin H Dedman, *The Origins and Development of the European Union 1945–2008: A History of European Integration* (2nd ed, Routledge, 1996) 55; Carol Ann Cosgrove, 'The Common Market and Its Colonial Heritage' (1969) Journal of Contemporary History vol 4 (1) pp 73–87 at 76

27 Hayter, French Aid (1966) 9–12

28 Hayter, French Aid (1966) 9–12 at 77; Van Der Lee, 'Association Relations Between the European Economic Community and African States' (1967) African Affairs vol 66 (264) pp 197–212

29 Treaty of Rome, Part IV Association of the Overseas Countries and Territories (hereinafter Rome Treaty) Article 131 of the www.consilium.europa.eu/media/29665/archives-enlargment-1.pdf accessed 20 June 2020

30 Rome Treaty 1957 Article 132 (2) Part IV

31 Van Der Lee (n 18)

32 Robert W Cox, 'Gramsci, Hegemony and International Relations: An Essay in Method' (1983) Millennium-Journal of International Studies vol 12 pp 163–72

Regarding the parties, Guy maintained that the associates were unequal and fundamentally exploitative through the economic policies implemented by the metropoles in their African territories.[33]

Several nations under colonial rule secured independence in the 1960s. Consequently, the associates' arrangement was transformed to the Yaoundé I and subsequently Yaoundé II Conventions.[34] The Convention preceded the Lomé Conventions. The first Lomé Convention was concluded in Togo, in 1975.[35] The second Lomé Convention came into effect in January 1981, and the third came into force in March 1985 for trade provisions and in May 1986 for aid. The fourth Lomé, unlike the previous Lomé, had a ten-year tenure and was signed in December 1989. The trade provision was in effect on 1 May 1990, and the rest of the provisions came into effect in September 1991.[36] Commenting on the strength of IV Lomé Conventions, the EU council president, Mr Solana, stated that the EU and ACP countries' cooperation represents what the Caribbean poet Derek Walcott calls, 'bread that lasts when systems have decayed.'[37] However, the ACP council president, Moi Avei, counter-argued that the cooperation provides no bread but hastens the system's decay.[38]

The Cotonou Agreement succeeded the Lomé Convention, which heralded the EPAs.[39] After most overseas territories gained independence in 1960, Guy[40] notes that it became imperative to renegotiate the 'Associate Status' between the six EEC and 18 African Associate and the Malagasy States. The first Yaoundé Convention of June 1964 to March 1969 replicated Part IV of the Rome Treaty without substantial improvement.[41] The second Yaoundé Convention from January 1971 to March 1975 brought some minor improvements.[42] However, it maintained the fundamental structure of the earliest agreement.[43] The series of the trade arrangement has its background in the European post-colonial settlement, after World War II, what Minta referred to as an 'unbroken historical continuum.'[44] After the 18 Associated States' trade

33 Guy Martin, 'Africa and the Ideology of Eurafrica: Neo-Colonialism or Pan-Africanism' (1982) The Journal of Modern African Studies vol 20 (2) p 226

34 John Ravenhill, 'Asymmetrical Interdependence: Renegotiating the Lomé Convention' (1979/1980) International Journal vol 35 (1) pp 150–69 at 152

35 Directorate-General for Development Commission of the European Community, 'Ten Years of Lomé. A Record of EEC-ACP Partnership, 1974–1984' Com (84) 398 Final, 17 July 1984, p 12

36 Reginald Herbold Green, 'The Lomé Convention: Updated Dependence or Departure Toward Collective Self Reliance?' 43 http://journals.co.za/docserver/fulltext/afre/6/1/182.pdf?expires=15927445028id=id accessed 21 June 2020

37 'The Finest and Most Complete Instrument of Cooperation Ever', The ACP-EU Countries NO 55, January-February 1996, Special Issue on the Revised Lomé Convention 3–4

38 'The Finest and Most Complete Instrument of Cooperation Ever', The ACP-EU Countries NO 55, January-February 1996, Special Issue on the Revised Lomé Convention 3–4

39 Ravenhill (n 34)

40 Guy op (n 33)

41 Reginald (n 36)

42 Kenneth J Twichett, 'Yaoundé Association and the Enlargement European Community' (1974) The World to Day vol 30 (2) pp 51–63

43 Kenneth J Twichett, 'Yaoundé Association and the Enlargement European Community' (1974) The World to Day vol 30 (2) pp 51–63

44 I.K. Minta, 'The Lomé Convention and The New International Economic Order' (1980) Howard L J 27953

relationship with the EEC, the following notable step took place when Britain acceded to the Common Market in 1973. Britain's accession to the EEC caused a significant restructuring of the trade arrangement between the EEC and African states.[45]

Contrary to the Yaoundé Convention, the Lomé Agreement granted preference based on non-reciprocity.[46] According to the ACP-EU *Courier*, under Lomé Conventions, several protocols produced a significant profit by allowing export products such as bananas, beef, rum, and sugar into the EU market.[47] Another point evident in the spirit of the New International Economic Order (NIEO) was aid, which formed a substantial component of the Lomé Convention, funded through the European Development Fund (EDF).[48] Also, a mechanism provided indemnity for countries that had experienced loss due to fluctuation of raw materials through the stabilisation of commodity-export earnings (STABEX).[49] Similarly, the Convention provided security for the manufacturing of certain minerals through stabilising mineral exports earnings (SYSMIN or MINEX).[50] According to Elgstrom, this 'insurance scheme' was put in place to cushion the effect of short-term drops in ACP export earnings.[51] The scheme was celebrated as ground-breaking; it was perceived as a solution to the challenges of raw material production by the least developed countries (LDCs).

Nevertheless, Dedman viewed that the provision of aid only created unhealthy dependency.[52] According to Nkrumah, the provision of assistance is used as a 'guise' to perpetuate neocolonialism.[53] Lister maintained that the SYSMIN did not succeed, as only 35% of the fund voted for SYSMIN was used on mineral projects.[54]

45 I.K. Minta, 'The Lomé Convention and The New International Economic Order' (1980) Howard L J 27953

46 Convention of Association between the European Economic Community and the African and Malagasy States Associated with that Community and Annexed Documents (herein after Convention of Association), Article 3 (3) (1970) International Legal Materials vol 9 (3) pp 484–506

47 The ACP-EU Courier, Special Issue on the Revised Lomé Convention, No 155 (January-February 1996) 6

48 The Lomé Convention, www.acp.int accessed 5 April 2021; Charlotte Bretherton and John Vogler, *The European Union as a Global Actor* (Routledge, 2006) 116

49 The Second Lomé ACP-EEC Lomé Convention, Articles 23 (1) and (2) and 24, No L 347/2 Official Journal of the European Communities (31 October 1979) www.evce.eu/obj/the_second_acp_eec_lome_convention_31october_1979-en-416ece3a-4e44-44771-8c0e-52a754f2e007.html accessed 21 June 2020

50 The Second Lomé ACP-EEC Lomé Convention Articles 49 and 50, No L 347/2 Official Journal of the European Communities 31 October 1979 www.evce.eu/obj/the_second_acp_eec_lome_convention_31october_1979-en-416ece3a-4e44-44771-8c0e-52a754f2e007.html accessed 21 June 2020

51 Ole Elgstrom, 'Lomé and Post-Lomé: Asymmetric Negotiation and the Impact of Norms' (2000) European Foreign Affairs Review vol 5 pp 175–95 at 177

52 Martin J Dedman, *The Origins and Development of the European Union 1945–2008: A History of European Integration* (2nd ed, Routledge, 2010) 182

53 Nkrumah (n 2) at 176

54 Majories Lister, *The European Union and the South: Relations With Developing Countries* (Routledge, 1997) 128

Many of the projects failed. For example, the SYSMIN projects in Togo and Papua New Guinea were abandoned.[55]

It is argued that the EU-ACP countries' trade relations have dual defects: first, according to Bretherton and Vogler; 'The Community effectively created the ACP group to facilitate its interaction with a large and diverse group of former colonies . . . the majority of which are economically weak.'[56] Second, to Ravenhill, the vast differences in power asymmetry show that ACP countries played the role of a 'demandeur.'[57] In the author's view, the ACP countries had little or no meaningful bargaining power over the EU.[58] As an alternative, the ACP falls back on what Ravenhill refers to as 'collective clientelism.'[59] Ravenhill described the ACP group as the 'embodiment of economic weakness'; hence, 'equal partnership' is illusory.[60] Similarly, according to Lang, these complex problems faced by ACP countries never found an outline in the multilateral trading system, believed to be 'embedded.'[61] In his discussion on European universalism, Wallerstein maintained that the global value promoted by the powerful is 'partial and distorted universalism.'[62] How the EU dramatically changed its views on the Cotonou Agreement to meet the requirement of Article XXIV through its green paper remained a point of interest.

According to Goldstein and Keohane, ideas are used to govern such an arrangement if a relationship is not symmetrical.[63] According to Blyth, ideas are used to 'delegitimate' the currently existing structure if it no longer serves the interest of the core.[64] In 1996, the EC published its green paper, which examined the trade relations between the EU and the ACP countries.[65] It declared that the Lomé

55 Majories Lister, *The European Union and the South: Relations With Developing Countries* (Routledge, 1997) 128

56 Charlotte Bretherton and John Vogler, *The European Union as a Global Actor* (1st ed, Routledge, 1999) 126

57 John Ravenhill, 'Back to the Nest? Europe's Relationship With the African, Caribbean and Pacific Group of Countries' (Working Paper PEIF-9, December 2000) 7–8 www.researchgate.net/publication/238105746 accessed 24 June 2020

58 John Ravenhill, 'Back to the Nest? Europe's Relationship With the African, Caribbean and Pacific Group of Countries' (Working Paper PEIF-9, December 2000) 7–8 www.researchgate.net/publication/238105746 accessed 24 June 2020

59 John Ravenhill, *Collective Clientelism: The Lomé Conventions and North-South Relations* (Colombian University Press, 1985) 4, 221

60 John Ravenhill, *Collective Clientelism: The Lomé Conventions and North-South Relations* (Colombian University Press, 1985) 4, 221

61 Andrew Lang, 'Reconstructing Embedded Liberalism: John Ruggie and Constructivist Approaches to the Study of International Trade Regime' (2006) Journal of International Economic Law vol 9 (1) pp 99–100

62 Immanuel Wallerstein, *European Universalism: The Rhetoric of Power* (The New Press, 2004) xiv

63 Goldstein and Keohane (n 4) at 30

64 Blyth (n 5) at 35–42

65 Commission of the European Communities, 'Green Paper on Relations Between the European Union and the ACP Countries on the Eve of the 21st Century: Challenges and Options for a New Partnership' (Brussel, 20/11/1996, COM) (96) (570 Final,) iii, https://eu-lex.europa.eu/legal-content/EN/TXT/pdf/?uri=CEL . . . accessed: 26 June 2020

Convention has unequivocally failed to realise its primary objectives.[66] The 'partnership enshrined in the Lomé Convention has diminished substantially and has not been fully realised.'[67] Although the EU green paper did not deny the value of the Lomé Convention, it posits, 'the value of the Lomé trade preferences has declined and stands to suffer further erosion.'[68]

Another element that forms part of the rationale to end the Lomé Convention was that the numerical strength of the EU increased.[69] It is claimed that, as the number enlarged, it insidiously weakened the considerable relevance of the ACP countries.[70] According to Elgstrom, for instance, as Spain and Portugal acceded to the EU, attention was shifted to Latin America in the EU.[71] According to Lister, upon the appointment of Spaniard Manuel Marin as development commissioner in 1988, the focus became more on the Community's relationship with Central and South America.[72] The grant of stabilisation of export earnings system (STABEX) in 1987 to Bangladesh, Bhutan, Haiti, Laos, the Maldives, Nepal, the Yemen Arab Republic, and the People's Republic of Yemen widened the scope of the Community's engagement and interests.[73] Another element that contributed to the marginalisation of the interests of the ACP countries was the fall of the Soviet Union. According to Lister's account, during the ACP-EU Joint Assembly meeting in 1989, ACP countries requested funds, but the EU declined. At the beginning of 1990 EU substantially established the East European Bank for Reconstruction and Development and made available extensive European Investment Bank loans to Eastern Europe. However, in October 1991, the European Council of foreign ministers declined to forgive €3 billion of ACP countries' debt but endorsed during the period €2 billion

66 Commission of the European Communities, 'Green Paper on Relations Between the European Union and the ACP Countries on the Eve of the 21st Century: Challenges and Options for a New Partnership' (Brussel, 20/11/1996, COM) (96) (570 Final,) iii, https://eu-lex.europa.eu/legal-content/EN/TXT/pdf/?uri=CEL . . . accessed: 26 June 2020

67 Commission of the European Communities, 'Green Paper on Relations Between the European Union and the ACP Countries on the Eve of the 21st Century: Challenges and Options for a New Partnership' (Brussel, 20/11/1996, COM) (96) (570 Final,) iii, https://eu-lex.europa.eu/legal-content/EN/TXT/pdf/?uri=CEL . . . accessed: 26 June 2020

68 Commission of the European Communities, 'Green Paper on Relations Between the European Union and the ACP Countries on the Eve of the 21st Century: Challenges and Options for a New Partnership' (Brussel, 20/11/1996, COM) (96) (570 Final,) iii, https://eu-lex.europa.eu/legal-content/EN/TXT/pdf/?uri=CEL . . . accessed: 26 June 2020; European Commission, Guideline for Negotiation of New Cooperation Agreements with the Africa, Caribbean and Pacific (Office for the Official Publications of the European Communities, L-2985, Luxembourg (COM (97) 29.10.1997 C) https://eur-lex.europaeu/legal-content . . . s accessed 26 June 2020

69 Faizel Ismail, 'The Changing Global Trade Architecture: Implications for Africa's Regional Integration and Development' (2017) Journal of World Trade vol 51 (1) p 7

70 Ole Elgstrom, 'The Cotonou Agreement: Asymmetric Negotiations and the Impact of Norms', in Ole Elgstrom and Christer Jonsson (eds), *European Union Negotiations* (Routledge, 2005) 186

71 Ole Elgstrom, 'The Cotonou Agreement: Asymmetric Negotiations and the Impact of Norms', in Ole Elgstrom and Christer Jonsson (eds), *European Union Negotiations* (Routledge, 2005) 186

72 Lister (n 54) at 146

73 Lister (n 54) at 146

of aid for the post-Soviet Union.[74] It became crystal clear, according to Lister, that the ACP countries were not on the top list of the EU priority.[75]

Another factor cited numerous times was the unfavourable ruling against the EU's banana protocol under General Agreement on Tariff and Trade and World Trade Organization (GATT/WTO). The WTO has been blamed for the demise of the Lomé Convention.[76] However, the original banana case that arose before the dispute settlement panel was not due to the Lomé Convention but to the single banana market in 1992,[77] which was an aspect of implementing the Single European Act.[78] In 1994, however, the GATT panel judged that the Lomé Convention does not comply[79] with most favoured nations (MFN) because it was neither a free trade area nor a customs union, as there was no reciprocity.[80] It does not also comply with the 1979 Enabling Clause because it discriminates against other developing countries.[81]

According to Ravenhill[82] and Dickson,[83] the EU cannot ignore the decisions of the WTO dispute or continue to weaken the fundamental principle of the trading system by sustaining a waiver, as the EU is well positioned to play a vital role in promoting its interests in the multilateral trading system.[84] Many observers believed that the banana dispute was the only useful disguise to back up the majority's argument within the EU.[85] According to Blyth, agent uses ideas as weapon to 'delegitimate' an existing structure.[86] As the EU carefully delegitimises the structure of its connection with the ACP countries, it sought a more WTO-compatible arrangement, hence the EPAs through the EU green paper.[87]

74 Lister (n 54) at 146
75 Lister (n 54) at 146
76 Karen J Alter and Sophie Meunier, 'Nested and Overlapping Regimes in the Transatlantic Banana Trade Dispute' (2006) Journal of European Public Policy vol 13 (3) pp 362–82 at 366
77 Commission Regulation (EEC) No. 1858/93, Articles 12, 15 and 17 (1993) *Official Journal of the European Communities,* Brussels 12 June 1993
78 Commission Regulation (EEC) No. 1858/93, Articles 12, 15 and 17 (1993) *Official Journal of the European Communities,* Brussels 12 June 1993
79 Eliza Patterson, The US-EU Banana Dispute (2000) American Society of International Law 6 (4) www.wto.org/english/res.e/booksp_e/dispu_settlement_e.pdf accessed 29 2020
80 The Appellate Body, European Communities-Regime for the Importation, Sale and Distribution of Bananas, WT/DS27/AB/R, adopted 25 September, 1997
81 The Appellate Body, European Communities-Regime for the Importation, Sale and Distribution of Bananas, WT/DS27/AB/R, adopted 25 September, 1997
82 Ravenhill 2000 (n 57)
83 Anna K Dickson, 'The Importance of Trade Preferences' in Karin Arts and Anna K Dickson (eds), *EU Development Cooperation—From Model to Symbol* (Manchester University Press, 2004) 42–59
84 Anna K Dickson, 'The Importance of Trade Preferences' in Karin Arts and Anna K Dickson (eds), *EU Development Cooperation—From Model to Symbol* (Manchester University Press, 2004) 42–59
85 Ravenhill (n 57)
86 Blyth (n 5)
87 Commission of the European Communities, *Green Paper on Relations Between the European Union and the ACP Countries on the Eve of the 21st Century: Challenges and Options for a New Partnership* (COM (96) 570 final, Brussels, 20 November 1996) xiii

4.3 Economic Partnership Agreements

The EPAs were negotiated among six regions: the Caribbean, Pacific, West Africa, Central, Eastern and Southern Africa (ESA), and Southern Africa (SADC-minus)—identified by the Commission.[88] In order to allow the ACP countries adequate time to prepare for the EPA negotiations, the EU applied for an extension to the WTO for a waiver, which was granted during the 2002 Doha Ministerial Meeting in Qatar.[89] The negotiation started in September 2002 and ended in 2007. The Cotonou Agreement made special provisions for LDCs, similar to Lomé (duty and quota) free preferences under what is now known as the Everything but Arms (EBA) Agreement of 2001.[90] The EBA met the requirement of WTO compatibility as the regime was in line with the 1979 Enabling Clause.[91]

As noted earlier, the parties agreed to extensively alter the structure of the Lomé Convention in 2000 to solve the incompatibility issues with the multilateral trade rules.[92] According to Hurt, the EU's interpretation of the GATT Article XXIV was rigid, therefore, not disposed toward flexibility.[93] Gibb maintained that the EU premeditated to put WTO compatibility ahead and, thus, presented the change to the Lomé Convention as the only alternative.[94] However, as noted previously, the Lomé Convention did not come under any categories listed exceptions permitted by WTO law.[95] Therefore, the EU asked other WTO members for a waiver of Article I, which was granted.[96]

The WTO members need concessions as a trade-off for allowing the waiver. Protecting the interests of the ACP countries had its price, which the EU could not

88 Cotonou Agreement Article 37 (1), Declaration XV Cotonou Agreement, also Declaration II, Joint Declaration on Article 68 of the Cotonou Agreement

89 EU, European Parliament's recommendations to the Commission concerning the negotiation of Economic Partnership Agreements with the ACP countries and regions (Thursday, 26 September 2002—Strasbourg) www.europarl.europa.eu/sides/getDoc.do?pubRef=-//EP//TEXT+TA+P5-TA-2002-0453+0+DOC+XML+V0//EN accessed 31 October 2021

90 EU, Regulation No 978/2012 Article 1 (2) (c) Official Journal of the European Union

91 Officially called the 'Decision on Differential and More Favourable Treatment, Reciprocity and Fuller Participation of Developing Countries' it was adopted under GATT 1979

92 Stephen R Hurt, 'Co-Operation and Coercion? The Cotonou Agreement Between the European Union and ACP States and the End of the Lomé Convention' (2003) Third World Quarterly vol 24 (1) pp 161–74 at 174

93 Stephen R Hurt, 'Co-Operation and Coercion? The Cotonou Agreement Between the European Union and ACP States and the End of the Lomé Convention' (2003) Third World Quarterly vol 24 (1) pp 161–74 at 174

94 Richard Gibb, 'Post Lomé: The European Union and the South' (2000) Third World Quarterly vol 21 (3) pp 457–81 at 477 https://doi.org/10.1080/713701046 accessed 6 May 2021

95 Achille Bassilekin, 'Possibility of Obtaining a New ACP-EC Waiver at the WTO' (ECDPM March 2007) 1–2 https://ecdpm.org/wp-content/uploads/2013/11/DP-71-New-ACP-EC-Waiver-WTO-2007.pdf accessed 31 October 2021

96 Achille Bassilekin, 'Possibility of Obtaining a New ACP-EC Waiver at the WTO' (ECDPM March 2007) 1–2 https://ecdpm.org/wp-content/uploads/2013/11/DP-71-New-ACP-EC-Waiver-WTO-2007.pdf accessed 31 October 2021

continue to pay much longer.[97] As a result, the WTO granted the EU leave to allow for the operation of the preference to be extended only for a time frame of another seven years, giving the parties time to negotiate a WTO-compatible agreement, EPA (2002–2007).[98] Instructively, the United States still grants preferential trade to sub-Saharan Africa through AGOA because it recognised the economic power asymmetry between the two regions.[99]

The Economic Community of West Africa States (ECOWAS) was founded on 28 May 1975, through the treaty of Lagos.[100] Its main objective was economic integration and cooperation among the members. ECOWAS comprised 16 member states, but in 2000, the Islamic Republic of Mauritania withdrew to join the Maghreb Union, consisting of Libya, Morocco, and Algeria.[101] However, for ease of EU-ECOWAS Economic Partnership negotiation, Mauritania joined ECOWAS. The ultimate aim of ECOWAS was to create an economic and monetary union to include free movement of persons, goods, capital, and services and common commercial policy and common external customs tariffs. In 1993, deeper cooperation on peace and security issues were made a part of the directive and objective. The West African Economic and Monetary Union (WAEMU or UEMOA),[102] established in 1994, is a sub-regional arrangement to respond to the devaluation of the CFA, *Communaute Financiere Africaine* (African Financial Community) franc relative to the French franc. It is a customs union and currency union. ECOWAS and UEMOA are far gone in the steps towards a West African single market.[103] The focus has been on trade liberalisation and the harmonisation of macroeconomic policies.[104]

The European Union was established after the Second World War.[105] In the beginning, the aim was to advance and encourage economic cooperation and interdependence and through the process minimise situations that would lead to

97 Achille Bassilekin, ‘Possibility of Obtaining a New ACP-EC Waiver at the WTO’ (ECDPM March 2007) 1–2 https://ecdpm.org/wp-content/uploads/2013/11/DP-71-New-ACP-EC-Waiver-WTO-2007.pdf accessed 31 October 2021

98 Achille Bassilekin, ‘Possibility of Obtaining a New ACP-EC Waiver at the WTO’ (ECDPM March 2007) 1–2 https://ecdpm.org/wp-content/uploads/2013/11/DP-71-New-ACP-EC-Waiver-WTO-2007.pdf accessed 31 October 2021; Hurt (n 92) at 166

99 Africa Growth and Opportunity Act (AGOA as amended), World Trade Organization for Trade in Goods, G/C/W/713 (16 July 2015) https://agoa.info>images>documents>wtowaiveragoa2015.pdf accessed 6 May 2019

100 Economic Community of West Africa States (ECOWAS): Basic Information www.ecowas.int accessed 6 May 2021

101 ‘Mauritania pulls out of ECOWAS’, 28 December 2000 www.thenewhumanitarian.org/news/2000/12/28/ Mauritania-pulls-out-ecowas accessed 31 October 2021; Michael Oduor, ‘Mauritania Signed Partnership Agreement With ECOWAS’ (African news, 8 May 2017) www.africanews.com/2017/05/08/mauritania-signs-partnership-agreement-with-ecowas// accessed 31 October 2021

102 UEMOA is an abbreviation of its more common French name ‘*Union Economique et Monetaire Quest Africaine*.’

103 Interview with official of ECOWAS (2020)

104 Interview with official of ECOWAS (2020)

105 Martin J Dedman, *The Origins and Development of the European Union 1945–2008: A History of European Integration* (2nd ed, Routledge, 1996) 51–81

violence, conflict, and war. After this initial step, the EU project has broadened more widely to include institutional, political, and cultural integration. The EU single market was formed in 1993 with a single currency.[106] Bretherton and Vogler succinctly describe the economic power status of the EU in the world.[107]

According to the document obtained from the ECOWAS archive,[108] trade between ECOWAS and the EU accounts for nearly 40% of the total EU-ACP countries' trade, and is therefore substantial for the economic relations between the EU-ACP countries. Nevertheless, ECOWAS's share of EU's total trade remains small at 1.2% of EU imports originating from ECOWAS.[109] Meanwhile, 1.3% of the EU's total export is directed to the ECOWAS region.[110] According to the ECOWAS report, the trade is mainly concentrated within a few countries in the region. The three non-LDCs, Nigeria, Ghana, and Côte d'Ivoire, account for almost all the exports to the EU. Nigeria alone accounts for 65% of ECOWAS exports to the EU—mainly crude oil and minerals.[111] Apart from oil, the EU also imports agricultural products from the region, while it exports mainly finished products and vehicles.[112] Trade between the regions had reduced in the past decade, but the EU continues to provide development aid to ECOWAS. For instance, in the eighth EDF (1996–2001), West Africa was granted €219m, while the tenth EDF (2008–2013) amounted to €645m to the West African region.[113]

Nevertheless, according to the ECOWAS report[114] examined, almost all the member states are preoccupied daily with the scourge of poverty. The HIV/AIDS pandemic, malaria, illiteracy, and conflicts have had an enormous 'impact on the region's governance, growth and stability.' The report states that the ECOWAS region is the poorest of zones in the world. Besides Cape Verde and Ghana, all other states are considered low-level human development by the United Nations

106 Martin J Dedman, *The Origins and Development of the European Union 1945–2008: A History of European Integration* (2nd ed, Routledge, 1996) 136
107 Charlotte Bretherton and John Vogler, *The European Union as a Global Actor* (Routledge, 2006) 59
108 ECOWAS, Negotiation of the Economic Partnership Agreement: West Africa-European Community, Report on the Reference Framework of the Economic Partnership Agreement (EPA) Between the West Africa Region and the European Community (hereinafter ECOWAS report) (Final) 11
109 ECOWAS, Negotiation of the Economic Partnership Agreement: West Africa-European Community, Report on the Reference Framework of the Economic Partnership Agreement (EPA) Between the West Africa Region and the European Community (hereinafter ECOWAS report) (Final) 11
110 ECOWAS, Negotiation of the Economic Partnership Agreement: West Africa-European Community, Report on the Reference Framework of the Economic Partnership Agreement (EPA) Between the West Africa Region and the European Community (hereinafter ECOWAS report) (Final) 11
111 ECOWAS, Negotiation of the Economic Partnership Agreement: West Africa-European Community, Report on the Reference Framework of the Economic Partnership Agreement (EPA) Between the West Africa Region and the European Community (hereinafter ECOWAS report) (Final) 11
112 E Anyidoho, 'ECOWAS-EPA Negotiations: State of Play, Seminar Tradecom/FEWACCI' (25–27 August 2010) AccraGhana www.fewacci.org/index.php?option=com_eventlist&view=details&id=2%ASeminar+Tradecom%2FFEWACCI&Itemid=20&lang=en accessed 7 May 2021
113 E Anyidoho, 'ECOWAS-EPA Negotiations: State of Play, Seminar Tradecom/FEWACCI' (25–27 August 2010) AccraGhana www.fewacci.org/index.php?option=com_eventlist&view=details&id=2%ASeminar+Tradecom%2FFEWACCI&Itemid=20&lang=en accessed 7 May 2021
114 ECOWAS Report (n 108) at 7

Development Programme (UNDP). The report mentioned earlier further states that social indicators remain unsatisfactory. An average of 50% of the total population lives below the poverty level. For zero to one year, the infant mortality rate is around 45.36% for sub-Saharan Africa. Primary and secondary school registration levitate around 65% and 15%, in sub-Saharan Africa and life expectancy is slightly above 50 years. The report further asserts that in the area of infrastructure, the ECOWAS region is impoverished.

The key sectors of the economy, according to the report, are agriculture, livestock, forestry, and fisheries. Agriculture represents between 30% and 60% of GDP in the region. It also employs the leading workforce ranging between 30% and 90%. The report further notes that in terms of industrialisation, the region is behind. With the production of 1.7 billion dollars, Côte d'Ivoire led West African manufacturing in 2000. Nigeria makes up 59% of the total manufacturing production of the region. The share increases to 80% when Senegal and Ghana are included. According to a respondent, the economic gap between the EU and West Africa is too wide for the region to engage in such an all-encompassing opening of markets.[115] This is what Lang alluded to when he stated that the issue of development never featured in embedded liberalism.[116] Similarly, in the bilateral and regional arrangement, the peripheral countries lack the capacity to negotiate favourable trade terms with core countries.[117] However, the EU assured the ACP countries of compliance with the Cotonou Agreement on flexibility and gradual liberalisation through special and differential treatment.[118]

4.4 GATT Article IV and Flexibility in the Cotonou Agreement

The Cotonou Partnership Agreement was signed in 2000.[119] It contains the fundamental principles guiding the EU and 79 ACP countries.[120] The EU-ACP redefines their trade relationship to comply with the WTO rules by general agreement. Article 1 of the Cotonou Agreement states the general aims of the agreement, while Article 19 (1) provides, explicitly, the main objective of the agreement between the EU-ACP countries as 'cooperation in poverty reduction and ultimately its eradication; sustainable development; and progressive integration of the ACP countries

115 Interview with official of Manufacturing Association of Nigeria (MAN) (2020)

116 Lang (61) 6 at 99–100

117 Yilmaz Akyuz, 'Multilateral Disciplines and the Question of Policy Space' in Julio Faundez and Celine Tan (eds), *International Economic Law, Globalisation and Developing Countries* (Elgars, 2012) 36; Stephen Woolcock, 'The Scope for Asymmetry in the World Trade Organisation (WTO)' in Sanoussi Bilal, Phillip Lombaerde and Diana Tussi (eds), *Asymmetric Trade Negotiations* (Routledge, 2016) 27

118 Peter Mandelson, 'The ACP-EU Relationship in the Global Economy' Speech/04/505, ACP-EU Ministerial (1 December 2004) 2–3

119 Cotonou Agreement, signed in Cotonou on 23 June 2000 Revised in Luxembourg on 25 June 2005, Revised in Ouagadougou on 22 June 2010

120 Cotonou Agreement Articles 1 and 2; Geert Laporte, 'The Cotonou Partnership Agreement: What Role in a Changing World? Reflection on the Future of ACP-EU Relations' (European Centre for Development Policy Management, November 2007) https://ecdpm.org/wp-content/uploads/2013/10/PMR-13-coto . . . accessed 30 June 2020

into the world economy.'[121] Paragraph 2 of Article 34 states, 'The ultimate objective of economic and trade cooperation is to enable the ACP countries to play a full part in international trade.' The basis for the provision in the sub-paragraph is for ACP countries to become active participants in trade negotiations in the multilateral trading system. Nevertheless, the outcome of negotiations revealed the contrary.[122] According to Oxfam, the trade agreement between the EU and the ACP states is a 'classic free trade.'[123] There is not much difference between it and the EU-Chile and EU-Mexico trade agreement.[124] Observers raised concerns that the agreement could be detrimental to ACP countries' development.[125] Weller and Ulmer[126] view the EPAs as another effort by developed countries (the EU) to impose an obsolete style of development founded on a neo-classical prescription that does not consider lessons from the historical development of advanced countries.[127]

There was a consensus on the EU-ECOWAS + Mauritania 'Road Map'[128] that there should be sufficient time to allow capacity building in ACP countries' public and private sectors.[129] Article 37 states that capacity building shall be provided by the provisions of Title I and Article 35 to ACP countries' public and private sectors during the negotiations of the Economic Partnership Agreements. The 'capacity building' is to improve the competitiveness and strengthen regional organisations, implement fiscal reform, and improve and rehabilitate infrastructure.[130] The agreement's aim

121 Cotonou Agreement Article 34
122 Christina Weller, *Dialogue of the Deaf: An Assessment of Europe's Developmental Approach to Trade Negotiations* (ICCO, 2008) 5 www.bibalex.org/baifa/Attachment/Documents/116861.pdf accessed 1 June 2020
123 Oxfam, 'Partnership or Power Play? How Europe Should Bring Development Into Its Trade Deals With African, Caribbean, and Pacific Countries' (2008) 6 www.oxfam.org/en/policy/bp110_EPAs_europe_trade_deals_with_acp_countries_0804 (2008)
124 Oxfam, 'Partnership or Power Play? How Europe Should Bring Development Into Its Trade Deals With African, Caribbean, and Pacific Countries' (2008) 6 www.oxfam.org/en/policy/bp110_EPAs_europe_trade_deals_with_acp_countries_0804 (2008)
125 Oxfam, 'Partnership or Power Play? How Europe Should Bring Development Into Its Trade Deals With African, Caribbean, and Pacific Countries' (2008) 6 www.oxfam.org/en/policy/bp110_EPAs_europe_trade_deals_with_acp_countries_0804 (2008)
126 Christina Weller and Karin Ulmer, 'Trade and Governance: Does Governance Matter for Trade?' (2008) www.aprodev.net/trade/files/Events/Trade-and-gov.pdf cited in Sanoussi Bilal, 'Asymmetric Trade Negotiations for Development: What Does the Experience From the ACP-EU Economic Partnership Agreement Tell Us?' in Sanoussi Bilal, Philippe De Lombaerde and Diana Tussie (eds) *Asymmetric Trade Negotiations* (Routledge, 2011) 57
127 Christina Weller and Karin Ulmer, 'Trade and Governance: Does Governance Matter for Trade?' (2008) www.aprodev.net/trade/files/Events/Trade-and-gov.pdf cited in Sanoussi Bilal, 'Asymmetric Trade Negotiations for Development: What Does the Experience From the ACP-EU Economic Partnership Agreement Tell Us?' in Sanoussi Bilal, Philippe De Lombaerde and Diana Tussie (eds) *Asymmetric Trade Negotiations* (Routledge, 2011) 57; Reinert S Erik, *How Rich Countries Got Rich and Why Poor Countries Stay Poor* (Constable and Robinson Ltd, 2007)
128 ECOWAS-EU, Joint ECOWAS-EC Technical Meeting on Negotiations of an Economic Partnership Agreement (Approved Road Map for Negotiation of the Economic Partnership Agreement Between West Africa and the European Community) (Abuja 11–12 March 2004, document obtained from the ECOWAS archive)
129 The Cotonou Agreement Articles 30 (a) and 35
130 The Cotonou Agreement Article 37 (1)

was to 'foster the smooth and gradual integration of the ACP States into the world economy, with due regard to their political choice and development priorities.'[131]

Some observers such as Reinert[132] have likened the contradictions to what Williamson called the 'Washington Consensus.'[133] For Rodrik, the Washington Consensus is held as the nucleus of the 'conventional understanding of a desirable policy framework for economic growth.' Rodrik calls for the Washington Consensus reform because it has obstructive outcomes on others.[134] Serra and Stiglitz hold that recent experiences in aiding developing countries through the Washington Consensus revealed that it failed because it is outdated.[135]

Perhaps, to distance itself from the Washington Consensus, the EU made provision for flexibility in the Cotonou Agreement. Article 7 provides that the economic impact of the trade measures to be adopted must allow the ACP countries to adjust to the process of liberalisation. Thus, flexibility should be the keyword.[136]

However, the extent of special and differential treatment proposals in the EU-ACP countries' EPA became the key controversial topic during the negotiation of the EPA. A respondent interviewed stated that the EU declined to negotiate the topics that are of interest to ACP countries and claimed it had passed that stage.[137] Several times, the ACP countries asked for flexibility but were refused. For instance, the Central Africans (CEMAC) proposed a liberalisation of 60% spread out over 25 years. The EU remained adamant and continues to rely on the textual reading of the WTO rules. An interviewee commented that the EU 'intentionally declined to pay attention to its obligation towards ECOWAS as provided under the Cotonou Agreement.' In Mandelson's own words,

> as I have said over again, limiting trade opening to 60 per cent will not survive WTO scrutiny, and I would not consider signing an agreement I could not successfully defend in Geneva. I believe that your development objectives are best served by going far beyond 80 per cent.[138]

131 The Cotonou Agreement Article 37 (1)

132 Reinert (n 127)

133 John Williamson, 'What Washington Mean by Policy Reform' in John Williamson (ed), *Latin American Adjustment: How Much Has Happened?* (Institute for International Economics, 1990) cited in Dani Rodrik, *One Economics, Many Recipes: Globalization, Institutions, and Economic Growth* (Princeton University Press, 2007) 16

134 John Williamson, 'What Washington Mean by Policy Reform' in John Williamson (ed), *Latin American Adjustment: How Much Has Happened?* (Institute for International Economics, 1990) cited in Dani Rodrik, *One Economics, Many Recipes: Globalization, Institutions, and Economic Growth* (Princeton University Press, 2007) at 57

135 Narcis Serra and Joseph E Stiglitz (eds), *The Washington Consensus Reconsidered: Towards a New Global Governance* (OUP, 2008) 42–7

136 The Cotonou Agreement Article 37 (4)

137 Interview with Oluwatoyin Durojaiye, Director of Manufacturer Association of Nigeria (MAN) Abuja, 2020

138 EPA Ministerial Meeting with Central Africa, Introduction Statement by Peter Mandelson (Brussels, 29 October 2007) cited in Christina Weller, *Dialogue of the Deaf: An Assessment of Europe's Developmental Approach to Trade Negotiations* (ICCO, 2008) 14

In other words, development needs are best served with strict application of GATT Article XXIV.[139]

The GATT was drafted in 1947. It was the aspiration of founding members to promote free trade to the most significant extent possible.[140] To achieve this objective, Article 1 (1) made provision for the MFN clause, which requires that any advantage or privilege extended by any member on any product originating in other member states shall be accorded immediately and unconditionally to all like the product of all other members.[141] Nevertheless, as GATT contracting parties could not agree on MFN treatment without exception; Article XXIV permitted a deviation from Article 1 (1) GATT for customs unions and free trade areas if the conditions as outlined in the clause are met.[142] According to Hilpold, Article XXIV stopped MFN from functioning stringently.[143] The focus in this chapter is Article XXIV:8 and XXIV:5. The provision of 'substantially all the trade' requires that in the establishment of a customs union and free trade area, duties and restrictive trade regulations should be eliminated between the members.[144] The application of Article XXIV has not been without controversy. The provision is believed to suffer ambiguity, as discussed later.

According to Jacob Viner, Article XXIV of GATT has become a veritable nuisance to scholars who have attempted to decipher its content. While agreeing to the reality that, to some extent, bilateral trade can reduce the barriers to trade with some economic gain, Viner, a devotee of classical liberalism and a fierce defender of the MFN principle, argued, 'customs union are not important, and are unlikely to yield more economic benefit than harm.'[145] The world has reverted to the 1930 'from which all sensible men and women had recoiled due to the rapid increase in Preferential Trade Agreement (PTA).'[146] In Bhagwati's words, 'PTA is a pandemic and a pox on the world trading system.'[147] Bhagwati et al. stated that PTA is 'a stumbling block to multilateral liberalisation,' 'developed countries prefer it

139 EPA Ministerial Meeting with Central Africa, Introduction Statement by Peter Mandelson (Brussels, 29 October 2007) cited in Christina Weller, *Dialogue of the Deaf: An Assessment of Europe's Developmental Approach to Trade Negotiations* (ICCO, 2008) 14

140 Jürgen Huber, 'The Practice of GATT in Examining Regional Arrangements Under Article XXIV' (1981) Journal of Common Market Studies vol XIX (3) at 281

141 Peter Van den Bossche and Werner Zdouc, *The Law and Policy of the World Trade Organization: Text, Cases and Materials* (4th ed, CUP, 2017) 306–7

142 Peter Van den Bossche and Werner Zdouc, *The Law and Policy of the World Trade Organization: Text, Cases and Materials* (4th ed, CUP, 2017) at 680–1

143 Peter Hilpold, 'Regional Integration According to Article XXIV GATT—Between Law and Politics' (2007) Max Planck Yearbook of United Nations Law vol 7 pp 219–60 at 232

144 GATT Article XXIV

145 Jacob Viner and Paul Oslington (eds) *The Customs Union* (OUP, 2014) xiv and xviii, Professor Paul Oslington in his introduction to the work of Viner described him as an astute believer of classical liberalism and protector of the MFN principle.

146 Jagdish Bhagwati, *Termite in the Trading System: How Preferential Agreements Undermine Free Trade* (OUP, 2008) 14

147 Jagdish Bhagwati, *Termite in the Trading System: How Preferential Agreements Undermine Free Trade* (OUP, 2008) at 15

because it is more advantageous to them as they can utilise their power to the maximum to make smaller countries accept meagre offers.' In a dissenting opinion, the WTO Panel in the case of Turkey made the pronouncement that PTA is 'a means of increasing freedom of trade.'[148] Article XXIV:4 provides that the contracting parties recognised the 'desirability of increasing freedom of trade by the development, through voluntary agreements, of closer integration between the economies of the countries, parties to such agreement.'[149] Bhagwati further questioned the policy underlying the creation of Article XXIV. He believes that it is not only 'an intellectual failure' to believe PTA would promote free trade, but the strict conditions provided in XXIV have been weakened due to a lack of compliance.[150]

Several reasons have been given as to why the GATT deviates from the MFN principle.

According to Patterson, Belgium, the Netherlands and Luxembourg (Benelux) countries delegation proposed that the non-discriminatory regulation be amended to allow The Organisation for Economic Cooperation and Development (OECD) countries to carry on discrimination among the members at the GATT meeting held in 1954.[151] The Benelux argument was that it would allow for closer economic integration.[152] The Canadian Minister of Trade, supported by several members, argued that, without doubt, the OEEC-European Payment Union (EPU) deal assisted its members in advancing their economies. Nevertheless, according to the minister, regional grouping is 'a notoriously weak and unstable basis for trade.'[153] It is only in exceptional situations that it can be formed for a short time and where unusual circumstances exist.[154] However, Patterson notes that the OEEC had become a stumbling block to multilateral progress, whether short or long term.[155]

As mentioned earlier, the method of interpretation of GATT Article XXIV has been a subject of controversy.[156] According to Obote Ochieng, applying a literal interpretation to Article XXIV would be problematic for the ACP countries.[157]

148 Report of the Panel, Turkey Restrictions on Imports of Textile and Clothing Products, WTO Doc. WT/DS34/R, para. 2.2 (31 May 1999) [hereinafter, Panel Report on Turkey's Restrictions on Textile].

149 Article XXIV:4, WTO Analytical Index, GATT 1994-Article XXIV (Jurisprudence) www.wto.org/english/res-e/publications-e/ai17_e/gatt19 accessed 3 July 2020; John Jackson, *The Jurisprudence of GATT & the WTO: Insight on Treaty Law and Economic Relations* (CUP, 2000) 64

150 Jagdish (n 147)

151 Gardner Patterson, *Discrimination in International Trade: The Policy Issue* 1945–1965 (Princeton University Press, 1966) 105

152 Gardner Patterson, *Discrimination in International Trade: The Policy Issue* 1945–1965 (Princeton University Press, 1966) at 105–6

153 Gardner Patterson, *Discrimination in International Trade: The Policy Issue* 1945–1965 (Princeton University Press, 1966)

154 Gardner Patterson, *Discrimination in International Trade: The Policy Issue* 1945–1965 (Princeton University Press, 1966)

155 Gardner Patterson, *Discrimination in International Trade: The Policy Issue* 1945–1965 (Princeton University Press, 1966)

156 Huber (n 140) at 282

157 Cosmas M Obote Ochieng, 'The EU–ACP Economic Partnership Agreements and 'Development Questions': Constraints and Opportunities Posed by Article XXIV and Special and Differential Treatment Provisions of the WTO' (2007) JIEL vol 10 (2) pp 363–95 at 364

Even under domestic laws, judges are observed to be wary of textual interpretations. For example, Ramanatha thinks that the criticisms against the literal rule are twofold: first, 'logical defects which constitute ambiguity, inconsistency, and incompleteness, and second, is absurdity or irrationality.'[158] Article XXIV seems to suffer from the defects enumerated by Ramanatha. The focus here is not to debate how rules are interpreted under the domestic legal system but to show that rules are interpreted in such a way that it would avoid substantial injustice—especially when it is couched in an ambiguous term. For example, in Article XXIV, according to Haight, the EU finds it vastly adaptable, while smaller countries consider it 'complex,' 'ambiguous' and 'vague.'[159] Onguglo and Ito have called for the provision to be redrafted to give it clarity.[160] Criticising the defectively drafted Article XXIV, Hilpold expresses that it is hard to 'discover an underlying settled economic theory' and how the GATT/WTO law[161] should faithfully implement it. An observer argued that an accurate description of the article is challenging.[162] According to Dam, Article XXIV is 'deceptive.'[163] On its face, the article gives the impression of being well thought out, but it 'makes little economic sense.' The most discouraging aspect of the law is that no free trade agreement (FTA) has complied with Article XXIV since its promulgation.[164] Nevertheless, the FTA agreements are implicitly or explicitly approved.[165]

No FTA agreement has squared up to the provision of Article XXIV.[166] Nevertheless, such an agreement had been tacitly or explicitly approved in the past.[167] For example, the Southern Rhodesia and Union of South Africa was the first customs union presented before the contracting parties in 1948. It came into force on 1 April 1949[168] and was an interim agreement.[169] Although it was intended that restrictions on other forms of internal trade would be removed and common tariffs

158 Aiyer P Ramanatha, *Law Lexicon* (2nd ed, LexisNexis, 2002) 1134

159 F.A. Haight, 'Customs Unions and Free Trade Areas Under GATT: A Reappraisal' (1972) Journal of World Trade Law vol 6 p 391

160 Bonapas Onguglo and Taisuke Ito, 'In Defence of the ACP Submission on Special and Differential Treatment in GATT Article XXIV' ECDPM Discussion Paper 67, ECDPM, Maastricht (2005)

161 Hilpold (n 143)

162 Kenneth W Dam, 'Regional Economic Arrangements and the GATT: The Legacy of a Misconception' (1963) The University Law Review vol 30 (4) pp 615–6 at 619

163 Kenneth W Dam, 'Regional Economic Arrangements and the GATT: The Legacy of a Misconception' (1963) The University Law Review vol 30 (4) pp 615–6 at 619

164 Kenneth W Dam, 'Regional Economic Arrangements and the GATT: The Legacy of a Misconception' (1963) The University Law Review vol 30 (4) pp 615–6 at 619

165 Kenneth W Dam, 'Regional Economic Arrangements and the GATT: The Legacy of a Misconception' (1963) The University Law Review vol 30 (4) pp 615–6 at 619

166 Huber (140) at 296

167 Huber (140) at 296

168 General Agreement on Tariffs and Trade, Report of Working Party 4 on South Africa-Southern Rhodesia Customs Union (Report to the Contracting Parties, Contracting Parties Third Session, 14 May 1949) (hereinafter, GATT/CP3/24) 9 https://docs.wto.org/gattdocs/q/GG/GATTCP3/24.PDF accessed 18 May 2021; Dam (n 163) at 619

169 General Agreement on Tariffs and Trade, Report of Working Party 4 on South Africa-Southern Rhodesia Customs Union (Report to the Contracting Parties, Contracting Parties Third Session, 14

adopted subsequently, there was no scheduling in the agreement stipulating a specific date for eliminating the tariff and adopting a common tariff.[170] The interim agreement violated Article XXIV of the GATT/WTO because of the failure to include a timetable of the customs union.[171]

The fundamental principle of the trade relationships between Southern Rhodesia and Southern Africa countries and the interim agreement was to eliminate quantitative restrictions in Articles 10, 11 and 12.[172] The restrictions were listed in Annexure D[173] and only provided for review from time to time, without specific dates.[174] The two governments were allowed to extend preferential treatment to each other about products that were not particularly competitive but were permitted to delay for five years before deciding on products, where eliminating tariffs would bring about fierce competition.[175] The parties to the customs union (CU) remedied the deficiency by taking responsibility. Another point argued was whether the ten-year period allowed for the parties to bring the CU into compliance was in excess. The Working Party agreed not to focus on the ten years because of the guarantee from the parties. The period provided was not 'a reasonable time' as envisaged by Article XXIV.[176] Nevertheless, the Working Party endorsed the interim agreement as modified by the parties.[177]

Another instance was the case of El Salvador and Nicaragua. In 1951, they signed a free trade agreement that was not in compliance with the provision of XXIV on two grounds:[178] the first ground was technical. El Salvador was not a signatory to GATT. As such, it contradicted Article XXIV:5, since free trade areas must be 'between the territories of contracting parties.' The second ground was 'substantially all the trade' as provided under Article XXIV:8 (b). The agreement allowed quantitative restrictions between the members in some situations.[179] The contracting parties granted a waiver under the provisions of paragraph 10 of Article XXIV that the government of Nicaragua was entitled to benefit from the

---

May 1949) (hereinafter, GATT/CP3/24) 9 https://docs.wto.org/gattdocs/q/GG/GATTCP3/24.PDF accessed 18 May 2021 at 9

170 General Agreement on Tariffs and Trade, Report of Working Party 4 on South Africa-Southern Rhodesia Customs Union (Report to the Contracting Parties, Contracting Parties Third Session, 14 May 1949) (hereinafter, GATT/CP3/24) 9 https://docs.wto.org/gattdocs/q/GG/GATTCP3/24.PDF accessed 18 May 2021 at 5–6

171 Dam (n 162) at 635

172 GATT/CP3/24

173 GATT/CP3/24

174 GATT/CP3/24

175 Dam (n 163) at 636

176 GATT/CP3/24 at 7

177 GATT/CP3/24 at 9

178 GATT, 'Item 23: Nicaragua–El Salvador Free Trade Area' (GATT, Contracting Parties, Sixth Session, GATT/CP.6/24/Add.1, 22 October 1952) https://docs.wto.org/gattdocs/q/GG/GATTCP6/24A1.PDF accessed 19 May 2021

179 GATT, 'Item 23: Nicaragua–El Salvador Free Trade Area' (GATT, Contracting Parties, Sixth Session, GATT/CP.6/24/Add.1, 22 October 1952) https://docs.wto.org/gattdocs/q/GG/GATTCP6/24A1.PDF accessed 19 May 2021 at 3–4

provisions of Article XXIV. However, contracting parties decided to review the decision based on the report furnished to it by the government of Nicaragua.[180]

The European Coal and Steel Community (ECSC) represents a classic example of non-compliance with GATT Article XXIV. First, according to Dam, there was a complete departure from the framework of Article XXIV. In his view, it is 'impossible to pretend that the article's requirements were met.'[181] ECSC did not meet the description of a customs union or free trade area within the context of Article XXIV; second, it was only coal and steel that were covered. It is thus far from 'substantially all the trade' between the constituent territories in products originating in the ECSC member countries.[182] Assuming the two issues could be ignored because ECSC was new and tested for the first time on compliance with Article XXIV, according to Dam, some provisions could not be overlooked because they were not in agreement with Article XXIV or the general provisions of GATT.[183] For example, as a high-cost manufacturer, Italy was to maintain barriers against other ECSC members. The Benelux countries were allowed to increase some duties to 'facilitate harmonisation of ECSC external tariffs.'[184] None was extended to other contracting parties as GATT requires.[185] Belgium was given an allowance to continue quantitative restrictions on coal for seven years. This was to enable it to protect weak collieries.[186]

Notwithstanding the apparent departure from the provisions of Article XXIV, a waiver was instantly and unanimously granted by the contracting parties.[187] Overwhelming support for the Six, according to Dam, could either be political, based on extreme faith in the economic assurance of the ECSC, or based on the absence of confidence in the GATT.[188] ECSC extended its coverage to other economies by forming the European Economic Community. The customs union and free trade area had to pass the Article XXIV test. In order to examine the Treaty of Rome and ensure its compliance with Article XXIV, four sub-groups were set up. Sub-Group A was to examine the common external tariff (CET). Sub-Group B had the task of examining quantitative restrictions. Sub-Group C was to examine agriculture.[189]

180 GATT, 'Item 23: Nicaragua–El Salvador Free Trade Area' (GATT, Contracting Parties, Sixth Session, GATT/CP.6/24/Add.1, 22 October 1952) https://docs.wto.org/gattdocs/q/GG/GATTCP6/24A1.PDF accessed 19 May 2021 at 3–4; Dam (n 162) at 637
181 Dam (n 162) at 138
182 GATT Article XXIV (8) (a) (i))
183 Dam (n 162) at 138
184 Dam (n 162) at 138; Patterson (n 151) at 106, 190
185 Mead Liesner and Christina Wells, 'Case Studies in European Economic Union (1962) 408–09 cite in Kenneth W Dam, 'Regional Economic Arrangements and the GATT: The Legacy of a Misconception' (1963) The University Law Review vol 30 (4) pp 615–6 at 368
186 Mead Liesner and Christina Wells, 'Case Studies in European Economic Union (1962) 408–09 cite in Kenneth W Dam, 'Regional Economic Arrangements and the GATT: The Legacy of a Misconception' (1963) The University Law Review vol 30 (4) pp 615–6 at 368
187 Patterson (n 151) at 128
188 The Report of the Working Party, GATT, Basic Instruments, 1st Supp., at 85 (1952); ECSC Treaty and the General Agreement GATT, Basic Instruments, 1st Supp., at 17–19 (1952) cited in Dam (n 162) at 368
189 Treaty of Rome, article 30–37, 104–9 (1957)

According to Dam's account, after examining the provision, the Working Party could not arrive at any concrete resolution on the legal issues raised.[190] The Working Party did not give due attention to the consequences of discrimination between members and the quantitative restrictions were imposed.[191] The provision in the Treaty of Rome on agriculture poses some unusual challenges.[192] Even though agricultural commodities regulation comes under GATT, overproduction and protectionism were the norm in industrialised countries.[193] It was argued that the Six confidently declared that agriculture could not flow freely in the Community.[194]

Sub-Group D examined the Association of Overseas Territories. As mentioned earlier, France, Belgium, and the Netherlands negotiated several preferential commercial arrangements with some colonies under the Rome Treaty.[195] The EEC made an effort to explain that the creation of the association was a free trade area, that it satisfied paragraph 8 (b) of Article XXIV.[196] This position from the EEC member states generated rancorous arguments among other contracting parties. For the sub-Group D, the EEC arrangement with the associated territories was an extension of a subsisting preferential commercial agreement with no breach of the MFN principle. The Six remained inflexible on all the legal issues raised and contended that no obligation could be imposed on the Six until provisions dealing with 'substantially all' had been adequately defined.[197] During the Thirteenth Session of October and November of 1958, the Working Party recommended, 'it would be more fruitful, if attention could be directed to specific and practical problems, leaving aside for the time being questions of law and debates about the compatibility of the Rome Treaty with Article XXIV.'[198]

The interpretation of the provisions of Article XXIV generated heated arguments between the EU and ACP groups.[199] As a result of the disagreement over the right interpretation of the article, the West African trade coalition commissioned a study to be carried out on Article XXIV.[200] The result of the research eventually formed part of the negotiating process. The EPA negotiating process in West Africa made use of non-state actors extensively. The 15 ECOWAS member states + Mauritania negotiating team was made up of public officials, 'private sectors representatives,'

190 Dam (n 162) at 644
191 Dam (n 162) at 644
192 Treaty of Rome, Articles 38–47
193 Charles Mutasa, 'A Critique of the EU's Common Agricultural Policy' in Adekeye Adebajo and Kaye Whiteman (eds), *The EU and Africa: From Eurafrique to Afro-Europa* (C. Hurst & Co Publishers Ltd, 2012) 138 CAP
194 Dam (n 162) at 644
195 Dam (n 162) at 644
196 Dam (n 162) at 644
197 Dam (n 162) at 644
198 GATT, Basic Instruments, 7th Supp. at 70 1958 cited in Dam (n 162) at 651
199 Obote Ochieng (n 157) at 364; Aniekan Ukpe and Ken Ukaoha, 'West Africa's EPA: Defining a Pro-Poor Market Access Offer' (2009) Trade Policy Monitor vol 2 (4) at 6–7
200 Interview conducted by Silke Trommer with Representatives Bathie Ciss and Cheikh Tidiane Dieye (16 and 28 July 2009, Dakar)

and 'civil society representatives.[201] There were four organisations: national civil society platforms representing farmers' associations, non-government organisations (NGOs), trade unions, and women's rights groups. The eight-member organisations are African development and global justice NGOs and two other trade unions—the National Association of Nigeria Traders (NANTS) and private sector representatives.[202] The coalition was made of 11 out of 16 negotiating countries with a civil and not well-organised on-trade policy in Cape Verde, Guinea-Bissau, Liberia, Mauritania, and Sierra Leone. Few members of the coalition enjoy international visibility, such as ENDA Third World (Senegal), Third World Network (Ghana), and National Association of Nigerian Traders (Nigeria). These three are no strangers to international trade campaign in Africa and at the global level.[203]

The West African Peasants' movement ROPPA observed in 2006 that ECOWAS could only afford to liberalise 50% with the EU to ensure food security.[204] The National Association of Nigeria Traders, a Nigerian-based organisation, for instance, did forecast that the large-scale trade liberalisation proposed by the EU can only bring about 'loss of government revenue, an influx of goods and import surge, capital flight, de-industrialisation, labour dislocation and job losses, insecurity and poverty escalation.'[205] The West African trade coalition that canvassed with ROPPA disapproved of the arrangement because of its impact on economic development if the proposed liberalisation was followed.[206] On the other hand, the EU argued that the extent of the market liberalisation was not on political grounds but in compliance with Article XXIV of the GATT.

Although the EU made an effort to make the ACP countries see the advantages of signing the EPAs, the coalition members did not believe the 'substantial all the trade' clause was in their economic interests.[207] The representative of the coalition questioned the textual reading of Article XXIV of the GATT and subsequently explored other ways of interpreting the GATT provision. El Hadi Diouf, the head of the EPA programme at the International Centre for Trade and Sustainable Development in Geneva, was commissioned by the coalition to examine Article XXIV's

201 Interview conducted by Silke Trommer with Representatives Bathie Ciss and Cheikh Tidiane Dieye (16 and 28 July 2009, Dakar)

202 POSCAO, Negotiation of an EPA Between West Africa and the European Community: Capacity Building Programme, Regional Strategic Planning Seminar (ENDA, Dakar, 2004)

203 Silke Trommer (n 200)

204 ROPPA, *proposition du ROPPA pour la mise en aeuvre et la defense de la politique agricole de la CEDEAO* (ECOWAP, Ouagadougou: ROPPA, 2007)

205 Ken Ukaoha, 'Reasons Why Nigeria Could Not Sign the EPA' Trade Policy Monitor', vol 1 (2) pp 1–11, UN-OHRLLS and UN-NGLS (2008) cited in Silke Trommer, 'Legal Opportunity in Trade Negotiations: International Law, Opportunity Structures and the Political Economy of Trade Agreements' (2014) New Political Economic vol 19 (1)

206 Ken Ukaoha, 'Reasons Why Nigeria Could Not Sign the EPA' Trade Policy Monitor', vol 1 (2) pp 1–11, UN-OHRLLS and UN-NGLS (2008) cited in Silke Trommer, 'Legal Opportunity in Trade Negotiations: International Law, Opportunity Structures and the Political Economy of Trade Agreements' (2014) New Political Economic vol 19 (1)

207 Goodison Paul, 'EU Trade Policy and the Future of Africa's Trade Relationship With the EU' (2007) Review of Africa Political Economy vol 34 (112) pp 247–66 at 249; Hurt (91)

content critically.[208] Diouf dissected the many parts of the provisions in his study. The chief concern in his study was 'substantially all the trade.' In the presentation of 'substantially all the trade,' Diouf posited that there is no benchmark of interpreting 'substantially all the trade' evident in international trade law.[209]

Contrary to the EU's view, jurisprudence and state practice allow flexibility if a textual interpreting the law in this way will create unnecessary difficulty for developing countries. The WTO Dispute Settlement Body (DSB) recognised that the rule of interpretation in the Vienna Convention on the Laws Treaties (VCLT) should apply in international jurisprudence.[210] This means that states' practice and judicial interpretation can be used for interpretation, as shown in legislative preparatory works.[211] In the Turkey-Textile case, the DSB panel stated that the wordings of Article XXIV are of sub-optimal clarity and have been the object of various, sometimes opposing views among individual contracting parties and members, as well as academic literature.[212]

4.5 Conclusion

Although it was declared by the proponent—France—that the association of the overseas countries and colonies would generate mutual benefit for the European powers and colonies, the African colonies did not negotiate or contribute to such an arrangement.[213] When the arrangement transitioned into Yaoundé and subsequent Lomé Conventions, it continued to follow an established colonial construct, protecting the interests of the European Community.[214] Nevertheless, ACP countries benefitted from the preferential agreement but only minimally—one of the reasons the EU in its green paper decided to resort to reciprocal agreement was to enhance the participation of the ACP countries in the global economy. However, negotiation and the textual interpretation of the GATT Article XXIV was not endorsed by the ACP countries.[215]

Cox's critical theory was applied to understand that the power employed by the EU to protect its interests in GATT was exported into its negotiations and trade relations with ACP countries.[216] The insight gained from critical theory assists in understanding the interests underlying the EU-ACP countries EPA. While the EU posits that the relationship is among equal partners, several observers doubt the

208 Interview with coalition representative Cheikh Tidiane Dieye, 27 April 2009, Geneva (2009) Interview conducted by Silke Trommer (n 200)

209 Interview with coalition representative Cheikh Tidiane Dieye, 27 April 2009, Geneva (2009) Interview conducted by Silke Trommer (n 200)

210 Appellate Body Report on United States—Standard for Reformulated and Conventional Gasoline, WT/DS2/AB/R, adopted 29 April 1996

211 Obote Ochieng (n 157)

212 Panel Report on Turkey -Restrictions on Imports of Textile and Clothing, WT/DS34/R, adopted 31 May 1999

213 Peo and Jonsson (n 22) at 156

214 Carol Ann Cosgrove, 'The Common Market and its Colonial Heritage' (1969) Journal of Contemporary History vol 4 (1) pp 73–87

215 Obote Ochieng (n 157)

216 Cox (n 3) at 128

genuineness of such partnerships between the parties because the economic power is asymmetrical.[217] Negotiations among unequal parties can only produce favourable results for industrialised countries.

Conventions and WTO Cases

Agreement Between the Governments of the Union of South Africa and Southern Rhodesia (Directed to the Re-establishment of a Customs Union) (GATT/CP.3/24/Annex, 1948) www.wto.org/gatt_docs/English/SULPDF/90320154.pdf accessed: 19 May 2021

Agreement Between the Governments of the Union of South Africa and Southern Rhodesia (Directed to the Re-establishment of a Customs Union) (GATT/CP.3/24/Annex, 1948), www.wto.org/gatt_docs/English/SULPDF/90320154.pdf accessed: 19 May 2021

Report of the Panel, Turkey—Restrictions on Imports of Textile and Clothing Products, WTO Doc. WT/DS34/R, para. 2.2 (31 May 1999) WTO Analytical Index, GATT 1994-Article XXIV (Jurisprudence) www.wto.org/english/res-e/publications-e/ai17_e/gatt19. accessed: 3 July 2020

European Union Treaty of Amsterdam, Treaty of Amsterdam, Amending the Treaty on European Union, The Treaty Establishing the European Communities and Certain Related Acts (2 October 1997), https://europa.eu/european-union/sites/europaeu/files/docs/b. . . accessed: 26 June 2020

Appellate Body Report on Turkey—Restrictions on Imports of Textiles and Clothing, WT/DS34/AB/R, adopted 22 October 1999

Appellate Body Report on the United States—Standard for Reformulated and Conventional Gasoline, WT/DS2/AB/R, adopted 29 April 1996

Appellate Body, European Communities-Regime for the Importation, Sale, and Distribution of Bananas, WT/DS27/AB/R, adopted 25 September 1997

Panel Report on Turkey -Restrictions on Imports of Textile and Clothing, WT/DS34/R, adopted 31 May 1999

Panel Report, European Communities-Regime for the Importation, Sale, and Distribution of Bananas-Recourse to Arbitration by the EC Under Article 22.6, WT/DS27/RW/EEC & Corr. I, 12 April 1999, DSR, 1999:11, 783

The decision by the Arbitration, European Communities—Regime for the Importation, Sale, Distribution of Bananas—Recourse to Arbitration by the European Communities under Article 22.6 of the DSU, WTT/DS27/ARB/ECU, 24, March 2000, DSR 2000, V

Treaty of Rome, Part IV, Association of the Overseas Countries and Territories, (hereinafter Rome Treaty) Article 131 of the www.consilium.europa.eu/media/29665/archives-enlargment-1.pdf accessed: 20 June 2020

Treaty on European Union as signed in Maastricht (Luxembourg: Office for Official Publications of the European Communities, 1992)

217 Rob de Vos, 'Europe, Africa and Aid: Towards a Genuine Partnership in Adekeye Adebajo and Kaye White (eds), *The EU and Africa: From Eurafrique to Afro-Europa* (OUP, 2012) 105; Guy Martin, 'Africa and the Ideology of Eurafrica: Neo-Colonialism or Pan-Africanism,' The Journal of Modern African Studies (1982) vol 20 (2) p 226

Bibliography

Adebajo A, & White K (eds), *The EU and Africa From Eurafrique to Afro-Europa* (C Hurst & Co Publishers Ltd, 2012)

African Growth and Opportunity Act (AGOA as Amended), World Trade Organization for Trade in Goods, G/C/W/713 (16 July 2015). https://agoa.info>images>documents>wtowaiveragoa2015.pdf (accessed 6 May 2019)

Akyuz Y, 'Multilateral Disciplines and the Question of Policy Space' in F Faundez & C Tan (eds), *International Economic Law, Globalisation and Developing Countries* (Edward Elgar, 2012)

Alter K J & Meunier S, 'Nested and Overlapping Regimes in the Transatlantic Banana Trade Dispute' (2006) Journal of European Public Policy vol 13 (3) pp 362–382

Anyidoho E, 'ECOWAS-EPA Negotiations: State of Play' Seminar Tradecom/FEWACCI, 25–27 August 2010. AccraGhana. www.fewacci.org/index.php?option=com_eventlist&view=details&id=2%ASeminar+Tradecom%2FFEWACCI&Itemid=20&lang=en (accessed 7 May 2021)

Bassilekin A, 'Possibility of Obtaining a New ACP-EC Waiver at the WTO' (ECDPM March 2007). https://ecdpm.org/wp-content/uploads/2013/11/DP-71-New-ACP-EC-Waiver-WTO-2007.pdf (accessed 31 October 2021)

Bhagwati J, *Termite in the Trading System: How Preferential Agreements Undermine Free Trade* (OUP, 2008)

Bhagwati J N, Krishna P, & Panagariya A (eds), *The World Trade System Trends and Challenges* (The MIT Press, 2016) 10

Bilal S, De Lombaerde P, & Tussie D (eds), *Asymmetric Trade Negotiations* (Routledge, 2011)

Blyth M, *Great Transformations: Economic Ideas and Institutional Change in the Twentieth Century* (CUP, 2002)

Bossche P, & Zdouc W, *The Law and Policy of the World Trade Organization: Text, Cases and Materials* (4th edn, CUP, 2017)

Bretherton C, & John Vogler J, *The European Union as a Global Actor* (2nd ed, Routledge, 2006)

Brown W, 'Restructuring North-South Relations: ACP-EU Development Cooperation in a Liberal International Order' (2000) Review of Africa Political Economy vol 85 pp 376-383

Camps M, *Britain and the European Community, 1955–1963* (Princeton University Press, 1964)

Chang H J, *Kicking Away the Ladder: Development Strategy in Historical Perspective* (Anthem Press, 2002)

Commission of the European Communities, 'Green Paper on Relations Between the European Union and the ACP Countries on the Eve of the 21ist Century: Challenges and Options for a New Partnership' (Brussels, 20 November 1996, COM) (96) (570 Final,) iii, https://eu-lex.europa.eu/legal-content/EN/TXT/pdf/?uri=CEL. . . (accessed 26 June 2020)

Commission of the European Communities, 'Green Paper on Relations Between the European Union and the ACP Countries on the Eve of the 21st Century: Challenges and Options for a New Partnership' (COM (96) 570 Final, Brussels, 20 November 1996)

Community Topics, Partnership in Africa: The Yaoundé Association, (European Community Information Service)

Convention of Association Between the European Economic Community and the African and Malagasy States Associated With That Community and Annexed Documents (May 1970) International Legal Materials vol 9 (3)

Cosgrove C A, 'The Common Market and Its Colonial Heritage' (1969) Journal of Contemporary History vol 4 (1)

Council Regulation (EEC) No. 1858/93, 13 February 1993, on Common Organization of the Market in Bananas' Official Journal of the European Communities, Brussels, 12 June 1993

Cox R W, 'Critical Theory' in T Weiss & R Wilkinson (eds), *International Organisation and Global Governance: What Matters & Why* (Routledge, 2014)

Cox R W, 'Gramsci, Hegemony and International Relations: An Essay in Method' (1983) Millennium-Journal of International Studies vol 12

Cox R W, 'Social Forces, States, and World Orders: Beyond International Relations Theory' (1981)

Dam K W, 'Regional Economic Arrangements and the GATT: The Legacy of a Misconception' (1963) The University Law Review vol 30 (4) pp 615–616

de Vos R, 'Europe, Africa, and Aid: Towards a Genuine Partnership' in A Adebajo & K White (eds), *The EU and Africa From Eurafrique to Afro-Europa* (C Hurst & Co Publishers Ltd, 2012)

Dedman M, *The Origins and Development of the European Union 1945–2008: A History of European Integration* (2nd ed, Routledge, 2010)

Dickson A K, 'The Importance of Trade Preferences' in A Karin & A K Dickson (eds), *EU Development Cooperation-From Model to Symbol* (Manchester University Press, 2004)

'Economic Community of West Africa States (ECOWAS): Basic Information' www.ecowas.int (accessed 6 May 2021)

Elgstrom O, 'Lomé and Post-Lomé: Asymmetric Negotiation and the Impact of Norms European' (2000) European Foreign Affairs Review vol 5 (2) pp 175–195

Elgstrom O, & Jonsson C (eds), *European Union Negotiations* (Routledge, 2005)

Elgstrom O, & Pilgaard J, 'Imposed Coherence: Negotiating Economic Partnership Agreements' (2008) European Integration vol 30 (3), pp 363–380

European Commission, *Guideline for Negotiation of New Cooperation Agreements With the Africa, Caribbean, and Pacific* (Office for the Official Publications of the European Communities, L-2985, Luxembourg (COM (97) 29.10.1997 C). https://eur-lex.europaeu/legal-content . . . s (accessed 26 June 2020)

European Commission, 'SYSMIN and Mining Development: Cooperation Between the European Union and the ACP States' DE 3 (January 1996). aei.pitt.edu/9665/4/9665.pdf (accessed 21 June 2020)

The European Commission, The STABEX System, and Export Revenue in ACP Countries' Development DE 93 (December 1997). aei.pitt.edu/7559/1/31735055261188_I.pdf (accessed 21 June 2020)

European Parliament, 'Relations With the Africa, Caribbean and Pacific Countries: From Yaoundé and Lomé to Cotonou Agreement'

European Parliament, 'Resolution on the European Parliament's Recommendations to the Commission Concerning the Negotiation of Economic Partnership Agreements With the ACP Countries and Regions (26 September 2002—Strasbourg). www.europarl.europa.eu/sides/getDoc.do?pubRef=-//EP//TEXT+TA+P5-TA-2002-0453 + 0+DOC+XML+V0//EN (accessed 31 October 2021)

'The Finest and Most Complete Instrument of Cooperation Ever' The ACP-EU Countries NO 55, January-February 1996, Special Issue on the Revised Lomé Convention

Gibb R, 'Post-Lomé: The European Union and the South' (2000) Third World Quarterly vol 21 (3) pp 457–481

Goldstein J, & Keohane R O (eds), *Ideas and Foreign Policy: Beliefs, Institutions, and Political Changes* (Cornell University Press, 1993)

Green R H, 'The Lomé Convention: Updated Dependence or Departure Toward Collective Self Reliance?' http://journals.co.za/docserver/fulltext/afre/6/1/182.pdf?expires=15927445028id=id (accessed 21 June 2020)

Haight F A, 'Customs Unions and Free Trade Areas Under GATT: A Reappraisal' (1972) Journal of World Trade vol 6 (4) pp 391–404

Hayter T, *French Aid* (Overseas Development Institute Ltd, 1966)

Heron T, 'Asymmetric Bargaining and Development Trade-Offs in the CARIFORUM-European Union Economic Partnership Agreement' (2011) Review of International Political Economy vol 18 (3) pp 328–357

Hilpold P, 'Regional Integration According to Article XXIV GATT—Between Law and Politics' (2007) Max Planck Yearbook of United Nations Law vol 7 pp 219–260

Huber J, 'The Practice of GATT in Examining Regional Arrangements Under Article XXIV' (1981) Journal of Common Market Studies vol XIX (3)

Hurt S R, 'Co-Operation and Coercion? The Cotonou Agreement Between the European Union and ACP States and the End of the Lomé Convention' (2003) Third World Quarterly vol 24 (1) pp 161–174

Ismail F, 'The Changing Global Trade Architecture: Implications for Africa's Regional Integration and Development' (2017) Journal of World Trade vol 51 (1)

Jackson J, *The Jurisprudence of GATT & the WTO: Insight on Treaty Law and Economic Relations* (CUP, 2000)

Keohane R O, & Nye J S, *World Politics and the International Economic System in Berdsten F C, The Future of the International Economic Order: An Agenda for Research* (Lexington Books, 1941)

Kottos L, 'A European Commonwealth: Britain, the European League for Economic Co-Operation, and European Debates on Empire, 1947–1957' (2012) Journal of Contemporary European Studies vol 20 (4) pp 497–515

Lang A, 'Reconstructing Embedded Liberalism: John Ruggie and Constructivist Approaches to the Study of the International Trade Regime' (2006) Journal of International Law vol 9 (1) p 84

Laporte G, *The Cotonou Partnership Agreement: What Role in a Changing World? Reflection on the Future of ACP-EU Relations* (European Centre for Development Policy Management, November 2007). https://ecdpm.org/wp-content/uploads/2013/10/PMR-13-coto. . . (accessed 30 June 2020)

Liesner M, & Wells C, 'Case Studies in European Economic Union' Cite in Dam K W, Regional Economic Arrangements and the GATT: The Legacy of a Misconception' (1963) The University Law Review vol 30 (4) pp 615–616

List F, & Lloyd S (trans), *The National System* of *Political Economy* (1909)

Lister M, *The European Union and the South: Relations With Developing Countries* (Routledge, 1997)

The Lomé Convention. www.acp.int (accessed 5 April 2021)

Long F, *The Political Economy of EEC Relations With African, Caribbean and Pacific States* (Pergamon Press, 1980)

Mandelson P, 'Open Markets, Open Trade: Europe's Global Challenge' *Market Access Symposium European Parliament* (Brussels, 19 September 2005)

Martin G, 'Africa and the Ideology of Eurafrica: Neo-Colonialism or Pan-Africanism' (1982) The Journal of Modern African Studies vol 20 (2) p 226

Mazower M, *Governing the World: The History of an Idea* (Penguin Books, 2011)

Mckenzie F, 'The GATT—EEC Collision: The Challenge of Regional Trade Blocs to the General Agreement on Tariffs and Trade' (2010) The International History Review vol 32 (2)

Minta I K, 'The Lomé Convention and the New International Economic Order' (1980) Howard Law Journal vol 27 p 953

Mutasa C, 'A Critique of the EU's Common Agricultural Policy' in A Adebajo & K Whiteman (eds), *The EU and Africa From Eurafrique to Afro-Europa* (C. Hurst & Co Publishers Ltd, 2012)

Narcis S, & Stiglitz J E (eds), *The Washington Consensus Reconsidered: Towards a New Global Governance* (OUP, 2008)

Nicaragua—El Salvador Free Trade Area (GATT, Contracting Parties, Sixth Session, GATT/CP.6/24/Add.1, 22, October 1952). https://docs.wto.org/gattdocs/q/GG/GATTCP6/24A1.PDF (19 May 2021)

Nkrumah K, *Africa Must Unite* (Heineman, 1963)

Ochieng C M O, 'The EU—ACP Economic Partnership Agreements and 'Development Questions': Constraints and Opportunities Posed by Article XXIV and Special and Differential Treatment Provisions of The WTO' (2007) JIEL vol 10 (2) pp 363–395

Ongulo B, & Ito T, 'In Defence of the ACP Submission on Special and Differential Treatment in GATT Article XXIV' ECDPM Discussion Paper 67, ECDPM, Maastricht (2005)
Patterson E, 'The US-EU Banana Dispute' (2000) American Society of International Law vol 6 (4), June. www.wto.org/english/res.e/booksp_e/dispu_settlement_e.pdf (accessed 2 September 2020)
Patterson G, *Discrimination in International Trade: The Policy Issues 195–1965* (Princeton University Press, 1966)
Peo H, & Jonsson S, *Eurafrican: The Untold History of European Integration and Colonialism* (Bloomsbury Publishing, 2014)
Ramanathan, A P, *Law Lexicon* (2nd ed, 2002)
Ravenhill J, 'Asymmetrical Interdependence: Renegotiating the Lomé Convention' (1979/1980) International Journal vol 35 (1) pp 150–169
Ravenhill J, 'Back to the Nest? Europe's Relationship With the African, Caribbean and Pacific Group of Countries' Working Paper PEIF-9, December 2000 pp 7–8. www.researchgate.net/publication/238105746 (accessed 24 June 2020)
Ravenhill J, *Collective Clientelism: The Lomé Conventions and North-South Relations* (Columbia University Press, 1985)
Rein C, 'The European Union and the African Union: A Strategic Partnership?' (2015) European Foreign Affairs Review vol 20 (4)
Reinert E S, *How Rich Countries Got Rich and Why Poor Countries Stay Poor* (Constable and Robinson, 2007)
The Report of the Working Party, GATT, Basic Instruments, 1st Supp, at 85 (1952)
Rodney W, *How Europe Underdeveloped Africa* (Bogie-L'Ouverture Publications, 1973)
Rodrik D, *One Economics, Many Recipes: Globalization, Institutions, and Economic Growth* (Princeton University Press, 2007)
ROPPA, *proposition du ROPPA pour la mise en aeuvre et la defense de la politique agricole de la CEDEAO* (ECOWAP, Ouagadougou: ROPPA, 2007)
Schmieg E, 'EU Economic Partnership Agreement in Sub-Saharan Africa' (German Institute for International and Security Affairs, January 2014)
The Second Lomé ACP-EEC Lomé Convention No L 347/2 Official Journal of the European Communities (31 October 1979). www.evce.eu/obj/the_second_acp_eec_lome_convention_31october_1979-en-416ece3a-4e44-44771-8c0e-52a754f2e007.html
Sékou Touré, 'Africa's Future and the World Foreign Affairs' (October 1962) vol 41 (1)
Smith R, 'EPA Provisions May Impact the Ability of Some Developing Countries to Respond to the Crisis, Trade Negotiation Insight' (2009) ECDPM/ICTSD vol 8 (4). www.acp-eu-trade.org/tni
Twichett K J, 'Yaoundé Association and the Enlargement European Community' (1974) The World to Day vol 30 (2) pp 51–63
Ukaoha K, 'Reasons Why Nigeria Could Not Sign the EPA' (2008) Trade Policy Monitor vol 1 (2) pp 1–11, UN-OHRLLS and UN-NGLS (2008), cited in Trommer S, 'Legal Opportunity in Trade Negotiations: International Law, Opportunity Structures and the Political Economy of Trade Agreements' (2014) New Political Economic vol 19 (1)
Ukpe A, & Ukaoha K, 'West Africa's EPA: Defining a Pro-Poor Market Access Offer' (2009) Trade Policy Monitor vol 2 (4)
UNCTAD & WTO, 'A Common Global Economy' (TAD/INF/PR/9628, 8 October 1996). www.unctad.org (accessed 31 August 2020)
'Understanding the West Africa European Union-Economic Partnership Agreement: Key Facts and Issues' (ECOWAS Commission, UEMOA Commission and the European Centre for Development Policy Management (ECDPM), Archival Document Abuja 2012, 2002)
Van Der Lee J J, 'Association Relations Between the European Economic Community and African States' (1967) African Affairs vol 66 (264) pp 197–212
Viner J, & Oslington P (eds), *The Customs Union* (OUP, 2014)

Wallerstein I, *European Universalism: The Rhetoric of Power* (The New Press, 2004)
Weil G L (ed), *A Handbook on the European Economic Community* (Fredrick A Praeger, 1965) 1. https://aei.pitt.edu/3216/1/8216.pdf (accessed 4 July 2020)
Weller C, & Ulmer K, 'Trade and Governance: Does Governance Matter for Trade?' (2008) www.aprodev.net/trade/files/Events/Trade-and-gov.pdf
Weller C, *Dialogue of the Deaf: An Assessment of Europe's Developmental Approach to Trade Negotiations* (ICCO, 2008) 5. www.bibalex.org/baifa/Attachment/Documents/116861.pdf (accessed 1 July 2020)
Wilkinson R, 'Of Butchery and Bicycles: The WTO and the 'Death' of the Doha Development Agenda' (2012) The Political Quarterly vol 83 (2)
Wilkinson R, *What's Wrong With the WTO and How to Fix* (Polity Press, 2014)
Williamson J, 'What Washington Mean by Policy Reform' in John Williamson (ed), *Latin American Adjustment: How Much Has Happen?* (Institute for International Economics, 1990)
Woolcock S, 'The Scope for Asymmetry in the World Trade Organisation (WTO)' in S Bilal, P Lombaerde, & D Tussi (eds), *Asymmetric Trade Negotiations* (Routledge, 2016)

5 The Ghana-EU Economic Partnership Agreement

5.1 Introduction

Ghana like most African countries has poor infrastructure, so exceptions such as the one provided by the EPA may have no benefit. It is against this background that it is argued that the Special and Differential Treatment (SDT) provided in the text of the EU-Ghana Economic Partnership Agreement (EPA) is insufficient to meet the economic development aspiration of Ghana. According to Stewart,[1] investment in infrastructures like energy, transportation, water, and communication is pivotal in advancing economic growth and poverty reduction.[2] Sahoo[3] recognised that a proficient infrastructure could minimise transaction costs and facilitate trade and foreign direct investment.[4] In the same way, it promotes intra-regional trade and encourages investment, creating a regional market and an efficient market. In other words, infrastructure has the potential to advance growth and alleviate poverty.[5] In the whole of the African continent, according to the World Bank, the infrastructure provided 99% basis points to per capita economic growth than did structural policies in the period between 1990 and 2005.[6] However, several African countries fall far behind in infrastructure development when juxtaposed with other developing countries, such as Latin America. It is further approximated that about 2% of the continent's yearly growth suffers from poor infrastructure. If there is adequate quality infrastructure in Africa, it will

1 James Stewart, 'The UK National Infrastructure Plan 2010' (2010) European Investment Bank Paper Luxembourg vol 15 (2) pp 28–32
2 Harold Coulombe, 'Ghana Census-Based Poverty Map: District & Sub-District Level Results' in Ernest Aryeeteh and Ravi Kanbur (eds), *The Economy of Ghana: Analytical Perspectives on Stability, Growth and Poverty* (James Currey Ltd & Woeli Publishing Service, 2008) 224
3 Pravakar Sahoo and Dash K Ranjan, 'Economic Growth in India: Role of Physical and Human Infrastructure' (2010) Journal of Economic Policy Reforms vol 13 (4) pp 409–29
4 Torsten Ehlers, 'Understanding the Challenges for Infrastructure Finance' (2014) Bank for International Settlements Working Papers No. 454
5 Coulombe (n 2) at 224; Rizwanul Islam and Jean Majeres, 'Employment-Intensive Growth for Poverty Reduction: What Can Labour-Based Technology in Infrastructure Contribute?' (2001) Urban Forum vol 12 (3) pp 279–96
6 Vivien Foster and Cecilia Briceño-Garmendia (eds), *World Bank African Infrastructure: A Time for Transportation* (World Bank, 2010)

DOI: 10.4324/9781032615059-5

boost the continent's productivity, according to the Africa Development Bank (AfDB) in 2013.[7]

Ryan[8] discussed with sharecroppers, migrants, and families on whose shoulders 'the world chocolate industry rests' in Côte d'Ivoire and Ghana. Ryan paints a vivid picture of the abject condition of farmers in those countries. The villages have no 'electricity, water, and decent schools.' According to those he interviewed, the farming and harvesting of cocoa is 'back-breaking and hard, carried out with nothing more sophisticated than a machete.' The World Economic Forum reported in 2020 that chocolate is a global $130 billion industry, mainly dependent on cocoa. However, cocoa farmers in Côte d'Ivoire and Ghana earn less than $1 a day.[9] The EPA, it is claimed, may heighten the dire situation in these countries. Oxfam quoted a farmer in Ghana, Tetteh Hormeku, who lamented that the EPA represents a crippling situation that generates excruciating discontentment, he states:

> I come from a small fishing village in Ghana. Members of my family fished for their livelihood, but fishing has become impossible since larger European fishing vessels came and fished our seas empty. The same happened with poultry. EU imports of frozen chicken wings destroyed the local market . . . EPAs are free to trade agreements, and as such, they will bring poverty to Africa.
>
> —Tetteh Hormeku, Third World Network, Accra, Ghana[10]

The African Competitive Report 2013 rated Ghana 86th in evaluating the general standard in the country's infrastructure, with a total of 3.7 out of 7.[11] Further dissection of the assessment revealed that Ghana's railway infrastructure was rated at 1.7, and the standard of roads, ports, and airport infrastructure was rated 3.5, 4.0, and 4.1 in the order mentioned. However, considerable growth has been witnessed in the infrastructure when placed side by side with low-income countries, but Ghana lagged in juxtaposition with other middle-income countries in Africa.[12] The government of Ghana has acknowledged the enormous positive impact that quality and adequate infrastructure could have on their economic development.[13] Therefore, it gave

7 AfDb, 'The Africa Infrastructure Development Index (AIDI, 2013) African Development Bank' www.icafrica.org/fileadmin/documents/Knowledge/AFDB/Economic_Brief_-_The_Africa_Infrastructure_Development_Index_01.pdf accessed 9 November 2021

8 Orla Ryan, 'Chocolate Is a Treat but Leaves a Sour Taste in Cocoa Farmers' Mouths' (Financial Times, December 2020) www.ft.com accessed 25 December 2020

9 Covind Bhutada, 'Cocoa's Bittersweet Supply Chain in One Virtualization' (World Economic Forum, 4 November 2020) www.weforum.org accessed 26 May 2021

10 Quoted in, OXFAM, Unequal Partners: How EU—ACP Economic Partnership Agreements (EPAs) could harm the development prospects of many of the world's poorest countries (September 2006)

11 Cathy Jabara, Michael Ferrantino, Isaac Wohl, et al., 'Sub Saharan Africa: Effects of Infrastructure Condition on export Competitiveness', Third Annual Report, United States International Trade Commission 2009 www.usitc.gov/publications/332/pub4071.pdf accessed 9 November 2021.

12 [1]691 Coulombe (n 2) at 225

13 Budget Statement, Budget Statement and Economic Policy of the Government of Ghana for the 2015 Financial Year, Ministry of Finance, Accra 2014, 10

priority to enlarged infrastructure, mainly in oil and gas, roads, and ports, ostensibly to encourage economic development.[14] This acknowledgment led the government to set up the Ghana Infrastructure Fund. The policies adopted by Ghana for economic development, according to Oxfam,[15] reflect the same level of consistency.

The rest of the chapter explores the justification for the signing of the legal instrument and voice of the opposition. The following sections dissect some of the terms of the agreements, signed in accordance with GATT Article XXIV to examine the key provisions on exceptions, meant to ensure Ghana's competitiveness with the EU.

5.2 Ghana-EU Economic Partnership Agreement Conundrum

The main characteristics of the EU-Ghana EPA text include, first, duty- and quota-free access into the EU for all imports originating in Ghana beginning from 1 January 2008. Second, Ghana was granted a transition period until 2010 for rice and 2015 for sugar. Third, Ghana committed to liberalising 80% of imports from the EU within the next 15 years. Fourth, trade defence is provided in the agreement to allow both parties to introduce duties or quotas if imports threaten their economy. It provides for technical barriers to trade (TBT) and sanitary and phytosanitary (SPS) measures and voluntary compliance terms to assist the Ghanaian exporters in complying with the EU requirements.[16] However, Appendix II subparagraph (a) provides that parties shall be responsible for ensuring compliance notwithstanding the lack of capacity on the side of Ghana.[17]

According to the EU, developing economies must participate in the process of globalisation through trade liberalisation.[18] This would enable it to boost trade exchanges, transform into an active player in the worldwide market, and advance its production.[19] To achieve this, it was argued that the economies of West Africa

14 Budget Statement, Budget Statement and Economic Policy of the Government of Ghana for the 2015 Financial Year, Ministry of Finance, Accra 2014, 10

15 Oxfam International, *Ghana Under Interim Economic Partnership Agreement With the European Union: Implications on Socio-Economic Development* (Oxfam Policy Brief, July 2013)

16 Annex D: Appendices to Chapter 3 Concerning Technical Barriers to Trade, and Sanitary and Phytosanitary Measures (Appendix I) of the Stepping Stone Economic Partnership Agreement Between Ghana of the one Part and the European Community and its Member States, of the other part (Brussels, 28 July 2016)

17 Annex D: Appendices to Chapter 3 Concerning Technical Barriers to Trade, and Sanitary and Phytosanitary Measures (Appendix I) of the Stepping Stone Economic Partnership Agreement Between Ghana of the one Part and the European Community and its Member States, of the other part (Brussels, 28 July 2016)

18 Cecilia Malmstrom, 'High Level Roundtable: Putting Partnership Into Practice' (European Commission, Speech at the Borschette Congree Centre, Brussels, 20 October 2017)

19 Interim Economic Partnership Agreement Between Ghana and the European Union-Factsheet- (European Commission, 2017) http://ec.europa.eu/trade/policy/countries-and-regions/regions/west-africa/; 2 Theophilus Acheampng, Michael Omane Achamfuor and Nii Annan Tawiah, 'The Economic Partnership Agreement Between Ghana and European Union: A Development Game Changer?' Ghana Growth and Development Platform Working Paper 2 (29 July 2014)

should not depend on the commodities they export: for instance, oil, cocoa, wood, or bananas, but commence the exportation of finished goods with added value, made locally.[20] According to the EU, the ECOWAS-EU Economic Partnership Agreement is better positioned to address these issues.

Notwithstanding the aforementioned benefits of trade liberalisation, in December 2012, the ACP heads of state and government declared in Sipopo, Equatorial Guinea, that the EPA failed to address the rapid increase of the 'EU regulations and legislation on non-tariff measures.'[21] The former ACP secretary Dr Mohamed Ibn Chambas called for the EU to shift 'their hardline position' in respect of Market Access Regulation 1528/2007.[22] According to Alhaji Muhammad Mumuni, ACP Secretary-General, the 'deadline' set by the EU harms the countries who negotiated the EPA.[23] The Africa Union (AU) trade ministerial meeting of 2011 in Accra argued that non-LDCs are at the same stage of development as LDCs. They also argued that the Everything but Arms (EBA) trade preference scheme should be extended to all the countries in Africa.[24] According to ITUC-Africa, the EPA will worsen the low employment in Africa.[25] An NGO expert, Paul Goodison,[26] stated that the EU approach was a call for unbridled liberalisation in the context of promoting its internal policy. Mandelson confirmed Goodison's argument when he stated, 'if our economic strength is built on trade, then our prosperity is directly linked to the openness of the markets we try to sell to.'[27]

The ratification of the EPA by Ghana generated active debate and controversy. During the negotiation process and the subsequent signing of the agreement, the advocates of the EPA were mainly government agencies such as the Ministry of Trade and Industry (MoTI) and Finance. Others are exporters and investment promotion authorities, various business groups, and industrial labour unions, which

20 Malmstrom (n 18)

21 European Parliament, 'African, Caribbean and Pacific (ACP) Countries Position on Economic Partnership Agreements (EPAs), Directorate-General for External Policies of the Union, Policy Department' Expo/ B/Deve/2012 (April 2014) (Retrieved from ECOWAS Commission, 2020) 15

22 European Parliament, 'African, Caribbean and Pacific (ACP) Countries Position on Economic Partnership Agreements (EPAs), Directorate-General for External Policies of the Union, Policy Department' Expo/ B/Deve/2012 (April 2014) (Retrieved from ECOWAS Commission, 2020) at 16

23 'EU Pressure Botswana to Sign Trade Agreement' (Sunday Standard, 5 May 2013) www.sundaystandard.info/eu-pressures-botswana-to-sign-trade-agreement/ accessed 15 November 2021

24 AU Conference of Ministers of Trade, 7th Ordinary Session, 29 November-3 December 2011, Accra cited in European Parliament, 'African, Caribbean and Pacific (ACP) Countries Position on Economic Partnership Agreements (EPAs), Directorate-General for External Policies of the Union, Policy Department, Expo/ B/Deve/2012 (April 2014) (Retrieved from ECOWAS Commission, 2020)

25 'Africa: Trade Liberalisation a Downturn to Economy' Says Unions, Daily Nations (Kenya), 7 October 2008 http://allfrica.com/stories/200810070814.html cited in European Parliament (n 24)

26 Paul Goodison, 'The Future of Africa's Trade With Europe: New EU's Trade Policy' (2007) Review of African Political Economy vol 34 (111) pp 139–51 at 144

27 Paul Goodison, 'The Future of Africa's Trade With Europe: New EU's Trade Policy' (2007) Review of African Political Economy vol 34 (111) pp 139–51 at 144; EC Staff Working Document, 'Global Europe: Competing in the World Economy: A Contribution to the EU's Growth and Jobs Strategy' Brussels, 4 October 2006, SEC (2006) 1230 https://eur-lex.europa.eu/LexUriServ/LexUriServ.do?uri=COM:2006:0567:FIN:en:PDF 3–5 accessed 24 June 2021

were convinced that Ghana would be harmed economically if the EPA was not signed. A study by MoTI and the World Bank provides very useful insights for this study on the effect of the EPA taken as key documents concerning the assessment of and insight regarding the effect of EPA on Ghana's economy. In the aforementioned study by MacLeod et al.,[28] the authors contend that the economic impact of the EPA will be quite minimal. However, an interviewee stated that it is good that Ghana signed, but he doubts Ghana will benefit because the country does not have what it takes to gain from such a trade agreement with a developed region.[29] A former ECOWAS trade director stated that Ghana was still negotiating with the EU as of 2020—that the level of liberalisation is beyond what the country can cope with, given its stage of development.[30]

The Federation of Associations of Ghanaian Exporters (FAGE), comprising over 2,500 members in the agricultural and manufacturing sectors, extensively advocated for the EPA. Supporters of the EPA pointed out that there are more disadvantages to the Generalised Scheme of Preferences (GSP) than advantages.[31] The tuna, cocoa, and fruit processing industries and yam, shea butter, and fruit (banana and pineapple) sectors would be the worst hit if they were subjected to GSP tariffs in Ghana.[32] The biggest processor, the Pioneer Food Cannery (Thai Union Group), employing about 1,800 employees, explicitly warned that it would withdraw from Ghana if the EPA were not signed. It was also reported that the cocoa sector would have been worse hit, as its primary market is the EU. Another report by the EU development cooperation programme, Trade Related Assistance and Quality Enabling Programme (TRAQUE),[33] asserted that different fruit and fruit processing industries exporting under the GSP tariff would have been forced to reduce exports or close down without an EPA (for instance, Golden Exotics, Volta River Estates, Pioneer Quality Farms). This would have contributed directly or indirectly to job losses.[34]

28 World Bank Group, 'Assessing the Economic Impact of the ECOWAS CET and Economic Partnership Agreement on Ghana', World Bank, Washington, DC https://openknowledge.worldbank.org/handle/10986/23242 License: CC BY 3.0 IGOk, accessed 12 November 2021

29 Interview with Official of ECOWAS (2020)

30 Interview with Former Trade Director, ECOWAS (2020)

31 The EU created the GSP in 1971 to assist developing countries to pay lower tariffs on their goods to the EU. It was revised in 2012 under Regulation (EU) No 978/2012) EUR-Lex https://eur-lex.europa.eu/EN/legal-content/glossary/generalised-system-of-preferences-gsp.html accessed 7 May 2024

32 Eurostat, 'Statistical Database' (2016) http://ec.europa.eu/eurostat; FAGE, 'How Is the Economic Partnership Agreement Benefitting Ghana's Economy' (Brochure published by the Federation of Association of Ghanaian Exporters with the support of the Related Assistance and Quality Enabling Programme, 2016) http://eurboghana.eu/ebo/wp-content/uplo . . . accessed 24 January 2021

33 Eurostat, 'Statistical Database' (2016) http://ec.europa.eu/eurostat; FAGE, 'How Is the Economic Partnership Agreement Benefitting Ghana's Economy' (Brochure published by the Federation of Association of Ghanaian Exporters with the support of the Related Assistance and Quality Enabling Programme, 2016) http://eurboghana.eu/ebo/wp-content/uplo . . . accessed 24 January 2021

34 Eurostat, 'Statistical Database' (2016) http://ec.europa.eu/eurostat; FAGE, 'How Is the Economic Partnership Agreement Benefitting Ghana's Economy' (Brochure published by the Federation of Association of Ghanaian Exporters with the support of the Related Assistance and Quality Enabling Programme, 2016) http://eurboghana.eu/ebo/wp-content/uplo . . . accessed 24 January 2021

Those opposed to the EPA are from academia and national and international NGOs such as the Third World Network (TWN).[35] Others are farmer organisations, local and regional business associations (for instance, the Private Enterprise Foundation and some sections of the Associations of Ghanaian Industries), and labour unions. These groups emphasise the anti-developmental nature of EPAs arising from policy space restrictions due to the inclusion of WTO requirements such as the level of market liberalisation, the MFN clause, the standstill clause, and export taxes. According to Ken Ukaoha, the safeguard measures inserted in the agreement's text were not negotiated by the West Africa region but the EU deemed fit to include it in the agreement.

TWN was the most active of the NGOs opposed to implementing the EPAs in general and in Ghana specifically. In 2013, TWN argued that the price of signing the EPA would amount to disruption in various industries.[36] Another challenge would be the cost of crowding out or hindering future development of domestically oriented businesses as in the case of the EPA (e.g., businesses in the plywood, veneer, and pharmaceutical sectors) on the one hand, or of regionally oriented businesses in the case of ECOWAS-EPA (e.g., businesses producing pharmaceutical, wood, wire, weavers, plastic, pasta, and other products) on the other. The loss of tariff revenue would be three to seven times larger than the total GSP tariff reduction on the export side during that time. On these grounds, they argued that it would be in the best interest of Ghana not to sign the EPA. However, in 2021 Bilal expressed the view that the EPAs may not be perfect but they have paved the way for Cameroon, Côte d'Ivoire, and Ghana's products to access the EU's market and that the negative prediction during the negotiation phase has been proven wrong.[37]

Furthermore, others argued that imports subject to liberalisation from the EU are essential goods that are not manufactured domestically and include materials used by local industries such as agricultural inputs, equipment, and machinery.[38]Also, the EU gave assurance that eliminating duties would be done gradually and systematically over many years to ensure that the inceptive revenue loss was retained at a lower level to reduce its impact over several years.[39] However, Borrmann and Busse argued that the EU failed to address how a significant institution can be put in place for Ghana to gain from the EPA.[40]

35 Third World Network, 'Ghana Should Not Sign the Interim Economic Partnership Agreement, Summary of Briefing to Ministerial Advisory Board of the Ministry of Trade and Industry, 16 October 2013

36 FAGE (n 32)

37 San Bilal, 'EU-Africa Trade Relations and the EPA Process: Ratification and Sustainable Development Perspective for Cameroon, Côte d'Ivoire and Ghana' Discussion Paper No. 304 ECDPM September 2021 https://ecdpm.org/work/eu-africa-trade-relations-and-the-epa-process-ratification-and-sustainable-development-perspectives-for-cameroon-cote-divoire-an accessed 5 May 2024

38 Acheampng and others (n 19) at 3

39 Mareike Meyn, *Economic Partnership Agreements: A 'Historic Step' Towards a 'Partnership of Equals?* (Overseas Development Institute, 2008) 10

40 Axel Borrman and Matthias Busse, 'The Institutional Challenge of the ACP/EU Economic Partnership Agreements' HWWI Research Paper www.hwwi.org/uploads/tx_wilpubdb/HWWI_Research_Paper_2-3.pdf

5.3 EU-Ghana Economic Partnership Agreement Key Provisions

On 28 November 2019, a Joint Communique was made between Ghana and the EU in the Charlemagne Building in Brussels. At the ceremonial opening, the Hon. Alan Kyerematen, Ghana's Minister of Trade and Industry, emphasised that Ghana and the EU were signing 'into a new phase of their partnership, with the start of liberalisation under the EPA in Ghana.' Deputy Director-General of Trade at the European Commission Helena Konig[41] expressed satisfaction that the EPA's implementation was now picking up steam and that parties were making good progress. However, this 'new phase of partnership' has been questioned and doubted by stakeholders, civil society, and NGOs. Oxfam[42] observed, 'European's mercantilist interests have taken precedence over the ACP's development and regional interest.' Whiteman pointed out that the term 'treaty between equal partners' is nothing but 'hypocritical for comfort'[43] as the partnership steadily deepens asymmetry.[44] Commenting on the deepening of asymmetry, Hurst asserts, 'the history of Lomé Convention and beyond reflects the increasing dominance of neoliberal ideas in the relationship.'[45] On their part, the ACP countries were hopeful of receiving substantial expansion in their economy by exporting duty-free to the EU markets. The specific provisions that will pave the way for the aforementioned overarching liberalisation will now be explored.

5.3.1 'Substantially All the Trade'

The preferential arrangement between the EU-ACP countries, including Ghana, has discriminatory effects on other developing countries.[46] According to the EU, compatibility with the WTO rules is fundamental to its trade relationship with the ACP countries going forward.[47] To prevent legal uncertainty and address the concerns enumerated by the EU, Article 17 (5) of the EU-Ghana EPA provides that 'free trade agreement' means substantial liberalisation of trade and eliminates all

41 Commission of The European Communities Brussels 10. 7 2008 COM (2008)) 441 FINAL, 2008/0137 (AVC), Proposal for Decision, accessed 25 January 2020

42 Oxfam International, 'Partnership or Power Play? How Europe Should Bring Development Into Its Trade Deals With African, Caribbean, and Pacific Countries' (Briefing Paper, 21 April 2008) 2

43 Kaye Whiteman, 'Africa, the ACP and Europe: The Lessons of 25 Years' (1998) Development Policy Review vol 16 pp 29–37 at 32

44 Kaye Whiteman, 'Africa, the ACP and Europe: The Lessons of 25 Years' (1998) Development Policy Review vol 16 pp 29–37 at 33

45 Stephen Hurst, 'Cooperation and Coercion? The Cotonou Agreement Between the European Union and the ACP States and the End of Lomé Convention' (2003) Third World Quarterly vol 25 (1) pp 161–76 at 162

46 Lonel Zamfir, 'An Overview of the EU-ACP Countries' Economic Partnership Agreements: Building a New Trade Relationship' (European Parliamentary Research Service, July 2018) www.europarl.europa.eu 5 accessed 25 February 2020

47 Lonel Zamfir, 'An Overview of the EU-ACP Countries' Economic Partnership Agreements: Building a New Trade Relationship' (European Parliamentary Research Service, July 2018) www.europarl.europa.eu 5 accessed 25 February 2020

forms of restriction. This could be at the entry into force of the agreement or based on a reasonable time frame. Regarding the 'reasonable length of time' when liberalisation should commence, the EU posited that, while the tariff on 'the bulk' of liberalised goods should come to zero within ten years, 'exceptional cases' require some level of flexibility in the EPAs, particularly for smaller countries.[48] At the start of the negotiations of the EPA, ACP countries, including Ghana, advocated for flexibility on tariff liberalisation and interpretation of the text of GATT Article XXIV.[49]

Babula and Baltzer[50] admitted that the general approval of 'nation-specific gains' ascribed to EPA should be taken with caution. The authors maintained that EPAs with the sub-Saharan African and ACP countries might significantly reduce regional government revenue.[51] However, there is a qualification to these revenue loss issues as Hinkle et al. (2006) argued that the revenue loss might be exaggerated for some reasons. First, tariff exemptions among the Sub-Saharan Africa (SSA) could alleviate the impact of revenue loss. Second, the SSA has the allowance to exempt those imports that increase tariff revenue from the EPA. Third, some ACP groups could reduce revenue loss by imposing value-added tax (VAT). Fourth, some SSA ACP groups are given 15 to 20 years to implement their obligations under the EPAs. Nevertheless, Onguglo and Ito noted that it is not often easy to increase VAT and collect inland revenue due to a lack of infrastructure to access the collection of revenues. Also, Ghana does not have competitive industries that will match the EU.[52]

It is a strenuous task to evaluate whether one FTA is more or less beneficial than another due to the dissimilarities in coverage of goods, services, and 'Singapore issues,' sectors that are not included, and a reasonable length of time. However, 80% liberalisation of the ACP countries' trade within a time frame of 15 years is more or less beneficial than the implied definition of substantially all the trade and reasonable period as shown in the following bilateral arrangement.

48 Lonel Zamfir, 'An Overview of the EU-ACP Countries' Economic Partnership Agreements: Building a New Trade Relationship' (European Parliamentary Research Service, July 2018) www.europarl.europa.eu 5 accessed 25 February 2020

49 Interview with Ken Ukaoha Director, NANTS official (2020)

50 Ronald A Babula and Kenneth Baltzer, 'Overview of Quantitative Analyses of Economic Partnership Agreements: Market and Revenue Effects of Liberalization of ACP Barriers and Enhanced EU Market Access' (Institute of Food and Resource Economics, 2007) 38–9 www.researchgate.net/publication/24255887_Overview_0f_Quantitative_analyzes_of_Economic_Part_nership_Agreements_Market_And_Revenue_Effects_of_Liberalization_of_ACP_Barriers_and_Ehanced_EU_Market_Access accessed 18 February 2020

51 Ronald A Babula and Kenneth Baltzer, 'Overview of Quantitative Analyses of Economic Partnership Agreements: Market and Revenue Effects of Liberalization of ACP Barriers and Enhanced EU Market Access' (Institute of Food and Resource Economics, 2007) 38–9 www.researchgate.net/publication/24255887_Overview_0f_Quantitative_analyzes_of_Economic_Part_nership_Agreements_Market_And_Revenue_Effects_of_Liberalization_of_ACP_Barriers_and_Ehanced_EU_Market_Access accessed 18 February 2020

52 Bonapas Onguglo and Taisuke Ito, 'In Defence of the ACP Submission on Special and Differential Treatment in GATT Article XXIV' Discussion Paper No. 67 (ECDPM October 2005)

Thailand-Australia had 20 years, Thailand-New Zealand 20 years, US-Australia 18, Canada-Chile 18, Korea-Chile 16, Canada-Costa Rica 15, EU-Morocco 12, EU-South Africa 12, US-Bahrain 10, US-Singapore 10, and US-Morocco 9. The US-Morocco is the shortest time in North-South FTAs.[53] However, product coverage is minimal; it was not a deep commitment to liberalisation as provided by Article XXIV. This means exclusionary rule barring certain goods is a significant factor in determining the scope of liberalisation. With the exclusion of the United States, bilateral agreements with Mexico and Chile and all other bilateral arrangements entered into by the United States failed to meet full liberalisation for the parties involved. Some goods were excluded or gradually eliminated over more than 20 years in most of the agreements.[54]

Although the United States FTAs try to comply with substantially all the trade, according to Obote Ochieng, it consistently ensures it excludes agriculture entirely from the coverage. For example, the USA-Canada FTA, named the North American Free Trade Agreement (NAFTA), would ensure a prolonged period before it phases out sensitive agricultural products, such as the USA-Australia FTA. This practice, according to the author, undermines substantially all the trade as provided in Article XXIV GATT. The EU, on the other hand, would exclude specific products instead of a whole sector. In its FTAs, such as the Trade Development and Cooperation Agreement (TDCA), EU-Chile, EU-Czech Republic, EU-Lithuania, and EU-Morocco, the EU committed to tariff reduction and not tariff removal and failed to commit to certain products, such as fish, cheese, and specific wines. These contradictory practices subvert the provision of Article XXIV. According to the evaluation of the interpretation of Article XXIV by Scollay and Grynberg of 15 FTAs—that is, North-South and North-North, it revealed that there are different interpretations of substantially all the trade and reasonable length of time—compatibility with GATT Article XXIV differs.[55]

Comparative analysis of other FTAs demonstrated that Ghana, like other ACP countries, EPAs seemed to commit to extensive liberalisation, even though it allowed for 15 years transition period. For instance, acknowledging power asymmetry between the European Free Trade Association-Chile, the arrangement permitted unspecified phase-out periods for many products.[56] In the same vein,

53 Gary Clyde Hufbauer and Richard Baldwin, 'The Shape of a Free Trade Agreement Between Switzerland and the United States, Report by the Institute for International Economic (27 September 2005 Washington DC) www.pii.com/publications/papers/hufbauer-Swiss-us-pdf 21 accessed 23 June 2021

54 Gary Clyde Hufbauer and Richard Baldwin, 'The Shape of a Free Trade Agreement Between Switzerland and the United States, Report by the Institute for International Economic (27 September 2005 Washington DC) www.pii.com/publications/papers/hufbauer-Swiss-us-pdf 21 accessed 23 June 2021

55 Robert Scollay and R Grynberg, 'Substantially All Trade: Which Definitions Are Fulfilled in Practice? An Empirical Investigation' A Report for the Commonwealth Secretariat, 15 August 2005' cited in Cosmas Milton Obote Ochieng, 'Legal and Systematic Issues in the Interim Economic Partnership Agreements: Which Way Now?' (Issue Paper No 2 International Centre for Trade and Sustainable Development, 2009) www.ictsd.org 10

56 Gary and Baldwin (n 53)

the United States, apart from FTA with Chile and Mexico, declined to eliminate agricultural barriers. For the US-Canada FTA, specific agricultural products are indefinitely subject to reduced tariff rates. Also, reduced tariffs remain on around 220 lines for dairy products and peanuts in the US-Israel FTA.[57] The next section explores the Economic Partnership Agreement text to show how the provisions may not support Ghana's development and trade interests.

Article 2 (e) of the Ghana-EU EPA provides for compatibility with GATT Article XXIV. Under the GATT/WTO, the provision prescribes that regional trade agreements must remove duties on 'substantially all the trade' within a 'reasonable length of time.' One significant deviation from the Cotonou Agreement in the EPA is the provision for a reciprocal liberalisation obligation. The Understanding on the Interpretation of Article XXIV of GATT 1994 was that a reasonable length of time should not be more than ten years, only in 'exceptional cases,'[58] but the term is not clarified. Therefore, the negotiations of the EPAs were fraught with divergent interpretations of Article XXIV.

The Cotonou Agreement, however, contains direction on how the WTO compatibility can be achieved. For example, Article 37 provides that in the negotiation of the EPA, the peripheral countries should be equipped. Article 37 provides that measures shall be put in place to 'enhance competitiveness.' Article 37 (4) of the Cotonou Agreement provides, 'Negotiations will be as flexible as possible' in determining the length of an adequate transitional period, the final product coverage—considering sensitive sectors—and the level of asymmetry in the tariff dismantling schedule, while complying with the prevailing WTO rules.

5.3.2 Standstill Provision

Article 15 of the Ghana-EU EPA provides:

> notwithstanding Article 23 and 24, no new customs duty on imports shall be introduced on trade between the Parties and those currently applied on trade between the Parties shall not be increased as from the date of entry into force of this Agreement.

The text of the final version of the EPA published on the Council's website does not reflect any significant change from the first version. However, a few changes on the standstill provision include the revision of the Common External Tariff in connection with regional agreements.[59] It states: Paragraph 2 of Article 15 provides, the 'finalisation of the implementation of the Economic Community of West African

57 Gary and Baldwin (n 53) at 2

58 GATT Article XXIV: 5 (C)

59 Sanoussi Bilal and Christopher Stevens, 'The Interim Economic Partnership Agreements Between the EU and African States: Contents, Challenges and Prospects' Overseas Development Institute, ECDPM Policy Management Report, Maastricht: ECDPM www.ecdpm.or/pmr17 126 accessed 01 July 2020

States (ECOWAS) common external tariff, Ghana may revise until December 2011 its basic custom duties applying to goods originating in the European Community.' Article 15 of Ghana-EU EPA means, 'tariffs would therefore be bound at the applied rate,' which is not so under the WTO, where tariff rates are lower in the WTO.[60] However, the main agenda pursued by developed countries during the Doha Round of trade negotiation was to finalise the liberalisation of trade in industrial products, which was termed 'non-agricultural market access' (NAMA). They advocated that all tariffs should eventually be bound.[61] Nonetheless, the proposed NAMA does not align with the historical experience of the developed countries.[62] As documented by scholars such as Bairoch, protectionism was the cornerstone, and free trade was used as an exception to the general rule.[63] In the aftermath of mercantilism that was present and apparent throughout earlier centuries, free trade began to take shape in 1840 but could not take root.[64] In 1870 agriculture and industry were heavily protected by Bismarck, and the French in a similar fashion returned to protectionism.[65] The argument for tariff harmonisation is strikingly different from what industrialised countries practised during the colonial era. Notwithstanding the want of trade policy freedom from external control in various colonies, the gunboat diplomacy forced the natives to sign free trade agreements with the core countries even when protectionism was the norm.[66] Thus it may be far from the truth if one is to argue that the standstill provision in EU-Ghana is a depiction of what Chang referred to as kicking away the ladder after the core countries achieved industrialisation.[67]

All the EPAs across ACP countries have standstill obligations, but the clauses are not the same. For example, in the Caribbean Forum (CARIFORUM),[68] SADC,[69]

60 Cosmas Milton Obote Ochieng, 'Legal and Systemic Issues in the Interim Economic Partnership Agreements: Which Way Now?' Issue Paper No 2 (International Centre for Trade and Sustainable Development, 2009) 16

61 Yilmaz Akyuz, 'WTO Negotiations on Industrial Tariffs: What Is at Stake for Developing Countries?' (2005) Economic and Political Weekly vol 40 (46) pp 4827–36

62 Yilmaz Akyuz, 'WTO Negotiations on Industrial Tariffs: What Is at Stake for Developing Countries?' (2005) Economic and Political Weekly vol 40 (46) pp 4827–36 at 4828

63 Paul Bairoch, *Economics and World History: Myths and Paradoxes* (The University of Chicago Press, 1993) 16–7

64 Ha-Joon Chang, *Kicking Away the Ladder: Development Strategy in Historical Perspective* (Anthem Press, 2002); Kevin H O'Rourke, 'Tariffs and Growth in the Late 19 Century' (2000) Economic Journal vol 10 (4) pp 456–83; Kevin O'Rourke and Jeffrey G Williamson, *Globalisation and Economic History: The Evolution of Nineteenth Century Atlantic Economy* (The MIT Press, 2002) 95

65 Kevin O'Rourke and Jeffrey G Williamson, *Globalisation and Economic History: The Evolution of Nineteenth Century Atlantic Economy* (The MIT Press, 2002) 95

66 Michael A Clemens and Jeffrey G Williamson, 'A Tariff-Growth Paradox? Protection's Impact the World Around 1875–1997' (NBER Working Paper, 8459 2001) 7

67 Chang (n 64)

68 Article 16 and Annex III OF CARIFORUM-EU EPA; 'The Signatory CARIFORUM States shall not be required to begin a phased elimination of the customs duties other than those listed in Annex III.' See, the Schedule of tariff liberalization of the CARIFORUM States Appendix I Annex III

69 Economic Partnership Agreement between the European Union and its Member States, of the one part, and the SADC EPA States, of the other (hereinafter SADC-EU EPA) Article 23 (2016) *Official Journal of the European Union* L 250/3 https://trade.ec.europa.eu/doclib/docs/2015/october/tradoc_153915.pdf accessed 23 June 2021

and Pacific EPA,[70] standstill provisions specifically apply to products listed to be subjected to the liberalisation scheme. However, the standstill provision in other regions such as the East African Community (EAC),[71] ESA,[72] and Ghana[73] covers the omitted products from liberalisation. Article 16 made it clear that new custom duty on exports or charges shall not be introduced on trade between the EU and Ghana and the charges that are currently applied shall not be increased whatsoever. However, the exception provided therein states that the Ghanaian party may be permitted if it shows a particular need in terms of revenue and protection of the infant industry; in those instances, interim customs duties on export could be introduced. As with core countries' exceptions, whether it creates stupefaction rather than clarity, which may amount to a particular need in a poor peripheral country like Ghana, the Agreement did not elaborate; this is a usual way for the core to embed an idea to gain acceptance. For instance, during the controversial debate about reciprocity in the now comatose Doha Round, the Doha Ministerial Declaration and Annex B of the July Package acknowledged that in negotiations on NAMA, particular needs and interests of developing countries would be taken into account as provided in Article XXVIII bis of GATT, with the specific mention of 'less than full reciprocity in reduction commitments' by developing countries. SDT has become a product of complexity not only in the multilateral trading system but also at the bilateral level.[74]

However, the rationalisation by Bilal and Stevens is that perhaps the EU included the standstill provision since the primary purpose of EPAs is trade liberalisation. In order to allow for flexibility for the tariff to be increased after signing the agreement, it would defeat the whole essence of the EPAs. Also, EU exporters would not want tariffs to be increased during the transition phase. Nevertheless, Goodison[75] believes that strictly enforcing a tariff bound immediately upon entering into force of the EPA may bring about the freezing of meagre import duties. With the provision of the WTO on compatibility, Bartels observed that the lowest level of

70 Interim Partnership Agreement between the European Community, of the part, and the Pacific States, of the other part (hereinafter Pacific-EU interim EPA) Article 14 (2009) Official Journal of the European Union https://eur-lex.europa.eu/legal-content/EN/TXTT/PDF/?u . . . accessed 23 June 2021

71 Economic Partnership Agreement between the East African Community Partners States, of the one part, and the European Union and its members on the other part (hereinafter EAC-EU EPA) Article 13 https://trade.ec.europa.eu/doclib/docs/2015/october/tr . . . accessed 23 June 2021

72 ESA-EU EPA Article 14 (2012) *Official Journal of the European Union* https://eur-lex.europa.eu/legal-content/EN/TXT/PDF/?uri=OJ:L:2012:111:FULL& . . . accessed 23 June 2021

73 Stepping Stone Economic Partnership Agreement between Ghana, of the one part, and the European Community and its Member States, of the other part (hereinafter Ghana-EU EPA) Article 15 (2016) *Official Journal of the European Union* L/287/3

74 Akyus (n 61) at 4834

75 Paul Goodison, 'Remarks at the ACP-EU Joint Parliamentary Assembly Committee on Economic Development' Finance and Trade Meeting Brussels, Belgium, 10 September 2008 cited in Sanoussi Bilal and Christopher Stevens (eds), *The Interim Economic Partnership Agreements Between the EU and African States: Contents, Challenges and Prospects* (Overseas Development Institute, ECDPM Policy Management Report, Maastricht: ECDPM, 2009) www.ecdpm.or/pmr17 accessed 1 July 2020

requirement for free trade in goods is what the WTO law prescribed.[76] It does not extend to liberalisation such as MFN and standstill clauses.[77]

Article 18 of Ghana's EPA provides, 'notwithstanding Articles 23, 24 and 25, all prohibitions or restriction on import or export between Parties, other than customs duties, taxes, fees and other charges provided for under Article 11, whether made effective through quotas, import or export licenses or other measures, shall be eliminated upon the entry into force of this agreement.' Ghana imposes duties and charges on some goods for a good number of reasons. Export taxes and restrictions are imposed in ACP countries on agricultural products, fishery products, mineral and metal products, and leather and skin products,[78] 'while most attention is focused on export duties, the restriction can also include export license and quotas.' The WTO does not proscribe the use of export taxes, but Article XI:1 of GATT provides a general ban on the usage of other types of export restrictions. The EU argued in the circumstances of the EPA that removing export taxes and restrictions is essential to meeting the criteria laid down in Article XXIV of GATT, which is the elimination of 'substantially all the trade' together with export and import measures.[79] Another key provision of concern to West Africa was the inclusion of national treatment, estopping Ghana from favouring itself more than the EU, in other words, Ghana shall not discriminate against the products of the EU, in like manner, the EU.

5.3.3 ***Provision of National Treatment in the EPA***

National treatment is one of the pillars of WTO laws, and it is provided for in the three main WTO agreements: General Agreement on Tariff and Trade (GATT),[80] Article 2.1 of the Technical Barrier to Trade addresses national treatment,[81] General Agreement on Trade in Services (GATS),[82] and Trade-Related Aspect of Intellectual Property Rights (TRIPS).[83] The Ghana EPA provision on national treatment is

76 Lorand Bartels, 'The Legal Status of the Initialled EPA' (ICTSD 1 April 2008) Trade Negotiation Insights vol 7 (3) www.ictsd.org accessed 25 February 2020; Sanoussi Bilal and Christopher Stevens, 'The Interim Economic Partnership Agreements Between the EU and African States: Contents, Challenges and Prospects' (Overseas Development Institute, ECDPM Policy Management Report, Maastricht: ECDPM (2009) 67 www.ecdpm.org accessed 1 July 2020

77 Melissa Julain, 'ACP-EU Council Discusses EPAs' (2011) Trade Negotiations Insights vol 10 (5) www.ictsd.org Accessed 25 February 2020

78 Roberta Piermartini, 'The Role of Export Taxes in the Field of Primary Commodities' (World Trade Publication Geneva, 2004) www.wto.org/english/res_e/booksp_e/discussion_papers4_e.pdf 14 accessed 23 June 2021

79 Sanoussi Bilal and Isabelle Ramdoo, 'Options to Address Contentious Issue in EPA Negotiations: A Question of Political Will' European Centre for Development Policy Management' (ECDPN 20 November 2010) 4 https://ecdpm.org/wp-content/uploa . . . accessed 4 November 2021

80 GATT Article III: 2

81 European Communities—Measure Prohibiting the Importation and Marketing of Seal Product, WT/DS400/AB/R paras.5. 118, 5.122

82 Article XVII General Agreement on Trade in Services (GATS) https://library.arcticportal.org/1587/1/gats.pdf accessed 6 May 2024

83 Agreement on Trade Related Aspect of Intellectual Property Rights (TRIPS) Article 3 www.wipo.int/wipolex/en/text/305736 accessed 6 May 2024

framed in the exact specification as GATT Article III.[84] As provided in both GATT and EPA, the national treatment principle stipulates that parties should provide the same treatment foreign goods that they provide to national products.[85] In other words, locally produced and foreign goods should compete at the same level once the goods have crossed the border.[86] This provision should be of no consequence to ACP members who are contracting parties to the WTO because they are conversant with implementing Article III of GATT. As provided in GATT, the national principle does not apply to government procurement, as the government can purchase locally made products on a preferential basis.[87]

Similar to the provision of CARIFORUM, Eastern and Southern Africa (ESA), East African Community (EAC), and Central Africa Economic and Monetary Community (CEMAC), the Ghana EPA provides in Article 19 (5), 'the provision of this article shall not apply to laws, regulations, procedures or practices governing public procurement.' A technical meeting on the EPA between the ACP-EU urged the EU to explicitly mention the national treatment in GATT to remove any ambiguity regarding the scope of the EPA. However, this went unheeded.[88]

Another point of disagreement is the provision that deals with subsidies. Article 19 (4) of the Ghana EPA states:

> the provisions of Article 19 shall prevent the payment of subsidies exclusively to national producers, including payments to national producers derived from proceeds of internal taxes or charges applied consistently with the provisions of this Article, and subsidies effected through governmental purchases of national products or for their benefit.

The ambiguity is that it is not clear whether Ghana can continue and introduce new subsidies. The WTO acknowledged the significance of subsidies as a policy tool. For instance, Bilal and Lui observed that the ACP countries are not bound to reduce tariffs or subsidies under the WTO law.[89] However, there are limits to how it can be used to avoid distortions to world trade. The provision of laws dealing with trade in goods can be found in the Agreement on Subsidies and Countervailing Measures (ASCM) and the Agreement on Agriculture (AoA). Domestic producers can be paid subsidies as long as they do not violate the ASCM and AoA. Based on Ghana's EPA provision, there is no clarity as to what subsidies entail. Under the WTO, developing countries who need to promote the industry by providing subsidies can

84 GATT Article III: National Treatment on Internal Taxation and Regulation of General Agreement on Tariff and Trade 1947
85 Article 19 (1) (2) (3) Ghana-EU EPA
86 Imported goods all not directly or indirectly be subject to internal taxes.' 'Parties shall not otherwise apply internal taxes or other internal charges so as to afford protection to national treatment'
87 GATT/WTO Article III 8 (a)
88 Commonwealth and ACP Secretariat in April 2008 (Commonwealth Secretariat, 2008)
89 Sanoussi Bilal and Dan Lui, 'Contentious Issues in the Interim EPAs Potential Flexibility in the Negotiations' Discussion Paper No. 89 European Centre for Development Policy Management Brussels Belgium (2009) 3

refer to Article XVIII: c to give other WTO members notice to start a consultation. Following that, the developing country is allowed to deviate from the GATT provision to take specific measures subject to some restrictions.

5.3.4 Bilateral Safeguard Measure and Infant Industry in the Ghana-EU EPA

Agreements on Safeguards are originally rules set forth that take measures pursuant to Article XIX of the GATT 1994. They are interpreted as emergency action when there is an import surge, which threatens injury to domestic products or industry.[90] Article 24 of the Ghana-EU EPA provides a multilateral safeguard measure in the EPA, while Article 25 makes provisions for bilateral EPA safeguards. Article 24 of the EPA protects the right of the EU and Ghana to invoke multilateral safeguard measures in line with Article XIX of GATT 1994, the WTO Agreement on Safeguards, and Article 5 of the WTO Agreement on Agriculture. The agreement further stated that notwithstanding paragraph 1, 'the EC Party shall' in the interest of, and due to the low level of development, 'exclude imports from Ghana on any measures taken pursuant to Article XIX of the GATT 1994, the WTO Agreement on Safeguards and Article 5 of the WTO Agreement on Agriculture.' The paragraph was meant to apply for five years and then be reviewed for developmental needs.[91]

In contradistinction, Article 25, which deals with bilateral safeguard measures, stipulates the framework in which the EU and Ghana may hold its tariff liberalisation obligation in abeyance in some situations.[92] The Ghana-EU EPA provides for the procedure to be followed. Paragraph 5 (a) states, the 'Ghanaian Party may take surveillance on safeguard measures limited to its territory following the procedure laid down in paragraphs 6 and 9.' The length of time that the safeguard measure will last is also provided.[93] Even though both parties must comply equally, any of the parties can take a unilateral step as provided in Article 25 (8).[94] Safeguards may be applied for a more extended period for Ghana, which is twice as long as for the EU.[95] However, the EU's outermost regions are treated the same as the Ghanaians, except that the period for Ghana is 200 days and 180 days for the EU.[96] It is observed that the difference is not much, given the different levels of development between the parties.

The level of protection given to nascent industries has been a subject of debate. In the EU-Ghana EPA, some provisions specifically protect infant industries,

90 GATT 1994 Article XIX: 2

91 Ghana-EU EPA Article 24 (3)

92 Ghana-EU EPA Article 24 Para (6) (b) 'Safeguard measures shall apply for a period not exceeding two years. If the circumstances warranting imposition of safeguard measures continue to exist, such measures may be extended for a further period of no more than two years . . .'

93 Ghana-EU EPA Article 25 (6) (a)

94 Ghana-EU EPA Article 25 (8) 'Where exceptional circumstances require immediate action, the importing Party concerned, whether the EC Party or the Ghanaian Party as the case may be, may take the measures provided for in paras 3, 4, 5 on a provisional basis without complying with Article 25 (7) (b) and (e)'

95 Ghana-EU EPA Article 25 (6) (b)

96 Ghana-EU EPA Article 25 (8) and (7) (b)

which is more like the traditional safeguard measures. For example, Article 25 (5) (b) provides:

> Ghana may take safeguard measures where a product originating in the EU Party . . . which is likely to cause or threaten to cause injury to infant industry producing products. (b) if the Ghanaian Party can show a specific need for the infant industry, customs duties on export or equivalent charges may be introduced,[97] for mainly raw material and equipment for existing and infant industries, the liberalisation will start on 1st January 2013 to be completed by 31st December 2017.[98]

The EU recognised the need for safeguard measures for Ghana in the EPA to avert any negative impact from the liberalisation of market access. It was argued during the EPA negotiation that the multilateral and bilateral safeguard takes care of a sudden surge in imports that may cause damage to local products.[99]

However, observers have noted some lack of clarification in the safeguards provision.[100] For instance, some terms that need to be adequately understood are not defined, such as 'serious injury.' This phrase originated from the WTO. Article XIX permits member states to suspend their obligations under GATT if there is import surge which threatens to cause serious injury to local producers of competing products so that it become a necessity to prevent the injury.[101] In the GATT/WTO language, the measure under Article XIX is a 'safeguard' step; this action is also known as 'escape clause.' Several countries signatory to the GATT, particularly the United States, EC, Canada, and Australia, have invoked Article XIX to protect industries threatened to be 'injured.'[102] It has been argued that Article XIX was designed mainly to protect the US steel industry.[103] From GATT to present WTO dispensation, it is mainly the developed countries that have invoked the safeguard measures.

These trade remedy tools are put in place by governments for remedial action against imports that could cause substantial injury to local industries. They include anti-dumping and countervailing measures to prevent increased imports of goods due to trade liberalisation. When national regulations are enacted and remedial

97 Ghana-EU EPA Article 16 (c)

98 Annex 2 Ghana-EU EPA

99 Interview with official of MoTI (2020)

100 Bilal and Stevens (n 59)

101 GATT Article XIX (1) (a)

102 Gary Sampson, 'Safeguards', in Michael J Finger and Andrzej Olechowski (eds), *Uruguay Round: A Handbook on the Multilateral Trade Negotiations* (World Bank, 1987) 143, 147

103 President Rejects Import Relief Plan for Steel Industry, Sets New Policy, 1 Intl Trade Rptr (BNA) 296 (1984); U.S. Opens VRA Talks with Foreign Producers; Dispute Erupts over Marketing Requirement, 1 Intl Trade Rptr (BNA) 1340 (1989) cited in Alan O Sykes, 'Protectionism as Safeguard: A Positive Analysis of the GATT Escape Clause With Normative Speculations' (1991) The University of Chicago Law Review vol 58 (1) pp 255–305 at 256; Marco CEJ Bronckers, *Selective Safeguard Measures in Multilateral Trade Relations: Issues of Protectionism in GATT European Community and United States Law* (Kluwer, 1985) 31–50

procedures are put in place, the WTO will need to be notified in accordance with WTO agreements. Several African countries have not notified the WTO of their domestic legislation, regulations, and procedures because most of them do not have the adequate laws and in some they are completely absent. Only South Africa and Egypt notified the WTO in 2010. In 2015, Zambia notified the WTO Committee on Safeguards of its initiation, a safeguard investigation on 'Flat-Rolled Products on Iron, Non-Alloy Steel,[104] Trailer and Semi-Trailers' and it imposed a 'safeguard measure' provisionally, to last for 180 days.[105] The challenges faced by African countries is the adequacy of national law and capacity, which include legal, institutional, human, and financial resources, and Ghana is not excluded from these challenges.

Ghana and ACP countries set off in trepidation as per interpretation of Article XIX of the WTO on safeguards and the strict meaning given to it by the Appellate Body.[106] Similar to other ACP countries, Ghana is anxious that the safeguard as presently structured may be too complicated for Ghana.[107] According to an interviewee, Ghana cannot take advantage of the safeguard measures as provided in the agreement's text. This is similar to how the GATT/WTO is believed to have made adequate balanced provisions in the name of embedded liberalism, but observers argued that it is only to benefit the core, who have the capacity to utilise such exceptions.[108]

5.3.5 The EU-Ghana EPA: Provision of Most Favoured Nation Clause

The most favoured nation is the founding principle of the GATT/WTO. GATT Article 1:1 requires WTO members to grant MFN treatment to like products of other WTO members concerning tariffs, regulations on exports and imports, internal taxes and charges on imported products, and internal regulations. Put another way, if a WTO member gives favourable treatment to one country, the same treatment must be provided to all the members.[109] This WTO principle is also provided in the EU-Ghana EPA. In the EPA, the MFN principle states that if Ghana signs a trade agreement with any 'major trading partner'[110] other than the EU country,

104 WTO, 'Notification Under Article 12.1 (A) of the Agreement on Safeguards on Initiation of an Investigation and the Reasons for it' (G/SG/N/6/ZMB/1 5 October 2015) https://docs.wto.org/dol2fe/Pages/SS/directdoc.aspx?filename=q:/G/SG/N6ZMB1.pdf&Open=True accessed 7 May 2024

105 Paul Kalenga, 'Safeguards and Trade Remedies in African Integration' Trade Law Centre, www.tralac.org accessed 7 May 2024

106 United States-Definitive Safeguard Measures on Imports of Circular Welded Carbon Quality Line Pipe from Korea WT/DS202/AP/R 15 February 2002 para 84

107 Jacques Berthelot, 'The Contradiction of Ghana's Interim EPA' (SOL, 8 October 2016), www.sol-asso.fr accessed 7 August 2020

108 Andrew Lang, 'Reconstructing Embedded Liberalism: John Ruggie and Constructivist Approaches to the Study of the International Trade Regime' (2006) Journal of International Economic Law vol 9 (1) pp 81–116

109 MFN Treatment is provided for in GATT Article 1, III:7, V, and XVIII

110 Ghana-EU EPA Article 17 (3) provides, 'if the Ghanaian Party obtains from a major trading partner a substantially more favourable treatment than the one offered by the EC Party, the Parties will enter into consultations and jointly decide on the implementation of the provisions of paragraph 2.'

'a joint consultation' will be held to decide the implementation method. 'A major trading partner'[111] means any developed country or any country accounting for a share of world merchandise exports above 1%, or a group of countries accounting collectively for a share of world merchandise exports above 1.5% in the year before the entry into force of the free trade agreement referred to in paragraph 2 of Article 17. The articles provide, 'the Ghanaian Party shall accord to the EC Party any favourable treatment applicable due to the Ghanaian Party becoming a party to a free trade agreement with any major trading partner after the signature of this agreement.'

The reverse shall be the case if the EU extends favourable treatment to another party. Bilal[112] argues that the EU could be exempted from this duty because it granted a duty-free quota-free (DFQF) market access to the ACP EPA countries.[113] However, the application of the MFN principle does not cover tariffs alone. It applies to all the chapters where it is found, including Articles 14 on rules of origin, 15 on a standstill, 24 on multilateral safeguards, and 25 on bilateral safeguards.[114] This would also mean that if the EU, for instance, granted less restrictive rules of origin to a non-ACP country, it would have to extend these to the ACP countries, including Ghana.

Even though the WTO does not explicitly require the inclusion of the MFN clause in an FTA, it is not unusual for parties to include it in the text of their agreement. Of the 20 regional trade agreements examined by the Organisation for Economic Co-operation and Development (OECD) in 2008, only five have no provision for an MFN clause.[115] The most prominent agreement with an MFN provision is the North American Free Trade Agreement. Others are the Central American-Dominican Republic Free Trade Agreement, the Japan-Mexico, Thailand-Australia, and USA-Morocco agreements. Nevertheless, Economic Partnership Agreements became the first in which the EU included the MFN clause in its FTAs with developing nations. For example, FTAs between the EU-Chile, EU-Mexico, and EU-South Africa agreements have no such provision.[116]

According to an interviewee, the MFN clause in the EPA is contradictory because the EU emphasises that the EPAs are all about development.[117] The respondent asserts that the clause will impede the economic development of Ghana as it would in the rest of the ACP countries.[118] The proviso is not necessitated under GATT

111 Ghana-EU EPA Article 17 (6)

112 Bilal and Stevens (n 59)

113 Ghana-EU EPA Article 12

114 Cheikh Tidiane Dieye and Victoria Hanson, 'MFN Provision in EPAs: A Threat to South-South Trade?' (March 2008) Negotiation vol 7 (2) ictsd.org accessed 14 February 2020

115 OECD, *International Investment Law: Understanding Concepts and Tracking Innovations* (Paris, 2008)

116 Christopher Stevens, Bilal Sanoussi and others, 'The New EPAs: Comparative Analysis of their Content and Challenges for 2008' Overseas Development Institute and the European Centre for Development Policy Management, London, UK, and Brussels Belgium (2008) www.odi.org/sites/odi.org.uk/files/odi-assets/pu . . . xiv accessed 22 January 2021

117 Interview with NANTS officials (2020)

118 Interview with ECOWAS official (2020)

Article XXIV, from whence the EPAs derive their stance, or the General Agreement on Trade in Services Article V that deals with the agreement on services. The reason is that GATS Article V is not similar to GATT Article XXIV. The MFN provision was not provided for under the Cotonou Partnership Agreement. Despite that, the MFN proviso is contained in all the EPAs' text. Examples include Articles 19, 70, and 79 in the EPA of the Caribbean Forum, a subgroup of the organisation of African, Caribbean, and Pacific States, or CARIFORUM. Other examples are Article 28 in the EU-SADC EPA, Article 15 in the East African Community (EAC) EPA, Article 16 in the Eastern and Southern Africa (ESA) EPA, and Article 17 of the Ghana EPA. All the provisions are similar in every detail.[119]

The EU's justification for the inclusion of the MFN is premised on two grounds: first, to protect EU interests, and second, it claims that the MFN protects the interests of the ACP countries.[120] For the EU interests, the EU contends that the MFN provision protects it against potentially less favourable treatment by ACP countries in future FTAs with third-country partners. According to EU former development commissioner Louis Michel, '[i]t is difficult to say that Europe should let our partner countries treat our economic adversaries better than us. We are generous but not naïve.'[121] Concerning the interests of the ACP countries, the EU argues that the EPA MFN clause would defend the ACP countries from the undue pursuit of interest from advanced developing countries such as Brazil, Russia, India, China, and South Africa (BRICS) block. The point is that the understanding that any favourable treatment they bring to bear upon the ACP countries will immediately be granted to the EU may deter advanced developing countries from taking advantage of the ACP's weak position in negotiations.

According to Obote Ochieng, while the EU's argument is cogent, it is made, to a large extent, to protect the EU's mercantilist's interests.[122] Obote Ochieng is of the view that the argument has three major flaws: first, if the ACP countries viewed the MFN provision as protecting them against an aggressive third party, why were many opposed to it? Second, there is no concrete provision in the EPAs to show that the ACP countries are protected from the economic weight and interests of the EU.[123] Third, the Enabling Clause regulates South-South FTAs; however, in the inclusion of some developing countries in its interpretation of key trading economies, the EPA MFN clause remains problematic 'to the purpose and functions of the Enabling Clause and the smooth functioning of the multilateral WTO system.'[124] The MFN is limited to goods only in most of the EPA's text, except for the CARIFORUM MFN clause which includes services and investment. Another point to explore is the dispute settlement mechanism.

119 Interview with ECOWAS official (2020)

120 Economic Partnership Agreement (EPAs) (European Commission, September 2018) 4 https://trade.ec.europa.eu/doclib/docs/2017/february/tr . . . accessed 21 January 2021

121 'Q&A: We Are Generous but Not Naïve' (Inter Press Service, Brussels, January IPA Interview with Louis Michel, EU Development Commissioner Louis Michel) www.ipsnews.net accessed 22 January 2020

122 Obote Ochieng (N 55) 13

123 Obote Ochieng (N 55) 13

124 Obote Ochieng (N 55) 13

5.3.6 Ghana-EU EPA Dispute Settlement Mechanism[125]

The dispute settlement mechanism is, in many respects, similar in all of the EPAs and the full CARIFORUM EPA.[126] For instance, Title V of the EU-Ghana EPA, Article 55 of the ESA, Article 38 and 39 of the EAC EPA,[127] and Part 111 of the SADC EPA are the same. Generally, the provisions are restrictive alterations of the WTO dispute settlement (DS) provision. The EPA DS mechanism reflects a preference for judicatory intervention instead of diplomacy.[128] The provisions are intended to reduce the difficulty experienced in trying to utilise the WTO DS.[129] Robert Hudec[130] succinctly explains the experience of developing countries, beginning from the era of GATT. According to him, 'the GATT dispute settlement system, at a margin, [is] more responsive to the interests of the strong than the interests of the weak.' He backs this assertion with evidence by pointing out the frequency of discontinuing disputes by developing countries before the panel's decision. This, to Hudec, reveals the extensive barriers developing countries face at the start of any dispute settlement procedure.[131]

Busch and Reinhardt[132] are in accord with Hudec. These scholars have ascertained that WTO severely impacts developing countries' capacity to participate in dispute settlement. Essentially, two key obstacles are faced by developing countries in the WTO DS.[133] First, countries like Ghana are bereft of human and financial

125 Interview with official of MoTI (2020)

126 Mehmet Karli, 'Assessing the Development Friendliness of Dispute Settlement Mechanisms in the Economic Partnership Agreements and an Analytical and Comparative Guide to the Dispute Settlement in the EU's FTAs' Occasional Paper, European Studies Centre, Oxford University, UK (2008) www.papers.ssrn.com 7 accessed 22 January 2021; Sanoussi Bilal and Dan Lui, 'Contentious Issues in the Interim EPAs Potential Flexibility in the Negotiations' Discussion Paper No. 89 European Centre for Development Policy Management Brussels Belgium (2009)

127 East African Community 'Agreement Establishing a Framework for an Economic Partnership Agreement With the East African Community Partner States One Part and the European Community and Its Member States on the Other Part' (EAC Secretariat, Arusha, United Republic of Tanzania)

128 Karli (n 126) at 7–8

129 Alavi Amin, 'African Countries and the WTO's Dispute Settlement Mechanism' (2007) Development Policy Review vol 25 (1) www.peacepalacelibrary.nl/ebooks/files/Alavi_African-Countries.pdf 25–42 accessed 21 January 2021; Bernard M Hoekman and Petros C Mavroidis, 'WTO Dispute Settlement, Transparency and Surveillance' (2000) The World Economy vol 23 (4) pp 527–42 at 527

130 Robert Hudec, 'Enforcing International Trade Law: The Evolution of the Modern GATT Legal System' (Butterworth Legal Publishers, 1993) 353 cited in Cosmas Milton Obote Ochieng, 'Legal and Systemic Issues in the Interim Partnership Agreement' (International Centre for Trade and Sustaining Development Issue Paper No 2 September 2009) 17

131 Robert Hudec, 'Enforcing International Trade Law: The Evolution of the Modern GATT Legal System' (Butterworth Legal Publishers, 1993) 353 cited in Cosmas Milton Obote Ochieng, 'Legal and Systemic Issues in the Interim Partnership Agreement' (International Centre for Trade and Sustaining Development Issue Paper No 2 September 2009) 17

132 Marc L Busch and Erick Reinhardt, 'Testing International Trade Law: Empirical Studies of GATT/WTO Dispute Settlement' Paper presented at the University of Minnesota Law School Conference on the Political Economy of International Trade Law 15–16 September 2000

133 Marc L Busch and Erick Reinhardt, 'Testing International Trade Law: Empirical Studies of GATT/WTO Dispute Settlement' Paper presented at the University of Minnesota Law School Conference on the Political Economy of International Trade Law 15–16 September 2000

resources to productively take part in the judicial procedure of the WTO DS, and second, they depend economically on developed countries. Countries like Ghana cannot thus gain from the WTO DS remedially. Article 19 of the WTO DS system allows for the termination of a breach as a remedy. In other words, the country causing the infringement takes steps to conform to WTO obligations.[134] Retaliatory trade measures such as the suspension of concessions and other legal commitments have been observed for a long time not to be feasible for developing countries.[135] In the Antigua and Barbuda-USA Gambling case, even though the United States lost, it did not promptly enforce the decision within the time frame stipulated. However, due to the economic costs to Antigua and Barbuda, they halted the suspension of concessions to the United States.[136]

Drahos has argued that 'rules and procedure, whether bilateral or multilateral,' do not automatically reduce the power asymmetry between peripheral countries and the core.[137] He states, 'What matters to the preservation or extension of an individual's economic interests ultimately rests on that individual's bargaining power.'[138] As a result of North-South asymmetry, SDT was created favouring developing countries within the WTO Dispute Settlement Understanding (DSU). Within the DSU system, SDTs are, for the most part, procedural; that is to say, developing countries may decide to select a quick procedure or ask for a more extended period or legal assistance from secretariats of the WTO. Various stages of WTO DS have their provisions. Article 4.10 of DSU allows for foreign digital services taxes (DSTs) in the consultations, with attention to be given to the interest of developing countries. Article 12.10 of the DSU permits the Settlement Body (DSB) chairperson to extend the time frame for peripheral countries to prepare for defence. Article 8.10 of the DSU provides for SDT at the panel, permitting the developing country to select or ask for the inclusion of a panellist from a developing country.

The EPA DS framework essentially copied the WTO DSU, but comparatively, the regulations are more restrictive. Most of the EPA DS does not have any special treatment for a developing country, even though it was a development-oriented package.[139] Instead of seven to eight months, the EPA DS reduced the panel to six months for filing submissions. According to Karli, these countries are at their critical stages of development, but their access to legal resources is relatively limited.[140] The short time frame in the EPA DS makes the regulation more restrictive than the

134 Alavi (n 129)
135 Bilal and Lui (n 89)
136 'United States—Measure Affecting the Cross-Borders Supply of Gambling and Betting Services' (WT/DS285/26 25 April 2013) www.wto.org accessed 29 January 2021
137 Peter Drahos, 'The Bilateral Web of Trade Dispute Settlement' Paper Presented to the Conference on WTO Dispute Settlement and Developing Countries, Centre for World Affairs and the Global Economy (University of Wisconsin-Madison, 2005) 14
138 Peter Drahos, 'The Bilateral Web of Trade Dispute Settlement' Paper Presented to the Conference on WTO Dispute Settlement and Developing Countries, Centre for World Affairs and the Global Economy (University of Wisconsin-Madison, 2005) at 14
139 Ghana-EU EPA Title V, ESA-EU Article 55; EAC-EU EPA Article 38, 39, and Part 111 SADC EPA
140 Mehmet Karli (n 126) at 29

WTO DS. The short panel stage in the EPA DS seemed to favour the EU, which has unmatched legal capacity. It has been argued that even if a more extended period is granted in the agreement, it would still not make any difference, given peripheral countries' constraints in financing and human resources.[141]

The Ghana-EU EPA did not altogether ignore Ghana's level of development. For example, Article 52 (2) provides that the 'complaining Party shall endeavour to select measures that least affect the attainment of this Agreement's objectives and shall consider their impact on the economy of the Party complained against.' The provision is soft in the sense that it is based on the thoughtfulness of the complaining party. There are, however, clauses that seem to strengthen this point of SDT by stating, 'under no circumstance will the appropriate measures referred to in the present paragraph affect development assistance in Ghana.' Subparagraph 3 of Article 56 called for 'due restraint in asking for compensation . . . pursuant to paragraph 1 or 2' not to impede development in Ghana. Also, Article 54 (3) of the Ghana-EU EPA allows an arbitration panel to consider 'constraint' that adopting a measure may bring about against the defendant.

5.4 Convergence Between Economic Partnership Agreement and Development

According to Ruggie, once a system is formed, it creates expectations, rules, organisational plans, and financial obligations.[142] Tussie believes that the regime becomes a place where the most powerful dominate to protect its interests eclipsing the peripheral countries.[143] Sometimes, the latter can resist the pressure to articulate its concerns but not to a large extent.[144]

In the negotiation of the EPA, the Economic Community of West African States countries called the EU's attention to the importance of building an agreement focusing on development and poverty reduction. The EU and ECOWAS agreed to draw up an EPA based on reciprocity and make it development oriented to pave the way for the new trade environment.[145] However, an interviewee asserts that the conclusion of EPA demonstrates no convergence in the views among the ECOWAS countries and the EU, and that the EPA will be a tool through which development will be delivered.[146] Several areas of interest to ECOWAS were excluded from

141 Mehmet Karli (n 126)

142 John Ruggie, *Constructing the World Polity* (Routledge, 1998) 56

143 Diana Tussie, 'Developmental Opposition in International Trade Regimes: Regional Groupings, State and Civil Society Coalition' (Working Paper, Rigway Centre for International Security Studies at the University of Pittsburgh, 2015) 1

144 Diana Tussie, 'Developmental Opposition in International Trade Regimes: Regional Groupings, State and Civil Society Coalition' (Working Paper, Rigway Centre for International Security Studies at the University of Pittsburgh, 2015) 1

145 Enda, 'Impact Study of the Economic Partnership Agreement Market Access Offer on West African Countries' (hereinafter Enda Impact Study) Impact Study (n 80) at 8

146 Interview with the official of ECOWAS (2020); Addis Ababa Ministerial Declaration on Economic Partnership Agreement Negotiations, adopted by the Conference of Ministers of the African Union at its third Extraordinary Session (Addis Ababa, 15–16 January 2007, document Ext/Exp/Trade/Decl. (2) III www.uneca.org

the EPA. According to Heron, it is plain that the exclusion of power-moderating institutions reinforced development trade-offs during the negotiation.[147] Langman and Price argued that asymmetrical negotiations were produced due to excessive dependency on the part of the ACP countries.[148] A respondent claims that the EU paid for the ECOWAS negotiators and the venue; to him, it is no surprise that the EU dictated to ECOWAS what should be the subject of negotiation.[149] In its document, however, the EU states that it supports flexibility and the development needs of the ACP countries, ECOWAS inclusive.[150]

However, EPA negotiations are described as 'commercial' trade talks and not portrayed as development negotiations. According to Bengtsson and Elgström,[151] the EU delineated itself during the EPA negotiations as 'a partner for development [and] . . . a promoter of norms.' The idea of a 'partnership' rather than 'conditionality' became the focal point for the World Bank discourse toward the end of the 1990s when it brought the Comprehensive Development Framework to the fore.[152] Lister considers that descriptions like 'even,' 'uneven,' 'unequal,' and 'asymmetrical' can be added to 'partnership' to show the 'unbalanced nature in practice.'[153] Further, Lister compared the 'partnership' to 'horse and a rider,'[154] rather like the Orwellian 'partnership' style in which the powerful, in this case, the EU, decide on what is best for the party with insufficient capacity (developing countries such as Ghana) and view them fundamentally as 'a historical burden.'[155]

147 Tony Heron, 'Asymmetric Bargaining and Development Trade-offs in Cariforum-European Union Economic Partnership Agreement' (2011) Review of International Political Economy vol 18 (3) pp 328–57 at 334

148 Mark Langman and Sophia Price, 'Extraversion and the West African EPA Development Programme: Realising the Development Dimension of ACP-EU Trade?' (2015) The Journal of Modern African Studies vol 53 (3) pp 263–87 at 278–80

149 Interview with ECOWAS official (2020)

150 Louis Michel, 'European Consensus on Development' December (European Commission, Directorate General for Development, June 2006), para 36 https://ec.europa.eu/international-partner . . . accessed 23 January 2021; Lonel Zamfir, 'An Overview of the EU-ACP Countries' Economic Partnership Agreements: Building a New Trade Relationship' (European Parliament, Briefing, July 2018) www.europarl.europa.eu/thinktank 8 accessed 9 January 2021

151 Rikard Bengtsson and Ole Elgström, 'Conflicting Role Conceptions? The European Union in Global Politics' (2012) Foreign Affairs Analysis vol 8 (1) pp 93–108 at 103

152 Pender John, 'From Structural Adjustment' to Comprehensive Development Framework: Conditionality Transformed?' (2001) Third World Quarterly vol 22 (3) pp 397–411

153 Marjorie Lister, 'European Development Policymaking: Globalisation and the Post-Lomé World' in Andrew Mold (ed), *EU Development Policy in a Changing World: Challenges for the 21st Century* (Amsterdam University Press, 2007) 77

154 Kunibert Raffer, Cotonou: Slowly Undoing Lomé's Concept of Partnership' Development Studies Association Paper (2001) https://pdfs.semanticscholar.org/60c0d/do36ce61be44 . . . 19 accessed 24 January 2021; Majories Lister, 'The European Union's Greene Paper on Relations With the African, Caribbean and Pacific Countries' (1988) Oxford Development Studies vol 26 (3) pp 375–90 at 381

155 Kunibert Raffer, Cotonou: Slowly Undoing Lomé's Concept of Partnership' Development Studies Association Paper (2001) https://pdfs.semanticscholar.org/60c0d/do36ce61be44 . . . 19 accessed 24 January 2021

Central to the EU's depiction of the EPA is its unwavering conviction regarding the gain from trade liberalisation for development.[156] However, according to Patel,[157] removing tariffs would lead to a loss of income for small farmers in West Africa, including Ghana, considering their lack of capacity compared with EU producers. Notably, Patel referred to the European Commission's own sustainability impact assessment (SIA) on an ECOWAS EPA. This projected a substantial sudden import increase of up to 16% for onions, 15% for potatoes, 16% for beef, and 18% for poultry. This displaced local production in the region.[158] He has argued that the current European subsidies for agricultural production under the Common Agricultural Policy (CAP) will end the likelihood of West Africa taking advantage of its comparative advantage in competitive sectors like dairy and millet rice. For example, the EU subsidies for dairy is about US$1 billion and $39.4 billion for millet, which cannot bring about a level playing field for the West African subsistence farmer whose source of income would be exposed to the possibility of losses due to the EPA.[159] A respondent asserted that in Ghana, there is no provision for subsidies to benefit farmers. He maintained that there is no basis for competing with the EU without substantial SDT provisions.[160]

The United Kingdom published its position in 2005 in a paper on making the EPA development oriented.[161] The UK remains resolute that the negotiation of the EPAs between the EU-ACP countries, including Ghana, 'should not be used as a backdoor means to prise open their markets.'[162] The EU described the UK publication as 'a major and unwelcome shift.'[163] The European Commission responded that the UK was undermining its mandate as given by the European Council's Commission.[164] The EU believed that development is an integral part of the EPA; however, the lack of concrete provisions dealing with development cooperation contrary to the overall aims of the EPAs defeat the purpose. It only set ambitious

156 Michel Louis, *Economic Partnership Agreements: Drivers of Development* (European Commission, Brussels, 2008) 16; Lorenz Ulrike, 'Negotiating Regions-Fostering Welfare. The Economic Partnership Agreements as a New Model of Development?' (2011) Journal of International Relations and Development vol 14 (1) pp 142–51

157 Mayur Patel, *Economic Partnership Agreements Between the EU and African Countries: Potential Development Implications for Ghana* (Realising Rights, 2007) 18

158 Mayur Patel, *Economic Partnership Agreements Between the EU and African Countries: Potential Development Implications for Ghana* (Realising Rights, 2007) 20

159 Mayur Patel, *Economic Partnership Agreements Between the EU and African Countries: Potential Development Implications for Ghana* (Realising Rights, 2007)

160 Interview with official of MoTI

161 Economic Partnership Agreements: Making EPAs Work for Development. (DTI and DFID paper, March 2005) cited in Alan Hudson, Case Study: Economic Partnership Agreement https://cdn.odi.org/media/documents/3671.pdf accessed 25 June 2021

162 Larry Elliott, 'EU Move to Block Trade Aid for Poor' (The Guardian, 19 May 2005) www.theguardian.com accessed 24 January 2021

163 Larry Elliott, 'EU Move to Block Trade Aid for Poor' (The Guardian, 19 May 2005) www.theguardian.com accessed 24 January 2021

164 Larry Elliott, 'EU Move to Block Trade Aid for Poor' (The Guardian, 19 May 2005) www.theguardian.com accessed 24 January 2021

terms in the agreement, for example, promote regional integration,[165] encourage sustainable development,[166] and transform the country into an active player in the global economy.[167]

While there are few texts on concrete forms of non-financial cooperation, for instance, exchange of information and expertise,[168] conducive business climate,[169] support for implementation of rules, and improvement of the productive sector;[170] in respect of financial cooperation, the provision only recognised the problem that elimination of customs duties posed to Ghana and called for 'dialogue and cooperation in this field.'[171] This represented the European Commission's position that aid be external to the EPA text; in other words, it is treated separately through the Regional Preparatory Task Force (RPTF), a Regional EPA Fund, Aid for Trade, and the European Development Fund.[172]

5.5 Conclusion

The evidence reviewed indicates that power asymmetry between the EU and Ghana played a significant role in bringing about the signing and subsequent ratification of the EPA. The argument put forward against the inclusion of the MFN and dispute settlement mechanism demonstrates that the instrument is mainly in the interest of the EU. Peripheral countries are hemmed in within the WTO system, and similarly, the EU-Ghana EPA may constrain economic development because Ghana cannot take advantage of these exceptions due to its lack of capacity. The arrangement remains a reflection of the colonial treaties, where the natives had treaties imposed on them, the only difference is that peripheral countries can negotiate with the core, but they do not have substantial influence, only the deepening of power asymmetry even though exceptions are made.

The various exceptions in the EU-Ghana Economic Partnership Agreement should advance the development of Ghana; however, it is demonstrated that Ghana might likely not take advantage of the exceptions due to a lack of capacity. It was in this regard that the majority of the civil society organizations (CSOs) in Ghana were concerned about excessive liberalisation of trade, mounting up to 80%. The EU insisted it was the minimum required by the provisions of GATT Article XXIV.

As shown, both the EU and the United States have allowed latitude for indefinite application of the provision of GATT Article XXIV, particularly, the phrases 'substantially all trade' and 'within a reasonable length of time'. However, no ACP

165 Larry Elliott, 'EU Move to Block Trade Aid for Poor' (The Guardian, 19 May 2005) www.theguardian.com accessed 24 January 2021 at 27
166 Preamble to the EPA between Ghana and the EU
167 Preamble to the EPA between Ghana and the EU
168 Ghana-EU EPA Article 43 (a)
169 Ghana-EU EPA Articles 5
170 Ghana-EU EPA Article 7
171 Ghana-EU EPA Article 8
172 West Africa EPA Negotiations: Preliminary Comments on the EC 'Draft EPA Text for West Africa' South Centre Geneva May 2007 4–5

countries benefitted per se from such asymmetrical provisions. Instead, the EU advocated and obtained a deep liberalisation in the ACP countries. Also, some of the agreement's text was examined, one being Article 2 (e) of the EU-Ghana EPA, which provides for compatibility with the WTO. The conflict of ideas that arose during the negotiation was about the proper interpretation to be given to 'substantially all trade,' where it was insisted that the proper interpretation was Ghana liberalising 80% of its trade. It was agreed in the Cotonou Partnership Agreement that there would be room for flexibility, but eventually, the EU ignored the provision and imposed terms that protect its interests. For instance, there is no permission to increase tariffs upon signing the agreement in the standstill provision, even for products exempted from liberalisation. It is rhetoric without concrete action with respect to development concerns in West Africa that led some to decline to sign the EPAs.

Bibliography

Acheampng T, Achamfuor M O, & Tawiah N, 'A Ghana Growth and Development Platform' Working Paper 2, 29 July 2014

Acheampng T, Omane-Achamfuor M, & Tawiah N A, 'The Economic Partnership Agreement Between Ghana and the European Union: A Development Game Changer?' Ghana Growth and Development Platform, Working Paper 2, 29 July 2014. https://mpra.ub.uni-muenchen.de/66232/1/MPRA_paper_66232.pdf 3 (accessed 24 June 2021)

ActionAid, Ghana Under the Interim Economic Partnership Agreement With the European Union: Implication on Socio-Economic Development (Policy Brief, July 2013)

Addis Ababa Ministerial Declaration on Economic Partnership Agreement Negotiations, Adopted by the Conference of Ministers of the African Union at Its Third Extraordinary Session (Addis Ababa, 15–16 January 2007, Document Ext/Exp/Trade/Decl. (2) III. www.uneca.org

Amin A, 'African Countries and the WTO's Dispute Settlement Mechanism' (2007) Development Policy Review vol 25 (1). www.peacepalacelibrary.nl/ebooks/files/Alavi_African-Countries.pdf 25–42 (accessed 21 January 2021)

Bartels L, 'The Legal Status of the Initialled EPA' (ICTSD, 1 April 2008) Trade Negotiation Insights vol 7 (3). www.ictsd.org (accessed 25 February 2020)

Berthelot J, *The Contradiction of Ghana's Interim EPA* (SOL, 8 October 2016). www.sol-asso.fr (accessed 7 August 2020)

Bilal S, & Lui D, 'Contentious Issues in the Interim EPAs Potential Flexibility in the Negotiations' Discussion Paper No. 89, European Centre for Development Policy Management Brussels, Belgium (2009)

Bilal S, & Ramdoo I, 'Options to Address Contentious Issue in EPA Negotiations: A Question of Political Will' European Centre for Development Policy Management (ECDPN, 20 November 2010) 4. https://ecdpm.org/wp-content/uploa. . . (accessed 4 November 2021)

Chang H J, *Kicking Away the Ladder: Development Strategy in Historical Perspective* (Anthem Press, 2002)

Dieye C T, & Hanson V, 'MFN Provision in EPAs: A Threat to South-South Trade?' (March 2008) Negotiation vol 7 (2). ictsd.org (accessed 14 February 2020)

Drahos P, 'The Bilateral Web of Trade Dispute Settlement' Paper Presented to the Conference on WTO Dispute Settlement and Developing Countries, Centre for World Affairs and the Global Economy, University of Wisconsin-Madison, Wisconsin, WI, USA, 2005

East African Community, 'Agreement Establishing a Framework for an Economic Partnership Agreement With the East African Community Partner States One Part and the

European Community and Its Member States on the Other Part' (EAC Secretariat, Arusha, United Republic of Tanzania)

EC Staff Working Document, 'Global Europe: Competing in the World Economy: A Contribution to the EU'S Growth and Jobs Strategy' Brussels, 4 October 2006, SEC (2006) 1230. https://eur-lex.europa.eu/LexUriServ/LexUriServ.do?uri=COM:2006:0567:FIN:en:PDF 3–5 (accessed 24 June 2021)

Economic Partnership Agreement Between the East African Community Partners States, of the One Part, and the European Union and Its Members on the Other Part (Hereinafter EAC-EU EPA). https://trade.ec.europa.eu/doclib/docs/2015/october/tr. . . (accessed 23 June 2021)

Economic Partnership Agreement Between the European Union and Its Member States, of the One Part, and the SADC EPA States, of the Other (Hereinafter SADC-EU EPA) (2016) Official Journal of the European Union L 250/3. https://trade.ec.europa.eu/doclib/docs/2015/october/tradoc_153915.pdf (accessed 23 June 2021)

'EU Pressure Botswana to Sign Trade Agreement' Sunday Standard, 5 May 2013. www.sundaystandard.info/eu-pressures-botswana-to-sign-trade-agreement/ (accessed 15 November 2021)

Goodison P, 'EU Trade Policy and the Future of Africa's Trade Relationship With the EU' (2007) Review of Africa Political Economy vol 34 (112) pp 247–266

Goodison P, Remarks at the ACP-EU Joint Parliamentary Assembly Committee on Economic Development, Finance and Trade Meeting Brussels, Belgium, 10 September 2008 cited in

Dan Lui and Sanoussi Bilal, 'Contentious Issues in the Interim EPAs: Potential Flexibility in the Negotiations' (2009) ECDPM Discussion Paper No 89

Heron T, 'Asymmetric Bargaining and Development Trade-Offs in Cariforum-European Union Economic Partnership Agreement' (2011) Review of International Political Economy vol 18 (3) pp 328–357

Hinkle L, Hoppe M, & Newfarmer R, 'Beyond Cotonou: Economic Partnership Agreements in Africa' in Richard Newfarmer (ed), *Trade, Doha and Development: A Window into the Issues* (The World Bank, 2006)

Hoekman B, & Mavroidis P, 'WTO Dispute Settlement, Transparency and Surveillance' (2000) The World Economy vol 23 (4) pp 527–542

Hudec R, *Enforcing International Trade Law: The Evolution of the Modern GATT Legal System* (Butterworth Legal Publishers, 1993)

Hufbauer G C, & Baldwin R, 'The Shape of a Free Trade Agreement Between Switzerland and the United States, Report by the Institute for International Economic' (27 September 2005, Washington DC). www.pii.com/publications/papers/hufbauer-Swiss-us-pdf 21 (accessed 23 June 2021)

Hurst S R, 'Cooperation and Coercion? The Cotonou Agreement Between the European Union and the ACP States and the End of Lomé Convention' (2003) Third World Quarterly vol 25 (1) pp 161–176

Hurst S R, 'The EU-SADC Economic Partnership Agreement Negotiations: Locking in the Neoliberal Development Model in Southern Africa' (2012) Third World Quarterly p 499. www.tandfonline.com/loi/ctwq20 (accessed 24 May 2020)

Ismail F, *Reforming the World Trade Organization: Developing Countries in the Doha Round* (Cuts International, 2009)

John P, 'From Structural Adjustment' to Comprehensive Development Framework': Conditionality Transformed?' (2001) Third World Quarterly vol 22 (3) pp 397–411

Julain M, 'ACP-EU Council Discusses EPAs, Trade Negotiations Insights' (15 July 2011) vol 10 (5). www.ictsd.org (accessed 25 February 2020)

Lang A, 'Reconstructing Embedded Liberalism: John Ruggie and Constructivist Approaches to the Study of the International Trade Regime' (2006) Journal of International Law vol 9 (1)

Lister M, 'European Development Policymaking: Globalisation and the Post-Lomé World' in Andrew Mold (ed), *EU Development Policy in a Changing World: Challenges for the 21st Century* (Amsterdam University Press, 2007)

Lister M, 'The European Union's Greene Paper on Relations With the African, Caribbean and Pacific Countries' (1988) Oxford Development Studies vol 26 (3) pp 375–390

Louis M, *Economic Partnership Agreements: Drivers of Development* (European Commission, Brussels, 2008)

Malmstrom C, *High Level Roundtable: Putting Partnership into Practice* (European Commission, Speech at the Borschette Congree Centre, Brussels, 20 October 2017)

Macleod J, Von Uexkull J E, & Shui L, *Assessing the Economic Impact of the ECOWAS CET and Economic Partnership Agreement on Ghana* (World Bank Group, 2015).

Mark L, & Sophia P, 'Extraversion and the West African EPA Development Programme: Realising the Development Dimension of ACP-EU Trade?' (2015) The Journal of Modern African Studies vol 53 (3) pp 263–287

Mehmet K, 'Assessing the Development Friendliness of Dispute Settlement Mechanisms in the Economic Partnership Agreements and an Analytical and Comparative Guide to the Dispute Settlement in the EU's FTAs' Occasional Paper, European Studies Centre, Oxford University, Oxford, UK (2008). www.papers.ssrn.com 7 (accessed 22 January 2021)

Meyn M, *Economic Partnership Agreements: A 'Historic Step' Towards a Partnership of Equals?* (Overseas Development Institute, 2008)

Michel L, *European Consensus on Development* (European Commission, Directorate General for Development, June 2006), para 36. https://ec.europa.eu/international-partner. . . (accessed 23 January 2021)

Ochieng C M O, *Legal and Systemic Issues in the Interim Economic Partnership Agreements: Which Way Now?* Issue Paper No. 2 (International Centre for Trade and Sustainable Development, 2009)

Ochieng C M O, *Legal and Systemic Issues in the Interim Partnership Agreement* Issue Paper No. 2 (International Centre for Trade and Sustaining Development, September 2009) 13

Patel M, *Economic Partnership Agreements Between the EU and African Countries: Potential Development Implications for Ghana* (Realizing Rights, 2007)

Piermartini R, *The Role of Export Taxes in the Field of Primary Commodities* (World Trade Publication, 2004). www.wto.org/english/res_e/booksp_e/discussion_papers4_e.pdf 14 (accessed 23 June 2021)

Richard B, & Elgstrom O, 'Conflicting Role Conceptions? The European Union IN Global Politics' (2012) Foreign Affairs Analysis vol 8 (1) pp 93–108

Ruggie J G, *Constructing the World Polity* (Routledge, 1998)

Stepping Stone Economic Partnership Agreement Between Ghana of the One Part and the European Community and Its Member States, of the Other Part (Brussels, 28 July 2016)

Stepping Stone Economic Partnership Agreement Between Ghana, of the One Part, and the European Community and Its Member States, of the Other Part (2016) Official Journal of the European Union L/287/3

Tussie D, 'Developmental Opposition in International Trade Regimes: Regional Groupings, State and Civil Society Coalition' Working Paper, Rigway Centre for International Security Studies at the University of Pittsburg, 2015

Ulrike L, 'Negotiating Regions-Fostering Welfare. The Economic Partnership Agreements as a New Model of Development?' (2011) Journal of International Relations and Development vol 14 (1) pp 142–151

United States—Measure Affecting the Cross-Borders Supply of Gambling and Betting Services, WT/DS285/26, 25 April 2013. www.wto.org (accessed 29 January 2021)

West Africa EPA Negotiations: Preliminary Comments on the EC 'Draft EPA Text for West Africa' South Centre Geneva May 2007 4–5

Whiteman K, 'Africa, the ACP, and Europe: The Lessons of 25 Years' (1998) Development Policy Review vol 16 pp 29–37

Woolcock S, 'The Scope for Asymmetry in the World Trade Organisation (WTO)' in Sanoussi Bilal, P Lombaerde, & D Tussi (eds), *Asymmetric Trade Negotiations* (Routledge, 2016)
World Bank Group, *Assessing the Economic Impact of the ECOWAS CET and Economic Partnership Agreement on Ghana* (World Bank). https://openknowledge.worldbank.org/handle/10986/23242 License: CC BY 3.0 IGOk (accessed 12 November 2021)
www.hwwi.org/uploads/tx_wilpubdb/HWWI_Research_Paper_2-3.pdf
Zamfir L, *An Overview of the EU-ACP Countries 'Economic Partnership Agreements: Building a New Trade Relationship* (European Parliamentary Research Service, July 2018). www.europarl.europa.eu 5 (accessed 25 February 2020)
Zamfir L, *An Overview of the EU-ACP Countries' Economic Partnership Agreements: Building a New Trade Relationship* (European Parliament, Briefing, July 2018). www.europarl.europa.eu/thinktank 8 (accessed 9 January 2021)

6 Nigeria-EU EPA Impasse and UK-Nigeria Trade Arrangement

6.1 Introduction

Nigeria declined to sign the Economic Partnership Agreement (EPA) despite its close trade relations with the EU and subsequently signed the Enhanced Trade and Investment Partnership with the United Kingdom (UK). Andriamananjara et al. posit that the economic impact of the EPA on Nigeria will be minimal because protected sectors are not part of liberalisation under the EPA arrangement.[1] However, using the World Bank's Tariff Reform Impact Simulation Tool (TRIST), the Bank forecast projected a magnitude of 17.3%–18.7% loss of tariff revenue. According to the Bank, this can only be prevented if a mechanism is put in place to check smuggling activities at the borders.[2] From the standpoint of respondents from the Manufacturer's Association of Nigeria (MAN), it was projected that the structural factors in Nigeria militate against industrialisation, and it is not wise for a country to begin to liberalise its markets up to 80% for EU goods. The respondent further stated that such an agreement would only stifle and impede Nigeria's diversification effort.[3]

In order to evaluate concerns raised by Nigeria during the negotiation of the EPA, a qualitative approach was used. This method offers an effective means to gain insight into the real issues contested by the opponents of the EPA and the current impasse in trade relations between Nigeria and the EU. To explore communicative discourse surrounding the EPA negotiations, the research relied on a series of speeches and articles by commissioners Peter Mandelson and Louis Michel, as well as factsheets on the EPA. The discourse employed by the EU officials during the EPAs negotiation was calculated to promote and win approval for the Commission's policy on trade liberalisation in Africa, Caribbean, and Pacific (ACP) countries under the guise of having no viable alternative. The chapter draws on

1 Soamiely Andriamananjara and Others, 'Assessing the Economic Impact of an Economic Partnership Agreement on Nigeria' www.elibrary.worldbank.org accessed 9 April 2021

2 World Bank, 'ECOWAS Economic Partnership Agreement With the EU and Nigeria Trade and Development' (30 September 2014) 14–5 www.openknowledge.worldbank.org accessed 9 April 2021

3 Interview with Oluwatoyin Durowaiye, Head of Manufacturing Association of Nigeria (hereinafter Oluwatoyin MAN) (2020)

DOI: 10.4324/9781032615059-6

the revisionist writers Wilkinson,[4] Cox,[5] Patterson[6] and Strange[7] for its analytical framework.

In 2018, Muhammadu Buhari, the president of the Federal Republic of Nigeria, explained to the EU ambassador to Nigeria, Ketil Iversen Karlsen, that the country would not sign the EPA. This was during the presentation of his letter of credence.[8] Commenting on his lack of interest to sign, he stated:

> We are not enthusiastic about signing the EPA because of our largely youthful population. We are still struggling to provide jobs for them, and we want our youth to be kept busy. Presently, our industries cannot compete with the more efficient and highly technologically driven industries in Europe. We have to protect our industries and our youths.[9]

This resistance to signing the EPA is not new. In 2016 at the Plenary Assembly of the European Parliament in France, Strasbourg, President Buhari reiterated why Nigeria would not sign the agreement. To the president, the lack of economic symmetry between the two regions (EU and ECOWAS) 'in terms of technology and manufacturing experience, must be considered.'[10] This means the EPA poses a threat to the industrialisation of Nigeria, hampering the creation of millions of jobs for the teeming youth. According to the president, the EU failed to address these concerns during the negotiation of the EPA.[11] The country is willing to sign the agreement if there is a mutuality of benefits.[12] Similarly, the Manufacturing

4 Rorden Wilkinson, *What Is Wrong With the WTO and How to Fix It* (Polity Press, 2014); Rorden Wilkinson, 'Language, Power and Multilateral Trade Negotiations' (2009) Review of International Political Economy vol 16 (4) pp 597–619; Rorden Wilkinson, 'Of Butchery and Bicycles: The WTO and the 'Death' of the Doha Development Agenda' (2012) The Political Quarterly vol 83 (2)

5 Robert W Cox and Gramsci, 'Hegemony and International Relations: An Essay in Method' (1983) Millennium-Journal of International Studies vol 12 (2); Robert W Cox with Michael G Schechter, *The Political Economy of a Plural World: Critical Reflections on Power, Moral, and Civilization* (Routledge, 2002)

6 Gardner Patterson, *Discrimination in International Trade: The Policy Issue 1945–1965* (Princeton University Press, 1966)

7 Susan Strange, 'Protectionism and World Politics' (1985) International Organisation vol 39 (2) pp 233–59

8 Jacques Berthelot, 'The EU Caught in the Trap of Nigeria's Refusal to Sign the West Africa Economic Partnership Agreement and the Continental Free Trade' (9 May 2018) www.eeas.europa/archives/delegations/nigeria/documents/press_corner/news/20160203_statement_by_president_buhari_03-02 CADTM accessed 9 February 2020

9 Press Release, 'Why Nigeria Won't Sign Economic Partnership Agreement With the EU' (Premium Times, 5 April 2018) www.premiumtimesng.com accessed 4 March 2020

10 'Statement by H.E. Muhamadu Buhari, President of the Republic of Nigeria' (Strasbourg, Eastern France, 3rd February 2016) www.eeas.europa/archives/delegations/nigeria/documents/press_corner/news/20160203_statement_by_president_buhari_03-02 accessed 9 February 2020

11 'Statement by H.E. Mohammadu Buhari, President of the Republic of Nigeria' (Strasbourg, Eastern France, 3rd February 2016) www.eeas.europa/archives/delegations/nigeria/documents/press_corner/news/20160203_statement_by_president_buhari_03-02 accessed 9 February 2020

12 'Statement by H.E. Mohammadu Buhari, President of the Republic of Nigeria' (Strasbourg, Eastern France, 3rd February 2016) www.eeas.europa/archives/delegations/nigeria/documents/press_corner/news/20160203_statement_by_president_buhari_03-02 accessed 9 February 2020

Association of Nigeria and the National Association of Nigeria Traders (NANTS) raised concerns over the EPA's negative impact on Nigeria's industrialisation programme.[13] This consternation is further explored later in this chapter.

According to some academic observers, private sector organisations wanted to ensure that the country benefits from the EPA arrangement.[14] As a result, business organisations such as the Lagos Chamber of Commerce and Industry; National Association of Chambers of Commerce, Industry, Mines, and Agriculture; Manufacturers Association of Nigeria; and National Association of Nigerian Traders, as well as the academics such as the Trade Policy Research and Training program at the University of Ibadan, opposed the idea of Nigeria signing the EPA.[15] They pointed to the power asymmetry that exists between the EU and Nigeria.[16]

Nevertheless, the EU remains optimistic that if Nigeria agrees to sign, the EPA will, in no small measure, benefit the country.[17] Mr Fillipo Amato, then head of the Trade and Economic Section of the EU Delegation to Nigeria and ECOWAS, advised the Nigerian government to sign the EPA to accelerate the country's industrial development. This was at a Lagos Chamber of Commerce and Industry (LCCI) event in 2017.[18] In response to Mr Fillipo Amato, Nike Akande emphasised that Nigeria would need a formidable infrastructure and vital industries to compete with the EU. She stated that the country could not get a fair deal because it is not competitive.[19] Despite the assurance, Nigeria maintains that it has salient concerns due to its historical and structural factors, according to a senior trade expert from the Federal Ministry of Industry Trade and Investment (FMITI) in Nigeria.[20]

The chapter examines the capacity of Nigeria to trade with the EU reciprocally. It then explores the reasons for Nigeria's refusal to sign the EPA. It discusses Nigeria's draft negotiating text and examines a development-oriented EPA in the context of 'substantially all the trade' (SAT) provision and reasonable length of time and communicative discourse. It then investigates some of the provisions in the Enhanced Trade and Investment Partnership between Nigeria and the UK, and whether there is a future in the steps taken by the parties in recent times.

13 Interview with the officials of NANTS and Oluwatoyin MAN (2020)

14 Franklin Alli and Naomi Uzor, 'EU Threaten to Stop Market Access for Nigerian Products Over EPA' (Vanguard 17 October 2016) www.vanguardngr.com accessed 19 May 2021; EU, 'ECOWAS Urge FG to Sign Economic Partnership Agreement' (Vanguard, 1 August 2017) www.vanguardngr.com accessed 19 May 2021

15 Samuel O Oloruntoba, *Regionalism and Integration in Africa: EU-ACP Economic Partnership Agreements and Euro-Nigeria Relations* (Palgrave Macmillan, 2016) 60

16 Samuel O Oloruntoba, *Regionalism and Integration in Africa: EU-ACP Economic Partnership Agreements and Euro-Nigeria Relations* (Palgrave Macmillan, 2016) 60

17 Peter Mandelson, Putting Development First: EU-ACP Relations, EPAs and the Doha Round (SPECCH/05/4, Georgetown, Guyana, 6 January 2005) 3

18 EU, 'ECOWAS Urge FG to Sign Economic Partnership Agreement' (Vanguard, 1 August 2017) www.vanguardngr.com accessed 19 May 2021

19 EU, 'ECOWAS Urge FG to Sign Economic Partnership Agreement' (Vanguard, 1 August 2017) www.vanguardngr.com accessed 19 May 2021

20 Interview with official of FMITI (2020)

6.2 Capacity of Nigeria to Compete With the EU

Since the Lomé Convention failed to produce its intended result, the EU activated its replacement in its 1996 green paper.[21] However, the curative measure for the failed Lomé Convention has not been without fierce criticism.[22] The Netherlands faulted the solution, stating, 'the economic remedy proposed by the EU was extreme: differentiation based around a commitment to free trade.'[23] In order to make the solution acceptable, the EU employed extensive language discourse to withdraw the legitimate status of the Lomé Convention.[24] Mark Blyth eruditely analyses how economic ideas and interests are used as weapons by agents to bring about changes through 'delegitimising' the current arrangement to replace it with a new institution that suits the agent's interests.[25] The 'delegitimisation' of the Lomé Convention was used to change the previous preferential trade arrangement, and thus, make a case for a reciprocal-based EPA.[26] The extensive delegitimisation and presentation of a different narrative failed to change Nigeria's position.

The question remains as to why Nigeria did not sign the EPA when Côte d'Ivoire and Ghana, who are also members of ECOWAS, signed. An interviewee, Oluwatoyin Durowaiye, the head of the Manufacturers Association of Nigeria, Abuja branch, stated that the new trade relation—EPA—is a continuation of colonial ideology. He stated frankly: the EPA as negotiated is 'a reminder of slavery and colonialism, a master/servant relationship.'[27] Durowaiye went on to expressly state that the EPA arrangement is not tenable. In his view, the 'GDP of the EU is 10 times higher than the combined GDP of West Africa, with a high-capacity economy while ours is a subsistence economy.' According to him, there is no basis to sign such an agreement. The respondents from the Federal Ministry of Industry, Trade and Investment referred to the electrical power supply situation as a classic example of the state of infrastructure in Nigeria. Durowaiye stated that power constitutes 43% of production cost in Nigeria, whereas in China it is 5%, and in Europe it is less than 5%. As such, there is no basis for competition.[28] Another extreme situation cited by the respondent was that of inadequate transportation.

21 European Commission, 'Green Paper on Relations Between the European Union and the ACP Countries on the Eve of the 21st Century: Challenges and Options for New Partnership' (Brussels 20 November 1996 COM (96) 570 Final) https://eu-lex.europa.eu/legal-content/EN/TXT/pdf/?uri=CEL . . . accessed 26 June 2020

22 Stephen R Hurt, 'The EU-SADC Economic Partnership Agreement Negotiations: "Locking in" the Neoliberal Development Model in Southern Africa?' (2012) *Third World Quarterly* vol 33 (3) pp 496

23 Martin Holland, '20/20 Vision? The EU's Cotonou Partnership Agreement' (2003) *The Brown Journal of World Affairs* vol 9 (2) pp 161–75 at 164

24 EU Green Paper (n 21); EU, 'Statement by EU Trade Commissioner Peter Mandelson Joint Parliamentary Assembly Bamako Mali Brochure' (19 April 2005)

25 Mark Blyth, *Great Transformations: Economic Ideas and Institutional Change in the Twentieth Century* (Cambridge University Press, 2002) 37–8

26 EU Green Paper (n 21) at 5–15

27 Oluwatoyin Durowaiye (N 3)

28 Oluwatoyin Durowaiye (N 3)

It is cheaper to move goods from Lagos to the EU than from Lagos to Maiduguri within Nigeria.[29]

However, a former trade director of the ECOWAS refused to subscribe to the views of the civil society, comparing the process of EU-ECOWAS negotiation to slavery and colonialism.[30] According to the ECOWAS former director of trade, ECOWAS, like the EU, negotiated its terms.[31] He remained convinced that the EPA aimed to assist the region's development, hence the special and differential treatment (S&DT) provisions in the agreement's text.[32] The senior ECOWAS trade expert, however, noted that the EU commissioners had access to the ECOWAS heads of state directly to give orders regarding the EPA negotiation, but pointed out that the ECOWAS trade commissioners or member states' ministers could not contact the EU's commissioners directly in the same manner. However, from the respondent's view, Nigeria would not have declined to sign if there was a more respectful and equal relationship between Nigeria and the EU. The Gambia too under Yahya Jammeh refused to sign and was not penalised. However, the interviewee explained the limitations faced by ECOWAS thus:

> At times, the EU had to support us; before we could attend meetings, we had looked for experts in different areas of negotiation. We were seriously limited, adversely affected—either we did not have the experts in the region, then we had to hire somebody from the EU or the USA who may not necessarily be talking strictly in our favour. . . . When we hire a consultant, the EU will give us support to pay the consultant, and the EU even pays for our hotel accommodation.[33]

According to the respondent, this lack of capacity and infrastructure severely impeded the performance of the region. Some academics such as Ascher and Krupp argued that the critical component of an advanced economy is infrastructure.[34] The 2030 Agenda for Sustainable Development brought the importance of infrastructure to the fore. It is argued that market access opportunities for Nigeria have not produced substantial benefits either regionally or outside West Africa. This includes preferences such as under the ECOWAS Trade Liberalisation Scheme (TLS) and preferences offered under the African Growth and Opportunity Act (AGOA). This is partly due to the appalling state of Nigeria's infrastructure, these academics contend. In 2013, Nigeria's Task Force on Trade Facilitation attributed the low performance at the local level to several factors: (a) an overwhelming informal trade

29 Oluwatoyin Durowaiye (N 3) (Maiduguri is located in the northeastern part of Nigeria)

30 Interview with former ECOWAS trade director, Abuja 2020

31 Interview with former ECOWAS trade director, Abuja 2020

32 Interview with former ECOWAS trade director, Abuja 2020

33 Interview with former ECOWAS trade director, Abuja 2020

34 William Ascher and Corrine Krupp, 'Distributional Implications of Alternative Financing of Physical Infrastructure Development' in William Ascher and Corrine Krupp (eds), *Physical Infrastructure Development: Balancing the Growth, Equity and Environment Imperatives* (Palgrave Macmillan, 2010) 32–68

and the smuggling of low-quality goods into Nigeria, a pattern that is detrimental to local manufacturers; (b) a cumbersome port administration with an inefficient, costly, non-transparent and time-consuming import, export and clearance procedure, with several checkpoints; and (c) poor information sharing and ineffective standard setting and certification activities.

While some respondents from Nigeria argued that there is no basis for competition between Nigeria and the EU,[35] other respondents in the ECOWAS Commission believed that the new agreement would boost the country's global trade competitiveness.[36] When asked whether the level of special and differential treatment/asymmetry provided in the agreement's text is sufficient, the ECOWAS respondent's answer was in the affirmative. He stated, 'The EU provides 100 per cent access to West Africa, so it takes care of asymmetry between the EU and Nigeria.'[37] According to the senior trade experts from ECOWAS, the EU had no ulterior motive other than 'following the obligations under the WTO.' When reminded that the United States still offers preference to sub-Saharan Africa under AGOA, he responded, '[the] United States is moving steadily toward reciprocity, already the USA is signing a reciprocal arrangement with some African countries.'[38] When asked about infrastructure and the lack of comprehensive trade policy for Nigeria to engage with a region like the EU, the respondent answered that the country has to put in more work for its benefit, as it cannot expect the EU to solve all its problems.[39] He further stated,

> There is no need to hide behind barriers because it is a global world. If free trade and fair trade is good, then it is good for everybody. Free trade is good for developing countries. It may be challenging in the short term, but in the long run, it is more beneficial.

He counselled countries in West Africa to start building capacity to engage concretely with the rest of the world. The respondent further stated that the money used by the EU to support Africa is from the taxpayers who have their interests as well.[40] This was also the view of the trade experts interviewed from the West Africa Economic and Monetary Union (WAEMU). Besides the aforementioned position, the EU was willing to protect the interests of Nigeria and the ACP countries.

Mandelson re-emphasises to the West African group that the EPA is for its benefit. According to the commissioner, the trade arrangement is solely in the interest of ECOWAS. In his speech in Brussels, he stated:

> What we want in exchange is not commercial. I have no European business leaders knocking at my door demanding greater access to the ACP

35 Interview with official of FMITI (2020)
36 Interview with official of ECOWAS (2020)
37 Interview with official of ECOWAS Commission (2020)
38 Interview with official of ECOWAS Commission (2020)
39 Interview with official of ECOWAS Commission (2020)
40 Interview with official of ECOWAS Commission (2020)

> market—but a commitment to improving the business climate in your countries, for your benefit. And domestic policies on good governance are part of the equation.[41]

On another occasion, Mandelson emphasised the importance of reciprocity in trade agreements, saying that it is far more profitable than preferential access to the EU market. The ACP countries (including Nigeria) believe that the agreement favours the EU.[42] When one of the respondents was asked whether asymmetrical provisions in the EPA text are sufficient to make ECOWAS competitive, he responded that the gap is wide and that 'it is not possible and feasible to compete with the EU.' The respondent further claimed that the agreement is exploitative, as 'it is solely to protect the interest of the EU and tie Nigeria down for years just like colonialism had done.' The respondent noted that ECOWAS and Nigeria cannot take advantage of the exceptions provided in the agreement. The question was, 'In your view, would the pattern of asymmetry further exacerbate and increase the unequal distribution of economic opportunity between the two regions?' Although some of the respondents from the ECOWAS Commission agreed that parties protect their interests in any negotiation, Ukaoha and trade experts from FMITI posited that the EU should have exercised some flexibility, given the vast nature of economic asymmetry between the two regions.

Rather than focus on negotiation, the ACP countries, including ECOWAS, were concerned about the EU relaxing its deadline and requesting the European Commission to remove Market Access Regulation 1528/2007.[43] In a delegate's words at the meeting,

> Instead of emphasis being placed on negotiating on substance . . . ACP countries [are pushed] into meeting their unilateral deadline set by the EU, which results in sub-optimal outcomes of the concerned regions. . . . We are committed to concluding a mutually beneficial agreement with the EU, but we should not be hurried to unduly follow a mutually agreed road map of negotiation.'[44]

It was reported that the Kenyan delegate at the meeting thought that the deadline was not set in 'good faith.' Instead, it put excessive pressure on the ACP countries.[45] Zambian Minister for Trade and Commerce Bob Sichinga stated that it is preferable not to have a deal at all, as the proposed agreement would be bad for the

41 Peter Mandelson, 'The ACP-EU Relationship in the Global Economy' (SPEECH/04/505, ACP-EU Ministerial, Brussels, 1 December 2004) 3

42 Interview with officials of FMITI, MAN and NANTS (2020)

43 ACP, 'ACP Ministers Resist "Unilateral Deadline" to Wrap Up EPAs' (Brussels, 10 December 2011/ ACP Newsdesk) www.acp.int accessed 10 April 2021

44 ACP, 'ACP Ministers Resist "Unilateral Deadline" to Wrap Up EPAs' (Brussels, 10 December 2011/ ACP Newsdesk) www.acp.int accessed 10 April 2021

45 ACP, 'ACP Ministers Resist "Unilateral Deadline" to Wrap Up EPAs' (Brussels, 10 December 2011/ ACP Newsdesk) www.acp.int accessed 10 April 2021

economy.[46] Instead, the EU had spoken clearly through its Executive Vice President and Commissioner for Trade Valdis Dombrovskis, expressing the resolve that every choice to reform around the world must consider 'our strategic interests and values.'[47]

6.2.1 Constructed Narrative in the EPA

Most ACP countries were not convinced by the EU's use of language, what Wilkinson referred to as the 'presentation of metaphor, historical logic as fact and common sense.' According to Blyth, various techniques could be utilised by an agent to protect its interests.[48] Blyth quoted John Maynard Keynes, who explored three techniques agents use to encourage ideas targeted at actors, for example, 'assume that the present is a much more serviceable guide to the future than a candid examination of the past.'[49] In the third hypothesis, Blyth asserts that ideas are weapons agents used to supplant the existing institution, believing that 'economic ideas not only facilitate collective action and radical policy change but are a prerequisite for them.'[50]

Mandelson states, 'My fellow Commissioner, Louis Michel, and I are both committed to working constructively together to reinforce the link between trade and development.'[51] During the speech, he assured the ACP countries that he was not unaware of the complexities of trade liberalisation. Consequently, he stated, market opening must be tailored to country's circumstances. It should be flexible and asymmetric. Mandelson gave his words on the protection of sensitive sectors and adequate time within which to transition.[52] In his speech to the 9th ACP-EU Joint Parliamentary Assembly in Mali, EU former trade commissioner Mandelson argued that EPAs would be 'both trade and development deals.' He emphasised the point that 'Tariff liberalisation on the ACP side will be progressive and we are prepared to take a very pragmatic and flexible approach.' Mandelson distanced himself from the position that the standard of the WTO should apply to the North-South strictly. He further declared, 'I am quite prepared to defend this

46 ACP, 'ACP Ministers Resist "Unilateral Deadline" to Wrap Up EPAs' (Brussels, 10 December 2011/ ACP Newsdesk) www.acp.int accessed 10 April 2021

47 EU, 'The Commission Sets Course for an Open Sustainable and Assertive EU Trade Policy' (18 February 2021) www.trade.ec.europa.eu/doclib/press/index.cfm?id=22438title=Commission-sets-course-for-an-open-sustainbale-and-assertive-EU-trade-strategy accessed 10 April 2021

48 Blyth (n 25) at 42

49 John Maynard Keynes, *The General Theory of Employment, Interest and Money* (Harcourt Brace, 1964) quoted in Blyth (n 25) at 42

50 John Maynard Keynes, *The General Theory of Employment, Interest and Money* (Harcourt Brace, 1964) quoted in Blyth (n 25) at 42

51 Peter Mandelson, 'The ACP-EU Relationship in the Global Economy' (SPEECH/04/505, ACP-EU Ministerial, Brussels, 1 December 2004) 3

52 Peter Mandelson, 'The ACP-EU Relationship in the Global Economy' (SPEECH/04/505, ACP-EU Ministerial, Brussels, 1 December 2004) 3

view should anyone wish me to do so.'[53] The European Parliament acknowledged these concerns when it called on the commissioner of trade to exercise utmost asymmetry and flexibility in the EPA negotiation.[54] It stated that the ACP-EU trade relations should be WTO compliant; however, it should not take pre-eminence over the development concerns of these countries.[55] However, Mandelson later began to employ the Smoot-Hawley metaphor, what Strange referred to as bicycle theory and Wilkinson termed crisis discourse. In his 2006 speech in Brussels, Mandelson began to warn about the danger of protectionism. According to Mandelson, the history of protectionist policies reveals that such policies are a 'dead end.' 'Protectionism deepened the economic recession of the 1930s.' He acknowledged the transitional protection to assist infant industries to grow, but protectionism planned to help established industries adjust is not practical.[56]

Thus, notwithstanding the positive declaration by some EU leaders such as former EU Trade Commissioner Peter Mandelson that the EU objective in the EPAs is to support the principles of cohesive 'partnership,' sustainable development, and making ACP countries viable players in the world economy,[57] many observers were not easily convinced about the feasibility of the EU EPA being a combination of trade and development instruments.[58] However, in his description of the ACP share of the world market, Mandelson stated that its share of the EU market had shrunk dramatically.[59] The broader picture is no better: 'Africa's share of world trade depreciated from 6 per cent in 1980 to 2 per cent in 2002.'[60] With the exclusion of South Africa, sub-Saharan Africa's total GDP is, to a large extent, lower than

53 Peter Mandelson, 'Economic Partnership Agreements: Progressive Trade Policy Into Practice' (Speech/05/241, ACP-EU Joint Parliamentary Assembly, Bamako Mali 19 April 2005)

54 European Parliament Report, 'On the Development Impact of Economic Partnership Agreements (EPAs)' in *Rapporteur: Luisa Morgantini, Committee on Development, Final A6–0053/2006* (Session Document, 2004–2009) para 10

55 European Parliament Report, 'On the Development Impact of Economic Partnership Agreements (EPAs)' in *Rapporteur: Luisa Morgantini, Committee on Development, Final A6–0053/2006* (Session Document, 2004–2009) at para 1

56 Peter Mandelson, 'Sustainable Trade: Observations on Trade and Protectionism' (SPEECH/06/187, Brussels, 21 March 2006) 2

57 Mandelson Peter, 'Statement to the Development Committee of the European Union Parliament' (Brussels, March 2005)

58 ACP Council of Ministers, 'Declaration of the ACP Council of Ministers at Its 86th Session Expressing Serious Concern on the Status of the Negotiations of the Economic Partnership Agreements' (Brussels, December 2007); Paul Goodison, 'EU Trade Policy and the Future of Africa's Trade Relationship With the EU' (2007) Review of African Political Economy vol 34 (112) pp 247–66; Stephen R Hurt, 'Co-operation and Coercion? The Cotonou Agreement Between the European Union and ACP States and the End of Lomé Convention' (2003) Third World Quarterly vol 24 (1) pp 161–76; Actionaid International, 'Trade Trap: Why EU-ACP Economic Partnership Agreements Pose a Threat to Africa's Development' p 29

59 Peter Mandelson, 'Economic Partnership Agreements Progressive Trade Policy Into Practice' (ACP-EU Joint Parliamentary Assembly Bamako Mali 19 April 2005 Speech/05/241) 2

60 Peter Mandelson, 'Economic Partnership Agreements Progressive Trade Policy Into Practice' (ACP-EU Joint Parliamentary Assembly Bamako Mali 19 April 2005 Speech/05/241) 2

that of Taiwan. According to Mandelson, the market share deflated because Africa insulated itself by relying on preferences. He claimed, '[a]rtificially insulat[ing] the ACP economies from the global economy creates dependency and therefore vulnerability.'[61] In other words, the unbridled opening of the market to global competition would solve the economic backwardness in Africa.[62]

While the EU promotes the ideas of free trade and a free market in Africa through its commissioner of trade, it effectively protects its sensitive sectors of the economy.[63] For example, the Common Agricultural Policy (CAP) is funded by the European Commission's Agricultural Guidance and Guarantee Fund (EAGGF).[64] According to Mutasa, the policy amounted to 60% of the EU budget in 1990, 49% in 2003, and 31% in 2010.[65] The subsidies aim to ensure the lowest price to producers, as subsidies are paid for crops planted and incentives granted to farmers in Europe to maximise productivity and efficiently use factors of production such as capital, enterprise, land, and labour.[66]

6.3 Nigeria's Refusal to Sign the EU-West Africa EPA

The EPA negotiations were set in motion in Brussels on 27 September 2002,[67] with only expectations and assurances that it would benefit the West African region.[68] The EPA negotiations were launched on 6 October 2003 and were scheduled to be concluded in 2007[69] as contained in the roadmap.[70] However, this could not be due to the many contentious issues between West African countries and the EU.[71]

61 Peter Mandelson, 'Economic Partnership Agreements Progressive Trade Policy Into Practice' (ACP-EU Joint Parliamentary Assembly Bamako Mali 19 April 2005 Speech/05/241) at 4
62 Peter Mandelson, 'Economic Partnership Agreements Progressive Trade Policy Into Practice' (ACP-EU Joint Parliamentary Assembly Bamako Mali 19 April 2005 Speech/05/241)
63 Charles Mutasa, 'A Critique of the EU's Common Agricultural Policy' in Adekeye Adebajo and Kaye Whiteman (eds), *The EU and Africa: From Eurafrique to Afro-Europa* (C Hurst & Co Publishers Ltd, 2012)
64 Charles Mutasa, 'A Critique of the EU's Common Agricultural Policy' in Adekeye Adebajo and Kaye Whiteman (eds), *The EU and Africa: From Eurafrique to Afro-Europa* (C Hurst & Co Publishers Ltd, 2012)
65 Charles Mutasa, 'A Critique of the EU's Common Agricultural Policy' in Adekeye Adebajo and Kaye Whiteman (eds), *The EU and Africa: From Eurafrique to Afro-Europa* (C Hurst & Co Publishers Ltd, 2012)
66 Charles Mutasa, 'A Critique of the EU's Common Agricultural Policy' in Adekeye Adebajo and Kaye Whiteman (eds), *The EU and Africa: From Eurafrique to Afro-Europa* (C Hurst & Co Publishers Ltd, 2012) at 138
67 Pascal Lamy and Poul Nielson, 'Economic Partnership Agreement: A New Approach in the Relations Between the European Union and the ACP Countries' (European Communities, Belgium, 2002) 1 www.ec.europa.eu accessed 24 November 2020
68 Pascal Lamy and Poul Nielson, 'Economic Partnership Agreement: A New Approach in the Relations Between the European Union and the ACP Countries' (European Communities, Belgium, 2002) 1 www.ec.europa.eu accessed 24 November 2020
69 The Cotonou Agreement Annex 1B (4),
70 'Economic Partnership Agreement' (ECOWAS) www.ecowas.int accessed 25 November 2020
71 European Union, 'EU-ACPs: Opening of Trade Negotiations With West and Central Africa' (IP/03/1334, Brussels, 02 October 2003) www.ec.europa.eu>commissioner>presscorner>detail accessed 24 November 2020

The significant disagreement concerns the extent of the liberalisation of the West African markets for imports from the EU,[72] the transition period, the level of development-oriented EPA and substantial funds to cushion the negative impact of the EPA.[73]

Some EU leaders, Pascal Lamy, Poul Nielson, and Peter Mandelson, assured ACP countries, including Nigeria, that the EU objective with respect to the EPAs was to support the principles of a cohesive partnership, sustainable development, and making ACP countries valuable players in the world economy.[74] However, Nigeria refused to be persuaded because the text did not meet its expectations. Even though the EPA has its legal standing, it is an indispensable part of the Cotonou Agreement.[75] EPAs are, above all, instruments for development.[76] According to the EU, it means two things: first, negotiations and implementation must be flexible to take account of the stage of development as provided in Article 37 (4) of the Cotonou Agreement, and second, economic, social, and environmental constraints to engaging in trade liberalisation must be taken into consideration.[77] Observers contended, however, that the EU would not accommodate Nigeria's need to examine and negotiate the various thorny clauses critically.[78]

Nevertheless, Nigeria carried out an impact analysis centred on generating empirical evidence on the likely impact of the EPA on the Nigerian economy.[79] It sought to establish the implications arising from Nigeria's signing of the EPA, the implications of Nigeria not signing the EPA, and the implications of Nigeria delaying the signing of the EPA.[80] The result of this modelling of the EPA on the country's economy revealed that its participation in the EPA would create significant revenue and economic loss,[81] even though most industrial and agricultural products such as food and beverages, tobacco, textiles, and leather were amongst the exclusion list. According to ENDA Tiers Monde's studies on West Africa, Nigeria's 'economy will pay the highest price for liberalisation of more than 65 per cent to the EU.' Conversely, however, Andriamananjara, Brenton, Von Uexkull, et al. considered that such an impact would be slight.[82]

72 Enda, 'Impact Study of the Economic Partnership Agreement Market Access Offer on West African Countries' (hereinafter Enda Impact Study) (Study Done by the Consortium *Pour La Recherche Economique et Sociale, Friedrich Ebert Stiftung*, July 2011) 1

73 Evita Schmieg, 'EU Economic Partnership Agreements in Sub-Saharan Africa: Avenues of Compromise for Constructive Outcome by September', 2014 *Stiftung Wissenschaft und Politic* (German Institute for International and Security Affairs, 8 May 2014) 4; Cotonou Agreement Article 39 (1) (2) (3)

74 Lamy and Nielson (n 67); Mandelson P., *Statement to the Development Committee of the European Union Parliament* (Brussels, March 2005)

75 Lamy and Nielson (n 67); Mandelson P., *Statement to the Development Committee of the European Union Parliament* (Brussels, March 2005)

76 The Cotonou Agreement Article 36 (2)

77 Lamy and Nielson (n 67)

78 Interview with MAN official (2020)

79 Interview with NANTS officials (2020)

80 Interview with NANTS officials (2020)

81 Interview with NANTS officials (2020)

82 Andriamanjara et al. (n 1)

One of the reasons for Nigeria's EPA negotiators facing significant challenges was concerns raised by Nigeria's public and private sectors that the EU and West African countries were not at the same level of development.[83] According to Wilkinson, negotiations among unequal partners produce an asymmetrical result, accompanied by 'heightened contestation and drama.'[84] A similar argument was made by Friedrich List in his work 'The National System of Political Economy.' According to him, free trade can only flourish among countries with the same level of economic development.[85] It is important to note that Nigeria set in motion a dual programme in 2014, namely, the Nigeria Industrial Revolution Plan and the National Enterprise Development Programme (NIRP), to dramatically change the nation's industrial prospects by expanding and encouraging development.[86] Former Minister of Industry, Trade and Investment Olusegun Aganga believed that the ratification of the EU-ECOWAS EPA would conflict with the aims and objectives of these programs. In the course of the launch of the programmes, President Goodluck Jonathan said, 'NIRP is the flagship industrialisation programme ever embarked upon by this country.' He extolled the programme's ability to 'fast-track industrialisation, accelerate inclusive economic growth, job creation, transform Nigeria's business environment and stop the drain on [the country's] foreign reserves, caused by importing what can [be] produced locally.'[87] At the Ministerial Monitoring Committee (MMC) meeting in February in Dakar, Nigeria's minister of trade and other ministers expressed their discontent with the EPA negotiations' proceedings and asked for a careful review of the repercussions.[88]

At the meeting, Nigeria raised ten concerns at the Council of Ministers held on 26 March 2014 in Yamoussoukro, namely: (a) the need to address the product mix in groups 'C' and 'D' in order not to hurt the economy; (b) provisions for an

83 Interview from MAN; European Commission, Economic Partnership Agreements (EPAs), New ACP-EU Trade Partnerships (July 2010) http://eu.europa.eu/trade/wider-agenda/development/economic-partnerships accessed 29 May 2018; Nigeria's Draft Position on the Economic Partnership Agreement (hereinafter Nigeria's draft Position) (Archival Doc/Nigeria Ministry of Industry, Trade and Investment, 2007); Ramdoo Isabelle and Bilal Sanoussi, 'EPA Negotiations: The Honey Moon is Over' Briefing Note 31 (2011) www.ecdpm.org/publications/ accessed 29 May 2018 at 3

84 Wilkinson 2014 (n 4) at 74

85 Friedrich List, The National System of Political Economy (tr by Sampson S Lloyd) (6 August 1789–30 November 1846) 4

86 'Nigeria Clarifies Reason for not Endorsing EU-ECOWAS EPAs' (15 May 2014) Bridges Africa vol 3 (4) www.ictsd.iisd.org accessed 1 December 2020; Kwasi Kpodo and Matthew Mpoke Bigg, 'African Economies Need Integration: Ghana President' (Reuters 07 April 2014) www.uk.reuters.com>article>Africa-summit-mahama>reut . . . accessed 14 December 2020; Favour Nnabugwu, 'EU/ECOWAS Trade Liberalisation Agreement Not Good for Nigeria' (Vanguard, 1 April 2014) www.vanguardngr.com>news accessed 14 December 2020

87 Matthew Mpoke Bigg, 'African Economies Need Integration: Ghana President' (Reuters 07 April 2014) www.uk.reuters.com>article>Africa-summit-mahama>reut . . . accessed 14 December 2020

88 Matthew Mpoke Bigg, 'African Economies Need Integration: Ghana President' (Reuters 07 April 2014) www.uk.reuters.com>article>Africa-summit-mahama>reut . . . accessed 14 December 2020

industrialisation drive in Nigeria and West Africa generally;[89] (c) the need for the development of a transparent support programme to enhance the competitiveness of products in group 'C' by the EU and ECOWAS Commission and annexed to the EPA agreement; (d) the agreement did not address the issue of the reimbursement of the financial loss for Nigeria and over 50% of the budgets of some least developed countries (LDCs) that rely on custom duties, as well as loss of investments and jobs that will arise from signing the EPA, and lack of clarity on how the fiscal/revenue loss will be recovered; (e) the €6.5 billion for the financing of the EPA Development Programme (EPADP) is unsatisfactory, as its sources, that is, European Development Fund (EDF) or EU member states funding, Aid-for-Trade, etc. all exist without an EPA. Nigeria wants to be assured of additional support funds; (f) the need for an additional safeguard clause/instrument as a declaration would become an integral part of the agreement. The regional supplementary protection measures should be annexed or embedded in the agreement; (g) the need to re-examine the text of the EPA should be guaranteed. For instance, Article 60 deals with transfers based on cooperation instead of legal guarantees to compensate for financial loss and ensure transfers into West African economies. The language used by the EU for the removal of the export subsidy is not binding; (h) a review clause is necessary, allowing for a review of the agreement every five years, using agreed indicators. Furthermore, member states should have the right to withdraw from the commitment if the agreement is disadvantageous to their economy; (i) the EU needs to work out specific modalities with its private sector and relate this to the EPA to locate production plants in West Africa in a joint venture arrangement to take advantage of raw materials for the EU market; and (j) monitoring and evaluation systems and benchmarks should be put in place. It is imperative for Nigeria, the only Generalised Scheme of Preferences (GSP) economy in ECOWAS, to be a member of the EPA monitoring group; and, finally, impact assessment measures for assessing the impact of EPA on member state's growth and industrialisation need to be put in place for the ECOWAS Commission and member states.[90] According to a respondent, the EU declined to consider the concerns raised, as according to them, it was too late to begin to return to these issues.[91]

6.3.1 Debate on Flexibility

During the EU's new trade strategy, EU Commissioner for Trade Mandelson emphasised the importance of special treatment for ACP countries. In his speech at the London School of Economics (LSC) on 9 October 2006, he unequivocally

89 Enda, 'Impact Study of the Economic Partnership Agreement Market Access Offer on West African Countries' (Study done by the Consortium *Pour La Recherche Economique et Sociale, Friedrich Ebert Stiftung*, July 2011) 1–8

90 'Nigeria's Draft Position on the Economic Partnership Agreement' (FMITI Doc, Nigeria); '13th Extraordinary Session of the ECOWAS Council of Ministers' (Yamoussoukro 26th March 2014) http://events.ecowas.int/wp-contentuploads/2014/03/draft . . . accessed 1 December 2020

91 Interviews with FMITI officials, 2020

stated that ACP countries' period for liberalisation would be prolonged and 'tailored to the needs of the countries themselves.'[92] In another address to the Party of European Socialists on 19 October 2006, he repeated that the EU had an obligation to 'build regional markets, build up production capacity and diversify ACP economies,' before their market could be liberalised.[93]

The European General Affairs and External Relations Council (GAERC) meeting in Brussels from 14 to 15 May 2007 declared that the Council had admitted that 'flexibility in favour of ACP states (exclusions of products, long transition periods and safeguard clauses) must be compatible with WTO rules.[94] Not long after this statement, Mandelson made it known that:

> in many areas, we are ready to give serious consideration to transition periods and, in some cases, very long transition periods—up to 25 years—together with substantial financial aid to help these countries implement their commitments so that EPAs genuinely act as a catalyst for policy reform in ACP Countries.[95]

Nevertheless, the EU concluded that the EPAs should ask for a minimum of 80% of liberalisation over a period of 15 years.[96] The UK Commission for Africa, set up in 2005, under the supervision of Prime Minister Tony Blair, proposed 20 years for the liberalisation of some sensitive products.[97] Similarly, the governments of Denmark, Ireland, and the Netherlands wrote to European Trade Commissioner Baroness Ashton, asking for the extensive use of flexibility and asymmetry as allowed under the laws of the WTO to demonstrate the different stages of development needs of ACP countries and various regions.[98] According to Julian,

92 Peter Mandelson, 'Bilateral Agreements in EU Trade Policy' London School of Economics, 9 October 2006 SPEECH 06/574-09/10/2006, https://ec-europa/Commission/presscorner/detail/en/SPEECH_06_574 accessed 14 December 2020

93 Peter Mandelson Commissioner Mandelson to the PSE-organised seminar on EPAs (SPEECH/10/612–19 October 2006), http://europa.eu/rapi/pressReleaseAction.do?reference=SPEECH/06/612&fromant=HTML&aged=0&language=EN&guiLanguage=en cited in Paul Goodison, 'The Future of Africa's Trade With Europe: New EU Trade Policy' (2007) Review of African Political Economy vol 34 (111) pp 143

94 press release, European General Affairs and External Relations Council (GAERC), 14–15 May 2007 www.concilium.europa.eu/ueDocs/cms-Data/dcos/pressData/en/gena/94116.pdf accessed 14 December 2020

95 Peter Mandelson, 'European Parliament Debate on EPAs' (22 May 2007) Strasbourg www.europarl.europa.eu accessed 14 December 2020

96 South Centre, 'EPA Negotiations: State of Play and Strategic Considerations for the Way Forward' (Analytical Note SC/AN/TDP/EPA/13, Geneva, Switzerland, February 2008) www.southcentre.org accessed 18 December 2021

97 Commission for Africa, 'Our Common Interests' (Report of the Commission for Africa 2005) www.bristol.ac.uk/poverty/downloads/keyofficialdocuments/Commission%20for%20Africa%20report.pdf accessed 16 May 2024

98 Letter to Commissioner Ashton by EU member states Denmark, Ireland and the Netherlands, dated 7 November 2007 published on the tralac, www.tralac.org

Baroness Ashton never relented in promising flexibility.[99] However, as negotiations progressed, the notion that the EPA would be flexible enough to accommodate different levels of development in ECOWAS became a mirage, according to a respondent.[100]

According to Goodison, despite several glowing speeches on the importance of flexibility during the EPA negotiations, the underlying intent was that the more extended period was more feasible to be dealt with only with some specific considerations and if the aim of the extensive liberalisation were accepted.[101] Goodison maintained this sent a mixed message to those engaged in the EU negotiations concerning an EPA with African countries:[102]

> flexibilities yes but not too much; longer time-frame, yes, but only in exceptional circumstances for susceptible areas . . . this can only happen if the African countries are willing to be bound by the long-term objective of full liberalisation across a wide range of areas.[103]

With this approach adopted by the EC's EPA negotiators, Goodison believes that the Commission is so focused on Europe's capacity and role to transform the world that it ignores the fundamental reality.[104] This means the EU's posturing is that the starting point for African countries is dissimilar to its gradual historical development.[105]

The method adopted for the negotiations of the EPAs was challenged during a debate in the European Parliament. The majority of the debaters argued in favour of flexibility and taking the development concerns of ACP countries into account. The following recommendations were made by Robert Sturdy (PPE-DE), that the EPA should be 'simplified, liberalised and more flexible rules of origin, full duty-free, quota-free market access for the ACP.' Sturdy supported a practicable safeguard, dispute settlement, and monitoring mechanism. According to him, actors must be

99 M Julian, 'EU Member States and New EC Trade Commissioner Committed to Flexibility in EPA Negotiations' EPA Updates (longer version), 2008/2009 Trade Negotiations Insight cited in Dan Lui and Sanoussi Bilal, 'Contentious Issues in the Interim EPAs: Potential Flexibility in the Negotiations' (2009) ECDPM Discussion Paper No 89 at 7–8; Amin Alavi, Peter Gibbon and Niels Jon Mortesen, 'EU-ACP Economic Partnership Agreements (EPAs): Institutional and Substantive Issues Danish Institute of for International Studies (2007) https://pire.dii.dk/ws/files/61466/EU-ACP_Economic_Partnership_Agreement_EPA_.pdf accessed 15 May 2024

100 Interview with NANTS Officials

101 Paul Goodison, 'What Is the Future for EU-Africa Agricultural Trade After CAP Reform?' (2007) Review of African Political Economy vol 34 (112) pp 279–95 at 143

102 Paul Goodison, 'What Is the Future for EU-Africa Agricultural Trade After CAP Reform?' (2007) Review of African Political Economy vol 34 (112) pp 279–95 at 143

103 Paul Goodison, 'What Is the Future for EU-Africa Agricultural Trade After CAP Reform?' (2007) Review of African Political Economy vol 34 (112) pp 279–95 at 143

104 Paul Goodison, 'What Is the Future for EU-Africa Agricultural Trade After CAP Reform?' (2007) Review of African Political Economy vol 34 (112) pp 279–95 at 143

105 Paul Goodison, 'What Is the Future for EU-Africa Agricultural Trade After CAP Reform?' (2007) Review of African Political Economy vol 34 (112) pp 279–95 at 143

armed with actual 'power to act' if the EPAs' negative impact becomes a cause for concern.[106]

On behalf of the Group of the European People's Party (Christian Democrats) and European Democrats, Jean-Pierre Audy stated that the EPAs must be in line with the spirit of the Cotonou Agreement. The EPA, the group argued, must not only become a free trade agreement as provided for by the WTO but must also provide an enabling environment for the development of the ACP countries. However, another view was offered by Leopold Józef Rutowicz, a member of the European Parliament (MEP), who argued that though he recognised the strong commitment made by the European Union, cooperation based on agreements that fail to take account of the global market and the principles laid down by the WTO would not advance such partnership agreement. He further recommended, 'European Union aid to these countries should aim first and foremost to stimulate production that will not represent competition for EU producers.' In other words, any financial aid should generate the minimum income needed for subsistence in the ACP countries and no more.

Vittorio Agnoletto, another MEP, argued that EPA negotiations conducted by the Commission and supported by the Council 'are threatening the economic and food security of the ACP countries and jeopardising any remaining possibility for these countries to consolidate their productive sectors.' MEP Jerzy Buzek pointed out that free trade 'does not by itself improve competitiveness.' Carl Schlyter challenged Mandelson by reminding him of the vast economic power asymmetries between the EU and ACP countries. He stated:

> These negotiations are not conducted on an equal footing. You, Mr. Mandelson, have hundreds of experts at your disposal. The ACP countries, on their part, have just a few. We have enormous economic power; they are scarcely able to buy food for the day. When condition differs so significantly, we need to listen to their demands and try to meet them.

In the course of the debate, Gabriele Zimmer objected to Mandelson's style of handling the EPAs negotiation, saying, 'when the WTO ruled that the advantages of the custom conferred by the EU countries on their former colonies amounted to putting other developing countries at a disadvantage, it was not calling for a new world order.'

Zimmer further stated that Mandelson's conduct of the negotiations was 'overreaching' and 'overestimating' his negotiating authorisation, creating a vast advantage for the EU market.[107] Based on Patterson's historical account of the GATT, the contradiction that is widespread in the multilateral trading system is indistinguishable from EPA negotiations. According to Patterson, the Community spokesmen for the OEEC noted that the anxiety expressed by Austria, Norway, and Sweden about industries in those countries being unlikely to survive discrimination was

106 European Parliament, 'The Economic Partnership Agreement' (Tuesday, 22 May 2007, Strasbourg) www.europarl.europa.eu>sides>getDoc>reference=20 accessed 14 December 2020

107 European Parliament, 'The Economic Partnership Agreement' (Tuesday, 22 May 2007, Strasbourg) www.europarl.europa.eu>sides>getDoc>reference=20 accessed 14 December 2020

'exaggerated.' The EEC counselled, 'that too rigid interpretation of the GATT was not advisable.' Therefore, GATT must consider that 'the changing condition of the world was necessary if the GATT were to survive and be useful.'[108] The contracting party decided that the GATT rule should not be strictly dwelt on; instead, there should be a practical way of finding solutions to problems.'[109]

Another instance is when the Netherlands, Belgium, and Luxembourg had a deficit challenge like the rest of the world. There was the postponement of liberalisation from 1946 to 1949 of 'both intra and extra-Benelux trade' by the Netherlands.[110] Similarly, when the UK had a severe diminution of reserves and imposed stringent 15% import surcharges, several developing countries requested that they be excluded from surcharges in goods. However, the UK and the United States refused, arguing that it 'would be discriminatory and hard to administer if such a request is granted.'[111] During the GATT years, the European Free Trade Association admitted that agriculture is vastly protected through government intervention in its various member countries.[112]

6.3.2 Reasonable Time for Transition Within the Context of the WTO

Article XXIV:5 (C) of GATT provided a transition period for liberalisation of SAT for parties to an FTA. The 1994 Understanding on Article XXIV of GATT provided for a 'reasonable length of time' within the context of an FTA. It states that the period should not be more than ten years, but a prolonged period may be permitted in exceptional circumstances.[113] In other words, a more extended period could be allowed. What amounts to 'exceptional circumstances' is a subject to be determined on a case-by-case basis.[114] Many FTAs have been permitted for a more extended period of transition in the past. This shows flexibility in applying a reasonable length of time.[115] In defence of the United States-Australia FTA that removes barriers to Australian beef exports after only 18 years, the two countries' justification for the long transition period was based on a pragmatic rationale.[116]

108 Gardner Patterson, *Discrimination in International Trade: The Policy Issue 1945–1965* (Princeton University Press, 1966) 128
109 Gardner Patterson, *Discrimination in International Trade: The Policy Issue 1945–1965* (Princeton University Press, 1966) at 157
110 Gardner Patterson, *Discrimination in International Trade: The Policy Issue 1945–1965* (Princeton University Press, 1966) at 190
111 GATT Press Release, 913, 21 December 1964 quoted in Patterson (n 108) at 196
112 GATT Press Release, 913, 21 December 1964 quoted in Patterson (n 108) at 196
113 Understanding on the Interpretation of Article XXIV of the General Agreement on Tariffs and Trade 1994, para 3
114 Understanding on the Interpretation of Article XXIV of the General Agreement on Tariffs and Trade 1994, para 3
115 South Centre, 'Revisiting EPAs and WTO Compatibility' www.southcentre.org/publications/AnalyticalNotes/Other/2005Jul_EPA_WTO.pdf accessed 1 December 2020
116 World Trade Organization, Free Trade Agreement Between the United States and Australia-Questions & Answers, para 19 WT/REG184/5; Lorand Bartels, 'Legal Issues Relevant to the Notification of EPAs Under Article XXIV GATT' www.acp-eu-trade.org/library/files/Bartels_EN_261007_Legal-issues-notification.pdf p 7

The United States posited that using more extended transition periods for complex products is more prosperous, and it encourages a solid and long-term agreement with maximum coverage.[117]

In justifying the more extended transition period in the agreement between the United States and Chile's FTA, the United States said:

> Neither GATT Article XXIV nor the 1994 Understanding on Article XXIV requires that transition periods to be limited to 10 years. Article XXIV does require, however, that the agreement eliminate tariffs on substantially all the trade. Focusing, therefore, on the requirement, the parties worked to negotiate as comprehensive an agreement as possible. In these negotiations, it became clear to each party that a limited number of agricultural products were susceptible and hence would require longer transition periods.[118]

The emphasis is that the mere length of a transition period for an FTA does not violate the WTO rule. Ultimately, the most important thing is that there is a high likelihood of the SAT requirement being met.[119] On several occasions, WTO members have used this logic to justify a more extended period than ten years.[120] In the Turkey-Textile case, it was observed by the Appellate Panel that the transition period of the interim agreement metamorphosing into the EC-Turkey customs union continued for 35 whole years.[121] In its defence of the extended transition period, Turkey made the point that the customs union was initially scheduled to conclude effectively upon utilising the long transition period. This therefore diffused and minimised criticisms that the period was excessively long to be regarded as 'reasonable.'[122] Due to this inherent contradiction in the trading system, the

117 World Trade Organization, 'Free Trade Agreement Between the United States and Australia: Question and Replies' (Committee on Regional Trade Agreements, Forty Seventh Session, WT/REG184/5, 3 September 2007) www.wto.org>DDFDocuments>Q>WT>REG>184-5 accessed 14 December 2020

118 World Trade Organization, 'Examination of the Free Trade Agreement Between the United States and Chile, Goods and Services' (Committee on Regional Trade Agreements Thirty-Ninth Session, WT/REG160/M/1 14 March 2005) 2, www.docs.wto.org>FE_search>DDFDocuments>WT>REG (14/12/2020); Bartels (n 116) 8; Cosmas M Obote Ochieng, 'The EU–ACP Economic Partnership Agreements and "Development Questions": Constraints and Opportunities Posed By Article XXIV and Special And Differential Treatment Provisions of The WTO' (2007) JIEL vol 10 (2) pp 363–95 at 364

119 Cosmas M Obote Ochieng, 'The EU–ACP Economic Partnership Agreements and "Development Questions": Constraints and Opportunities Posed By Article XXIV and Special And Differential Treatment Provisions of The WTO' (2007) JIEL vol 10 (2) pp 363–95 at 364

120 CRTA, 'Examination of the EC-Jordan Euro-Mediterranean Agreement' (WT/REG14/M/1, 28 April 2004, para 8) cited in Aniekan Iboro Ukpe, 'Will the EU-Africa Economic Partnership Agreements Foster the Integration of African Countries Into the Global System' www.paper.ssrn.com accessed 14 December 2020

121 Turkey Restrictions on Imports of Textiles and Clothing (Turkey-Textile) adopted on 31 May 1999, WT/DS34/R, para 6.126, www.worldtradelaw.net>reports>wtopanels>turkey . . . accessed 14 December 2020

122 Turkey Restrictions on Imports of Textiles and Clothing (Turkey-Textile) adopted on 31 May 1999, WT/DS34/R, para 6.126, www.worldtradelaw.net>reports>wtopanels>turkey . . . accessed 14 December 2020

concerns for its nascent industries, and some advantages that it could leverage such as the export of petroleum and entering into an arrangement with the UK, Nigeria declined to sign the agreement.

6.4 Nigeria-United Kingdom Partnership

The ties between Nigeria and Britain go back to the colonial era. However, the current relationship between the two countries revolves around economic and political interests. Nigeria is the second largest exporter to the UK after South Africa with trade worth £6.7 billion.[123] It was claimed by a respondent that while Nigeria declined to sign the EPAs, it had hoped to sign a trade agreement with Britain post-Brexit. Brexit was perceived as a great opportunity for developing countries to secure better access and aid from Britain.[124] It was in light of this that in 2019, the British Minister of State for Africa, Harriet Baldwin, and the Chairperson of the African Union Commission, Moussa Faki Mahamat, agreed to an MOU concerning a partnership between AU and the UK. The objective of the strategy was to promote further engagement between Africa and the UK, leading to generating investment in Africa to bring about sustainability and transformation. In addition, the partnership aimed to encourage UK-Africa trade and investment, the AfCFTA, and tackle demographic benefits.[125]

In 2024, the UK and Nigeria signed a memorandum of understanding termed Enhanced Trade and Investment Partnership (ETIP). Article 7 (b) of the ETIP provides that the arrangement does not represent or create any legal obligation but that the parties are committed to acting in good faith. The principle of good faith is recognized as both a general principle of law and a principle of customary international law. As such, the WTO Appellate Body acknowledged good faith as simultaneously a general principle of law and a principle of general international law.[126] The WTO Appellate Body's decision in US—Shrimp[127] highlights the use of the principle of good faith in interpreting treaty provisions within the broader framework of international law. In this case, the Appellate Body applied the principle of good faith through the doctrine of *abus de droit* while interpreting the Chapeau of Article XX of the GATT.[128]

123 Department for Business & Trade, 'Signature of Enhanced Trade and Investment Partnership Between the Government of the United Kingdom of Great Britain and Northern Ireland and the Government of the Republic of Nigeria' (12 February 2024) www.committees.parliament.uk accessed 11 May 2024

124 Nick Westcott, 'Breaking Away: The Developing World and the Future of Multilateralism, Africa, Europe and Britain After Brexit' (2019) Great Insights vol 7 (3) pp 11–3

125 Giovanni Faleg and Carlo Palleschi, *The UK Strategy Post-Brexit* (European Union Institute for Security Studies, 2020)

126 Appellate Body Report, United States—Tax Treatment for Foreign Sales Corporations', WTO Doc WT/DS108/AB/R (20 March 2000) para 166; Appellate Body Report, United States—Standards for Reformulated and Conventional Gasoline, WTO Doc WT/DS2/AB/R (20 May 1996) para 16–17

127 United States—Import Prohibition of Certain Shrimp and Shrimp Products, WTO Doc WT/DS58/AB/R (6 November 1998) para 114

128 Marrakesh Agreement Establishing the World Trade Organisation annex IA, open for signature 15 April 1994, 1867 UNTS 3 entered into force 1 January 1995)

In the case of *Mark Faulkner & Ors v Vollin Holdings Limited & Ors*,[129] the Court of Appeal emphasised the relevant principles that shape contractual good faith instruments. The judgment made it clear that, at a minimum, a party under a good faith clause must act honestly. Nevertheless, good faith could go beyond the minimum duty, and the scope of its application must be considered based on the specific provision, contextualising the particular good faith provisions.[130] In essence, the ETIP is not the same as an FTA with a focus on effectively addressing non-tariff barriers to trade. In other words, the UK does not have a formal trade agreement with Nigeria. However, parties are meant to comply with the MOU based on good faith, a principle recognised by the general principle of international law, invariably meaning making it an agreement that the parties are bound in principle.

Before the MOU, the parties conduct trade through the UK's Developing Countries Trading Scheme (DCTS) and the WTO and still do so. The DCTS was launched in 2023 by the UK government as an international development strategy to assist developing countries to integrate into the global economy.[131] Under the Annex, the parties seek to sign an MOU in the future on investment under the ETIP. It provides in the Annex that the parties will work to enhance the business climate in Nigeria to attract quality foreign direct investment in key areas of the economy. However, the MOU does not state the mode this work would take to enhance the business climate. Recently the National Assembly amended the Companies and Allied Matters Act to promote the ease of doing business. Also, the Economic Diversification Working Group will assist the Nigerian party to diversify by exploring opportunities in non-oil products to the UK.[132] The parties will address areas to building capacity and sensitise Nigerian exporters on how to take advantage of the UK market. However, the area that has generated controversies is the legal services sector, provided in the Annex.

The MOU under the Annex defines 'Legal Service' to mean 'services provided by qualified legal professionals such as the provision of legal advice, assistance or representation in connection with the application of the law or with any form of resolution of legal disputes including arbitration, conciliation, and mediation.' It went on to say, 'Qualified legal professional' 'means a natural person who is qualified to supply legal services under a home jurisdiction profession title.' How does this bring about cooperation to enhance this commitment in good faith? It states that the UK and Nigeria sectors can deepen the ties that already existed between the parties. The legal technical working group (the LST Working Group) would include both UK and Nigeria legal service sectors, to ensure collaboration and knowledge sharing to improve bilateral trade in legal services.

This provision has been interpreted as allowing UK lawyers to practice in Nigeria. This has generated some protests among lawyers, claiming that it will

129 (2022) EWCA Civ 1371

130 Oliver E Browne and Alex Cox, 'Meaning of "Good Faith" Under English Law: Latest Clarification' (Latham and Watkins 10 November 2022) www.latham.london accessed 14 May 2024

131 Department for Business & Trade, 'Developing Countries Trading Scheme: Government Policy Response'

132 See 'Annex to the Enhanced Trade and Investment Partnership Arrangement Between Nigeria and the United Kingdom' (Department for Business and Trade) www.gov.uk accessed 9 May 2024

erode the revenue of lawyers in Nigeria. The Nigerian Bar Association (NBA) through its president, Mr Yakubu Maikyau, said that the body had no knowledge of the bilateral agreement with the UK. Uzoka-Anitie, the Minister of Industry, Trade and Investment stated on her X handle: 'I am delighted to announce the official signing of a groundbreaking agreement between the UK and Nigeria, allowing British lawyers to practice within Nigeria. This agreement reaffirms our dedication to nurturing economic and trade alliances, especially in critical sectors like energy, legal, and financial services. The NBA described the statement as 'unpatriotic and uninformed. It is indeed unfortunate that this tragic reminder of our colonial past is being gleefully celebrated at the highest level of the government of Nigeria.' He wondered how such a serious decision could be taken without consultation with the people of Nigeria, especially the NBA. The NBA noted, 'it is truly tragic' that whereas the government of the UK desire to provide opportunities for its lawyers beyond their environment, the government of Nigeria is making an effort to deprive Nigerian lawyers and their dependents of a means of securing necessities of life. The NBA president expressed the point that he is not unaware of the reality of globalization and open 'borders for transnational trade and exchange of services, this must be done strategically, purposely, without endangering the already exposed and weakened Nigerian Market.' He calls for a review of ETIP and AfCFTA for the interest and development of the ECOWAS sub-region.[133] Dania is of the view that a UK lawyer can practice in Nigeria as the latter is still applying the law handed by the colonialists. However, the former's law has been amended several times to meet the modern times, their court systems are global tech compliant, and due to technological advancement, a Nigerian lawyer may find it difficult to practice in the UK. The competition will not be fair.[134] The attempt by the minister of trade and investment to clarify and allay the fears of the NBA fell on deaf ears.

The ETIP did not categorically give the right to UK lawyers to practice in Nigeria or Nigeria to do so in the UK, but it is that lawyers from the two jurisdictions can provide legal service anywhere in the jurisdiction. However, it defines 'host jurisdiction' to mean 'a qualified legal professional has not acquired a professional title but where they are providing services in their home jurisdiction law and international.' For the purpose of clarity, the interesting part of the Annex is reproduced here:

> The Parties aspire to facilitate in their respective jurisdictions the provision of legal services by each other's qualified legal professionals in relation to the law of their home jurisdiction, public international law, arbitration, conciliation, and mediation. This will exclude the provision of legal services in host jurisdiction law, rights of audience, and litigation in the host country's domestic courts.

133 Onozure Dania, 'Lawyers Reject Deal Allowing Britons to Practice Law in Nigeria' (Punch Newspapers 22 February 2024)

134 Onozure Dania, 'Lawyers Reject Deal Allowing Britons to Practice Law in Nigeria' (Punch Newspapers 22 February 2024)

At the moment, the MOU is an aspiration by both parties to promote legal services. Interestingly, the service will not extend to the application of the law of a host state. For instance, a Nigerian providing legal service in the UK will not apply the law of UK but only international law, arbitration, conciliation, and mediation and shall have no right to be heard in the UK court or right to represent litigants in the UK. The same applies if a UK-based legal professional has to provide legal services in Nigeria. It is a systematic inclusion of trade in services as stipulated in the GATT/WTO, which both parties are expected to carry out in good faith. The partnership in the legal sector could be an advantage to the Nigerian legal sector because it could improve legal service in Nigeria, build further capacity, and advance technological compliance through the sharing and transfer of knowledge. It is for this reason that the ETIP provided for a legal technical working group for both parties to work together to advance the legal sector. However, the NBA, which represents this sector, was unaware of the negotiation and process leading to the signing of the MOU.

Why the inclusion of trade in service in the MOU? The Law Society of England and Wales is an independent professional body that works worldwide to provide support and represent 220,000 English and Welsh solicitors. It is the largest profession in the UK, and it ensures the highest standards and the rule of law.[135] According to the body, trade in legal services is a huge opportunity to grow the UK economy, support job creation, and make the UK the leading place to do business. It encourages the UK government to give support to solicitors and law firms exporting services. The advantages are that it generates a trade surplus and assists in offsetting the UK's trade in goods deficit. In 2021, the net exports of UK legal services stood at £250 billion of global mergers and acquisitions and 40% of global corporate arbitrations.[136] The body noted that FTA is a useful tool in support of the exports of legal services, but concrete steps need to be taken to assist solicitors and law firms who export the services in the area of understanding the rules and regulations to operate in a foreign market, connect and create the client base for overseas lawyers, and increase exports by UK businesses—all of which means business for solicitors and law firms.

Since Brexit the market for the UK legal sector has shrunk. As a result, the body tasked the UK government to push implementation of the provisions under the EU-UK Trade and Cooperation Agreement (TCA), which allows a UK lawyer to practice under the home title, especially in Greece and Luxemburg.[137] In 2023, the Recognition of Professional Qualifications agreement with Switzerland contained an annex dealing with legal services. It provides for UK lawyers to register and

135 The Law Society of England and Wales Respond to the Business and Trade Committee Inquiry on Export Led Growth (Written Submission from the Law Society of England and Wales (ELG0012)) www.committees.parliament.uk accessed 12 May 2024

136 Oxera Report, 'Economic Value of English Law' (5 October 2021) https://legaluk.org/wp-content/uploads/2021/09/The-value-of0english-law-to-the-UK-economy.pdf

137 Articles 192 193 and 194 EU-UK Trade and Cooperation Agreement (2021) Official Journal of the European Law. L 149/10 https://eur-lex.europa.eu/legal-content/EN/TXT/?uri=CELEX%3A22021A0430%2801%29 accessed 14 May 2024

practice under the home title and requalify as Swiss lawyers after three years of registration and practice in the country without a need for a Swiss law degree or taking any local exams. The UK has a similar arrangement with Korea. Korea is the non-EU to have liberalised its legal service sector through its FTA, but it has yet to commit to joint practice between Korean and foreign lawyers; in other words, the market in the legal service sector is still protected. The UK-Australia FTA signed in 2021 came into force in 2023 and created a framework for bespoke legal services, to work together with relevant bodies such as the Law Society of England and Wales and the Law Council of Australia. However, ETIP did not mention the NBA. Before signing the 2023 regulation that would allow foreign lawyers to practice in India, the India Bar Council was consulted by the government of India and other stakeholders. The UK-Nigeria Economic Development Forum (EDF), a government-to-government initiative launched in 2018, included the Legal Services Technical Working Group to end the barriers for UK and Nigeria lawyers.

The NBA president has likened the provision of legal service to the colonial era, where treaties were imposed on the natives. Is there any need to be concerned since the MOU is not a legally binding instrument? What is the position of international law on MOU? MOU is well received as a legal tool under international law and practice. Lord McNair, in his classic work on the law of treaties, viewed the MOU as 'an informal but legal agreement' between two parties.[138] After the Second World War, the US and the UK entered into several bilateral MOUs in the defence sector dealing with military assistance, operation, and atomic energy, and agreements were duly registered with the United Nations under Article 102 of the Charter.[139] The US was taken aback when the UK questioned the legality of those instruments. This action on the part of the UK and US generated the US-UK arbitration regarding Heathrow Airport user charges. The UK strongly contended that the document at issue in the US-UK MOU of 6 April 1983 on airport user charges was not legally binding.[140]

In the commentary on the 1969 Vienna Convention on the Law of Treaties, the International Law Commission recognised that MOUs 'are undoubtedly international agreements subject to the law of treaties.' McNair acknowledged that the Vienna Convention is not the title or other appellation given to a diplomatic document that determines whether it is a legal instrument but the intention of those who drafted the document that is governed by international law. Documents that are intended to have a 'moral or political' force do not give rise to legally binding international agreements.[141] The intention of the parties is made known through

138 Arnold Duncan McNair, The Law of Treaties 15 (OUP, 1961); Hans & Jirina H. Emersion, The Treaty Maker's Handbook (1973) vol 7, pp 316

139 United Nations Charter Article 102

140 First Memorandum of the United Kingdom of Great Britain and Northern Ireland, US/UK Arbitration Concerning Heathrow Airport User Charges (31 May 1990) para 5.143, at 108–9

141 John H McNeill, 'International Agreements: Recent US-UK Practice Concerning the Memorandum of Understanding' (1994) The American Journal of International Law vol 88 (4) pp 821–6 at 923–4

the terminology used, such as 'the parties' and 'agree' the use of the final clauses noting the term and date of entry into force. The British position on the intent to be bound by an MOU is demonstrated in a list of terms produced by the UK Ministry of Defence in 1991. According to the UK Ministry, several terms are to be avoided to make an MOU not legally binding, words such as 'arrangement' to replace 'agreements' and 'will' for 'shall,' a 'section' instead of 'Article' 'mutually consents,' instead of 'undertakes.'[142] However, the UK-Nigeria MOU used the words: 'Parties,' 'Article,' and referred to invoking international law, and the use of arbitration in the event of disagreement between the Parties, giving it the force of law.

Given the serious nature of MOU in international law and practice, all stakeholders in Nigeria, especially the NBA, should have been consulted. In other agreements mentioned earlier, which the UK had with other countries, the stakeholders were involved in the negotiations and subsequent signing of such an agreement. Nigeria is still in the process of building capacity; this backdoor inclusion of trade in legal service is a reminder of how the colonialists undermined the natives. The ETIP provides for the review of the MOU every five years, so there is still an opportunity for balanced scrutiny of the trade in service in the legal sector. It is yet to be seen how as this agreement differs from the EPAs, which Nigeria refused to sign. Perhaps it is the genteel manner of easing Nigeria into a full-blown FTA that is more acceptable. The MOU uses the same rhetoric as in development assistance, such as taking into account different levels of development between Nigeria and the UK, 'endeavour to be mindful of the principles of progressivity.'[143] After Nigeria declined to sign the EPA, one would have thought that it would have negotiated a trade deal that protected its interests.

6.5 Conclusion

In this chapter, the primary question was why Nigeria refused to sign the EPA despite its close trade relations with the EU. It was determined that Nigeria recognised the built-in asymmetrical nature of the trade agreements—as, indeed, did other ECOWAS countries—and, almost uniquely amongst its ECOWAS and ACP countries, was in a position to refuse to acquiesce on this basis. Specifically, Nigeria had concerns about the interpretation of Article XXIV of GATT.

It reveals that complying with the provisions of GATT Article XXIV would be detrimental to its efforts to diversify its economy.[144] Unlike other ECOWAS countries, such as Ghana, Nigeria was not dependent on the EU for its exports. In addition, it exports crude oil to the EU market without payment of duties, and its main EU export destination was the UK which has exited the EU. In other words, Nigeria could withstand the economic power asymmetry favouring the EU because

142 Ministry of Defence to British Army Staff (Washington); John H McNeill, 'International Agreements: Recent US-UK Practice Concerning the Memorandum of Understanding' (1994) The American Journal of International Law vol 88 (4) pp 821–6 at 824

143 ETIP Article 32024

144 Interview with MAN, NANTS, and FMITI (2020)

it was looking forward to a trade deal with a dominant core (UK) when it exited the EU. Nigeria recently signed an MOU with the UK, and of course, there are some controversies; however, certain concerns, which were raised during the EPA negotiation, such as reviewing the agreement every five years, were addressed in the Nigeria and the UK ETIP. This finding corresponds to Drahos's argument that 'rules and procedure, whether bilateral or multilateral,' do not automatically subdue the economic power asymmetry between peripheral countries and the dominant core.[145] He states, 'What matters to the preservation or extension of an individual's economic interests ultimately rests on that individual's bargaining power.'[146] The documentation and interviews indicate that the EU adopted a posture that sought to impose its views on Nigeria rather than consider its concerns.[147]

The contradictions observed have shown that while the EU promotes the ideas of free trade and attempts to impose it on Nigeria and the rest of West Africa, in practice, the former has distanced itself from the GATT tenets, except when compliance would protect its interests. If the EU applies the provisions of GATT to itself, it does so with leniency. However, with countries in West Africa, it ensures strict compliance with the GATT Article XXIV provisions, even if it harms peripheral countries economically.

Conventions and Cases

The Cotonou Partnership Agreement

EU-UK Trade and Cooperation Agreement, (2021) Official Journal of the European Law. L 149/10 https://eur-lex.europa.eu/legal-content/EN/TXT/?uri=CELEX%3A22021A0430%2801%29 accessed 14 May 2024

Enhanced Trade and Investment Partnership Arrangement Between Nigeria and the United Kingdom

United Nations Charter Chapter XVI, Miscellaneous Provisions

First Memorandum of the United Kingdom of Great Britain and Northern Ireland, US/UK Arbitration Concerning Heathrow Airport User Charges

Turkey-Restrictions on Imports of Textiles and Clothing (Turkey-Textile) adopted on 31 May 1999, WT/DS34/R, www.worldtradelaw.net>reports>wtopanels>turkey. . . accessed 14 December 2020

United States-Import Prohibition of Certain Shrimp and Shrimp Products WT/DS58/AB/R para. 158

Mark Faulkner & Ors v Vollin Holdings Limited & Ors (2022) EWCA Civ 1371

145 Peter Drahos, 'The Bilateral Web of Trade Dispute Settlement' (Centre for World Affairs and the Global Economy University of Wisconsin-Madison, 2005) 14 cited in Cosmas Milton Obote Ochieng, Legal and Systematic Issues in the Interim Economic Partnership Agreements: Which Way Now? (2009) No 2 International Centre for Trade and Sustainable Development

146 Peter Drahos, 'The Bilateral Web of Trade Dispute Settlement' (Centre for World Affairs and the Global Economy University of Wisconsin-Madison, 2005) 14 cited in Cosmas Milton Obote Ochieng, Legal and Systematic Issues in the Interim Economic Partnership Agreements: Which Way Now? (2009) No 2 International Centre for Trade and Sustainable Development

147 Interview with MAN officials (2020)

Bibliography

13th Extraordinary Session of the ECOWAS Council of Ministers (Yamoussoukro, 26th March, 2014). http://events.ecowas.int/wp-contentuploads/2014/03/draft. . . (accessed 1 December 2020)

ACP Council of Ministers, 'Declaration of the ACP Council of Ministers at its 86th Session Expressing Serious Concern on the Status of the Negotiations of the Economic Partnership Agreements', Brussels, December 2007

Actionaid International, 'Trade Trap: Why EU-ACP Economic Partnership Agreements Pose a Threat to Africa's Development'

Alli F, & Uzor N, 'EU Threaten to Stop Market Access for Nigerian Products Over EPA' (*Vanguard*, 17 October 2016). www.vanguardngr.com (accessed 19 May 2021)

Andriamanjara S, Brenton P, and others, 'Assessing the Economic Impact of an Economic Partnership Agreement on Nigeria' www.elibrary.worldbank.org (accessed 9 April 2021)

Annex to the Enhanced Trade and Investment Partnership Arrangement Between Nigeria and the United Kingdom's Department for Business and Trade. www.gov.uk (accessed 9 May 2024)

Ascher W, & Krupp C, 'Distributional Implications of Alternative Financing of Physical Infrastructure Development' in W Ascher & C Krupp (eds), *Physical Infrastructure Development: Balancing the Growth, Equity and Environment Imperatives* (Palgrave Macmillan, 2010)

Bartels L, 'Legal Issues Relevant to the Notification of EPAs Under Article XXIV GATT' www.acp-eu-trade.org/library/files/Bartels_EN_261007_Legal-issues-notification.pdf p 8

Berthelot J, 'The EU Caught in the Trap of Nigeria's Refusal to Sign the West Africa Economic Partnership Agreement and the Continental Free Trade' (9 May 2018). www.eeas.europa/archives/delegations/nigeria/documents/press_corner/news/20160203_statement_by _president_buhari_03-02 CADTM (accessed 9 February 2020)

Blyth M, *Great Transformations: Economic Ideas and Institutional Change in the Twentieth Century* (Cambridge University Press, 2002)

Browne O E, & Cox A, 'Meaning of 'Good Faith' Under English Law: Latest Clarification (Latham & Watkins 10 November 2022)' www.latham.london (accessed 14 May 2024)

The Commission for Africa Commission for Africa, 'Our Common Interests' Report of the Commission for Africa, 2005. www.bristol.ac.uk/poverty/downloads/keyofficialdocuments/Commission%20for%20Africa%20report.pdf (accessed 16 May 2024)

Cox R W, 'Gramsci, Hegemony and International Relations: An Essay in Method' (1983) Millennium-Journal of International Studies vol 12 (2) pp 162–75

Cox R W, & Schechter M G, *The Political Economy of a Plural World: Critical Reflections on Power, Moral, and Civilization* (Routledge, 2002)

CRTA, 'Examination of the EC-Jordan Euro-Mediterranean Agreement', WT/REG14/M/1, 28 April 2004, para 8), cited in Aniekan Iboro Ukpe, 'Will the EU-Africa Economic Partnership Agreements Foster the Integration of African Countries into the Global System' www.paper.ssrn.com (accessed 14 December 2020)

Dania O, 'Lawyers Reject Deal Allowing Britons to Practice Law in Nigeria' (*Punch Newspapers*, 22 February 2024) www.punchng.com accessed 1 October 2024

Department for Business & Trade, 'Developing Countries Trading Scheme: Government Policy Response'

Department for Business & Trade, 'Signature of Enhanced Trade and Investment Partnership between the Government of the United Kingdom of Great Britain and Northern Ireland and the Government of the Republic of Nigeria' 12 February 2024. www.committees.parliament.uk (accessed 11 May 2024)

Drahos P, *The Bilateral Web of Trade Dispute Settlement* (Centre for World Affairs and the Global Economy, University of Wisconsin-Madison, 2005)

Economic Partnership Agreement (ECOWAS). www.ecowas.int (accessed 25 November 2020)

Emersion J H, *The Treaty Maker's Handbook* (Dag Hammarskjold Foundation, 1973)

Enda, Impact Study of the Economic Partnership Agreement Market Access Offer on West African Countries (Hereinafter Enda Impact Study) (Study Done by the Consortium *Pour La Recherche Economique et Sociale, Friedrich Ebert Stiftung*, July 2011)

Enda, Impact Study of the Economic Partnership Agreement Market Access Offer on West African Countries (Study Done by the Consortium *Pour La Recherche Economique et Sociale, Friedrich Ebert Stiftung*, July 2011)

EU, 'ECOWAS Urge FG to Sign Economic Partnership Agreement' (*Vanguard*, 1 August 2017). www.vanguardngr.com (accessed 19 May 2021)

EU, 'The 'Commission Sets Course for an Open Sustainable and Assertive EU Trade Policy' (18 February 2021). www.trade.ec.europa.eu/doclib/press/index.cfm?id=22438title= Commission-sets-course-for-an-open-sustainable-and-assertive-EU-trade-strategy (accessed 10 April 2021)

European Commission, 'Economic Partnership Agreements (EPAs), New ACP-EU Trade Partnerships' (July 2010). http://eu.europa.eu/trade/wider-agenda/development/economic-partnerships (accessed 29 May 2018)

European Commission, 'Green Paper on Relations Between the European Union and the ACP Countries on the Eve of the 21st Century: Challenges and Options for New Partnership' (*Brussels*, 20 November 1996 COM (96) 570 Final). https://eu-lex.europa.eu/legal-content/EN/TXT/pdf/?uri=CEL. . . (accessed 26 June 2020)

European Parliament, 'The Economic Partnership Agreement' (Tuesday, 22 May 2007, Strasbourg). www.europarl.europa.eu>sides>getDoc>reference=20 (accessed 14 December 2020)

European Parliament Report, *On the Development Impact of Economic Partnership Agreements' (EPAs)* (Rapporteur: Luisa Morgantini, Committee on Development, Final A6–0053/2006) (Session Document, 2004–2009)

European Union, *EU-ACPs: Opening of Trade Negotiations with West and Central Africa* (IP/03/1334, Brussels, 2 October 2003). www.ec.europa.eu>commissioner>presscorner>detail (accessed 24 November 2020)

Evita Schmieg, 'EU Economic Partnership Agreements in Sub-Saharan Africa: Avenues of Compromise for Constructive Outcome by September', 2014 Stiftung Wissenschaft und Politic, German Institute for International and Security Affairs, 8 May 2014

Faleg G, & Palleschi C, 'The UK Strategy Post-Brexit' (2020) European Union Institute for Security Studies https://data.europa.eu/doi/10.2815/297320 Chaillot Paper/158

First Memorandum of the United Kingdom of Great Britain and Northern Ireland, US/UK Arbitration Concerning Heathrow Airport User Charges (31 May 1990)

Friedrich List, The National System of Political Economy (trans by Sampson S Lloyd, 6 August 1789-30 November 1846)

GATT Press Release, 913, 21 December 1964 quoted in Patterson, (n 108) at 196

Goodison P, 'EU Trade Policy and the Future of Africa's Trade Relationship With the EU' (2007) Review of African Political Economy vol 34 (112) pp 247–266

Goodison P, 'What is the Future for EU-Africa Agricultural Trade After CAP Reform?' (2007) Review of African Political Economy vol 34 (112) pp 279–295

Holland M, '20/20 Vision? The EU's Cotonou Partnership Agreement' (2003) The Brown Journal of World Affairs vol 9 (2) pp 161–175

Hurt S R, 'Co-operation and Coercion? The Cotonou Agreement Between the European Union and ACP States and the End of Lomé Convention' (2003) Third World Quarterly vol 24 (1) pp 161–176

Hurt S R, 'The EU-SADC Economic Partnership Agreement Negotiations: 'Locking in' the Neoliberal Development Model in Southern Africa?' (2012) Third World Quarterly vol 33 (3)

Julian M, 'EU Member States and New EC Trade Commissioner committed to Flexibility in EPA Negotiations' EPA Update (Longer Version), Trade Negotiations Insight (2008/ January 2009)

Keynes J M, *The General Theory of Employment, Interest and Money* (Harcourt Brace, 1964)

Kpodo K, & Bigg M M, 'African Economies Need Integration—Ghana (President) John Mahama)' Reuters-Summit-West (7 April 2014). www.uk.reuters.com>article> Africa-summit-mahama>reut. . . (accessed 14 December 2020)

Lamy P, & Nielson P, Economic Partnership Agreement: A New Approach in the Relations Between the European Union and the ACP Countries (European Communities, Belgium, September 2002) 1. www.ec.europa.eu (accessed 24 November 2020)

The Law Society of England and Wales Respond to the Business and Trade Committee Inquiry on Export Led Growth (Written Submission from the Law Society of England and Wales (ELG0012). www.committees.parliament.uk (accessed 12 May 2024)

Letter to Commissioner Ashton by EU Member States Denmark, Ireland, and the Netherlands, Dated 7 November 2007 published on the tralac. www.tralac.org

Mandelson P, 'Bilateral Agreements in EU Trade Policy' (*London School of Economics*, 9 October 2006) SPEECH 06/574–09/10/2006. https://ec-europa/Commission/presscorner/ detail/en/SPEECH_06_574 (accessed 14 December 2020)

Mandelson P, 'Economic Partnership Agreements Progressive Trade Policy into Practice' (ACP-EU Joint Parliamentary Assembly, Bamako, Mali, 19 April 2005 Speech/05/241) 2

Mandelson P, 'European Commissioner for Trade, Economic Partnership Agreements: Progressive Trade Policy into Practice' (Speech/05/241, ACP-EU Joint Parliamentary Assembly, Bamako Mali, 19 April 2005)

Mandelson P, 'PSE-Organised Seminar on EPAs (SPEECH/10/612–19/10/2006)' http:// europa.eu/rapi/pressReleaseAction.do?reference=SPEECH/06/612&fromant=HTML& aged=0&language=EN&guiLanguage=en cited in Goodison P, 'The Future of Africa's Trade With Europe: New EU Trade Policy' (2007) Review of African Political Economy vol 34 (111)

Mandelson P, 'Putting Development First: EU-ACP Relations, EPAs and the Doha Round' (SPECCH/05/4, Georgetown, Guyana, 6 January 2005)

Mandelson P, 'Statement to the Development Committee of the European Union Parliament' (Brussels, March 2005)

Mandelson P, 'Sustainable Trade: Observations on Trade and Protectionism' (SPEECH/ 06/187) (Brussels, 21 March 2006)

Mandelson P, 'The ACP-EU Relationship in the Global Economy' (SPEECH/04/505, ACP-EU Ministerial, Brussels, 1 December 2004)

Mandelson P, 'The ACP-EU Relationship in the Global Economy' (SPEECH/04/505, ACP-EU Ministerial, Brussels, 1 December 2004)

Mandelson P, European Parliament Debate on EPAs, 22 May 2007, Strasbourg. www. europarl.europa.eu (accessed 14 December 2020)

Mandelson P, Statement to the Development Committee of the European Union Parliament (*Brussels*, March 2005)

McNair A D, *The Law of Treaties* (OUP, 1961) 15

McNeill J H, 'International Agreements: Recent U.S-UK Practice Concerning the Memorandum of Understanding' (1994) The American Journal of International Law vol 88 (4) pp 821–826

Ministry of Defence to British Army Staff (Washington)

Mutasa C, 'A Critique of the EU's Common Agricultural Policy' in A Adebajo & K Whiteman (eds), *The EU and Africa From Eurafrique to Afro-Europa* (C Hurst & Co Publishers Ltd, 2012)

'Nigeria Clarifies Reason for Not Endorsing EU-ECOWAS EPAs' (15 May 2014) *Bridges Africa* vol 3 (4). www.ictsd.iisd.org (accessed 1 December 2020)

'Nigeria's Draft Position on the Economic Partnership Agreement' (Archival Doc/Nigeria Ministry of Industry, Trade and Investment, 2007)

'Nigeria's Draft Position on the Economic Partnership Agreement' (FMITI Doc, Nigeria)

Nnabugwu F, 'EU/ECOWAS Trade Liberalisation Agreement not Good for Nigeria' (*Vanguard*, 1 April 2014). www.vanguardngr.com>news (accessed 14 December 2020)

Ochieng C M O, 'The EU—ACP Economic Partnership Agreements and 'Development Questions': Constraints and Opportunities Posed by Article XXIV And Special And Differential Treatment Provisions of The WTO' (2007) JIEL vol 10 (2) pp 363–395

Oloruntoba S O, *Regionalism, and Integration in Africa: EU-ACP Economic Partnership Agreements and Euro-Nigeria Relations* (Palgrave Macmillan, 2016)

Oxera Report, 'Economic Value of English Law' 5 October 2021. https://legaluk.org/wp-content/uploads/2021/09/The-value-of0english-law-to-the-UK-economy.pdf

Patterson G, *Discrimination in International Trade: The Policy Issue 1945–1965* (Princeton University Press, 1966)

Press Release, European General Affairs and External Relations Council (GAERC), 14–15 May 2007. www.concilium.europa.eu/ueDocs/cms-Data/dcos/pressData/en/gena/94116.pdf (accessed 14 December 2020)

Press Release, 'Why Nigeria Won't Sign Economic Partnership Agreement With the EU' (*Premium Times*, 5 April 2018). www.premiumtimesng.com (accessed 4 March 2020)

Ramdoo I, & Bilal S, 'EPA Negotiations: The Honey Moon is Over' Briefing Note 31 (2011)' www.ecdpm.org/publications/ (accessed 29 May 2018)

South Centre, 'EPA Negotiations: State of Play and Strategic Considerations for the Way Forward' (Analytical Note SC/AN/TDP/EPA/13, Geneva, Switzerland, February 2008). www.southcentre.org (18 December 2021)

South Centre, 'Revisiting EPAs and WTO Compatibility' www.southcentre.org/publications/AnalyticalNotes/Other/2005Jul_EPA_WTO.pdf) (accessed 1 December 2020)

Statement by EU Trade Commissioner Peter Mandelson Joint Parliamentary Assembly Bamako Mali Brochure (19 April 2005)

Statement by H.E. Mohammadu Buhari, President of the Republic of Nigeria (Strasbourg, Eastern France, 12–12:30, 3 February 2016). www.eeas.europa/archives/delegations/nigeria/documents/press_corner/news/20160203_statement_by_president_buhari_03-02 (accessed 9 February 2020)

Strange S, 'Protectionism and World Politics' (1985) International Organisation vol 39 (2) pp 233–259

Westcott N, 'Breaking Away: The Developing World and the Future of Multilateralism, Africa, Europe, and Britain After Brexit' (2019) Great Insights vol 7 (3) pp 11–13

Wilkinson R, 'Language, Power and Multilateral Trade Negotiations' (2009) Review of International Political Economy vol 16 (4) pp 597–619

Wilkinson R, 'Of Butchery and Bicycles: The WTO and the 'Death' of the Doha Development Agenda' (2012) The Political Quarterly vol 83 (2)

Wilkinson R, *What is Wrong With the WTO: How to Fix It* (Polity Press, 2014)

World Bank, 'ECOWAS Economic Partnership Agreement With the EU and Nigeria Trade and Development' (30 September 2014) www.openknowledge.worldbank.org (accessed 9 April 2021)

World Trade Organization, 'Examination of the Free Trade Agreement Between the United States and Chile, Goods and Services' (Committee on Regional Trade Agreements Thirty-Ninth Session, WT/REG160/M/1, 14 March 2005) 2. www.docs.wto.org>FE_search>DDFDocuments>WT>REG (accessed 14 December 2020)

World Trade Organization, 'Free Trade Agreement Between the United States and Australia-Questions & Answers', WT/REG184/5

World Trade Organization, 'Free Trade Agreement between the United States and Australia: Question and Replies' (Committee on Regional Trade Agreements, Forty Seventh Session, WT/REG184/5 (3 September 2007). www.wto.org>DDFDocuments>Q>WT>REG>184-5 (accessed 14 December 2020)

WTO, Understanding on the Interpretation of Article XXIV of the General Agreement on Tariffs and Trade 1994 https://www.wto.org/english/docs_e/legal_e/10-24.pdf

7 The Chinese Approach to African Development

7.1 Introduction

China's relationship with Africa is not a panacea for the challenges faced by the latter.[1] However, Chinese investment has played a role in initiating the systematic integration of Africa into global economic supply chains by diversifying exports.[2] Nonetheless, the African Centre for Economic Transformation (ACET) has expressed concerns that Chinese investment primarily focuses on projects that do not contribute to the capacity building of local communities. ACET has also criticised the unpredictable nature of investment in the manufacturing sector.[3] China's activities have been labelled as colonial agenda by the West and their supporters.[4] However, in 2008, President of Senegal Abdoulaye Wade vaunted the Chinese approach to African development. He states that Chinese economic activities in Africa have raised:

1 Sanusha Naidu, 'China and Africa's Natural Resources Sector: A View From South Africa' (2007) Centre for Strategic and International Studies www.csis.org/analysis/china-and-africas-natural-resource-sector-view-south-africa accessed 18 May 2024

2 Larry Hanauer and Lyle J Morris, *Chinese Engagement in Africa: Drivers, Reactions, and Implications* (RAND Corporation, 2014) 5–9; David H Shinn and Joshua Eisenman, *China and Africa: A Century of Engagement* (University of Pennsylvania Press, 2012) 142; Marcus Vinicius de Freitas, *The Impact of Chinese Investment in Africa: Neocolonialism or Cooperation* (2023) Policy Brief p 5 www.policycenter.ma/sites/default/files/2023-08/PB_30-23_Marcus%20Freitas.pdf accessed 18 May 2024

3 Barfour Osei, Edward K Brown and Kofi Blankson-Ocansey, 'Looking East: China-Africa Engagements: Ghana Country Case Study' (ACET, December 2009) 6–7 https://acetforafrica.org/research-and-analysis/reports-studies/multi-country-studies/looking-east-chinas-engagements-with-africa/ accessed 26 January 2024; ACET, 'Looking East: China-Africa Engagements: Rwanda Country Case Study' (Kigali December 2009)

4 Ralph Peters, 'The Undecided Continent' (2006) Armed Forces Journal, cited in Barry Sautman and Yan Hairong, 'East Mountain Tiger, West Mountain Tiger: China, the West, and "Colonialism" in Africa' (2006) Maryland Series in Contemporary Asian Studies vol 5 https://core.ac.uk/download/pdf/56353973.pdf accessed 19 May 2024; Diana Games, 'Chinese the New Economic Imperialists in Africa' (BusinessDay 21 February 2005); Nick Van Mead, 'China in Africa: Win-Win, or Colonialism' (Guardian 31 July 2018); Jean-Christoph Servants, 'China's Trade Safari in Africa' (Le Monde diplomatique 2005) http://archive.niza.nl/docs/200610161553573288.pdf accessed 19 May 2024; Johan Norberg, 'China Paranoia Derails Free Trade' (2006) Eastern Economic Review vol 196 (1) pp 46–9

DOI: 10.4324/9781032615059-7

> the standard of living for millions of Africans, not just an elite few. In Senegal, a Chinese company cannot be awarded an infrastructure-related contract unless it has partnered with a Senegalese company. In practice, Chinese companies are not only investing in Senegal but transferring technology, training, and know-how to Senegal at the same time.[5]

Accordingly, Africa can leverage the multipolarity resulting from its trade and investment engagement with China and the policy space it affords.[6] China's relationship with Africa is seen as the most viable alternative due to shared historical experiences, as both China and Africa were former colonies.[7] The impressive development and practical knowledge that China has demonstrated since the mid-1970s have instilled hope in the African continent. It is believed that China's interest in Africa offers an alternative model to the Western structural adjustment programmes of the 1980s and other conditionalities inherent in the agreements entered into between the West and African countries. In 1995, the EU suspended developing countries for gross violation of human rights or engaging in coup d'état.[8] The possibility of this action emanated from the provision of the Lomé Convention, which defines the rule of law, human rights, and democratic principles as crucial to the enforcement of the legal instrument between the EU and the ACP countries.[9] Article 9 (1) of the Cotonou Agreement provides respect for human rights and democracy based on the rule of law and accountable governance.[10] Article 96 broadens the essential elements of the procedure to follow if there is a breach of Article 9 by either of the parties. Article 97 stipulates that where corruption has occurred the party in question must step in to remedy the situation without delay. However, if the breach of the 'essential elements' continues, the appropriate measure would be to suspend the party.[11] Suspension means development aid will not be extended to the party who has breached the terms of the Convention—essential elements. While the Western countries impose human rights, good governance, and so forth, China distances itself from imposing these conditionalities and invests in Africa in exchange for raw materials.[12]

5 Abdoulaye Wade, 'Time for the West Practise what It Preaches' (Financial Times 23 January 2008) www.ft.com accessed 9 February 2024
6 Shinn and Eisenman (n 2) 128–4; Fantu Cheru and Cyril Obi (eds), *The Rise of China and India in Africa: Challenges, Opportunities and Critical Interventions* (Zed Books, 1988) 1
7 Eric Olander, 'China May Be a Lot of Things in Africa, but It Is Not a Coloniser' (23 July 2017) https://medium.com/@eolander/china-may-be-a-lot-of-things-in-africa-but-its-not-a-colonizer-628285cda6a0 accessed 19 May 2024; Brook Larmer, 'Is China the World's New Colonial Power' (The New York Times, 2 May 2017)
8 Karen Del Biondon, 'EU AID Conditionality in ACP Countries: Explaining Inconsistency in EU Sanctions Practice' (2011) Journal of Contemporary European Research vol 7 (3) pp 380–92
9 Karen Del Biondon, 'EU AID Conditionality in ACP Countries: Explaining Inconsistency in EU Sanctions Practice' (2011) Journal of Contemporary European Research vol 7 (3) pp 380–92 at 381
10 The Cotonou Agreement (2000) Article 9 (2)
11 The Cotonou Agreement Article 97 (3)
12 Arkebe Oquabay and Justin Yifu Lin, 'Introduction to China-Africa and Economic Transformation' in Arkebe Oquabay and Justin Yifu Lin (eds), *China-Africa and an Economic Transformation* (OUP, 2019) 2–8

African leaders and governments praised China's contribution to various African countries' infrastructure, the enlarged and visible economic projects, leading to job creation for the local workers with tangible construction and improvement to roads, rails, bridges, and transportation networks that have profited the common person.[13] Also, it has been pointed out that Chinese cooperation has improved services and quality of life. Censorship of China has been minimal because, according to David Shinn, there is no plan to 'kill the goose that is laying the golden egg.'[14] However, the major consternation posed by Chinese relations with Africa is the encroachment on the sovereign immunity of African states through the terms of agreements entered into between China and some African countries. Some of the terms of the agreement between China and Kenya are explored in this chapter from a commercial context to ascertain the extent to which it diminishes the sovereignty of Kenya.

The question remains whether the European Union style of relationship is preferable or whether the Chinese method would advance the African quest for development. The EU approach is succinctly stated in Article 2 of the Cotonou Partnership Agreement, 'ACP states shall determine the development strategies for their economies and societies in all sovereignty.'[15] This principle structures and directs all areas of cooperation between the EU and ACP. In reality, the EC is to provide support to existing national development plans and engage, for the most part, institutions and capacities in ACP countries; it supports national budgets but does not fund projects or programmes solely on its own. Article 8 of the Cotonou Agreement gave priority to political cooperation, which is discussed later in this chapter to understand the extension of EC interventionism and why China failed to follow the same path.

The chapter discusses China's engagement with Africa, with a particular focus on Kenya's relations with China. It examines the controversies surrounding Chinse encroachment into the sovereignty of African countries and analyses the position of the law, where countries have commercial transactions if sovereign states can still invoke and use sovereignty as a cloak. The chapter then explores the conditionalities imposed by the Western countries—why China has failed to apply the same rules in its relationship with African countries and whether this makes the Chinese approach to African development a preferred one.

7.2 China and Africa Engagement

China's quest for natural resources mounts because of its growing economy.[16] As a result, it is willing to invest in the extractive industries as well as transport, telecommunications, tourism, and other sectors in countries classified as high-risk

13 Wade (n 5)
14 Shinn and Eisenman (n 2)
15 The Cotonou Agreement 23 June 2000
16 Linda Yuen, 'China's Economic Emergence and Implications for Africa' in Arkebe Oquabay and Justin Yifu Lin (eds), *China-Africa and an Economic Transformation* (OUP, 2019) 25

because of insecurity—Sudan, Nigeria, and Angola.[17] China's obliviousness to the democratic agenda, spearheaded by the EU and the USA, has earned China many attributes of pursuing a colonial strategy, and their agenda is nothing short of self-interested mercantilist as it systematically tightens its grip on the African leaders.[18] The Chinese involvement in Africa cannot be described as a colonialist agenda, rather, as described by A'zami, it is a relationship between 'unequal equals.'[19] In contra-distinction to nineteenth-century imperialism, the rising hegemon has made substantial investments in Africa's infrastructure, notwithstanding that the infrastructure is directly linked to resource extraction.[20] The promoters of the democracy agenda in Africa may not win the fight against China because central to the Chinese agenda is the rehabilitation of infrastructure, which is key to Africa's development course.[21]

Jack Straw, a former home secretary from 1997 to 2001, foreign secretary from 2001 to 2006, and leader of the House of Commons, declared that Chinese activities bear semblance to what most of the British did in Africa for 150 years.[22] A former German Development Ministry official warned Africans to be critical of China as they may be facing a new form of colonialism.[23] A UK newspaper raises concerns about China being a new colonial power in Africa.[24] One wonders why the concerns about practicing colonialism in Africa have become a source of worry to the West. Top politicians in the UK declared that colonialism was advantageous and profitable for the colonised. For example, Margaret Thatcher expressed the view in 1988 that 'the story of how Europeans explored and colonised and yes, without apology-civilised much of the world, is an extraordinary tale of talent, skill and courage.'[25] Tony Blair in 1997 advised the Labour Party to extol and express pride in the British empire.[26] The academics are not left out in the praise of empire form of governance. Peter Bauer opined that the West did not cause the poverty of developing countries; rather, the contact of colonised countries with the West through colonialism brought much needed progress.[27] Niall Ferguson

17 Naidu (n1); David Luke, Kulani McCartan-Demie and Geofray Guepie, 'Africa's Trade Arrangements With the European Union and China' in David Luke (ed), *How Africa Trades* (LSE Press, 2023) 70
18 Sautman and Hairong (n 4)
19 Darius A'zami, 'China in Africa': From Under-Researched to Under-Theorised' (2015) Millennium Journal of International Studies vol 3 (2) pp 724–34
20 Jing Men and Benjamin Barton (eds), *China and the European Union in Africa in Africa: Partners or Competitors?* (Ashgate, 2011) 10–2, 32
21 Sautman and Hairong (n 4)
22 Quoted in Stevenson, 'Chinese Moves Spur a New Order, but There Is Nothing New About Colonisation (Daily Telegraph' 23 August 2006) 4
23 Brook Larmer, 'Is China the World's New Colonial Power' (The New York Times, 2 May 2017); Joseph Kahn, 'China Courts Africa, Angling for Strategic Gains NYT' (3 November 2006) 1
24 Conal Walsh, 'Is China the New Colonial Powers in Africa?' (The Observer 29 October 2006) www.theguardian.com/business/2006/oct/29/china.theobserver accessed 19 May 2024
25 Margaret Thatcher, 'Speech to the College of Europe' (The Brugers Speech)
26 John Kampfner, *Blair's Wars* (Free Press, 2004) 4
27 Peter T Bauer, *Equality, the Third World and Economic Delusion* (Harvard University Press, 1988) 70

recommended an empire style of governance in this twenty-first century, arguing that independence is a cataclysm. He advised that third world countries' sovereignty should be put on hold.[28] Andrew Robert argued that Britain's empire brought nothing but 'freedom and justice.'[29] Robert Cooper, Blair's foreign policy expert, head of the defence, and overseas secretary from 1999 to 2003, argued that when the West deals among themselves, they should apply the rule of law, and when they relate to the other 'traditional kinds of nations,' brutal force should be applied, what he termed the 'rule of the jungle.'[30]

Colonialism was a disastrous enterprise; its impacts on the colonised cannot be measured.[31] Contrary to the USA, who clandestinely supported colonialism and apartheid,[32] China was vehement in its opposition against these systems.[33] The African cannot forget in a hurry the assistance of the People's Republic of China (PRC) to end colonialism and apartheid on the continent.[34] Therefore, the label of China as colonialist or neocolonialist, according to Premier Wen Jiabao, does not stick as the Chinese also experienced the evils of colonialism.[35]

Since 1996, China has been the main investor in Sudan. The China National Petroleum Corporation (CNPC), which invests in oil exploration, production, and transportation infrastructure, owns 40% of the Greater Nile Petroleum Operating Company.[36] China has been criticised for failing to keep to the terms of the agreement of employing 80% of Sudanese. However, President Omar al-Bashir is not too concerned as Sudanese are employed and more people are obtaining technical training in China.[37] The China Petroleum and Chemical Corporation (Sinopec) constructed a 1,500 km pipeline to increase oil exports through Port Sudan. In

28 Niall Ferguson, *Empire: The Rise and Demise of the British World Order and the Lessons for Global Power* (Basic Books, 2004)

29 Andrew Robert, 'Why We Need Empires' (Sunday Telegraph 16 January 2005); Andrew Robert, 'Recolonise Africa' (DM, 8 January 2005) 20 cited in Barry Sautman and Yan Hairong, 'East Mountain Tiger, West Mountain Tiger: China, the West, and "Colonialism" in Africa' (2006) Maryland Series in Contemporary Asian Studies p 45, https://core.ac.uk/download/pdf/56353973.pdf accessed 19 May 2024; Robert Cooper, 'The New Liberal Imperialism' (The Guardian, 7 April 2002)

30 Robert Cooper, 'The Post Modern State' in Mark Leonard (ed), *Re-Ordering the World* (Foreign Policy Centre, 2002)

31 Sautman and Hairong (n 4) 45

32 Evelyn Colbert, 'The Road Not Taken: Decolonisation and Independence in Indonesia and Indochina' (1972) FA vol 51 (3); Robert Massie, *Loosing the Bonds: United States and South Africa in the Apartheid Years* (Nan A Talese/Doubleday, 1977)

33 Ian Taylor, *China and Africa: Engagement and Compromise* (Routledge, 2006) 28–31

34 Soutman and Hairong (n 22)

35 'China Premier Wen Jiabao, Gives Press Conference in Cairo' (Xinhua 19 June 2006) www.chinadaily.com.cn/china/2006-06/19/content_620692_2.htm

36 Joseph Hammond, 'Sudan: China's Original Foothold in Africa the Diplomat' (2017) https://thediplomat.com/2017/06/sudan-chinas-original-foothold-in-africa/ accessed 18 May 2024; Edward Yeranian, 'China Seeks Stronger Ties With Sudan Amid Regional, International Tug-of-War' (30 May 2023) www.voanews.com/a/china-seeks-stronger-ties-with-sudan-amid-regional-international-tug-of-war-/7115426.html accessed 18 May 2024

37 Joseph Hammond, 'Sudan: China's Original Foothold in Africa the Diplomat' (2017) https://thediplomat.com/2017/06/sudan-chinas-original-foothold-in-africa/ accessed 18 May 2024

2001, Harbin Power Engineering Company (HPE) constructed the Sudan Power Station with the assistance of a $110 million loan from China Export Import Bank of China (Eximbank).[38]

Since 1997, Chinese companies invested $24 million in a textile mill in Zambia and more than $300 million into mines, manufacturing projects, construction companies, and agriculture. However, the company employs more Chinese and pays a meagre salary to the local workers. Notwithstanding, the Zambians are glad that China is able to invest in an area that the West never would.[39] China's Eximbank granted a $2 billion credit line to Angola to rebuild infrastructure, assisting Sinopec to get concessions for oil exploration. 'The loan was connected to the guaranteed delivery of 10,000 barrels of oil per day.'[40] In 2006, China National Offshore Oil Corporation (CNOOC) signed a production-sharing contract in Equatorial Guinea.[41] CNOOC purchased a 45% stake in a Nigerian oil and gas field for $2.3 billion.[42]

It is interesting to know that Chinses interests are not restricted to oil exploration but to other natural resources as well.[43] COBEC, a Beijing-based company, offered to rehabilitate the Kamatanda copper and cobalt mines and other processing plants in Katanga province, Democratic Republic of the Congo, in a deal worth $27.5 million.[44] There has been negotiation to increase the Congolese stake in a cobalt and copper joint venture with Chinese firms to 70% from 32%; Congo is demanding $6 billion in infrastructure for a mineral agreement.[45] In Gabon, the China National and Machinery and Equipment Import and Export Corp invested $3 billion involving a 560-kilometre construction of the railway linking Belinga to Transgabonais, a deeper water mining port at Santa Clara, a hydroelectric dam, and a steel mill. In

38 Maglad Nour Eldin A, 'Scoping Study on Chinese Relations With Sudan' (2008) AERC 1–17 www.econstor.eu/bitstream/10419/93162/1/587559012.pdf accessed 18 May 2024

39 Chicago Tribune, 'China's Investment and Growing Clout in Africa Cause Concern' (Chicago Tribune 19 February 2006) www.chicagotribune.com/2006/02/19/chinas-investment-and-growing-clout-in-africa-cause-concern/ accessed 18 May 2024

40 Chicago Tribune, 'China's Investment and Growing Clout in Africa Cause Concern' (Chicago Tribune 19 February 2006) www.chicagotribune.com/2006/02/19/chinas-investment-and-growing-clout-in-africa-cause-concern/ accessed 18 May 2024; Sanucha Naidu, 'China and Africa's Natural Resources Sector: A View From South Africa' www.csis.org/analysis/china-and-africas-natural-resource-sector-view-south-africa

41 'CNOOC Inks Oil Deal With Equatorial Guinea' (Xinhua News Agency 19 February 2006) www.china.org.cn/english/2006/Feb/158520.htm accessed 18 May 2024

42 'Chinese Firm CNOOC to Buy 45% Stake in Nigeria Oil Filed' (Los Angeles Times 10 January 2006); Dulue Mbachu, 'Nigeria Resources: Changing the Playing Field' (2006) South African Journal of International Affairs vol 13 (1) pp 77–82

43 Chris Alden and Ana Christina Alves, 'China and Africa's Natural Resources: The Challenges and Implications for Development and Governance' (2009) Occasional Paper 41, SAIIA, at 6 https://saiia.org.za/wp-content/uploads/2009/09/Occasional-Paper-41.pdf accessed 19 May 2024

44 Sonia Rolley, 'Exclusive: Congo to Hike Stake in Copper, Cobalt Venture With China' (24 May 2023) www.reuters.com/markets/commodities/congo-hike-stake-copper-cobalt-venture-with-china-2023-05-24/ accessed 18 May 2024

45 Sonia Rolley, 'Exclusive: Congo to Hike Stake in Copper, Cobalt Venture With China' (24 May 2023) www.reuters.com/markets/commodities/congo-hike-stake-copper-cobalt-venture-with-china-2023-05-24/ accessed 18 May 2024

exchange, China is given the right to mine for iron ore in Belinga.[46] The China Rail Construction Corporation (CRCC), a subsidiary of China Civil Engineering Construction Corporation (CCECC), endorsed a contract with Nigeria's Federal Ministry of Transportation valued at $3.02 billion. The contract includes the rehabilitation of the railway from Port Harcourt to Maiduguri. The rail connection is to pass through 12 states. Besides reconstruction work, the current eastern railway projection is making additional construction of branch tracks. It is believed this project would facilitate the industrialisation of Nigeria.[47] The chairman of the CRCC, Mr. Dai-Hegen, reported to the president of Nigeria that they are near completion of the rail project linking Lagos-Ibadan and the Federal Capital Territory, the rail project of Kaduna-Kano will be completed in 2026. About 180,000 tons of cargo have been transported through the Abuja-Kaduna and Lagos-Ibadan Railway; also, the China Railway Construction Corporation (CRCC) signed an investment agreement with 119 companies in Nigeria, which stimulated $3 billion and created jobs for 4,000 in the country as well as paid $125 million in taxes.[48] Despite the potential profitability of the aforementioned investments, they have not been without disagreements and debates.

7.3 Loan Agreement Between Kenya and China

Kenya railway, which was built by the British a century ago, was in terrible shape[49] in 2006, with the World Bank's assistance, it was granted to the Private Rift Valley Railway Consortium, but years later, it was only able to handle 5% of the region's shipping.[50] To meet the United Nations' 2030 Strategic Development Goal,[51] the government in Kenya launched the Vision 2030 strategic plan in 2008.[52] In January 2009 the East African Railways Master Plan for the EAC was completed.[53] The Canadian consultants carried out a study and concluded that with US $1.2 billion, the old meter gauge railway could be renovated and would be able to handle 6.7% of regional demand, but only for 10 to 20 years.[54] While

46 AIDDATA, 'China Eximbank Pledge Loan for Belinga Iron Ore Project' (AIDDATA) https://china.aiddata.org/projects/630/ accessed 18 May 2024

47 AIDDATA, 'Nigeria's CCECC Secures $3.02 Billion Nigerian's Eastern Railway Contract' (29 April 2021) Railway Technology www.railway-technology.com/news/ccecc-nigerian-eastern-railway-contract/?cf-view accessed 18 May 2024

48 Deji Elumoye, 'Tinubu to Chinese Construction Executive: Your Investments Are Secure in Nigeria' (Arise News, 17 May 2024)

49 'World Bank, *Kenya Economic Update* (The World Bank, 2013) 3 www.worldbank.org/content/dam/worldbank/document/Africa/Kenya-economic-update-june-2013.pdf

50 Brendon Cannon, 'Inland Container Depots and the Future of Handling East Africa's Cargo' (Kenya Engineer 18 January 2018)

51 The UN Sustainable Development Goals (SDGs), Negotiated to Cover the Period 2015–2030, a Follow Up to the UN Millennium Development

52 Kenya, 'Towards a Globally Competitive and Prosperous Nation' (Kenya Vision Flagships Projects Progress Report (2008–2017)) https://vision2030.go.ke/wp-content/uploads/2021/11/KENYA-VISION-2030-FLAGSHIP-Projects-Progress-Report-2008–2017.pdf

53 CPCS, 'East African Railway Masterplan Study' (Final Report 2009)

54 Deborah Brautigam and Others, 'How Africa Borrows From China: And Why Mombasa Port Is Not Collateral for Kenya's Standard Gauge Railway' (China-Africa Research Initiative Working Paper 2022) 7–8

the government was considering how to approach the situation, China Road and Bridge Corporation (CRBC), a state-owned engineering firm that built part of the Shanghai-Beijing high-speed rail project, was invited by a notable Kenya industrialist, who then introduced the CRBC to the Kenyan president.[55]

On 12 August 2009, CRBC and the Kenya government signed a memorandum of understanding (MOU) that charged the CRBC to carry out a feasibility study and initial design for a brand-new standard gauge railway between Mombasa and Nairobi, without charge.[56] The feasibility study submitted in 2011 concluded that phase 1 of the railway could have an economic internal rate of return of almost 15%.[57] The construction contract was signed by the Kenya government for phase 1 of the Standard Gauge Railway (SGR), from Mombasa to Nairobi (470 km) with CRBC. Armed with the feasibility study carried out by CRBC, the Kenya government applied to China's export credit agency, China Eximbank, for financing.[58]

A multibillion dollar mega project like the SGR would naturally involve several parties and a diverse set of legal agreements to stipulate the reciprocal obligations of all the parties to the transaction.[59] In 2015 the OECD report on infrastructure finance observed that the intricate legal instruments are set up to allow for 'risk-sharing to align the incentive of all parties.'[60] The principal stakeholders were the Eximbank, China Road and Ridge Corporation, Kenya National Treasury, Kenya Port Authority (KPA), Kenya Rail Corporation (KRC), Sinosure (Chinese export credit insurance company), Kenya Revenue Authority and Auditor General (AG). Having established a brief background, the chapter now explores the controversy concerning using Mombasa Port as collateral for a Chinese loan.

According to Brautigam et al., the use of Kenya's Mombasa Port as collateral generated so much controversy that it revealed the rising geopolitical tensions between the West and China.[61] In 2019, a reporter for the *Sunday Nation* managed to obtain a copy of the preferential export buyer's credit loan between Kenya's National Treasury and China Eximbank.[62] 'Kenya's key strategic assets at home and abroad will not be protected by "sovereignty" and risk being seized by the

55 Deborah Brautigam and Others, 'How Africa Borrows From China: And Why Mombasa Port Is Not Collateral for Kenya's Standard Gauge Railway' (China-Africa Research Initiative Working Paper 2022) 7–8

56 Kenya National Assembly, Eleventh Parliament-Second Public Investments Committee, Special Report on the Procurement and Financing

57 China Road and Bridge Corporate, 'Chapter XII Economic Evaluation' in Feasibility Study Report of Kenya-Mombasa-Nairobi Railway Project (China Road and Bridges Corporation, 2011) 128

58 Kenya National Assembly, Eleventh Parliament-Second Session, 'Report of the Department Committee on Transport.' A Kenyan Appellate Court subsequently ruled that government breached the public procurement rules with the manner in which it handled the contract, see section 227 (1) of the constitution and section 6 (1) and 29 of the Public Procurement and Disposal Act, 2005 in the procurement of the SGR project.

59 Brautigam and others (n 54) 8–15

60 OECD, *Infrastructure Financing Instruments and Incentives* (OECD, 2015)

61 Brautigam and others (n 54) at 16

62 Edwin Okoth, 'SGR Pact With China a Risk to Kenya Sovereignty Assets' Nations 12 January 2019; Brautigam and others (n 54) at 17

Chinese government should there be a default.'[63] The Chinese ambassador to Kenya, Wu Pen, stated categorically,

> I can assure you that any loan agreement between China and Kenya is in line with common international practice. None of Kenya's national assets has been mortgaged for the SGR loan and neither can any of Kenya's assets be seized by the Chinese. I discussed these issues with my colleagues in Beijing and with the banks.[64]

However, Clause 15.5 of the loan contract provides that Kenya waive its right to sovereign immunity to all assets. There is no specific mention of the port in the agreement, however, but the clause makes assets a subject of collateral. Besides the point that the port was used as collateral, there was the claim of non-disclosure of the content of the agreement to the general public as required by the Kenya constitution.

Article 201 of Kenya's 2010 constitution provided that the public should be informed about public spending.[65] The Access to Information Act of 2016 requires all government information should be disclosed, subject to some limitations.[66] This also was a subject of debate in Kenya as to the extent of disclosure that should be allowed for public consumption. In 2019, the attorney general of Kenya made an intervention stating that provisions in commercial contracts are not required to be made public unless they are specifically obliged by Kenya law.[67] Nonetheless, in 2022, the court ordered that the loan contract between Kenya and China document be made public.[68] Another clause that generated the most controversy was Article 17.5 which provides that the parties, that is the Borrower, KRC, and KPA, agree to waive their sovereign immunity. The insertion of the sovereign immunity clause in the Kenya and China agreement sent a shockwave not only in Kenya but also throughout the continent of Africa. The clause on the governing law and sovereign immunity provides as follows: 'This Agreement and the rights and obligations of the parties hereunder shall, in all respects, be governed by and construed in accordance with the laws of China.'[69] Article 15.3 of the Agreement provides concerning jurisdiction:

> Any dispute arising out of or in connection with this Agreement shall be resolved through friendly consultation. If no settlement can be reached

63 Edwin Okoth, 'SGR Pact With China a Risk to Kenya Sovereignty Assets' Nations 12 January 2019
64 Amin Wako, 'Chinese Ambassador Explains Why SGR Contract Is Still "Top Secret" Nairobi News' (22 May 2019) https://nairobinews.nation.africa/chinese-ambassador-sgr-contract/ accessed 19 May 2024
65 The Constitution of Kenya, 2010
66 Access to Information Act No 31/2016 Articles 4 and 6 (1)
67 Philip Muyanga, 'AG Fights Quest for Disclosure of SH450bn SGR Contract With China' (Nation 23 August 2021)
68 Eric Olander, 'Kenyan Court Orders Government to Publish Loan Contract for SGR' (China Global South Project 16 May 2022) https://nation.africa/kenya/counties/mombasa/ag-fights-quest-for-disclosure-of-sh450bn-sgr-contract-with-china-3522310 accessed 19 May 2024
69 The Export-Import Bank of China and the Government of the Republic of Kenya Represented by the National Treasury of Kenya for the Kenya Mombasa-Nairobi Standard Gauge Railway Project 2014 Article 15.1

> through such consultation, each party shall have the right to submit such dispute to the China International Economic and Trade Arbitration Commission (CIETAC) for arbitration. The arbitration shall be conducted in accordance with the CIETAC's arbitration rules in effect at the time of applying for arbitration. The arbitral award shall be final and binding upon both parties. The arbitration shall take place in Beijing.[70]

Enormous projects such as the SGR would involve several parties with complex sets of legal agreements, to spell out the reciprocal obligations of all the parties.[71] According to the OECD report on infrastructure finance, a multipartite set of legal agreement structures are put in place to allow for 'risk-sharing to align the incentives of all parties.'[72] However, the clause could be perceived as biased because if there is a default or dispute between the parties, the matter would be referred to arbitration in China, where justice and fairness may not be assured. Clause 15.4 states that the 'Borrower irrevocably and unconditionally waives any objection.' China International Economic and Trade Arbitration Commission was initially called the Foreign Trade Arbitration Commission of the China Council for the Promotion of International Trade, presently used as its name 'Arbitration Institute of the China Chamber of International Commerce.'

Globally, arbitration in international commercial dispute resolution is recognised because of the benefits it affords parties. It is flexible, fast, and has a binding force. Although there are cultural differences, other forms of dispute resolution, mediation, and conciliation are the second most important model after arbitration. Also, mediation and conciliation have gained popularity in international and domestic commercial practice as a substitute for litigation. The United Nations Commission on International Trade Law (UNCITRAL) issued a model law on international commercial conciliation to provide for the ever-increasing development of international trade and e-commerce. According to the UNCITRAL Model Law, mediation and conciliation mean the same process of dispute resolution. A neutral third party is used to work with the parties to settle their dispute resulting from contractual transactions in a cordial manner. In arbitration, the arbitrators would make an arbitral award after hearing the parties.[73]

In Asia, based on the influence of Confucianism which emphasises the value of harmonious coexistence, informal mediation has been practised in China, Japan, and

70 'Export-Import Bank of China and The Government of the Republic of Kenya: Buyer Credit Loan for the Kenya Nairobi-Naivasha Standard Gauge Railway Project' (Contract No BLA201505)

71 Brautigam (n 54)

72 OECD, *Infrastructure Financing Instruments and Incentives* (OECD, 2015) 8, www.oecd.org.org/finance/private-pensions/Infrastruture—Financing-Instrument-and-Incentives-pdf accessed 19 November 2023

73 UNCITRAL Model Law on International Commercial Conciliation (2002,) Article 1; ICC, 'Guidance Notes on Resolving Belt and Road Disputes Using Mediation and Arbitration' https://iccwbo.org/content/uploads/sites/3/2019/02/icc-guidance-notes-belt-and-road-disputes-pdf.pdf/ accessed 2019

South Korea.[74] In Africa, Asia, and Europe, regional agreements on mediation have been reached, for instance, the '1964 Protocol of the Commission of Mediation and Arbitration of the Organisation of African Unity.' Again, the legal cultural values of the Asian society support mediation under the Belt and Road Initiative (BRI), which if integrated into economic cooperation, will be of immense gain to the parties, especially African countries in BRI. As seen in the prior provision, Article 15.3, China has blended mediation with arbitration. The orientation at the international level has been to integrate mediation with arbitration, and the result depends on what the parties accept.[75] It was reported by the China International Economic and Trade Arbitration Commission (CIETAC), that in 2016, 121,527 cases were resolved using mediation.[76] CIETAC published in its 2022 statistics and work plan that it saw steady growth in caseload and dispute. There is an indication of improved diversification of the types of disputes, geographical origins of parties, spoken languages of arbitration, governing laws, and involvement of arbitrators that are not in China, including in connection to arbitrators and funding for third parties. The main effort according to CIETAC is to globalise the rule of arbitration and further improve IT infrastructure and digital management in 2023.[77] CIETAC registered 4,086 new arbitration cases in 2022 and the total was approximately US $18.64 billion, being the fifth successive year that the amount in dispute in the cases registered by CIETAC exceeded Renminbi (RMB) 100 billion yuan (approximately US $14.69 billion). There were about 642 foreign cases with a total amount in dispute of RMB 37.4 billion, approximately $5.49 billion, almost one-third of the total amount in dispute for 2022, and CIETAC finished up 3,822 cases in 2022 with about 3,201 cases pending.

In 2022 international cases amounted to 83 cases where none of the parties was from the China mainland, as parties from 69 jurisdictions used CIETAC. The cases were connected to 83 countries and regions, as well as 32 countries and regions along the 'Belt and Road' area. Besides the PRC law, a variety of governing laws were applied to the dispute brought before CIETAC, comprising the United Nations Convention on Contracts for the International Sale of Goods (CISG), the laws of Hong Kong, Singapore, England, and Wales, and so on. In 115 cases, parties opted to use English or both English and Chinese as the languages of the arbitration. CIETAC'S panel comprised 591 arbitrators who were not in mainland China, and about 87 arbitrators not within mainland China took part in 83 cases.

Article 1 (2) of the CIETAC Arbitration Rule provides:

> where an arbitration agreement provides for arbitration by the China Council for the Promotion of International Trade/China Chamber of International

74 Lim Lan Yuan, *Court Mediation in Singapore* (F T Law & Tax Asia Pacific, 1997)

75 Wang Guiguo, 'On the Dispute Resolution Mechanism of the Belt and Road' in *Chinese Law Science* (Digest, 2017) 6, 56–71

76 CIETAC, 'Annual Report of China International Commercial Arbitration' www.cietac.org/Uploads/201710/59df3824b2849.pdf/ accessed 2016

77 'CIETAC 2022 Statistics Show Its Endeavours in Line With International Practices' (16 February 2023) https://hsfnotes.com/arbitration/2023/02/16/cietac-2022-statistics-show-its-endeavour-in-line-with-international-practices/

> Commerce, or by the Arbitration Commission or the Arbitration Institute of the China Council for the Promotion of International Commerce, or refers to CIETAC's previous names, it shall be deemed that the parties have agreed to arbitration by CIETAC.

Article 2 (3) states where CIETAC is located in Beijing, provisions are made for sub-commissions or arbitration centres. The aforementioned branches of CIETAC receive and conduct arbitration cases with CIETAC's authorisation. One would have expected that since China's commercial activities in Africa are high, it should have cited a branch of the CIETAC in Africa—this would allay the fears of bias and minimise the cost of travel for African countries that contract with China. However, the parties—China and Kenya—agreed to arbitration in the event of breach of the terms of the agreement. Article 4 (2) provides, 'parties have agreed to refer their dispute to CIETAC for arbitration, they shall be deemed to have agreed to arbitration in accordance with these Rules.' Article 6 (4) of the arbitration rules provides an allowance for a party to object to the jurisdiction of CIETAC before the hearing of the substantive matter.[78] Thus the Kenya party can always object to the jurisdiction of CIETAC, and if it has merit as provided in paragraph 7 of Article 6, the arbitrator may dismiss the case. However, the arbitration rules provide in Article 7 that if 'the parties have agreed on the place of arbitration, the parties' agreement shall prevail.' The rules further went on to state that even if the choice of a forum of the arbitration is not precise, then the location shall be the domicile of CIETAC. Paragraph 2 of Article 7 suggests that China at all times would prefer the domicile of CIETAC.

As mentioned earlier, clause 15.4 of the China-Kenya provision generated controversy, it provides:

> The Borrower irrevocably and unconditionally waives, any immunity to which it or its property may at any time be or become entitled, whether characterised as sovereign immunity or otherwise, from any suit, jurisdiction of any arbitral institutional or arbitral tribunal, judgment, arbitral award, service of process upon it or any agent, execution on judgment, enforcement of the arbitral award, set-off, attachment prior to judgment, attachment in aid of execution to which it or its assets may be entitled in any legal action or proceedings or arbitral proceedings with respect to this Agreement or any of the transactions contemplated hereby or hereunder.

According to Kidane, the provisions of the agreement reveal the underlying symmetrical power dynamics between China and Africa; these are sound signals that the relationship will be sustained due to the precise nature of the enforcement of the power symmetry.[79] Again, under Chapter 40 of the Laws of Kenya

78 CIETAC Arbitration Rules Article 6 (4) (5) (6)

79 Won L Kidane, 'Agreements and Dispute Settlement in China-Africa Economic Ties' in Arkebe Oqubay and Justin Yifu Lin (eds), *China-Africa and an Economic Transformation* (Oxford University Press, 2019) 224

(the 'Government Proceeding Act'), the agreement and transactions considered together amounted to commercial activities and not governmental or public activities of the Kenya government, which falls under private commercial law. As such, the Kenya government waives any immunity concerning the aforementioned provision.[80]

Sovereign immunity waivers are standard clauses in international commercial loan contracts.[81] Generally, sovereign states are not subject to litigation in international law.[82] In contrast to actors in the private market, such as individuals and corporations, a state cannot be coerced to appear before an international judge or arbitration tribunal, for instance by creditors if there is a default.[83] In the same way, the state is immune from the enforcement of a foreign judgment given against it, and government property cannot be converted to pay off its debt or seized.[84] Nevertheless, only a few international lenders are willing to give loans without legal means to recover the loan when the borrower defaults. According to Hoffman, 'in agreements with the host government and with entities controlled by the government, a waiver of sovereign immunity is required.'[85] Evidence of non-Chinese commercial project finance loan contracts released by the government of Cameroon revealed that banks from Belgium, Germany, Spain, Turkey, Austria, and the UK all demand sovereign immunity waivers.[86] Currently, the concerns over the waiving of sovereign immunity continue in Kenya and other parts of Africa.[87] However, as discussed later, waiver of immunity by a sovereign does not reduce in any way the sovereignty of a state even when a state permits itself to be a defendant in the lawsuit.[88] The concept of sovereign immunity in international law is not clear to many; for instance, it was reported that 'a leaked report by the Auditor General's office shows that the Kenyan government has in 2013 waived the port's sovereign

80 See Government Proceedings Act 1958 CAP 40 Sections 16 and 17

81 George Kahale III, 'State Loan Transactions: Foreign Law Restrictions on Waivers of Immunity and Submissions to Jurisdiction' (1982) The Business Lawyer vol 37 (4) pp 1549–68

82 Scott L Hoffman, *The Law and Business of International Project Finance* (2nd ed, Transnational Publishers, Inc., 1957) 158

83 Scott L Hoffman, *The Law and Business of International Project Finance* (2nd ed, Transnational Publishers, Inc., 1957) 158

84 August Reinisch, 'European Court Practice Concerning State Immunity From Enforcement Measure' (2006) EJIL vol 17 (4) pp 803–36 at 804–5

85 Scott LL Hoffman, *The Law and Business of International Project Finance* (CUP, 2012)158

86 Brautigam and others (n 54)

87 Press Release, 'Amaechi Explains Sovereignty Clause in $500M Chinese Railway Loan' (Premium Times, 2 August 2020); 'Chinese Loans and Our Sovereignty' (Vanguard, 8 August 2021); 'Chinese Loan and Nigeria's Sovereignty' (The Guardian 11 August 2020); Joseph Siegle, 'The Creeping Loss of African Sovereignty' (African Centre for Strategic Studies, 8 February 2023) https://africacenter.org/experts/creeping-loss-african-sovereignty/ accessed 19 May 2024

88 'China to Take Over Kenya Main Port Over Unpaid Huge Chinese Loan' (Hellenic Shipping News 22 November 2019) www.hellenicshippingnews.com/china-to-take-over-kenyas-main-port-over-unpaid-huge-chinese-loan/; George Omond, 'Mombasa Port at Risk as Audit Finds It Was Used to Secure SGR Loan' (The East African, 5 July 2020) www.theeastafrican.co.ke/tea/business/mombasa-port-at-risk-as-audit-finds-it-was-used-to-secure-sgr-loan-1408886

immunity to use it as a security for the Chinese loan.'[89] Yet, there is a difference between a standard sovereign immunity waiver endorsed by all parties to a contract and a particular property to be used as collateral.[90] A security, that is collateral in an agreement, is a backup payment mechanism that can only be activated when the borrower defaults on the loan.

Legal contracts between sovereign states are fundamentally not similar to those reached between private individuals, as the sovereign is immune from court action. In the year 1976, the US adopted a Foreign Sovereign Immunities Act (FSIA); in law, foreign governments are immune from lawsuits except if they expressly waive this immunity.[91] Once there is a waiver of sovereign immunity, it permits the state to sue in a foreign court or allow for international arbitration. However, the challenges of enforcement remain if the borrower is adjudged to be liable. It is important to note that waiver of immunity from enforcement is not the same as the first waiver, which is for the aim to be proceeded against in a court action or arbitration and is accompanied by serious technical legal difficulties about the sovereign immunity laws of the involved jurisdictions. Sovereign assets that are not for commercial purposes are completely protected.

Arguments remain that it is impossible for an equal to exercise control over another equal.[92] Nevertheless, in recent times in continental European countries, the paradigm has shifted toward restrictive immunity. The swing toward this acceptance may be due to the need for stable, fair play, good faith, and substantial justness in the modern world of commercial transactions.[93] Several renowned scholars have made suggestions that a distinction between *acta jure imperii* and *acta jure gestionis* should be established as an overture setting up restrictive immunity. In other words, a state that engages in private transactions should not enjoy immunity but like a private individual should be subjected to liability.[94] Even though the majority of legal scholars have agreed that immunity be restricted in international law, there is no informed law acceptable to all committees of nations that will regulate such restriction.[95]

89 Deborah Brautigam and Won Kidane, 'China, Africa, and Debt Distress: Fact and Fiction About Asset Seizures' (Policy Brief, China Africa Research Initiative 2020) www.sais-cari.org; Laure Deron, Thierry Pairault and Paola Pasquali Montenegro, 'China and Media: A Highway to Disinformation' (Briefing Paper, Briefing Paper No 17/2021, China Africa Research Initiative 2021)

90 Christina Bohannan, 'Beyond Abrogation of Sovereign Immunity: State Waivers, Private Contracts, and Federal Incentives' (2002) NYU Law Review vol 77 (273) pp 288, 292 at 303–4

91 United Nations 94th Congress, The Foreign Sovereign Immunities Act (FSIA) of 1976, Title 28, 1330, 1332, 1391 (f), 1441 (d), and 1602–1611, Washington DC: United States Public Law 94–583, Accessed

92 Ernest K. Bankas, *The State Immunity Controversy in International Law: Private Suites Against Sovereign States in Domestic Courts* (Springer, 2005)

93 Ian Brownlie, *Principles of Public International Law* (OUP, 1990) 323–45; Rosalyn Higgins, 'Certain Unresolved Aspects of the Law of State Immunity' (1982) NYIL vol 29, pp 265–6

94 F A Mann, 'The State Immunity Act 1978' (1979) BYIL vol 50 (1) pp 43–60; Brownlie (n 93) at 332-345

95 United Nations, Yearbook of the International Law Commission vol II Part one (ILC Report 1986) 25 Article 12 of the Draft Article on Jurisdiction Immunities of State and Their Property; M Sornarajoh, 'Problems in Applying the Restrictive Theory of Sovereign Immunity' (1982) ICLQ vol 31 pp 661–85

The logic for the wide acceptance of the concept of restrictive immunity is that states do not always act in a public capacity but sometimes as a private person, which falls out of the conventional functions of the state.[96] Professor Hyde, an advocate of restrictive immunity, refused to side with the prior argument that a state can act in a dual capacity. According to the author, a state never operates in a private capacity, even when engaging in activities typically managed by private individuals even if the act is usually carried out by private citizens.[97]

According to Judge Weiss, the objective test aids in determining if the nature of the business transacted by the state can be designated as one by essence or form to be sovereign or an act carried out by an individual. Therefore, if the act is depicted as *acta jure imperii* then to Weiss immunity must be permitted;[98] but if it is an act that an individual can undertake, then immunity must be denied.[99] Sir General Fitzmaurice was vehement against making any form of distinction between sovereign and non-sovereign acts.[100] However, the USA after dragging with the decision of the Supreme Court, led by Chief Justice Marshall in the *locus classicus* case of sovereign immunity—*Schooner v McFadden*,[101] altered its stands in 1952 when the Tate letter was issued from the department to deviate from absolute immunity.[102] *Alfred Dunhill of London, Inc v Republic of Cuba*[103] *seemed to have followed the path of the Tate letter when it nearly agreed with the principle of restrictive immunity. It gave a decision that rescinding commercial debt cannot be defined as an act of state and, as such, declined immunity. Chief Justice Marshall in the case of Bank of the United States v Planters Bank of Georgia*, states,[104]

> it is, we think, a sound principle, that, when a government becomes a partner in any trading company, it divests itself, so far as concerns the transactions of that company, of its sovereign character, and takes that of a private citizen. Instead of communicating to the company its privileges and its prerogatives, it descends to a level with those with whom it associates itself, and takes the

96 The Philippine Admiral (owner) v Wallem Shipping (Hong Kong) and Another (1977) AC 373 (JC); Trendtex Trading v Central Bank of Nigeria (1977) QB 529 (CA); I Congreso del Partico (1983) 1 AC 244 (HL)

97 Charles Cheney Hyde, *International Law* (Little Brown, 1945) 12–844

98 Andre Weiss, 'Competence ou Incompetence des Tribunaux a Legard des Etats Estrangers' (1923–1) Hague Recueil p 523 cited in Ernest K Bankas, *The State Immunity Controversy in International Law: Private Suits Against Sovereign States in Domestic Court* (Springer, 2005) 75

99 Andre Weiss, 'Competence ou Incompetence des Tribunaux a Legard des Etats Estrangers' (1923–1) Hague Recueil p 523 cited in Ernest K Bankas, *The State Immunity Controversy in International Law: Private Suits Against Sovereign States in Domestic Court* (Springer, 2005) 75

100 Gerald G Fitzmaurice, 'State Immunity From the Proceedings in Foreign Courts' (1933) 14 BYIL 101 p XIV

101 (1976) 336 F. 2d 354 2nd Civ

102 Simon G Jerome, 'Throwback Thursday: The Tate Letter and Foreign Sovereign Immunity' (26 May 2022) Litigation Blog https://tlblog.org/throwback-thursday-the-tate-letter-and-foreign-sovereign-immunity/ accessed 21 May 2024

103 (1976) 425 U.S 682

104 (1824) 9 Wheat. 904, 22 U.S 904

character which belongs to the associates, and to the business which is to be transacted.[105]

The power of the court in the USA to examine cases of commercial disputes between sovereign states and private companies was given to the State Department before the enactment of the Foreign Sovereign Immunity Act, which to a large extent structured the theory of immunity.

Article 1602 Foreign Sovereign Immunity Act vested power in the judiciary to determine if a particular activity of foreign states is commercial. Section 1010 of the act provides among other things for the enforcement of a judgment against foreign governments if it is well defined and unambiguous.[106] The provision of Articles 1609 to 1611 eliminates *in rem* and quasi *in rem* jurisdiction over foreign states[107] but permits jurisdiction over a foreign state with regards to *in personam* jurisdiction.[108] Action in court against foreign sovereigns in the US court is now possible after the enactment of the FSIA when the subject matter is commercial. In the case of the *National American Corp v the Federal Republic of Nigeria*,[109] the defendant invoked the maxim *par in parem nom habet imperium* to evade liability; the court gave judgment that the transaction and the kernel of the matter dealing with a letter of credit met the criterion stipulated in section 1605 (a) (2) of the act. Consequently, the sovereign immunity was denied as the beneficiary of the contract suffered a loss in the USA. In respect of attachment of property, the US court has always maintained that sovereign states must be accorded immunity from execution, arrest, and attachment of property.[110] This position has been changed in the US court under section 1610 of the FSIA; therefore, if a certain condition exists, immunity will not avail a foreign state if the property is situated in the US and used for commercial activity, or where the foreign state voluntary without coercion waives immunity.[111] The previous analysis demonstrated that the inclusion of a waiver of immunity clause in Chinese-Kenya and other African loan agreements follows international law best practices and municipal laws.

7.4 Western Conditionality and Beijing Non-Interventionism

The Washington Consensus reduced the role of government to pro-market interventions, like security and protection of lives and property rights, investments,

105 (1976) (n 103) at 425 U.S. 696

106 Beverly May Carl, 'Foreign Sovereign in American Courts: The United State Foreign Sovereign Immunities Act in Practice' (1979) Southwestern Law Journal vol 33 p 1009; Mark B Feldman, 'The United States Foreign Sovereign Immunities Act of 1976 in Perspective: A Founder's View' (1986) ICLQ vol 35 p 302

107 28 USC 1609–1611

108 Carl Pennoyer v Neff (1877) 95 US 714

109 (1978) 448 F. Supp. 622

110 Ian M Sinclair, 'The European Convention on State Immunity' (1973) ICLQ vol 22, p 254; Ian Sinclair I, *The Law of Sovereign Immunity, Recent Developments* (vol 167, Sijthof, 1980) 222

111 Section 1610 of FSIA

infrastructure, and other services such as education.[112] For the Chinese, the dogma of the market remains that economic development can only happen with a strong role for the state; in other words, a strong state presence in market affairs is best for growth. Before a country becomes actively engaged in global competition, the country must allow the industries to grow strong and stable enough to withstand foreign competition. The prior description is what China represents for Africa—state involvement in the process of development.

There were several innovative ideas of cooperation in the Lomé Conventions and the Cotonou Agreement that were purposed to practically address the diverse problems faced by ACP countries. Thus, Article 8 of the Cotonou Agreement gave priority to political cooperation. It provides, 'The parties to the Agreement shall regularly engage in a comprehensive, balanced and deep political dialogue leading to commitments on both sides.' While the series of Lomé Conventions focused on economic cooperation, the Cotonou Agreement emphasised politics, strengthening democratic processes, the rule of law, and various reforms for good governance in ACP countries.[113] A partner could impose sanctions if parties breach these essential elements which are the foundation of the agreement, for example, human rights. For instance, some ACP countries were sanctioned for not complying with essential elements of the Lomé Conventions; Mauritania in 2005 and 2008, Fiji in 2007, Guinea in 2009, and Madagascar in 2009 were sanctioned for coup d'état, which is a violation of Article 9 and triggered Article 97 (3). Also, in 2001 Zimbabwe was sanctioned for a steady rise in violence and insecurity, lack of freedom of expression, pre-electoral violence, and illegal occupation of land. Liberia was suspended for lack of freedom of the press and freedom of expression, including violations of human rights. The EU believes that the provision of development aid for the alleviation of poverty may work in the short term but without sound policies such as respect for the rule of law, it may not be sustainable.[114] Also, adequate trade policies need to be in place, with fair international rules for the aid to be of help to ACP countries.

A communication, entitled in 2005 'EU Strategy for Africa: Toward a Euro-Africa Pact to Accelerate Africa's Development,' the key focus was to meet up with Millennium Development Goals (MDGs). It was purposed to find a solution to make aid more coherent and effective for development. It was believed that peace, security, and good governance must take place before meaningful development could occur.[115] The point continues to be emphasised by the high representative for Common Foreign and Security Policy (CFSP), Javier Solana, wherein the promotion

112 Thomas I Palley, 'From Keynesianism to Neoliberalism: Shifting Paradigms in Economics' (Foreign Policy in Focus, 5 May 2004) https://fpif.org/from_keynesianism_to_neoliberalism_shifting_paradigms_in_economics/ accessed 20 May 2024

113 The Cotonou Agreement Articles 9 and 10

114 The Cotonou Agreement Article 9 (3)

115 EC, 'EU Strategy for Africa: Towards a Euro-Africa Pact to Accelerate Africa's Development' (Brussels 12 October 2005, COM 489) https://eur-lex.europa.eu/LexUriServ/LexUriServ.do?uri=COM:2005:0489:FIN:EN:PDF accessed 20 May 2024

of peace and security in Africa was seen as key to the CFSP.[116] The EU Parliament unanimously believed that there is a need for one coherent policy toward Africa and utilised conditionality for the advancement of human rights and democratic values.[117] The EU stated again strongly its commitment to peace and security by reinforcing the African Peace Facility, and political conditionality was then replaced by the African Peer Review Mechanism (APRM), which was set by African governments.[118] The strategy was faulted due to lack of wide consultation with all parties.

Similarly, the Africa Growth Opportunity Act (AGOA) under the eligibility clause, section 104, lists several conditions that must be met to participate in AGOA. Sub-paragraph (A) of 1 provides for minimising 'government interference in the economy through measures such as price controls, subsidies, and government ownership of economic assets.' Paragraph 2 disqualifies any country that takes part in an act that threatens the 'foreign policy interest' of the United States. Paragraph 3 makes ineligible any country that facilitates or takes part in 'gross violations of internationally recognised human rights or provide[s] support for acts of international terrorism and cooperate[s] in international efforts to eliminate human rights violations and terrorist activities.'

In the reauthorisation of AGOA talks in South Africa 2023, Anthony Blinken remarked, 'new jobs, new investment, less corruption, and greater human and labour rights, will translate to new and powerful partnership.'[119] It was in the same forum that some African countries were ejected from AGOA because they did not live up to the standard of Western ideas of protection of human rights. The AGOA programme was launched in 2000 for the promotion of 'economic growth, good governance and free markets in Africa.' The essence of AGOA was not formed to penalise African countries whose policies do not align with those of developed countries. Yet, this is what it has become, according to Odrek Rwabwogo, special presidential adviser to President Yoweri Museveni. In the trade moves to delist Uganda, the US is informing the Ugandans that 'their already slim prospects for economic prosperity are contingent on whether they vote in line with the values of whoever happens to hold high office in the US, not their own.' The officials in Uganda have connected the country's removal from AGOA as an attempt to coerce them to invalidate the anti-homosexuality law, passed by parliament in May 2023.[120]

116 Maurizio Carbone, 'Better Aid Less Ownership: Multi-Annual Programming and the EU's Development Strategies in Africa' (2008) Journal of International Development vol 20 pp 118–229; Solana Javier, 'Challenges for EU-China Cooperation in Africa' (China Daily, 7 February 2007)

117 Maria Martens, 'A Development Strategy for Africa' (European Parliament 27 October 2005, Report-A6–0318/2005) www.europarl.europa.eu/doceo/document/A-6-2005-0318_EN.html accessed 17 May 2024

118 Stephen Kingah, 'The New EU Africa Strategy: Grounds for Cautious Optimism' (2006) European Foreign Affairs Review vol 11 (4) pp 527–53; Siegmar Schmidt, 'Toward a New EU-Africa Relationship- a Grand Strategy for Africa?' (2008) Foreign Policy in Dialogue vol 8 (24) pp 8–18, cited in Maurizio Carbone, 'The EU in Africa: Increasing Coherence, Decreasing Partnership' https://is.muni.cz/el/fss/podzim2015/EVS188/um/Carbone.pdf?lang=en

119 Anthony J Blinken, 'Secretary of State's Address at South Africa's Future' (African Institute, 9 August 2022) www.agoa.info accessed 12 November 2023

120 Isaac Kaledzi, 'Uganda Criticises US Plan to Exclude It From Duty-Free Trade Programme' (November 2023) www.agoa.info

In 2015, the East Africa Community (EAC) heads of state adopted to start the process of phasing out used clothes and footwear.[121] The aim was to promote textile and leather factories, to produce enough and export the surplus, in line with the region's industrial policy.[122] This will enable the region to take advantage of the African Growth and Opportunity Act market, which has granted favourable access to exports from Africa. Before the ban, it was estimated that the EAC imported used clothes worth $274 million.[123] The EU, the US, and China were listed as the leading exporters of used clothes to Africa and other part of the world. The organisation called the Secondary Materials and Recycled Textiles Association (SMRTA) in the US filed a petition with the office of the US Trade Representative (USTR) regarding the EAC's ban on second-hand clothes. The complaint was that the EAC ban caused 'significant economic hardship' in the used clothing industry in the US. It is reported that the EAC ban could cause the loss of 40,000 jobs in the US and $124M in exports. By 2017 USTR warned the four countries, Kenya, Uganda, Tanzania, and Rwanda, in East Africa to backpedal or be removed from the category of AGOA as beneficiaries. The threat was potent. In the middle of 2017, Kenya announced that it would 'comply' with the terms of AGOA and allow the dumping of used clothes. It has been suggested that Kenya withdrew because it benefitted more from exports under AGOA than Rwanda. Exports under AGOA are worth $600m compared to only $43m. Tanzania and Uganda surrendered to the threat and pressure from the US as well. However, Rwanda refused to be cowed into withdrawal but is refused access to the US market under AGOA.

The aforementioned conditionalities, according to Cheru and Obi,[124] were the reason African leaders accepted Chinese aid and the latter's influence in the oil sector in Africa, which was initially leased to Western countries. According to Naidu and Corkin,[125] the Chinese leadership proposed a sturdy development assistance package for Africa during the first Heads of State Summit of the Forum on China-Africa Cooperation (FOCAC) in Beijing. However, a British newspaper stated in 2006 that all likelihood of change has been utterly defeated in Africa because China dealt with kleptocrats.[126] Nonetheless, at FOCAC, the Chinese emphasised the protection of the interest of Africa; there was no mention of

121 The East African Community, 17th Extra-Ordinary Summit of Heads of State of East Africa Community (EAC) 2016 (EAC/17/2016) https://www.eac.int/communique/552-953-770-communique-17th-extra-ordinary-summit-of-heads-of-state-of-the-east-african-community

122 East Africa Community Industrialisation Policy 2012-2032: Structural Transformation of the Manufacturing Sector Through High-Value Addition and Product Diversification Based on Comparative and Competitive Advantages of the Region (https://bdears.busitema.ac.ug/server/api/core/bitstreams/9a7d12b1-2adc-4534-96e5-f266b913c0ff/content)

123 Alice Kagina, 'Africa: AfCFTA-African Ministers Adopt Ban on Trade of Second-Hand Clothes' (The New Times, 2 June 2023)

124 Fantu Cheru and Cyril Obi, *The Rise of China and India in Africa* (Zed Books, 2010) 186

125 Sanusha Naidu and Lucy Corkin, 'Who Was the Real Winner in China?' (Business Day, 9 November 2006)

126 'China Winning Resources and Loyalties of Africa' (Financial Times, 2006)

oil-rich Africa and its benefit to China.[127] Chinese official development assistance (ODA) is embraced because it is unencumbered from the all-pervasive Western aid conditionalities. Therefore, African leaders see an alternative approach to OECD terms of agreement promoted by the Washington Consensus.[128] In the early 2000s, like most African countries, Kenya's foreign aid originated solely from Western countries—about US $750 million.[129] The presence of China in Kenya means that the latter permutated external sources of development aid, for instance, were reported in 2018 to be approximately USD $4.75 billion in Chinese loans.[130] The policymakers in Kenya appraised China's aid as unencumbered by burdensome conditions, and as such favour it in contradistinction with Western aid, which is only granted based on good governance, democracy, and signing some international treaties.

7.4.1 The Chinese Alternative

During the FOCAC meeting in Beijing in 2006, the government of China made a promise to increase development in 2009, provide more loans and debt relief, and establish a China-Africa Development Fund with more technical assistance.[131] The Chinese policy towards Africa was welcomed wholeheartedly by the latter's leaders. For instance, President Museveni declared, 'the Western ruling groups are conceited, full of themselves, ignorant of our conditions. Whereas Chinese just deal with you, you represent your country, they represent their interests, and you do business.'[132] President Mogae of Botswana also states, 'I find that the Chinese treat us as equals. The West treats us as former subjects. Which is a reality. I prefer the attitude of the Chinese to that of the West.'[133]

China's cooperation with Africa is based on eight constructs, articulated by Zhou Enlai in 1964: mutual benefit; no conditionality; no increase of the debt burden;

127 Cisse Dawouda, FOCAC: Trade, Investments and Aid in China-Africa Relations' Centre for Chinse Studies, Stellenbosch University 2012 at 6

128 Horace Campbell, 'China in Africa: Challenging US Global Hegemony' (2008) Third World Quarterly vol 28 (1) pp 89–105 at 90–2; Bin Xu, 'China's Economy: Historical Perspective and Future Outlook' (CEIBS Research, 31 August 2023) www.ceibs.edu/new-papers-columns/23641

129 Annalisa Prizzon and Tom Hart, *Age of Choice: Kenya in the New Development Finance Landscape* (Overseas Development Institute, 2016) 13 https://media.odi.org/documents/10986.pdf

130 Anzetse Were, 'Debt Trap? Chinse Loans and Africa's Development Options' (2018) South African Institute of International Affairs, Policy insight, No. 6, at 3, https://saiia.org.za/wp-content/uploads/2018/09/Policy-Insights-66.pdf

131 Ian Taylor, *The Forum on China–Africa Cooperation (FOCAC)* (Routledge, 2011)

132 Stephan Stephen Halper, *The Beijing Consensus: How China's Authoritarian Model Will Dominate the Twenty-First Century* (Basic Books, 2010) 100

133 Sunday Standard Reporter, 'Chinese Envoy tries to Snatch Friendship From the Jaws of Xenophobia' (2013) 2 cited in Frank Youngman, 'Strengthening Africa-China Relations: A Perspective From Botswana' (5 November 2013) Discussion Paper 6 http://ias.zjnu.edu.cn/_upload/article/files/5f/18/6ba18a914b2db3af607d5930ed65/1b4719b5-d8f6-49ec-90a5-232fe455b86a.pdf accessed 21 May 2024

development of national economies without any form of dependence; focus on the project with return; high-quality support at market value; technological transfer; and no extra benefit for the Chinese experts working in Africa.[134] There are other principles in connection with foreign assistance adopted in the 1950s: peaceful coexistence, non-aggression, non-interference, respect for sovereignty, and territorial integrity.

The institutionalisation of mutual relations under the Forum on China-Africa Cooperation (2000) included new principles concerning human rights and good governance.[135] The message from China to Africa is straightforward, which is that every state's sovereignty should be respected and free to determine its method of achieving development; in other words, no external actor should interfere in the domestic policies of another. 'China believes that its successful "growth at any cost" strategy at home can be applied in Africa and is not shy about it.'[136] China's policy toward Africa was well captured in the speech by the Chinese president at the United Nations in September 2015, that the country would increase investment in the least developed countries, mostly in Africa, by no less than $12 billion by 2023.

Nevertheless, China's 'benevolence' in Africa has been questioned in some quarters. For instance, former Central Bank of Nigeria governor Lamido Sanusi warned Africa about the extractive policies of China and likened China's activities in Africa to the colonial powers in the nineteenth century.[137] Africa's Chinese approach to development is seen as a threat and an attempt to eliminate the effort made so far by Western institutions to improve the protection of human rights and ensure transparency on the continent of Africa. For example, the relationship of China with Sudan and Zimbabwe in the past had been a source of worry for the mainstream media. In the midst of what the EU and USA have called genocide in Darfur, China continues to import oil from Darfur and supply weapons used by the government forces and militia against rebellious forces.[138] Moyo depicted China as 'shrewd, selfish, calculating, greedy and primitive because it prioritises its economic and political interests over ordinary people's human rights in its dealing with African countries.'[139] China was blamed for the human rights violation in Guinea in 2009.[140] China engages in government-to-government

134 'Friend Doesn't Cancel a Visit—Premier Zhou Enlai's Visits to 10 African Countries' (Global Times, 18 June 2021) www.globaltimes.cn/page/202106/1226506.shtml

135 Ian Taylor, *African Rising? BRICS—Diversifying Dependency* (James Currey, 2014) 89–92

136 Madison Condon, 'China in Africa: What the Policy of Non-Intervention Adds to the Western Development Dilemma' (2012) The Fletcher Journal of Human Security vol 27 (1) pp 1–25 at 6

137 William Wallis, 'Africa Told to View China as Competitor' (Financial Times, 11 March 2013)

138 Last Moyo, 'China's Role in African Politics Appalling' (AllAfrica, 18 July 2008) https://allafrica.com/stories/200807180654.html

139 Last Moyo, 'China's Role in African Politics Appalling' (AllAfrica, 18 July 2008) https://allafrica.com/stories/200807180654.html

140 Matthew Berger, 'Deal With Guinea Raises Questions About Chinese Role' (AllAfrica, 16 October 2009) https://allafrica.com/stories/200910161163.html

agreements and requires that foreign aid contracts be granted to Chinese contractors behind closed doors. Contrary to Western loans, which put in place tight measures against corruption, China has weak measures against corruption in its overseas dealings as its officials are not precluded from bribing foreign governments or officials.

Deborah Brautigam, an expert on China-Africa relations, expressed the view in an interview that China believes that a focus on economic development, through building industries, job creation, and generation of investment, would automatically raise the standard of living and improve good governance, and democracy would be a natural process as everyone is empowered economically. This was seen in the case of Taiwan, Korea, and Japan as economic development proceeded with their democracy after advanced industrialisation. China is aware of the poor governance in Africa but believes that economic development should kick start and stabilise and all else will be a natural consequence. However, the West holds a different perspective. First, there has to be good governance, democracy, and protection of human rights, then economic development will take place.

While the Western world continues to amplify the negative impact of China's practices in Africa, the latter did not shy away from its position. For instance, Li Ruogu, the head of China Export-Import (EXIM) Bank, informed an audience in Cape Town, 'Transparency and good governance are good terminologies, but achieving them is not a precondition of development; it is rather the result of it.'[141] Also, another concern is the speed with which China is cutting deals to secure the supplies of oil, copper, timber, natural gas, zinc, cobalt, iron, and other natural resources. China's investment and development aid to Africa is tied to securing raw materials in countries rich in the aforementioned resources. The West has criticised China for taking undue advantage of African countries by using investment needs and providing funds to obtain extraction rights. It is hard to back that claim. However, it was alleged that China pledged a US $5 billion loan to obtain 50% equity in a US $40 billion platinum concession.[142] This generated so much controversy because at the time Zimbabwe was under Western sanctions. In Mozambique, Chinese companies engaged in extensive logging while it protected its forest in China.[143]

Concerning labour practice, Chinese companies employ a minimal number of locals and engage more of their own professionals and labourers to handle projects in Africa. In Angola, Chinese companies employed not less than 70% to 80% of their labour from China. But 90% of Chevron's employees are Angolan, including

141 Richard Behar, 'China Surpasses US as Leader in Sub-Sahara' (Fast Company, 6 January 2008) www.fastcompany.com/849681/china-surpasses-us-leader-sub-sahara

142 Max Hamata and Wonder Guchu, 'China-Africa Deal a Lose-Lose Situation' (2009) www.pairault.fr/sinaf/index.php/15-references/80-informante-china-africa-deal-a-lose-lose-situation accessed 20 May 2024

143 Richard Behar, 'China Saps Mozambique of Time Resources' (Fast Company, 6 January 2008) www.fastcompany.com/849679/china-saps-mozambique-timber-resources

specialised personnel like engineers and managers, whereas Chinese oil companies' local workers are not up to 15% and are usually at the bottom of the cadre.[144] Thus, according to Hitchens, the Chinese are invaders and not investors.[145] The Chinese are also accused of flouting domestic laws, as they are alleged not to have regard for safety measures and pay less than the country's prescribed minimum wage.[146]

Responding to the criticism levelled at China's activities in Africa, Beijing launched a counter to the accusation. In 2009, at the FOCAC summit, China's assistant foreign minister made it clear that China did not intend to display any form of hegemonic power and had no plan to engage in colonialism in Africa. Unlike the West, imperialism is not on its agenda.[147] China, in turn, accused the USA and the EU of duplicity, stating that their relationship with Africa has not been anything close to magnanimity or any example to show from past to present.[148] China does not burden Africa with economic restructuring that always accompanies Western countries and international aid agencies enforced on Africa.[149]

Notwithstanding that the attitude of China was warmly embraced by African leaders, the EU policy towards Africa has not changed, as the EU continues to impose its conditions.[150] For example, the EU did not alter its previous positions on foreign aid, the Economic Partnership Agreement (EPA), and agriculture policy. According to Carbone, the concerns of African leaders are that the EU failed to maintain their promises in terms of development assistance and that trade barriers and agriculture subsidies are protected against African markets by the EU, and this has obstructed the capacity to trade as equals.[151] Also, the EU continues to impose its normative agenda of human rights and democratic governance.[152]

144 Loro Horta, 'Food Security in Africa: China's New Rice Bowl' (2009) China Brief vol (1) https://jamestown.org/program/food-security-in-africa-chinas-new-rice-bowl/; Loro Horta, 'The Zambezi: China's First Agricultural Colony (20 May 2008) Centre for Strategic and International Studies www.csis.org/analysis/zambezi-valley-chinas-first-agricultural-colony

145 Peter Hitchens, 'How China Has Created a New Slave Empire in Africa' (Mail Online, 28 September 2008)

146 George Ofosu and David Sarpong, 'The Evolving Perspective on the Chinese Labour Regime in Africa' (2022) Economic and Industrial Democracy vol 43 (4) pp 1747–66 at 1748–9

147 Atoaneta Bezola, 'Latest Africa Foray: Altruism or Hegemony' (Global Issues, 2009) www.globalissues.org/news/2009/11/09/3436

148 Barry Sautman and Hairong Yan, 'African Perspective on China-Africa Links' (2009) The China Quarterly vol 199 pp 728–59; Lydia Polgreen, 'As Chinese Investment in Africa Drops, Hope Sinks' (New York Times, 25 March 2009)

149 Lydia Polgreen, 'As Chinese Investment in Africa Drops, Hope Sinks' (New York Times, 25 March 2009)

150 R Marchal, 'The EU and China in Africa: Opportunities and Differences in Peter Ludlow (ed), *EU and China* (European Strategy Forum, 2007) 92–106; Emma Mawdsley, 'FU Machu Versus Dr Livingstone in the Dark Continent: Representing China, Africa and the West in British Broadcast Newspapers' (2008) Political Geography vol 27 (5) pp 509–29

151 Maurizio Carbone, 'The European Union and China's Rise in Africa: Competing Visions, External Coherence and Trilateral Cooperation' (2011) Journal of Contemporary African Studies vol 29 (2) pp 203–21 at 210

152 Maurizio Carbone, 'The European Union and China's Rise in Africa: Competing Visions, External Coherence and Trilateral Cooperation' (2011) Journal of Contemporary African Studies vol 29 (2) pp 203–21 at 210

The EU exports 'good governance' to African countries, but the concept is based on the EU representation of political and economic development founded on economic liberalisation and rules of the market, democratic norms and practices, and the protection of human rights.[153] Article 6 and 11 of the Treaty of the European Union provides for the promotion of democratic principles, the rule of law, and human rights. These doctrines emanate from the EU experience and are then cloaked with universality for other countries to emulate and, where necessary, it is exported and imposed. China's work in Africa has been negatively targeted as a result of the refusal to adopt the human rights canon and to make it a condition precedent for development assistance.

In the 2000s, the European Commission released its official communication on governance in the European Consensus on Development—Towards a Harmonised Approach Within the European Union. Point 13 of the aforementioned document stated, 'development is a central goal by itself, and that sustainable development includes good governance, human rights and political, economic social and environmental aspects.'[154] The values declared were that in partnering with third world countries, the EU would promote respect for human rights, fundamental freedoms, peace, democracy, good governance, gender equality, the rule of law, solidarity, and justice.[155] The EU delegation to the African Union emphasised the EU's support for the New Partnership for African Development (NEPAD), which is largely based on the commitment to core values, particularly, 'democracy, human rights, good governance and the rule of law.'[156] 'The EU strongly supports the political values at the heart of NEPAD, because they correspond with the "essential elements" of the EU's external cooperation policy regulated by the Maastricht Treaty and completed by the Lomé/Cotonou principles, the Mediterranean process, and the Agreement with South Africa.'[157]

Instructively, the EU formula for 'good governance' draws upon the international financial institutions that are generally agreed upon as global best practices of the ways of managing the domestic economy.[158] The 'good governance' credo by the EU is connected to the supremacy of technical experts' neoliberal idea and non-acceptance that the European policies failed to yield substantial fruits in Africa. According to Weaver, 'governance and anti-corruption issues ran first

153 Stephania Panebianco and Rosa Rossi, 'EU Attempts to Export Norms of Good Governance to the Mediterranean and the Western Balkans' (2004) Jean Monnet Working Papers in Comparative and International Politics p 6 http://aei.pitt.edu/6109/1/jmwp53.pdf

154 European Commission, 'The European Consensus on Development' (2006) https://international-partnerships.ec.europa.eu/system/files/2019-10/publication-the-european-consensus-on-development-200606_en.pdf accessed 20 May 2024

155 European Commission, 'The European Consensus on Development' (2006) https://international-partnerships.ec.europa.eu/system/files/2019-10/publication-the-european-consensus-on-development-200606_en.pdf accessed 20 May 2024

156 EU Delegation to the African Union 2002

157 Ian Taylor, 'Governance and Relations Between the European Union and Africa: The Case of NEPA' (2010) Third World Quarterly vol 31 (1) pp 51–67 at 53

158 IMF, 'Good Governance: The IMF's Role' (IMF, 1997) www.imf.org/external/pubs/ft/exrp/govern/govern.pdf accessed 17 May 2024

into the economic technocratic and apolitical features of the Bank's "intellectual culture." '[159] The trained economists who work with the World Bank are recruited from academia who have no experience in government and do not appreciate non-economic factors, which come into play in development.[160]

The entrance of China into Africa as a major player seemed to have made the EU good governance project beside the point. According to Taylor, China's engagement is the most significant development in Africa since the Cold War era.[161] China is the second if not first most important trading partner, coming directly behind the USA but way ahead of France and the United Kingdom. As activities and influence of China grow in Africa so also does the criticism and accusation that China is the new 'colonising' power engaging in crass exploitation of raw materials, flooding Africa with poor-quality and low-priced goods, and refusing to call the tyrants in Africa to account. The Western concerns about China's exploits in Africa are palpable.[162] China is usually projected as a violator of United Nations norms. However, it would be erroneous to disregard what Chinese sources call China's human rights outlook, which is grounded in native tradition, as one-dimensional—and thus, by inference, inimical to the international human rights regime.[163] As part of a long-established custom and practice, the Chinese idea of human rights is founded on and focused on creating a prosperous and formidable society.[164] This concept has been fortified as a Chinese position since 1949 and the central Chinese policy. The nature of human rights from China's perspective is communitarian with an emphasis on solidarity and responsibility for others, which originates from Confucian ideology centred on promoting amity.[165]

7.5 Conclusion

The approach to African development adopted by China is extolled by leaders on the continent. China, it is believed, does not impose conditionalities as is done by the West and its institutions but invests in Africa. The chapter further examines the conditionality imposed by the West when they transact with African countries, which has never been a welcome idea to African leaders. As such, the leaders have

159 Catherine Weaver, *Hypocrisy Trap: The World Bank and the Poverty of Reform* (Princeton University Press, 2008)

160 Catherine Weaver, *Hypocrisy Trap: The World Bank and the Poverty of Reform* (Princeton University Press, 2008)

161 Ian Taylor, *China's New Role in Africa* (Lynne Rienner, 2010)

162 Rory Carroll, 'China's Goldmine' (The Guardian, 28 March 2006) www.theguardian.com/business/2006/mar/28/china.g2; Joseph Kahn, 'China Opens Submit for African Leader' (The New York Times, 2 November 2006) www.nytimes.com/2006/11/02/world/asia/02cnd-china.html

163 Joel S Fetzer and Christopher J Sooper, *Confucianism, Democratization, and Human Right in Taiwan* (Lexington Book, 2012)

164 Joel S Fetzer and Christopher J Sooper, *Confucianism, Democratization, and Human Right in Taiwan* (Lexington Book, 2012)

165 Joel S Fetzer and Christopher J Sooper, *Confucianism, Democratization, and Human Right in Taiwan* (Lexington Book, 2012)

embraced China because the latter treats them as equal and not former subjects or colonies that are in perpetual need of guardians. China believes in human rights, the rule of law, and democracy but applies it through the belief that when development takes place, good governance and protection of rights are natural consequences. Thus China adopted noninterventionism and focused on investment. Burstein and Keijzer stated that the Chinese believe that the right to food, clothing, shelter, economic development, and security are of prime importance, not the traditional creed of the West's concept of individual freedom.[166]

However, the Chinese foray into Africa has not been without controversies. China in Africa has equated with colonialism as practised by the European powers in the nineteenth century. Africans have been warned to be critical of China's activities. The warnings and labelling of China as a colonialist come from the West. The paradox is that in recent times, top politicians and academics in the West have called for recolonising Africa. The call for a re-awakening of the British Empire was not out of interest for the colonised but for easy access to raw materials. The labelling of China as a colonialist does not stick; the rhetoric undermines the enormity of the disaster of colonialism. However, this does not mean African leaders should close their eyes to China's activities.

China has invested in Africa—infrastructure improvement, job creation, and overall economic growth are positive outcomes that enhance connectivity, trade, and transportation on a continent where integrating infrastructure has long been a challenge.[167] However, the commercial transactions between Africa and China have not been without controversies as demonstrated in the loan agreement between Kenya and China. The agreement generated controversy concerning some assets of the state being collaterised. The chapter argues that it has become a practice for countries to restrict sovereignty if the relationship is commercial in nature.

For the African leaders, China's contractual relation with Africa has provided some form of balancing. The African continent has gained, by China investing in Africa, a good example in Kenya and other places. This is not to say that China's presence in Africa is a panacea to the latter's problems. Africa needs to become economically active through diversification of its economy, through an acute awareness of its interests and ways and means of securing it, and to recognise and appreciate its strategic position in the global geopolitics.

Conventions and Cases

The Cotonou Agreement, signed in Cotonou on 23 June 2000, revised in Luxembourg on 25 June 2005, revised in Ouagadougou on 22 June 2010, and multiannual financial framework 2014–20, Publications Office, 2014, *https://op.europa.eu/*

166 Daniel Burstein and Arne de Keijzer, *Big Dragon: Future of China—What It Means for Business, the Economy and the Global Order* (Touchstone, 1999) 136

167 Marcus Vinicius de Freitas, *The Impact of Chinese Investment in Africa: Neocolonialism or Cooperation* (Policy Centre for the New South, 2023) 2 https://www.policycenter.ma/sites/default/files/2023-08/PB_30-23_Marcus%20Freitas.pdf accessed 1 October 2024

en/publication-detail/-/publication/c030c886-b15c-4456-930d-c9488db9cd0a, Accessed: 9 February 2024
Constitution of Kenya 2010
Access to Information Act (Kenya, 2016)
Public Procurement and Disposal Act, (Kenya, 2005)
UNCITRAL Model Law on International Commercial Conciliation (2002)
African Growth Opportunity Act (2000)
The Foreign Sovereign Immunities Act (FSIA) of 1976
China International Economic Arbitration and Commission (IETAC) Arbitration Rules, 2015
Government Proceedings Act 1958
ILC, Draft Article on Jurisdiction Immunities of State and Their Property;

Cases

The Philippine Admiral (1977) AC 373 (JC)
Trendtex Trading v Central Bank of Nigeria (1977) QB 529 (CA)
Congreso del Partico (1983) 1 AC 244 (HL)
Pennoyer v Neff (1877) 95 US 714
Schooner v McFadden (1976) 336 F. 2d 354 2nd Civ
United States v Planters Bank of Georgia (1824) 9 Wheat. 904, 22 U.S 904
Alfred Dunhill of London, Inc v Republic of Cuba (1976) 425 U.S 682

Bibliography

ACET, 'Looking East: China-Africa Engagements: Ghana Country Case Study Accra' (December 2009). https://acetforafrica.org/research-and-analysis/reports-studies/multi-country-studies/looking-east-chinas-engagements-with-africa/ (accessed 26 January 2024) 6–7

ACET, *Looking East: China-Africa Engagements: Rwanda Country Case Study* (Kigali, December 2009)

Alden C, & Alves A C, 'China and Africa's Natural Resources: The Challenges and Implications for Development and Governance' (2009) Occasional Paper 41, SAIIA, at 6. https://saiia.org.za/wp-content/uploads/2009/09/Occasional-Paper-41.pdf (accessed 19 May 2024)

Amin W, 'Chinese Ambassador Explains Why SGR Contract Is Still 'Top Secret' (*Nairobi News*, 22 May 2019). https://nairobinews.nation.africa/chinese-ambassador-sgr-contract/ (accessed 19 May 2024)

Bankas E K, *The State Immunity Controversy in International Law: Private Suites Against Sovereign States in Domestic Courts* (Springer, 2005)

Bauer P T, *Equality, the Third World and Economic Delusion* (Harvard University Press, 1988) 70

Behar R, 'China Saps Mozambique of Time Resources' (*Fast Company*, 6 January 2008). www.fastcompany.com/849679/china-saps-mozambique-timber-resources

Behar R, 'China Surpasses US as Leader in Sub-Sahara' (*Fast Company*, 6 January 2008). www.fastcompany.com/849681/china-surpasses-us-leader-sub-sahara

Berger M, 'Deal With Guinea Raises Questions About Chinese Role' (AllAfrica, 16 October 2009). https://allafrica.com/stories/200910161163.html

Bezola A, 'Latest Africa Foray: Altruism or Hegemony' (*Global Issues*, 2009). www.globalissues.org/news/2009/11/09/3436

Blinken A J, 'Secretary of State' (*South Africa*, November 2023). www.agoa.info
Bohannan C, 'Beyond Abrogation of Sovereign Immunity: State Waivers, Private Contracts, and Federal Incentives' (2002) New York University Law Review vol 77 (273)
Brautigam D, Bhalaki V, Deron L, & Wang Y, 'How Africa Borrows From China: And Why Mombasa Port Is Not Collateral for Kenya's Standard Gauge Railway' (2002) (China-Africa Research Initiative Working Paper, 2022)
Brautigam D, & Kidane W, 'China, Africa, and Debt Distress: Fact and Fiction About Asset Seizures' Policy Brief (China Africa Research Initiative, 2020). www.sais-cari.org
Brownlie I, *Principles of Public International Law* (OUP, 1990)
Burstein D, & Keijzer A, *Big Dragon: Future of China—What It Means for Business, the Economy and the Global Order* (New York Touchstone, 1999)
Campbell H, 'China in Africa: Challenging US Global Hegemony' (2008) Third World Quarterly vol 28 (1) pp 89–105
Cannon B, 'Inland Container Depots and the Future of Handling East Africa's Cargo' (*Kenya Engineer*, 18 January 2018)
Carbone M, 'Better Aid Less Ownership: Multi-Annual Programming and the EU's Development Strategies in Africa' (2008) Journal of International Development vol 20 pp 118–229
Carbone M, 'The European Union and China's Rise in Africa: Competing Visions, External Coherence and Trilateral Cooperation' (2011) Journal of Contemporary African Studies vol 29 (2) pp 203–221 at 210
Carl B M, 'Foreign Sovereign in American Courts: The United States Foreign Sovereign Immunities Act in Practice' (1979) Southwestern Law Journal vol 33 p 1009
Carroll R, 'China's Goldmine' (*The Guardian*, 28 March 2006). www.theguardian.com/business/2006/mar/28/china.g2
Cheru F, & Obi C (eds), *The Rise of China and India in Africa: Challenges, Opportunities and Critical Interventions* (Zed Books, 1988)
'China Eximbank Pledge Loan for Belinga Iron Ore Project' AIDDATA. https://china.aiddata.org/projects/630/ (accessed 18 May 2024)
'China Premier Wen Jiabao, Gives Press Conference in Cairo' Xinhua, 19 June 2006. www.chinadaily.com.cn/china/2006-06/19/content_620692_2.htm
'China to Take Over Kenya Main Port Over Unpaid Huge Chinese Loan' (*Hellenic Shipping News*, 22 November 2019). www.hellenicshippingnews.com/china-to-take-over-kenyas-main-port-over-unpaid-huge-chinese-loan/
'China Winning Resources and Loyalties of Africa' (*Financial Times*, 2006)
'China's Investment and Growing Clout in Africa Cause Concern' (*Chicago Tribune*, 19 February 2006). www.chicagotribune.com/2006/02/19/chinas-investment-and-growing-clout-in-africa-cause-concern/ (accessed 18 May 2024)
'Chinese Firm CNOOC to Buy 45% Stake in Nigeria Oil Filed' (*Los Angeles Times*, 10 January 2006)
'Chinese Loan and Nigeria's Sovereignty' (*The Guardian*, 11 August 2020)
CIETAC, 'Annual Report of China International Commercial Arbitration' www.cietac.org/Uploads/201710/59df3824b2849.pdf/. 2016
CIETAC, '2022 Statistics Show Its Endeavours In Line With International Practices 16 February 2023' https://hsfnotes.com/arbitration/2023/02/16/cietac-2022-statistics-show-its-endeavour-in-line-with-iinternational-practices/
'CNOOC Inks Oil Deal With Equatorial Guinea' (*Xinhua News Agency*, 19 February 2006). www.china.org.cn/english/2006/Feb/158520.htm (accessed 18 May 2024)
Colbert E, 'The Road Not Taken: Decolonisation and Independence in Indonesia and Indochina' (1972) FA vol 51 (3)
Condon M, 'China in Africa: What the Policy of Non-Intervention Adds to the Western Development Dilemma' (2012) The Fletcher Journal of Human Security vol 27 (1) pp 1–25
Cooper R, 'The New Liberal Imperialism' (*The Guardian*, 7 April 2002)

Cooper R, 'The Post Modern State' in M Leonard (ed), *Re-Ordering the World* (Foreign Policy Centre, 2002).
CPCS, 'East African Railway Masterplan Study' (Final Report, 2009)
Dawouda C, 'FOCAC: Trade, Investments, and Aid IN China-Africa Relations' Centre for Chinse Studies, Stellenbosch University, 2012 at 6
de Freitas M V, 'The Impact of Chinese Investment in Africa: Neocolonialism or Cooperation' 2023 Policy Brief 5. www.policycenter.ma/sites/default/files/2023-08/PB_30-23_Marcus%20Freitas.pdf (accessed 18 May 2024)
Del Biondon K, 'EU AID Conditionality in ACP Countries: Explaining Inconsistency in EU Sanctions Practice' (2011) Journal of Contemporary European Research vol 7 (3) pp 380–392
Deron L, Pairault T, & Montenegro P, 'China and Media: A Highway to Disinformation' (Briefing Paper No 17/2021, China Africa Research Initiative, 2021)
The East Africa Community (EAC), 'The East African Community Industrialisation Policy 2012–2032: Structural Transformation of the Manufacturing Sector Through High-Value Addition and Product Diversification Based on Comparative and Competitive Advantages of the Region' (2012) East African Community Secretariat. http://repository.eac.int/bitstream/handle/11671/539/Final%20%20EAC%20%Industrialisation%20policy.pdf?sequence=1&isAllowed=y
The East Africa Community (EAC), '17th Extra-Ordinary Summit of Heads of State of East African Community' (EAC), 2016A P 17, EAC Reports Database (EAC/SHS 17/2016)
EC, 'EU Strategy for Africa: Towards a Euro-Africa Pact to Accelerate Africa's Development' (Brussels, 12 October 2005), COM 489. https://eur-lex.europa.eu/LexUriServ/LexUriServ.do?uri=COM:2005:0489:FIN:EN:PDF (accessed 20 May 2024)
European Commission, 'The European Consensus on Development' (2006). https://international-partnerships.ec.europa.eu/system/files/2019-10/publication-the-european-consensus-on-development-200606_en.pdf (accessed 20 May 2024)
'Export-Import Bank of China and the Government of the Republic of Kenya: Buyer Credit Loan for the Kenya Nairobi-Naivasha Standard Gauge Railway Project' (Contract No BLA201505)
Fantu Cheru F, & Obi C, *The Rise of China and India in Africa* (Zed Books, 2010)
Feldman, Mark B, 'The United States Foreign Sovereign Immunities Act of 1976 in Perspective: A Founder's View' (1986) ICLQ vol 35
Ferguson N, *Empire: The Rise and Demise of the British World Order and the Lessons for Global Power* (Basic Books, 2004)
Fetzer J S, & Sooper J C, *Confucianism, Democratization, and Human Rights in Taiwan* (Lexington Book, 2012)
Fitzmaurice G, 'State Immunity from the Proceedings in Foreign Courts' (1933) BYIL vol 14 (101) pp XIV
'Friend Doesn't Cancel a Visit—Premier Zhou Enlai's Visits to 10 African Countries' (*Global Times*, 18 June 2021). www.globaltimes.cn/page/202106/1226506.shtml
Games D, 'Chinese the New Economic Imperialists in Africa' (*Business Day*, 21 February 2005)
Grannell F, 'The European Union and the New Partnership for Africa's Development (NEPAD)' in Taylor I, 'Governance and Relations between the European Union and Africa: The Case of NEPA' (2010) Third World Quarterly vol 31 (1) pp 51–57
Guiguo W, 'On the Dispute Resolution Mechanism of the Belt and Road' (2017) Chinese Law Science (Digest) vol 6 pp 56–71.
Halper S, *The Beijing Consensus: How China's Authoritarian Model Will Dominate the Twenty-First Century* (Basic Books, 2010) 100
Hamata M, & Guchu W, 'China-Africa Deal a Lose-Lose Situation' 2009. www.pairault.fr/sinaf/index.php/15-references/80-informante-china-africa-deal-a-lose-lose-situation (accessed 20 May 2024)
Hammond J, 'Sudan: China's Original Foothold in Africa' (*The Diplomat*, 2017). https://thediplomat.com/2017/06/sudan-chinas-original-foothold-in-africa/ (accessed 18 May 2024)

Higgins R, 'Certain Unresolved Aspects of the Law of State Immunity' (1982) NYIL vol 29 p 265

Hitchens P, 'How China Has Created a New Slave Empire in Africa' (*Mail Online*, 28 September 2008)

Hoffman S L, *The Law and Business of International Project Finance* (2nd ed, Transnational Publishers, Inc., 1957)

Horta L, 'Food Security in Africa: China's New Rice Bowl' (2009) China Brief vol (1). https://jamestown.org/program/food-security-in-africa-chinas-new-rice-bowl/

Horta L, 'The Zambezi: China's First Agricultural Colony' (20 May 2008) Centre for Strategic and International Studies. www.csis.org/analysis/zambezi-valley-chinas-first-agricultural-colony

Hyde C C, *International Law* (Little Brown and Company, 1945)

ICC, 'Guidance Notes on Resolving Belt and Road Disputes Using Mediation and Arbitration' https://iccwbo.org/content/uploads/sites/3/2019/02/icc-guidance-notes-belt-and-road-disputes-pdf.pdf/ (2019)

IMF, *Good Governance: The IMF's Role* (IMF, 1997). www.imf.org/external/pubs/ft/exrp/govern/govern.pdf (accessed 17 May 2024)

Javier S, 'Challenges for EU-China Cooperation in Africa' (*China Daily*, 7 February 2007)

Kagina A, 'Africa: AfCFTA-African Ministers Adopt Ban on Trade of Second-Hand Clothes' (*The New Times*, 2 June 2023)

Kahn J, 'China Courts Africa, Angling for Strategic Gains' (*NYT*, 3 November 2006)

Kahn J, 'China Opens Submit for African Leader' (*The New York Times*, 2 November 2006). www.nytimes.com/2006/11/02/world/asia/02cnd-china.html

Kaledzi I, 'Uganda Criticises US Plan to Exclude It From Duty-Free Trade Programme' (November 2023). www.agoa.info

Kampfner J, *Blare's Wars* (Free Press, 2004) 4

Kenya, 'Towards a Globally Competitive and Prosperous Nation' Kenya Vision Flagships Projects Progress Report (2008–2017)' https://vision2030.go.ke/wp-content/uploads/2021/11/KENYA-VISION-2030-FLAGSHIP-Projects-Progress-Report-2008-2017.pdf

Kenya National Assembly, 'Special Report on the Procurement and Financing of the Construction of Standard Gauge Railway from Mombasa to Nairobi' (29 April 2014) Eleventh Parliament-Second Public Investments Committee, 'Environmental and Social Impact Assessment Study Report for the Proposed Mombasa-Nairobi Standard Gauge Railway Project' (October 2012). https://africog.org/wp-content/uploads/2017/06/SGR-EAS-Impact-report.pdf

Kidane, W L, 'Agreements and Dispute Settlement in China-Africa Economic Ties' in A Oqubay & J Y Lin (eds), *China-Africa and an Economic Transformation* (Oxford University Press, 2019)

Kingah S, 'The New EU Africa Strategy: Grounds for Cautious Optimism' (2006) European Foreign Affairs Review vol 11 (4) pp 527–553

Larmer B, 'Is China the World's New Colonial Power' (*The New York Times*, 2 May 2017)

Lauterpacht H, *Private Law Sources and Analogies in International* (Longmans, 1927) 28

Maglad NEA, 'Scoping Study on Chinese Relations with Sudan' (2008) AERC pp 1–17. www.econstor.eu/bitstream/10419/93162/1/587559012.pdf (accessed 18 May 2024)

Mann FA, 'The State Immunity Act 1978' (1979) BYIL vol 50 p 43

Marchal R, 'The EU and China in Africa: Opportunities and Differences' in P R Ludlow (ed), *EU and China* (European Strategy Forum, 2007) 92–106

Martens M, EU Parliament, 'A Development Strategy for Africa' European Parliament (27 October 2005), Report-A6–0318/2005. www.europarl.europa.eu/doceo/document/A-6-2005-0318_EN.html (accessed 17 May 2024)

Massie R, *Loosing the Bonds: United States and South Africa in the Apartheid Years* (Nan A Talese/Doubleday, 1977)

Mawdsley E, 'FU Machu Versus Dr Livingstone in the Dark Continent: Representing China, Africa and the West in British Broadcast Newspapers' (2008) Political Geography vol 27 (5) pp 509–529

Mbachu D, 'Nigeria Resources: Changing the Playing Field' (2006) South African Journal of International Affairs vol 13 (1) pp 77–82

Mead N V, 'China in Africa: Win-Win, or Colonialism' (*Guardian*, 31 July 2018)

Moyo L, 'China's Role in African Politics Appalling' (*AllAfrica*, 18 July 2008). https://allafrica.com/stories/200807180654.html

Muyanga P, 'AG Fights Quest for Disclosure of SH450bn SGR Contract with China' (*Nation*, 23 August 2021)

Naidu S, 'China and Africa's Natural Resources Sector: A View From South Africa' www.csis.org/analysis/china-and-africas-natural-resource-sector-view-south-africa

Naidu S, & Corkin L, 'Who Was the Real Winner in China?' (2006)

'Nigeria's CCECC Secures $3.02 billion Nigerian's Eastern Railway Contract 29 April 2021 Railway Technology. www.railway-technology.com/news/ccecc-nigerian-eastern-railway-contract/?cf-view (accessed 18 May 2024)

Norberg J, 'China Paranoia Derails Free Trade' (2006) Eastern Economic Review vol 196 (1)

OECD, *Infrastructure Financing Instruments and Incentives* (OECD, 2015). www.oecd.org.org/finance/private-pensions/Infrastruture—Financing-Instrument-and-Incentives-pdf (accessed 19 November 2023)

Ofosu G, & Sarpong D, 'The Evolving Perspective on the Chinese Labour Regime in Africa' (2022) Economic and Industrial Democracy vol 43 (4) pp 1747–1766

Okoth E, 'SGR Pact With China a Risk to Kenya Sovereignty Assets' (*Nations*, 12 January 2019)

Olander E, 'China May Be a Lot of Things in Africa, But It Is Not a Coloniser' 23 July 2017. https://medium.com/@eolander/china-may-be-a-lot-of-things-in-africa-but-its-not-a-colonizer-628285cda6a0 (accessed 19 May 2024)

Olander E, 'Kenyan Court Orders Government to Publish Loan Contract for SGR' (*China Global South Project*, 16 May 2022). https://nation.africa/kenya/counties/mombasa/ag-fights-quest-for-disclosure-of-sh450bn-sgr-contract-with-china-3522310 (accessed 19 May 2024)

Omond G, 'Mombasa Port at Risk as Audit Finds It Was Used to Secure SGR Loan' (*The East African*, 5 July 2020). www.theeastafrican.co.ke/tea/business/mombasa-port-at-risk-as-audit-finds-it-was-used-to-secure-sgr-loan-1408886

Palley T I, 'From Keynesianism to Neoliberalism: Shifting Paradigms in Economics' (*Foreign Policy in Focus*, 5 May 2004). https://fpif.org/from_keynesianism_to_neoliberalism_shifting_paradigms_in_economics/ (accessed 20 May 2024)

Panebianco S, & Rossi R, 'EU Attempts to Export Norms of Good Governance to the Mediterranean and the Western Balkans' (2004) Jean Monnet Working Papers in Comparative and International Politics, p 6. http://aei.pitt.edu/6109/1/jmwp53.pdf

Peters R, 'The Undecided Continent' (2006) Armed Forces Journal, cited in Sautman B and Hairong Y, 'East Mountain Tiger, West Mountain Tiger: China, the West, and 'Colonialism' in Africa' (2006) Maryland Series in Contemporary Asian Studies vol 5. https://core.ac.uk/download/pdf/56353973.pdf (accessed 19 May 2024)

Polgreen L, 'As Chinese Investment in Africa Drops, Hope Sinks' (New York Times, 25 March 2009)

Press Release, 'Amaechi Explains Sovereignty Clause in $500M Chinese Railway Loan' (*Premium Times*, 2 August 2020); 'Chinese Loans and Our Sovereignty' (*Vanguard*, 8 August 2021)

Prizzon A, & Hart T, *Age of Choice: Kenya in the New Development Finance Landscape* (Overseas Development Institute, 2016) 13. https://media.odi.org/documents/10986.pdf

Reinisch A, 'European Court Practice Concerning State Immunity From Enforcement Measure' (2006) EJIL vol 17 (4) pp 803–836

Robert A, 'Why We Need Empires' (*Sunday Telegraph*, 16 January 2005); Andrew Robert, 'Recolonise Africa' (*DM*, 8 January 2005) 20 cited in Sautman B & Hairong Y, 'East Mountain Tiger, West Mountain Tiger: China, the West, and 'Colonialism' in Africa (2006) Maryland Series in Contemporary Asian Studies vol 45. https://core.ac.uk/download/pdf/56353973.pdf (accessed 19 May 2024)

Rolley S, 'Exclusive: Congo to Hike Stake in Copper, Cobalt Venture With China' 24 May 2023. www.reuters.com/markets/commodities/congo-hike-stake-copper-cobalt-venture-with-china-2023-05-24/ (accessed 18 May 2024)

Sanusha N, 'China and Africa's Natural Resources Sector: A View From South Africa' (2007) Centre for Strategic and International Studies. www.csis.org/analysis/china-and-africas-natural-resource-sector-view-south-africa (accessed 18 May 2024)

Sautman B, & Yan H, 'African Perspective on China-Africa Links' (2009) The China Quarterly vol 199 pp 728–759.

Schmidt S, 'Toward a New EU-Africa Relationship - A Grand Strategy for Africa?' (2008) Foreign Policy in Dialogue vol 8 (24) pp 8–18, cited in Schmidt M, 'The EU in Africa: Increasing Coherence, Decreasing Partnership' https://is.muni.cz/el/fss/podzim2015/EVS188/um/Carbone.pdf?lang=en

Servants J C, 'China's Trade Safari in Africa' (*Le Monde diplomatique*, 2005). http://archive.niza.nl/docs/200610161553573288.pdf (accessed 19 May 2024)

Shinn D H, & Eisenman J, *China and Africa: A Century of Engagement* (University of Pennsylvania Press, 2012)

Siegle J, 'The Creeping Loss of African Sovereignty' (*African Centre for Strategic Studies*, 8 February 2023). https://africacenter.org/experts/creeping-loss-african-sovereignty/ (accessed 19 May 2024)

Sinclair I M, 'The European Convention on State Immunity' (1973) ICLQ vol 22 p 254

Sinclair I M, 'The Law of Sovereign Immunity' (1980) Recent Developments vol 167 (Sijthof)

Sornarajoh M, 'Problems in Applying the Restrictive Theory of Sovereign Immunity' (1982) ICLQ vol 31 pp 661–685

Stevenson T, 'Chinese Moves Spawn a New Order' (*Daily Telegraph*, 23 August 2006)

Taylor I, *African Rising? BRICS—Diversifying Dependency* (James Currey, 2014) 89–92

Taylor I, *China and Africa: Engagement and Compromise* (Routledge, 2006)

Taylor I, *China's New Role in Africa* (Lynne Rienner, 2010)

Taylor I, *The Forum on China—Africa Cooperation (FOCAC)* (Routledge, 2011)

Thatcher M, 'Speech to the College of Europe' (*The Brugers Speech*, 20 September 1988)

The UN Sustainable Development Goals (SDGs), Negotiated to Cover the Period 2015–2030, a Follow Up to the UN Millennium Development

UNCITRAL Model Law on International Commercial Conciliation (2002) Article 1

United Nations, *Yearbook of the International Law Commission Vol II Part One* (ILC Report, 1986)

Wade A, 'Time for the West Practise What It Preaches' (*Financial Times*, 23 January 2008). www.ft.com (accessed 9 February 2024)

Walsh C, 'Is China the New Colonial Powers in Africa?' (*The Observer*, 29 October 2006). www.thegua rdian.com/business/2006/oct/29/china.theobserver (accessed 19 May 2024)

Weaver C, *Hypocrisy Trap: The World Bank and the Poverty of Reform* (Princeton University Press, 2008)

Were A, 'Debt Trap? Chinse Loans and Africa's Development Options' (2018) South African Institute of International Affairs, Policy Insight, No. 6, at 3. https://saiia.org.za/wp-content/uploads/2018/09/Policy-Insights-66.pdf

The World Bank, 'Time to Shift Gears: Accelerating Growth and Poverty Reduction in the New Kenya' (2013) Kenya Economic Update. www.worldbank.org/content/dam/Worldbank/document/Africa/Kenya/kenya-economic-update-june-2013.pdf (accessed 17 May 2024)

Xu B, 'Chin's Economy: Historical Perspective and Future Outlook' (*CEIBS Research*, 31 August 2023). www.ceibs.edu/new-papers-columns/23641

Yeranian E, 'China Seeks Stronger Ties With Sudan Amid Regional, International Tug-of-War' 30 May 2023. www.voanews.com/a/china-seeks-stronger-ties-with-sudan-amid-regional-international-tug-of-war-/7115426.html (accessed 18 May 2024)

Yuan L L, 'The Theory and Practice of Mediation' (*Singapore F T Law & Tax Asia Pacific*, Singapore 1997)

8 Breaking the Unbroken Continuum

Asymmetries between the EU and ACP countries are believed to be a continuity of colonialism, embedded in unequal multilateral/WTO and bilateral/EPA trade agreements.[1] However, the asymmetry of the colonial relationship is quite different from the modern era power asymmetry. The former was based on the use of force to protect the interest of the colonialists while the latter focused on granting aid and development promises without legal commitment and sometimes employed subtle threats and coercion to secure its interests. Faundez and Tan argue that trade arrangements such as the EPAs are highly affected by the colonial past with its damaging effects.[2] The authors believed that a genuine partnership between the core and peripheral countries is impossible. Kwame Nkrumah's perspective was that, for the gap between the core and peripheral countries to shrink, there has to be a deviation from the 'patron-client relationship.'[3]

According to observers, the EU-Africa relationship is inextricably linked to the colonial constraint.[4] Minta referred to the relationship as an 'unbroken historical continuum.'[5] Mandelson famously stated that the new structure of the trade relationship must discard whatever remains of the idea of colonialism. The general view is that the nomenclature of the EU and ACP countries may change, but the crux of the idea underlying the relationship is hardly altered.[6] For instance, Article 131 of Part IV of the Rome Treaty provides that the Community should foster the associates' economic and social development. Also, Article 132 subparagraphs enjoined the parties to promote progressive development investment in the associated states. The research finds this manner of presenting every

1 Kwame Nkrumah, *Neo-Colonialism: The Last Stage of Imperialism* (International Publishers, 1966) 17–9
2 Julio Faundez and Celine Tan, *International Economic Law, Globalisation and Developing Countries* (Edward Elgar, 2012) 15
3 Nkrumah (n 1) at 176
4 Adekeye Adebajo and Kaye White (eds), *The EU and Africa: From Eurafrique to Afro-Europa* (C Hurst & Co Publishers Ltd, 2012) 239; Nkrumah (n 2) at 176
5 I.K. Minta, 'The Lomé Convention and The New International Economic Order' (1980) Howard L J vol 27 p 953
6 I.K. Minta, 'The Lomé Convention and The New International Economic Order' (1980) Howard L J vol 27 p 953

DOI: 10.4324/9781032615059-8

agreement as the interests of Africa have not changed.[7] The General Act of the Berlin or other treaties between European powers made Africa to be imagined and treated through the prism of helpless infant in need of a guardian. Mandelson, in declaring the EPAs as being homegrown, said, 'Let there be no mistake: as with New Economic Partnership Africa's Development (NEPAD), you are in the driving seat, and we will support your priorities and your ambitions.'[8] According to Wilkinson, this manner of speaking constrains others from questioning such discourse.[9]

Not all the interviewees agreed that the EU merely protected its interests in the EPAs agreement. According to a trade expert from ECOWAS Trade Commission, the EU was generous because it recognised Ghana's development level and provided exceptions in the agreement.[10] However, other interviewees lamented that the exceptions exist, but Ghana and other ACP countries lack the necessary structures to take advantage of such provisions.[11] Another respondent expressed that it would not have signed the agreement if Ghana had a robust civil socsiety and private sector like Nigeria.[12] As a result of the weakness, the EU curried favour with government officials and some private sector actors and they signed the agreement without the popular support of the masses.[13]

Article 2 (e) of the Ghana-EU EPA provides for compatibility with Article XXIV of the WTO. As GATT Article XXIV provides, the regional agreement must remove duties on 'substantially all the trade' and do so within a 'reasonable length of time.' The insertion of the clause is a significant departure from the Cotonou Agreement in the EPA, which provided for reciprocal liberalisation obligation. The interpretation of GATT XXIV: 5 (C) was that reasonable time should not be more than ten years, only in a special circumstance, but what constitutes 'exceptional cases' remains abstruse. Thus, the EPA negotiations were fraught with different interpretations of Article XXIV.

However, Articles 37 and 38 (4) of the Cotonou Agreement contain directions on how WTO compliance is to be achieved between the EU-ACP EPA. Paragraph 4 of 38 of the Cotonou Agreement provided flexibility and sufficient time for the ACP countries to transition to full implementation gradually. However, the EU-Ghana standstill provision in Article 15 provides that new import duty shall not be introduced, and Article 18 provides for the elimination of all forms of import restrictions. The EU argued that removing export taxes and restrictions is essential to meeting the criteria laid down in Article XXIV of GATT.

7 Interview with senior academic staff (Zaria, 2020)

8 Peter Mandelson, 'The ACP-EU Relationship in the Global Economy' (SPEECH/04/505, ACP-EU Ministerial, Brussels, 1 December 2004) 2–3

9 Rorden Wilkinson, *What's Wrong With the WTO and How to Fix It* (Polity Press, 2014) 20–79; Wallerstein Immanuel, *The Modern World System* (Academic Press, 1974); Wallerstein Immanuel, *The Capitalist World-Economy* (CUP, 1979) 9

10 Interview with MoTI officer of (Ghana 2020)

11 Interview with MoTI official (Ghana 2020)

12 Interview with ECOWAS official (Abuja 2020)

13 Interview with official of FMITI (Abuja 2020)

It is found that Ghana signed the agreement because its economy relies on exports of cocoa.[14] Even though the country discovered crude oil, it has yet to reach Nigeria's production capacity. In summary, the EU still influences Ghana due to high-level power asymmetry, which has its origin in colonialism. Initially, the government of Ghana stood firm against endorsing the agreement as it was not in the country's favour due to its level of development.[15] According to an interviewee, Ghana signed after much pressure with a promise to extend assistance to Ghana and emphasis on the GSP not being a good alternative.[16]

Nigeria withstood the EU's pressure because the country is an established exporter of crude oil duty-free to the EU. According to the interviewee, petroleum products make up 90% of Nigeria's exports. As such, it could afford not to sign the EPAs. However, some interviewees in Nigeria maintained that the country refused to sign because the EU failed to address its concerns. Besides, due to its strategy to diversify its economy, it cannot liberalise beyond 65% and for less than a reasonable period of 25 years.[17] It is perceived that respondents interviewed in Nigeria, particularly from civil society and the private sector, believe it withstood the pressure from the EU because they have built some level of capacity; for them, it is no longer business as usual, and unless the EU adequately addresses the country's concerns, it would not sign.[18]

Another reason that Nigeria did not succumb to the coercion and economic power of the EU is far from the issue of diversification. A respondent stated that Nigeria eagerly looks forward to signing an agreement with the United Kingdom (UK) once Brexit is concluded.[19] Approximately 80% of non-oil products in Nigeria are exported to the UK market.[20] In 2023 an agreement was signed between the UK and Nigeria.[21] The country can access the UK market, of course, but it cannot compete, except for the advantage of crude oil export and raw materials. The UK still has a strong influence on Nigeria but it is forging a stronger alliance with China, who is investing in the country.

China never colonised Africa, and the economic relations between China and the continent is promising. Industrialisation is top on the list in Africa-China relations, also, globally, Sustainable Development Goals (SDGs) place a premium on 'building resilient infrastructure, promote inclusive and sustainable industrialization and foster innovation,' under Goal 9.[22] This has been echoed in Agenda 2063

14 Interview with MoTI official (2020)
15 Interview with ECOWAS official (2020)
16 Interview with ECOWAS official (2020)
17 Interview with former state Minister of Trade, Industry and Investment and Interview with NANTS official (2020)
18 Interview with Ken Ukaoha (2020)
19 Interview with FMITI official (2020)
20 Former senior government official, who started the negotiation process on behalf of Nigeria (2020)
21 The Enhanced Trade and Investment Partnership Between Nigeria and the UK, www.gov.uk/government/news/uk-signs-landmark-economic-partnership-with-nigeria accessed 17 April 2024
22 United Nations, Sustainable Development Goals, www.undp.org/sustainable-development-goals/industry-innovation-and-infrastructure accessed 17 April 2024

by the Africa Union, articulating a framework to transform the economic landscape of Africa.[23] It then means that China's relations with Africa offer prospects for substantial and concrete gains for Africa. For instance, China does not impose conditionalities on Africa but treats its partners as equals. However, China-Africa relations is not without controversy, such as China's encroachment on sovereignty. The book explored the agreement between China and Kenya specifically and addressed the concerns of encroachment on sovereignty from the perspective of international law. If the relations between countries are commercial in nature, the law allows for immunity to be restricted in the event of default. Also, it is acknowledged that China-Africa relations are not a panacea to the latter's challenges but that there is a need for it to be more critical and cautious in its negotiations and agreements and ensure that its interests are adequately protected.

The African Continental Free Trade Agreement (AfCFTA) offers an opportunity for these countries to develop a trade relationship that will benefit all parties in the final analysis—as the power asymmetry will be absent, or at least minimal in size. This is a sobering conclusion; there may not be much that can be done when the existing power asymmetry is significant. However, the hope is that trade agreements like the AfCFTA can achieve what the ideological framework purports to; economic development from trade liberalisation—but the right kind of liberalisation and with the right partners, such opportunities can help the continent. Article 3 (b) of the Treaty Establishing the Economic Community of Central African States (ECCAS) makes 'solidarity and collective self-reliance' a core principle to be adopted by the members.[24] Similarly, Article 4 (b) of the ECOWAS Treaty provides 'solidarity and collective self-reliance' as a basic principle,[25] the process of African countries controlling their economic affairs is an idea that pervades during the first generation of regional integration attempts after the period of colonialism.[26]

It is encouraging that, in the case of Nigeria, the country can withstand the pressure from the EU, but the reason it could do so is not sufficient to bring about development and diversification of its economy. Ghana seems to have a more promising and forward-looking approach to its economic growth, even though the structural factor still militates against its progress. Ghana has a tremendous capacity to formulate a strategy, but the issue noted is that it is mainly controlled by foreign elements that may negatively impact its economic success.[27] Having a more robust private as well as public sector could assist it in withstanding the economic and political power of the West. Even though Africa has an asymmetrical economic relationship

23 African Union, Linking Agenda 2063 and SDGs, https://au.int/en/agenda2063/sdgs accessed: 17 April 2024

24 Treaty Establishing the African Economic Community of Central African States para 3, Oct 19 1983, 23 I L M 945 (1984) Article 3 (b)

25 Treaty of Economic Community of West African States (ECOWAS) 28 May 1975, Article 4 (b) available at https://ecowas.int/wp-content/uploads/2022/08/Revised-treaty-1.pdf accessed 1 October 2024

26 Nkrumah (n 1) at 101; James Thuo Gathii, 'African Regional Trade Agreements as Flexible Legal Regimes' (2009) 35 North Carolina Journal of International Law 571 at 601

27 Interview with trade expert, ECOWAS representative to AFCFTA Secretariat (Ghana 2020)

with the EU and the rest of the world, it does not mean it should operate in an insular manner.[28] Therefore, as observed by Gammage, 'multipolarity' could be an opportunity for the ACP countries to variegate their partnership and to make good progress toward new relationships with countries outside the EU.[29] This does not mean that Africa should cut ties with the EU; rather, they should strategise and reinforce their skill in negotiating with the EU to receive favourable terms.

28 James Thuo Gathii, 'African Regional Trade Agreements as Flexible Legal Regimes' (2009) North Carolina Journal of International Law 35 (3) 571 at 607

29 Clair Gammage, 'Symposium ACP-EU Cooperation: Challenges and Opportunities for the Post-2020 Relationship' (27 May 2019) African International Economic Law Network www.afronomicslaw.org accessed 1 August 2022

Index

For Product Safety Concerns and Information please contact our EU
representative GPSR@taylorandfrancis.com
Taylor & Francis Verlag GmbH, Kaufingerstraße 24, 80331 München, Germany

www.ingramcontent.com/pod-product-compliance
Ingram Content Group UK Ltd.
Pitfield, Milton Keynes, MK11 3LW, UK
UKHW020006200926
475702UK00015B/2496
9781032615066